S0-AGA-842

CRIMSON HERO

VOL. 4
The Shojo Beat Manga Edition

This manga volume contains material that was originally published in English in *Shojo Beat* magazine, July–October 2006 issues.

STORY AND ART BY
MITSUBA TAKANASHI

Translation & English Adaptation/Naoko Amemiya
Touch-up Art & Lettering/Mark Griffin
Graphics & Cover Design/Courtney Utt
Editor/Nancy Thistlethwaite

Managing Editor/Megan Bates
Editorial Director/Elizabeth Kawasaki
VP & Editor in Chief/Yumi Hoashi
Sr. Director of Acquisitions/Rika Inouye
VP of Sales & Marketing/Liza Coppola
Exec. VP of Sales & Marketing/John Easum
Publisher/Hyoe Narita

Printed in Canada

Published by VIZ Media, LLC
P.O. Box 77010
San Francisco, CA 94107

Shojo Beat Manga Edition
10 9 8 7 6 5 4 3 2 1
First printing, December 2006

www.viz.com
store.viz.com

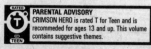

Crimson Hero™

Story & Art by
MITSUBA TAKANASHI

CONTENTS

STORY THUS FAR

Nobara Sumiyoshi is a first-year student in high school who lives for her one passion, volleyball. She's the successor to the Japanese ryotei, "Seiryu," the high-class ryotei restaurant her family runs, but she enrolled in Crimson High express-ly to play volleyball. When Nobara's mother arranged to have the girl's volley-ball team eliminated, an angered Nobara ran away from home, and ended up living and working in the Crimson Dorm, where the boys' volleyball scholarship students live. Her goal: to rebuild a girls' team. Finally, the day of their first prac-tice match arrived!!

That very day Nobara had to rescue her sister Souka from an obligatory date. Nobara ended up late for the game and got a major tongue-lashing at home to boot. Her mother finally let her play volleyball when Nobara agreed to become the successor to Seiryu, saying, "I'll do it. But for my three years in high school, I want to play volleyball."

Through all her trials, Nobara's sole support was Yushin, a volleyball player on the boys' team. But ever since she spotted him with his girlfriend, her heart has

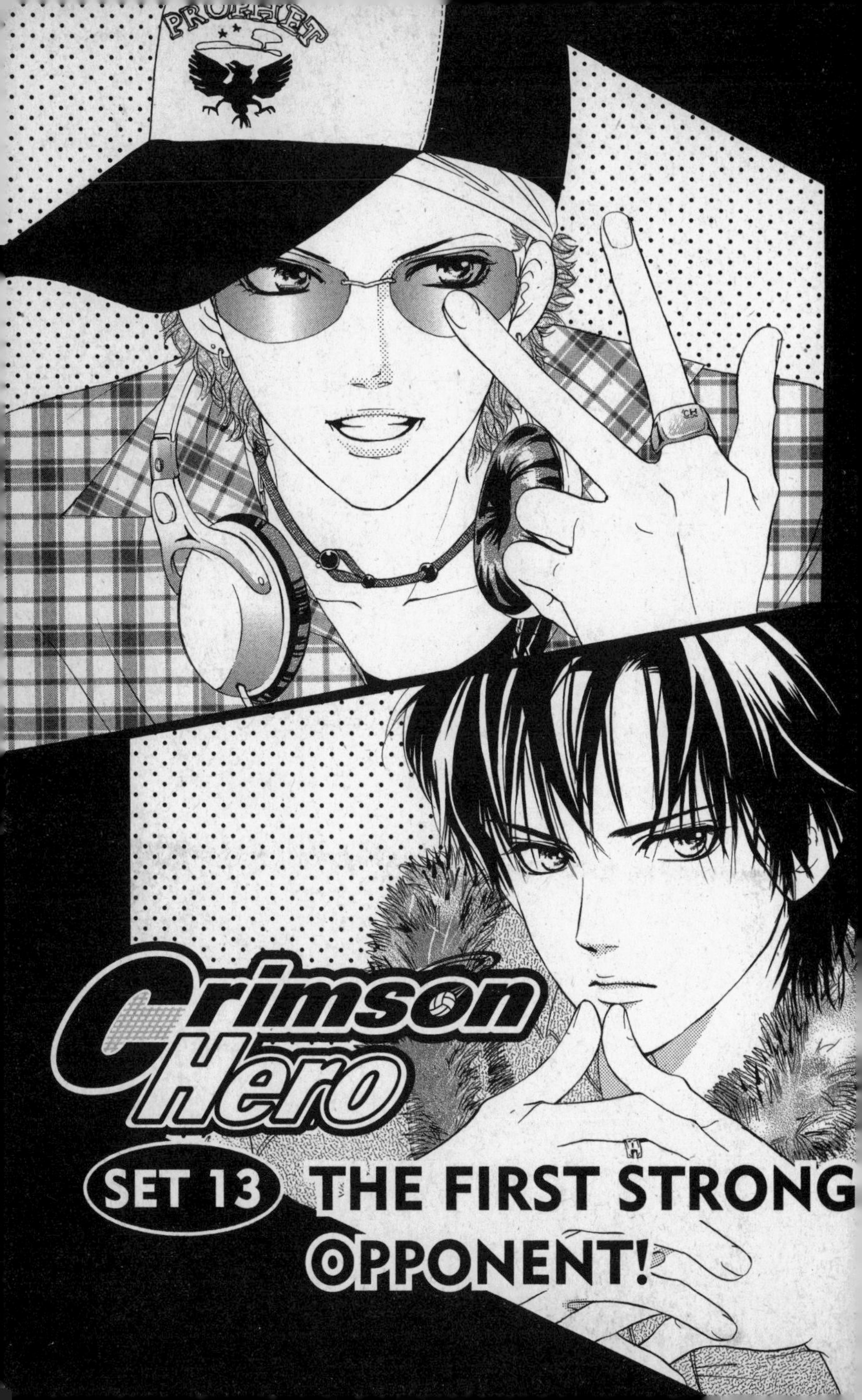
PROPHET
Crimson Hero
SET 13 THE FIRST STRONG OPPONENT!

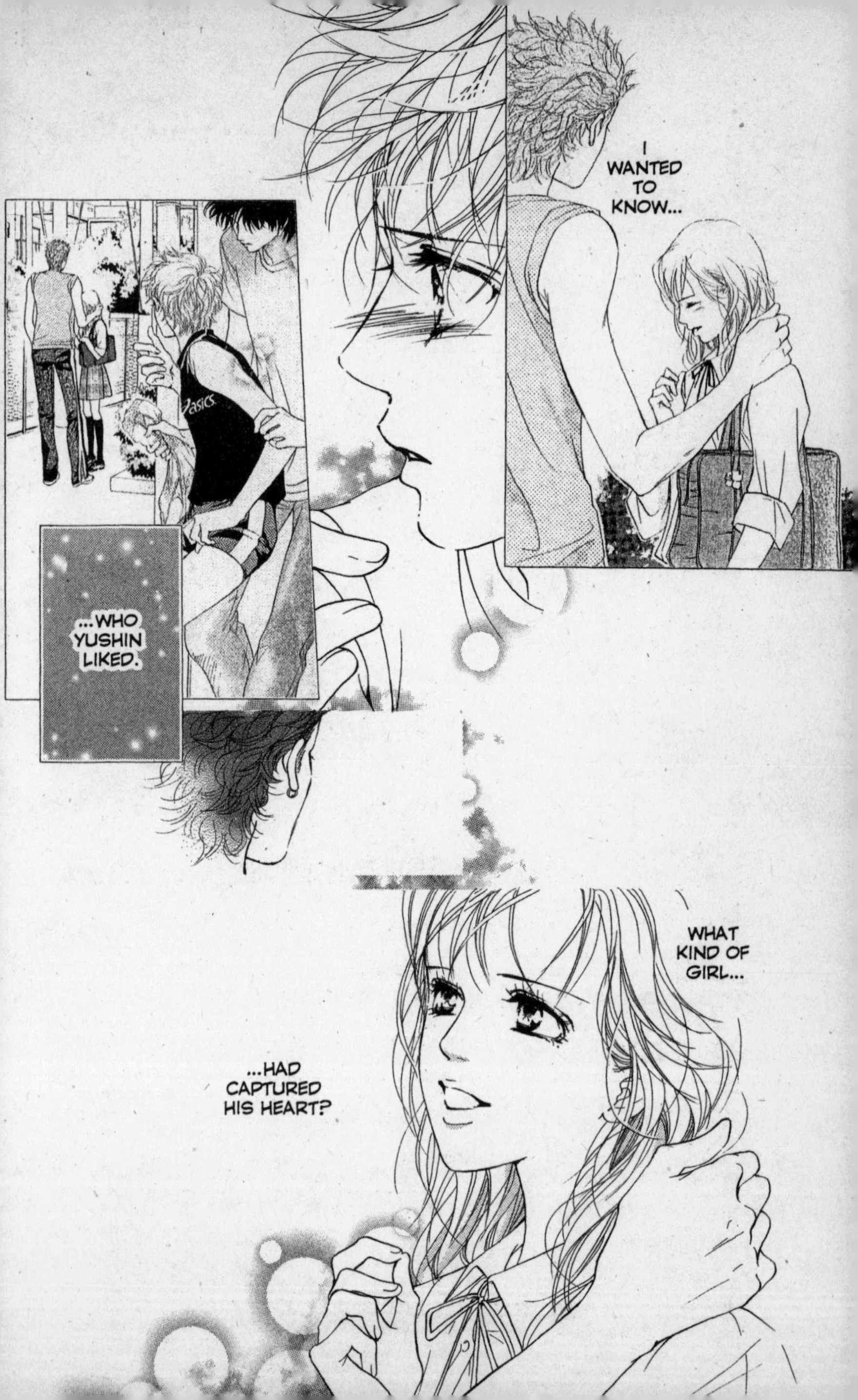
I WANTED TO KNOW...
...WHO YUSHIN LIKED.
WHAT KIND OF GIRL...
...HAD CAPTURED HIS HEART?

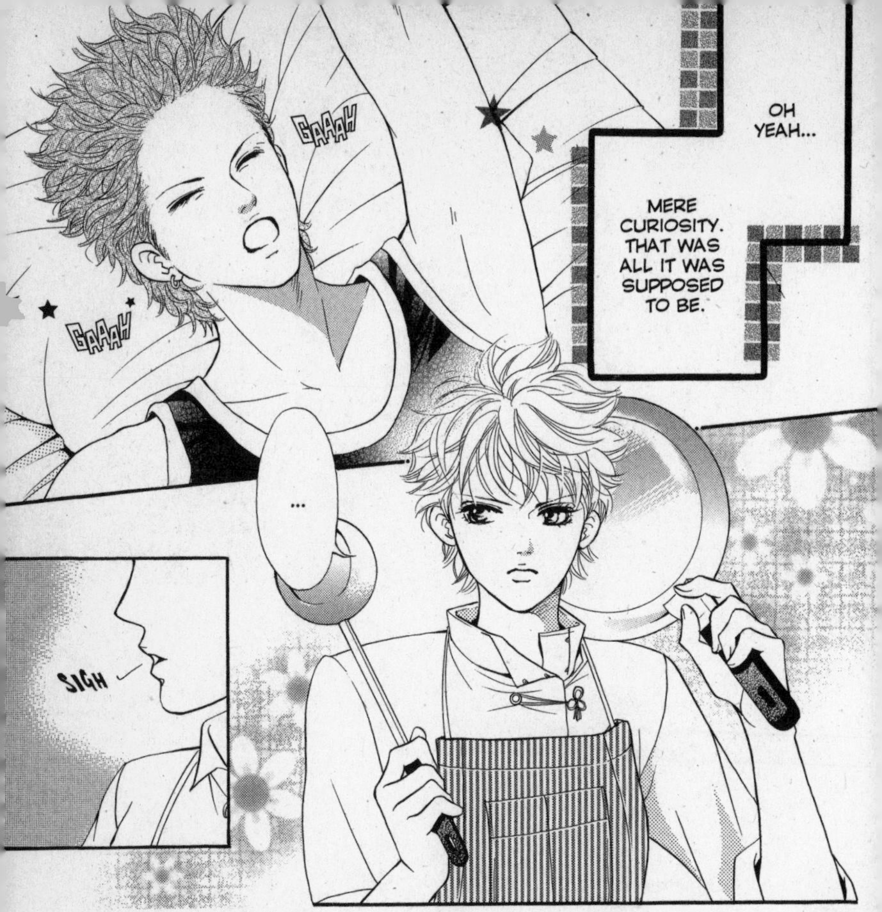
OH YEAH...
MERE CURIOSITY. THAT WAS ALL IT WAS SUPPOSED TO BE.
GAAAH
GAAAH
...
SIGH

THE MAKING OF CRIMSON HERO

Vol. 1

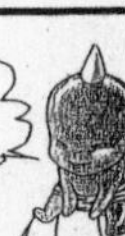

HELLO!★ TAKANASHI HERE. HOW HAVE YOU ALL BEEN? IN NO TIME AT ALL, WE'RE AT VOL. 4 OF CRIMSON HERO. I FEEL LIKE EVERY DAY I'VE JUST BEEN DRAWING AND DRAWING FOR THIS TITLE. ESPECIALLY SINCE THERE ARE GAME SCENES THIS TIME--I FEEL LIKE I DRAW AND I DRAW AND I'M NEVER DONE! WHOA!! ACTUALLY, WHATEVER THE SCENE, IT'S ALWAYS VERY DIFFICULT DRAWING AND WORKING HARD IN THE HOPE THAT READERS WILL FIND IT AT LEAST A LITTLE BIT ENTERTAINING. NOW THAT I'VE COME THIS FAR, I'VE BEEN REALIZING HOW MANY CHARACTERS THERE ARE! AND HOW MANY OF THEM HAVE NAMES? I HAVEN'T EVEN COUNTED. MY AUTHOR'S PICK FOR VOL. 4 WOULD HAVE TO BE YABESHO'S SHOJI. I LIKE HOW SHE'S REALLY PERSISTENT ABOUT BEING STRONG AND HOW SHE DOESN'T SEEM TO HAVE CONFIDENCE IN ANYONE BESIDES HERSELF. PERSONALLY, I LIKE HER. OR RATHER, MAYBE BECAUSE I'M BLOOD-TYPE A, I LIKE PEOPLE WHO DO AS THEY WANT--LIKE MOMOKO, FOR EXAMPLE. IT'S SATISFYING TO DRAW HER.

BY THE WAY, AS I WAS WORKING ON THE STORYBOARDS I HAD A DISCUSSION WITH THE STAFF ABOUT WHETHER SHOJI WOULD WEAR HER SCHOOL UNIFORM TO CLASS. I WONDER. IT'D BE OKAY TO HAVE HER WEAR IT, BUT TAKANASHI THOUGHT THAT IT'D BE INTERESTING IF SHE ALWAYS WORE WORKOUT CLOTHES. OH, BUT HER CHEST IS WAY BIGGER THAN NOBARA'S.

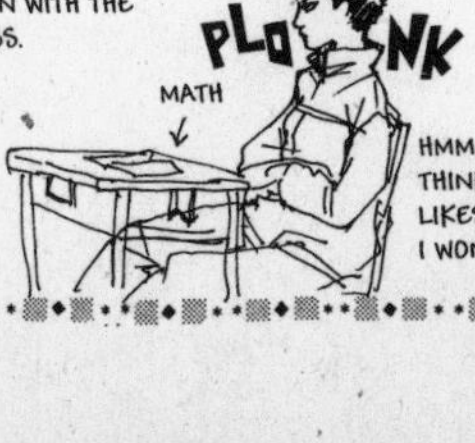
PLONK
MATH

HMM. DO YOU THINK SHE LIKES BOYS? I WONDER...

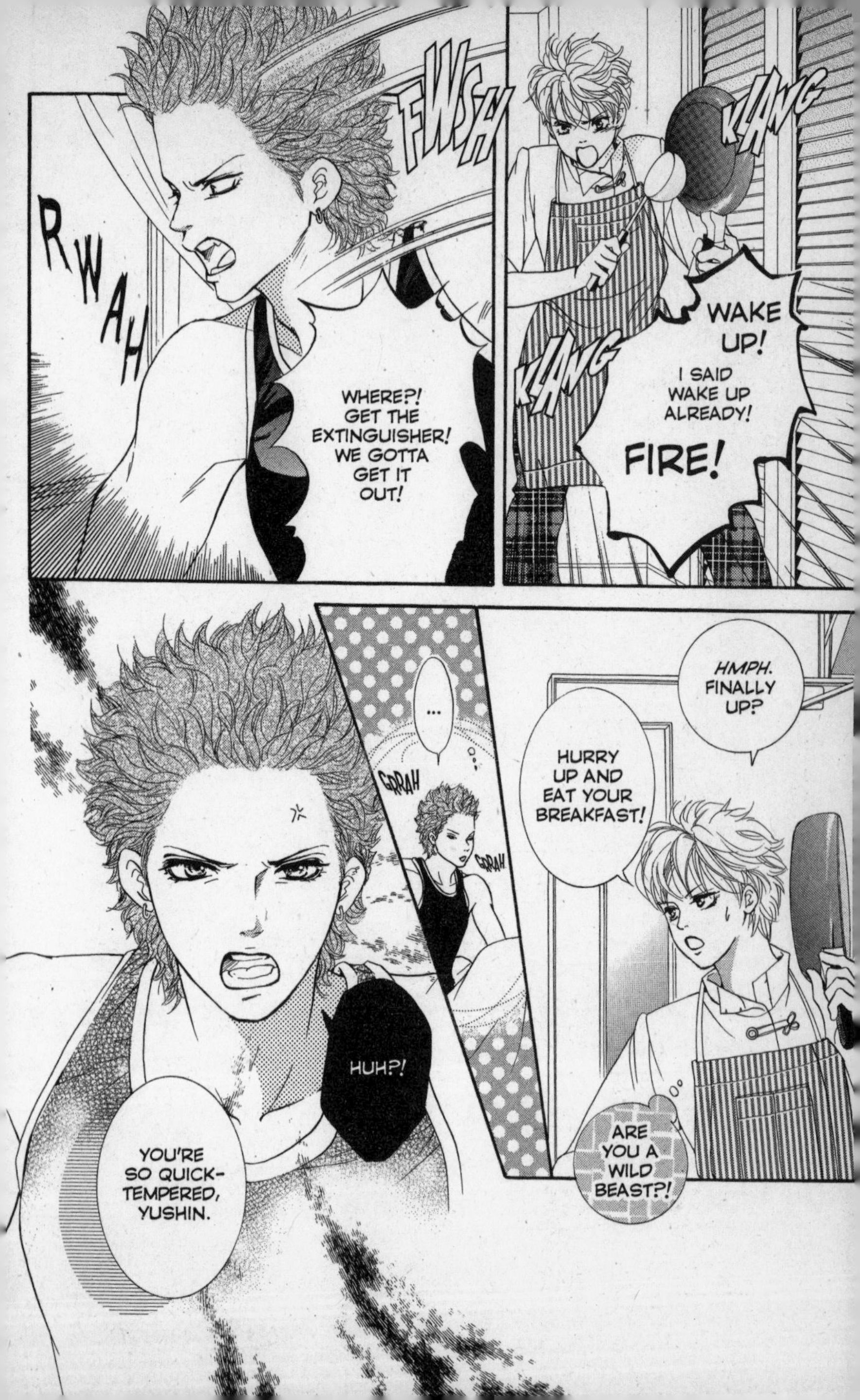
KLANG
WAKE UP!
I SAID WAKE UP ALREADY!
FIRE!
KLANG
FWSH
RWAH
WHERE?! GET THE EXTINGUISHER! WE GOTTA GET IT OUT!
HMPH. FINALLY UP?
HURRY UP AND EAT YOUR BREAKFAST!
ARE YOU A WILD BEAST?!
...
GRRAH
GRRAH
HUH?!
YOU'RE SO QUICK-TEMPERED, YUSHIN.

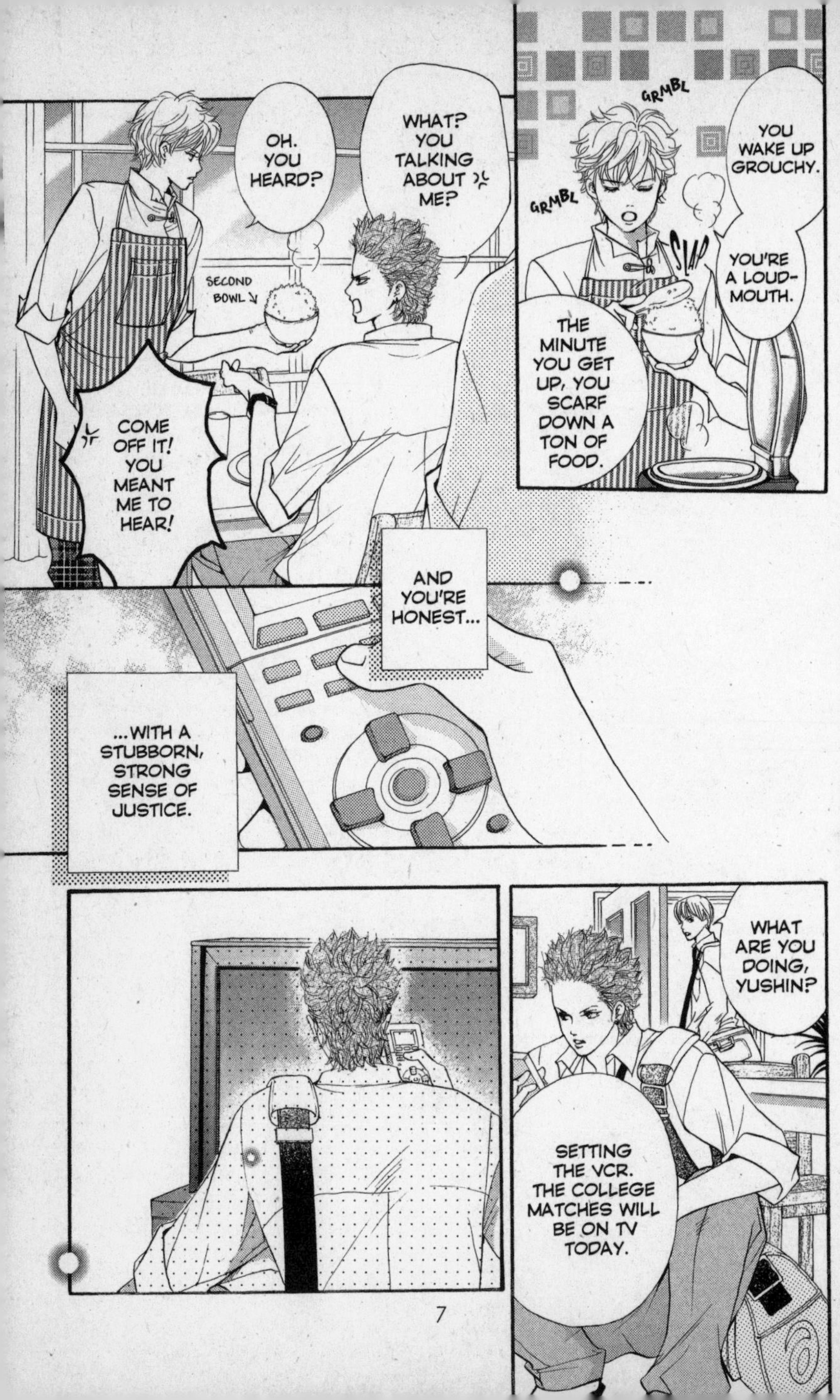
GRMBL
GRMBL
YOU WAKE UP GROUCHY.
SLAP
YOU'RE A LOUD-MOUTH.
THE MINUTE YOU GET UP, YOU SCARF DOWN A TON OF FOOD.
WHAT? YOU TALKING ABOUT ME?
OH. YOU HEARD?
SECOND BOWL
COME OFF IT! YOU MEANT ME TO HEAR!
AND YOU'RE HONEST...
...WITH A STUBBORN, STRONG SENSE OF JUSTICE.
WHAT ARE YOU DOING, YUSHIN?
SETTING THE VCR. THE COLLEGE MATCHES WILL BE ON TV TODAY.

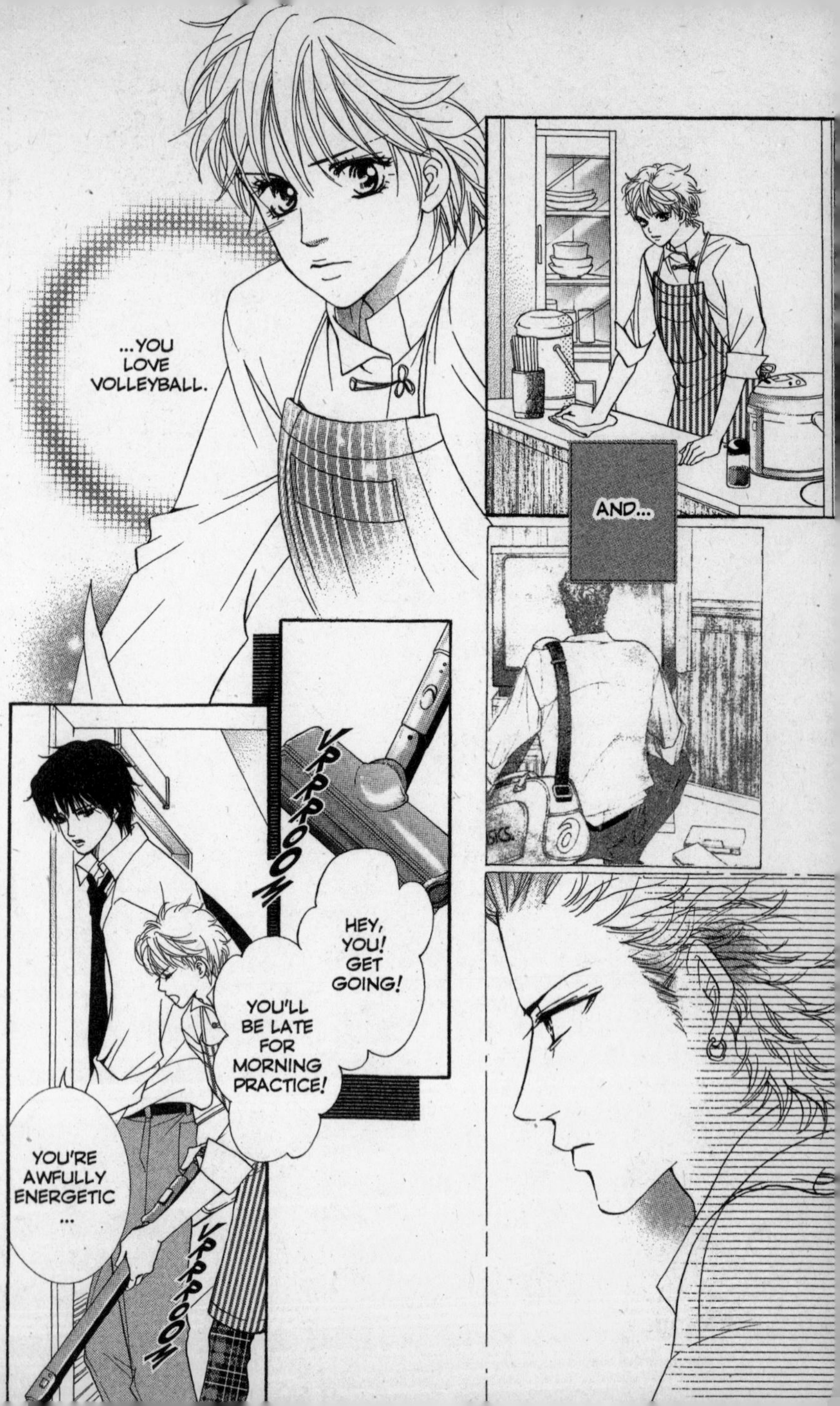
...YOU LOVE VOLLEYBALL.
AND...
VRRROOM
HEY, YOU! GET GOING!
YOU'LL BE LATE FOR MORNING PRACTICE!
YOU'RE AWFULLY ENERGETIC ...
VRRROOM

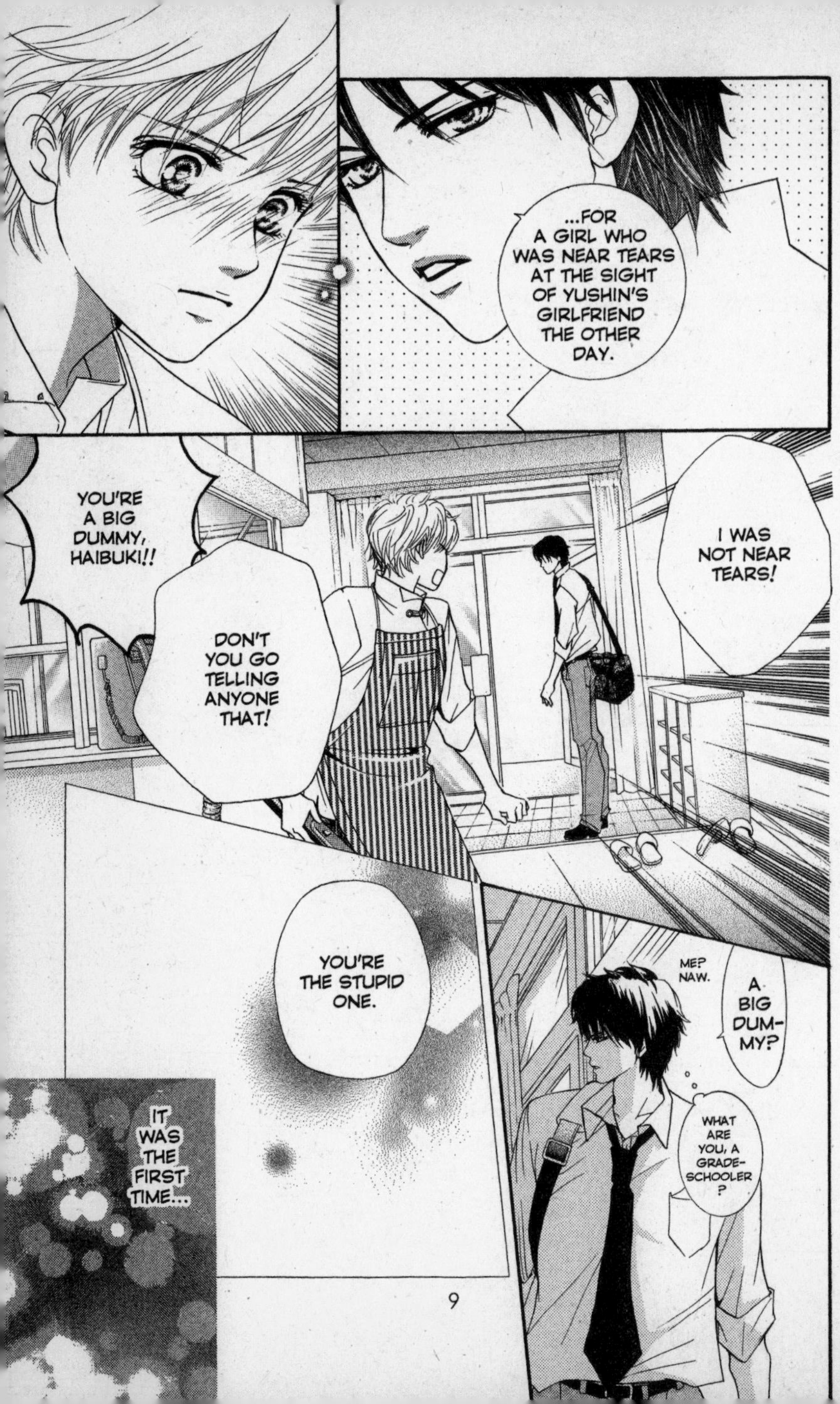
...FOR A GIRL WHO WAS NEAR TEARS AT THE SIGHT OF YUSHIN'S GIRLFRIEND THE OTHER DAY.
I WAS NOT NEAR TEARS!
YOU'RE A BIG DUMMY, HAIBUKI!!
DON'T YOU GO TELLING ANYONE THAT!
A BIG DUM-MY?
ME? NAW.
WHAT ARE YOU, A GRADE-SCHOOLER?
YOU'RE THE STUPID ONE.
IT WAS THE FIRST TIME...

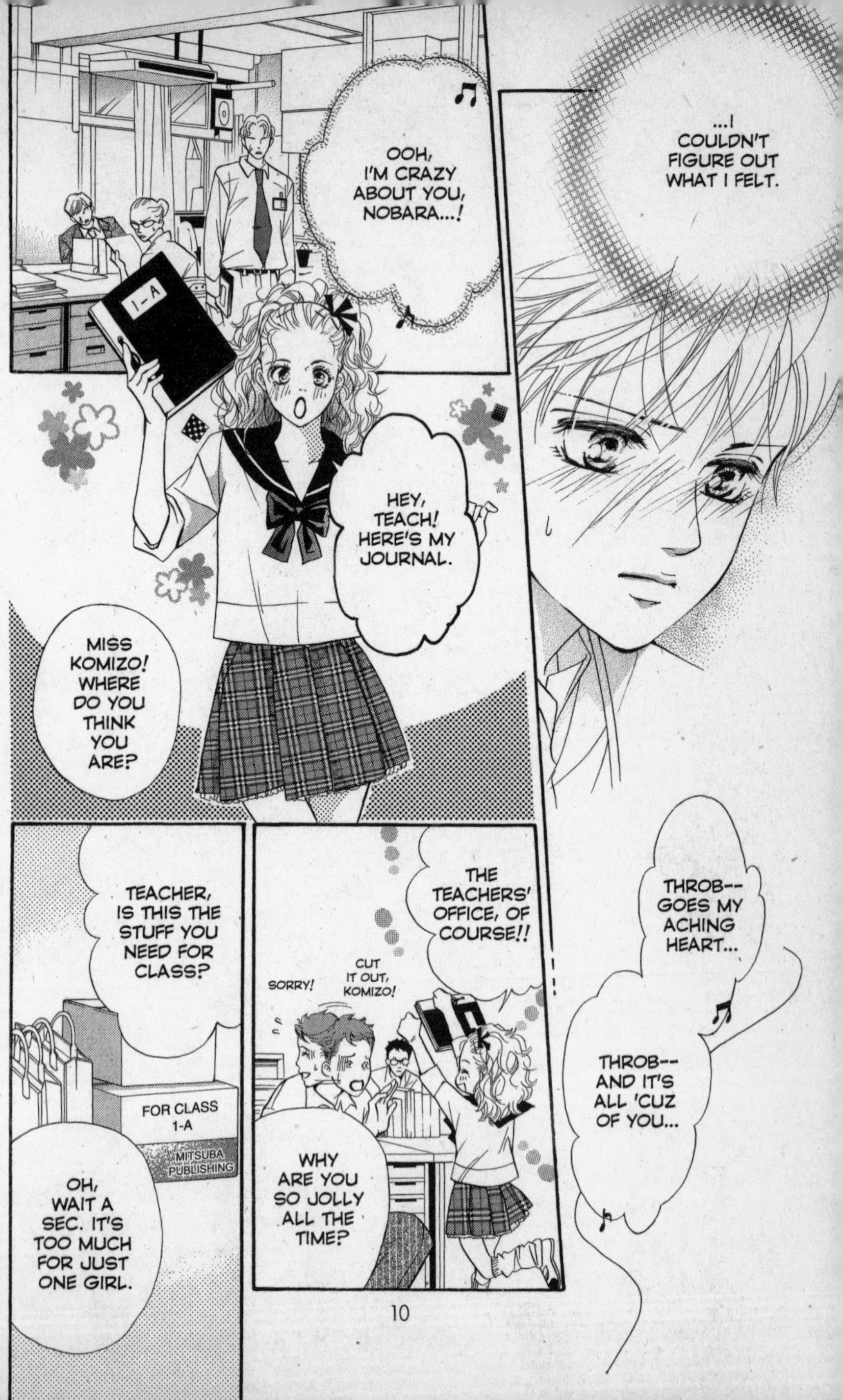
...I COULDN'T FIGURE OUT WHAT I FELT.
THROB-- GOES MY ACHING HEART...
THROB-- AND IT'S ALL 'CUZ OF YOU...
OOH, I'M CRAZY ABOUT YOU, NOBARA...!
1-A
HEY, TEACH! HERE'S MY JOURNAL.
MISS KOMIZO! WHERE DO YOU THINK YOU ARE?
THE TEACHERS' OFFICE, OF COURSE!!
CUT IT OUT, KOMIZO!
SORRY!
WHY ARE YOU SO JOLLY ALL THE TIME?
TEACHER, IS THIS THE STUFF YOU NEED FOR CLASS?
FOR CLASS 1-A
MITSUBA PUBLISHING
OH, WAIT A SEC. IT'S TOO MUCH FOR JUST ONE GIRL.

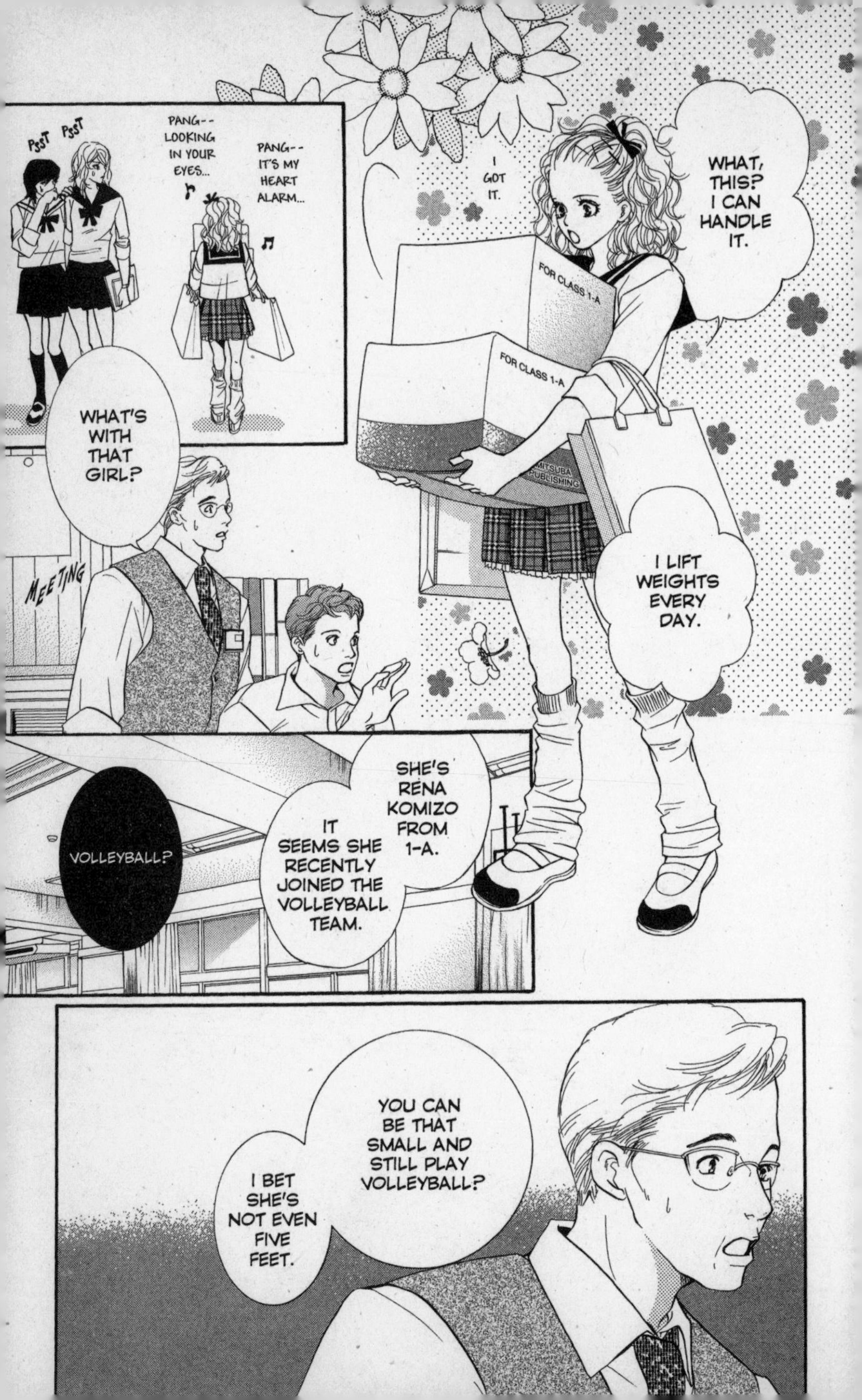
WHAT, THIS? I CAN HANDLE IT.
I GOT IT.
FOR CLASS 1-A
FOR CLASS 1-A
MITSUBA PUBLISHING
I LIFT WEIGHTS EVERY DAY.
PANG-- IT'S MY HEART ALARM...
PANG-- LOOKING IN YOUR EYES...
PSST PSST
WHAT'S WITH THAT GIRL?
MEETING
SHE'S RENA KOMIZO FROM 1-A.
IT SEEMS SHE RECENTLY JOINED THE VOLLEYBALL TEAM.
VOLLEYBALL?
YOU CAN BE THAT SMALL AND STILL PLAY VOLLEYBALL?
I BET SHE'S NOT EVEN FIVE FEET.

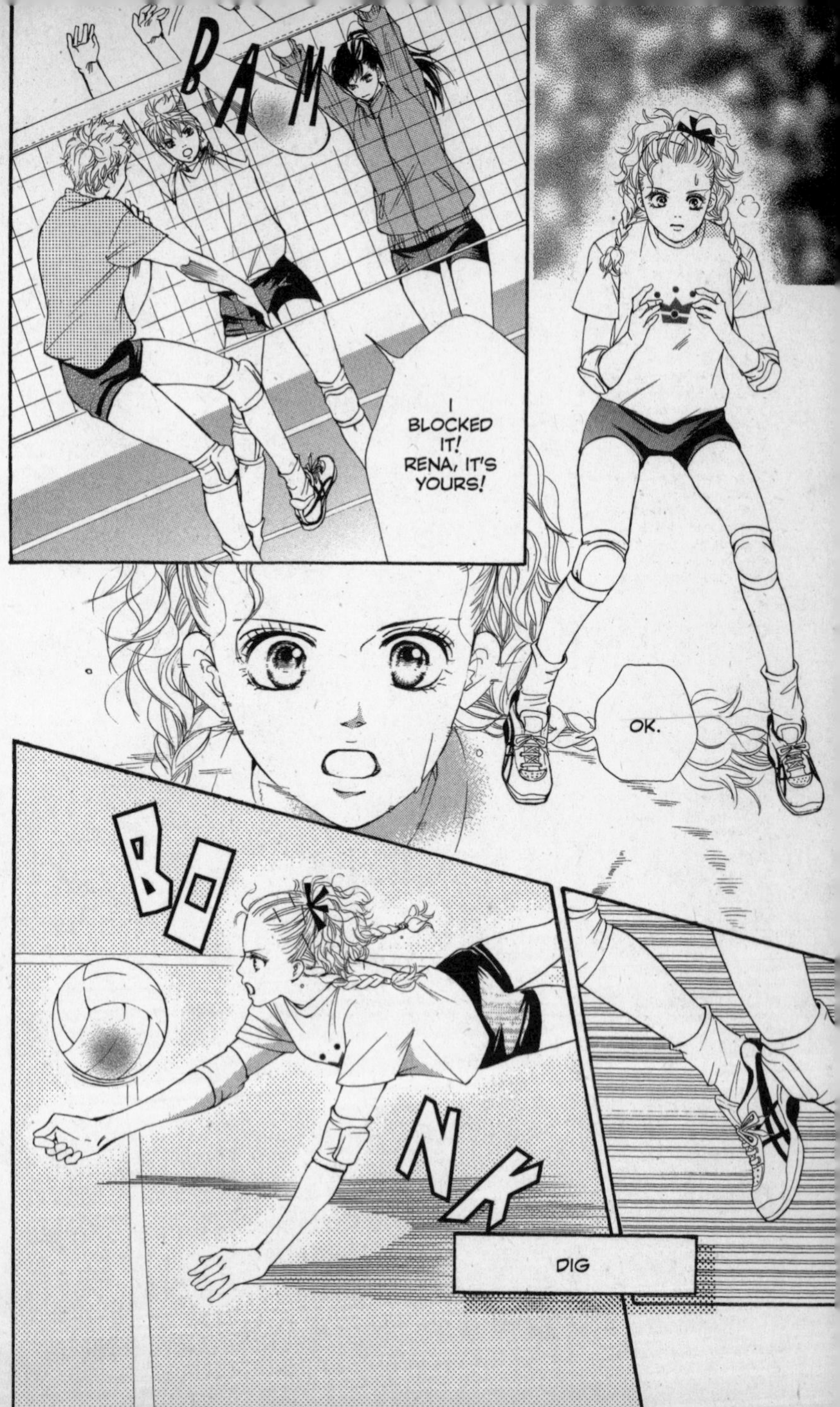
BAM
I BLOCKED IT! RENA, IT'S YOURS!
OK.
BOINK
DIG

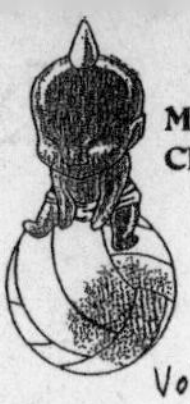

MITSUBA CLUB

Vol. 1

"THAT'S WRONG, TAKANASHI-SAN."

EVERY MONTH IN BETSUMA THERE'S SOMETHING WE CALL A "PREVIEW CUT." YOU GET A REQUEST FOR SOMETHING THAT GOES WITH THAT MONTH--THINGS LIKE A SWIMSUIT SHOT IN SUMMER OR AN EATING SCENE IN AUTUMN (SINCE AUTUMN IS THE BEST SEASON FOR EATING). THE REQUEST COMES BY PHONE. ONE MONTH THEY WANTED A SHAMPOO SCENE! I FORGET WHICH MONTH IT WAS FOR, BUT SHAMPOO? HUH? WAS THE THEME SOMETHING LIKE BETSUMA SUPPORTS PURE AND CLEAN ROMANCE? OKAY, THEN! SHAMPOO IT IS! SO I DREW NOBARA HAPPILY SHAMPOOING HER HAIR AND SENT IT IN...ONLY TO FIND THAT THEY DIDN'T WANT "SHAMPOO." THEY WANTED "JUMP." (NOTE: "JUMP" IN JAPANESE IS "JAMPU.") IT WOULD'VE BEEN STRANGE FOR MY CUT TO FEATURE A SHAMPOO SCENE WHEN ALL THE OTHER TITLES FEATURED A JUMP SCENE, SO I REDREW MINE.

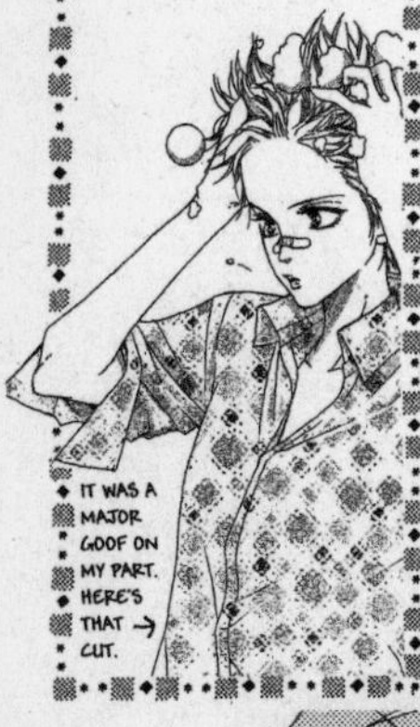

◆ IT WAS A MAJOR GOOF ON MY PART. HERE'S THAT → CUT.

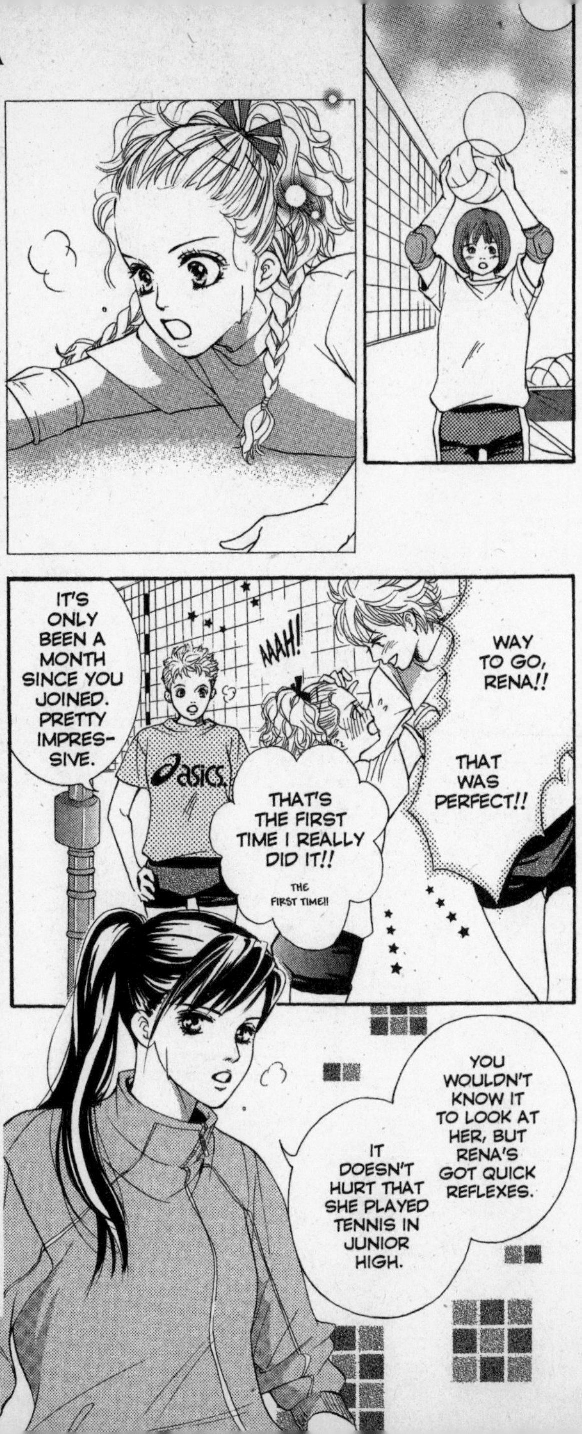
WAY TO GO, RENA!!
THAT WAS PERFECT!!
AAAH!
THAT'S THE FIRST TIME I REALLY DID IT!!
THE FIRST TIME!!
IT'S ONLY BEEN A MONTH SINCE YOU JOINED. PRETTY IMPRESSIVE.
asics
YOU WOULDN'T KNOW IT TO LOOK AT HER, BUT RENA'S GOT QUICK REFLEXES.
IT DOESN'T HURT THAT SHE PLAYED TENNIS IN JUNIOR HIGH.

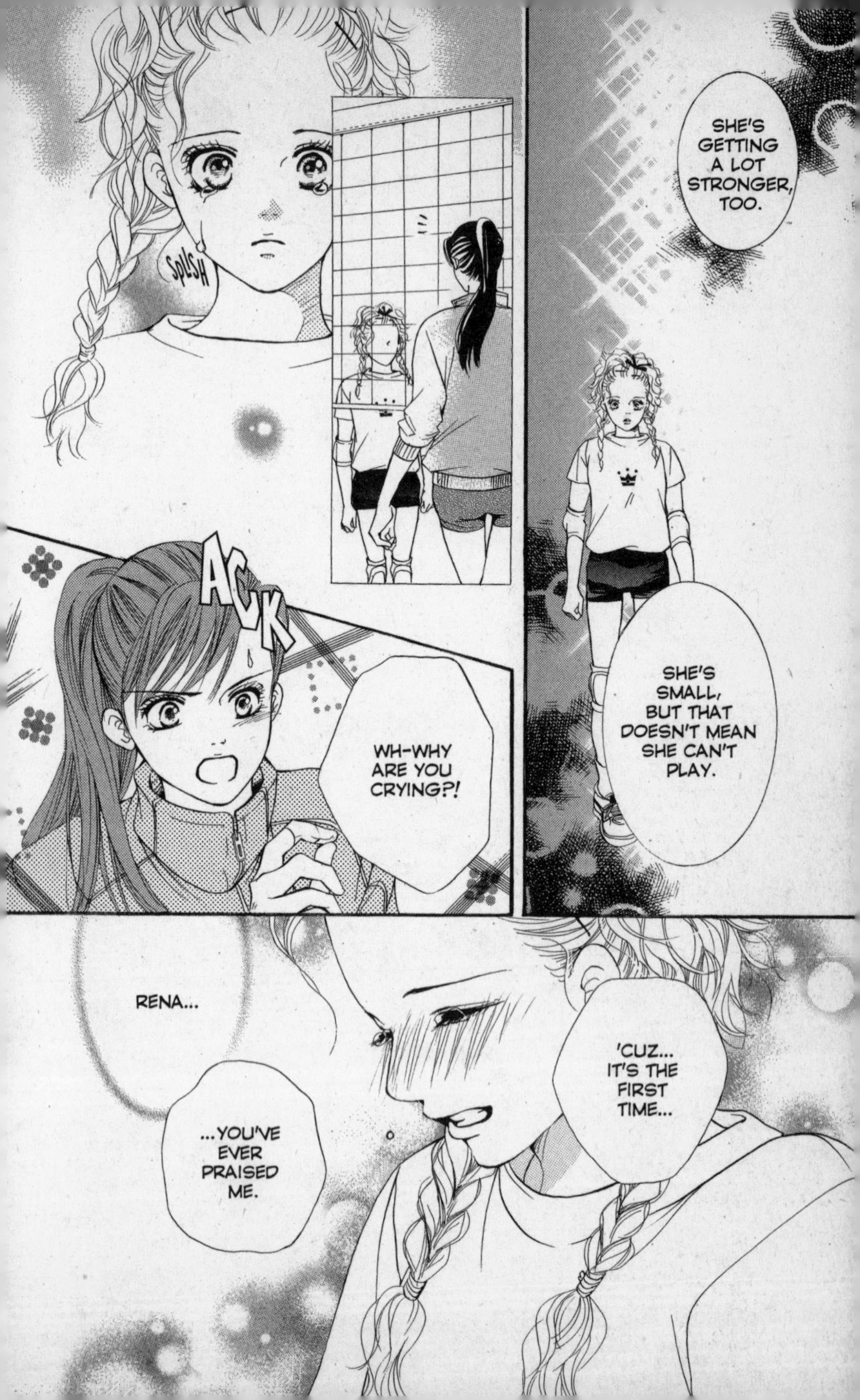
SHE'S GETTING A LOT STRONGER, TOO.
SHE'S SMALL, BUT THAT DOESN'T MEAN SHE CAN'T PLAY.
SPLISH
ACK
WH-WHY ARE YOU CRYING?!
'CUZ... IT'S THE FIRST TIME...
RENA...
...YOU'VE EVER PRAISED ME.

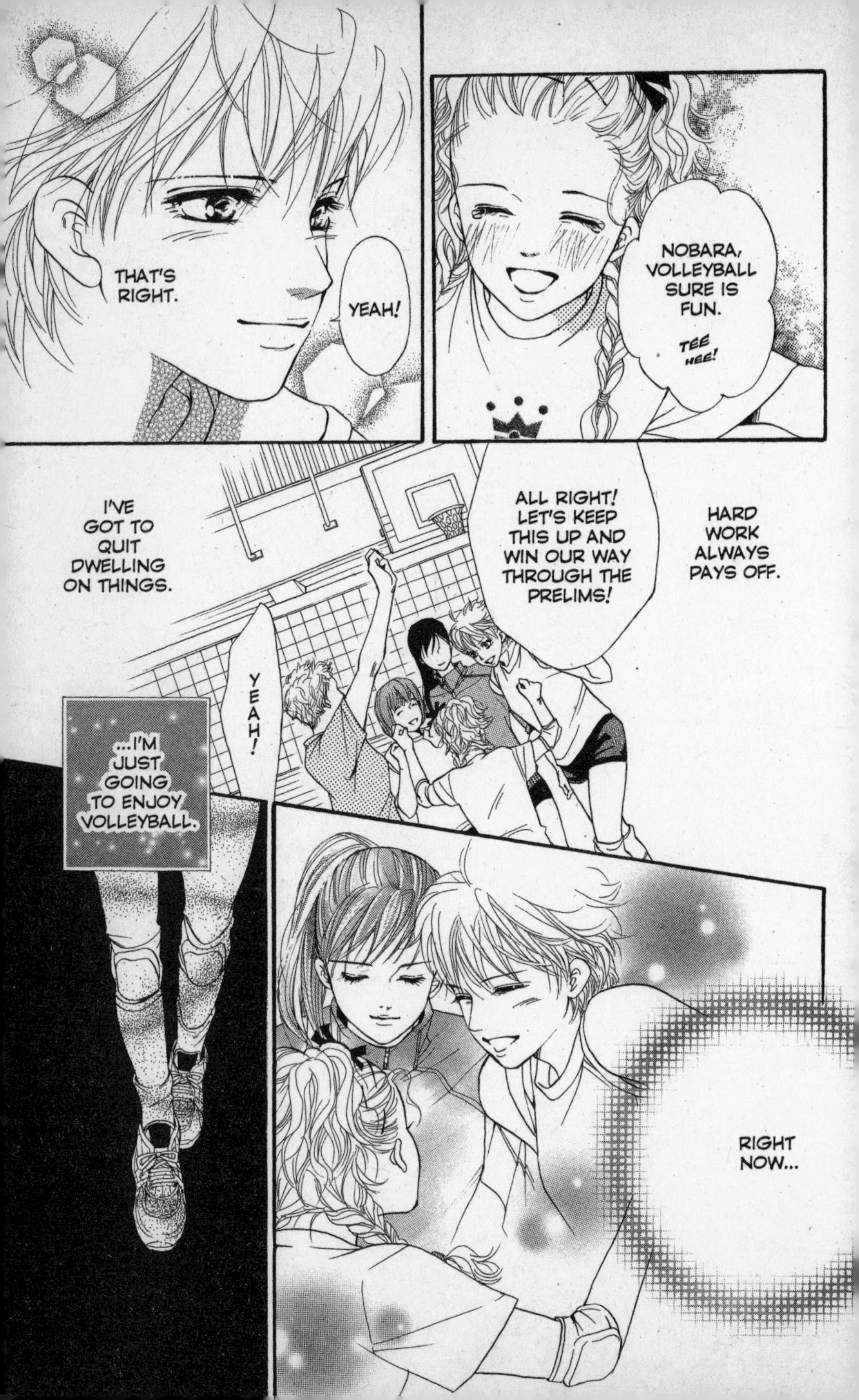
NOBARA, VOLLEYBALL SURE IS FUN.
TEE HEE!
YEAH!
THAT'S RIGHT.
HARD WORK ALWAYS PAYS OFF.
ALL RIGHT! LET'S KEEP THIS UP AND WIN OUR WAY THROUGH THE PRELIMS!
YEAH!
I'VE GOT TO QUIT DWELLING ON THINGS.
RIGHT NOW...
...I'M JUST GOING TO ENJOY VOLLEYBALL.

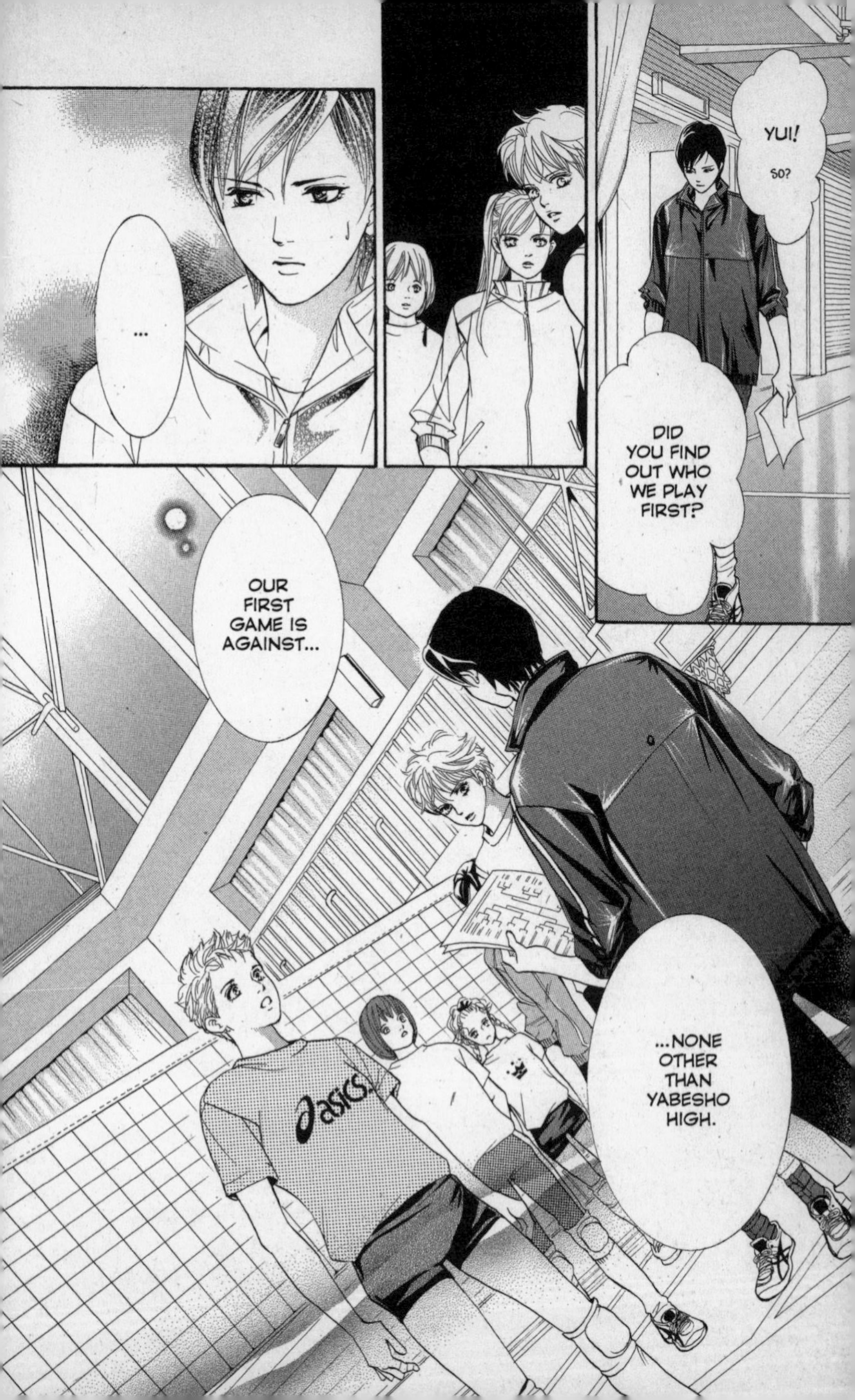
YUI!
SO?
DID YOU FIND OUT WHO WE PLAY FIRST?
...
OUR FIRST GAME IS AGAINST...
...NONE OTHER THAN YABESHO HIGH.

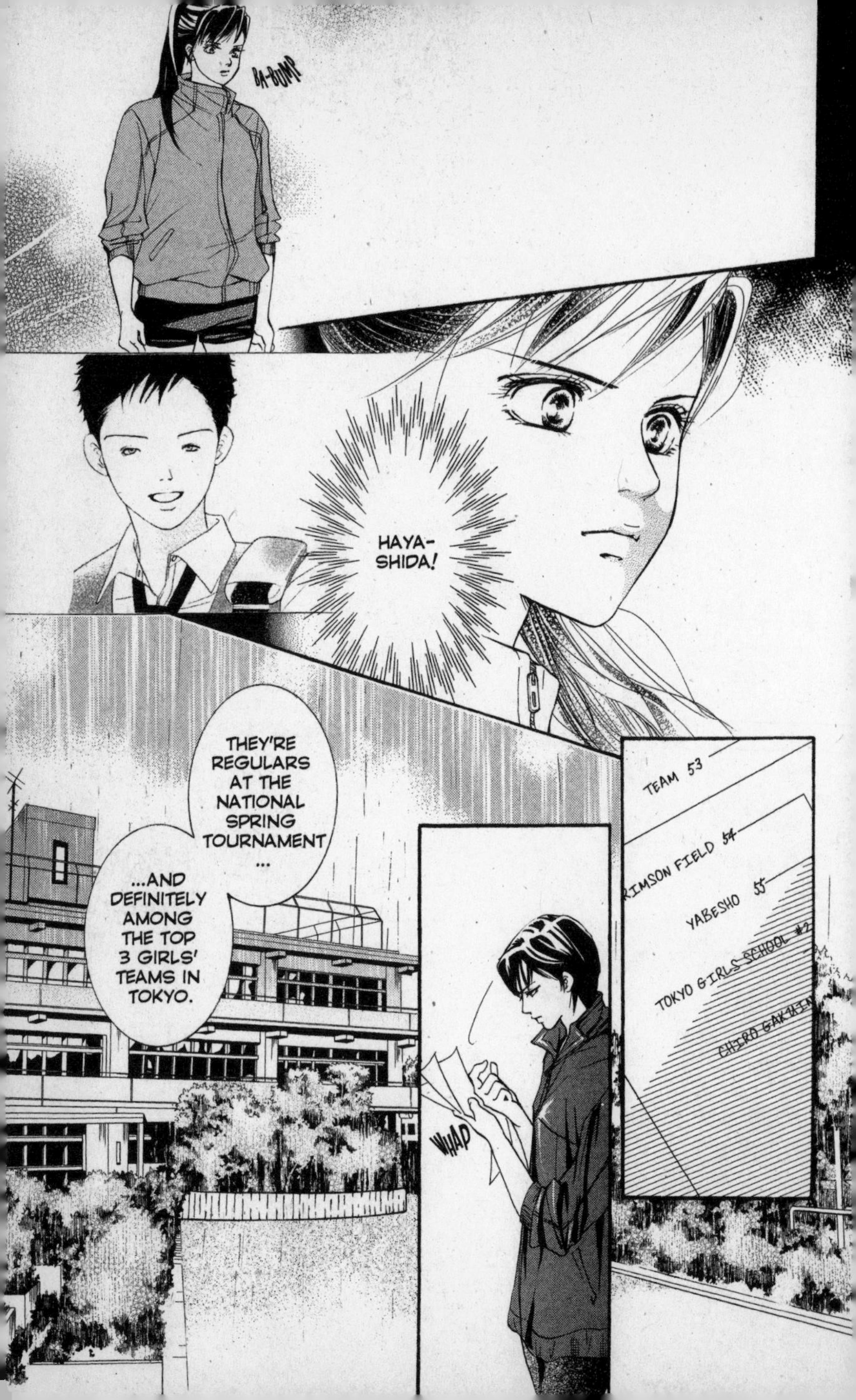
BA-BUMP
HAYA-SHIDA!
TEAM 53
RIMSON FIELD 54
YABESHO 55
TOKYO GIRLS SCHOOL #2
CHIRO GAKUIN
WHAP
THEY'RE REGULARS AT THE NATIONAL SPRING TOURNAMENT...
...AND DEFINITELY AMONG THE TOP 3 GIRLS' TEAMS IN TOKYO.

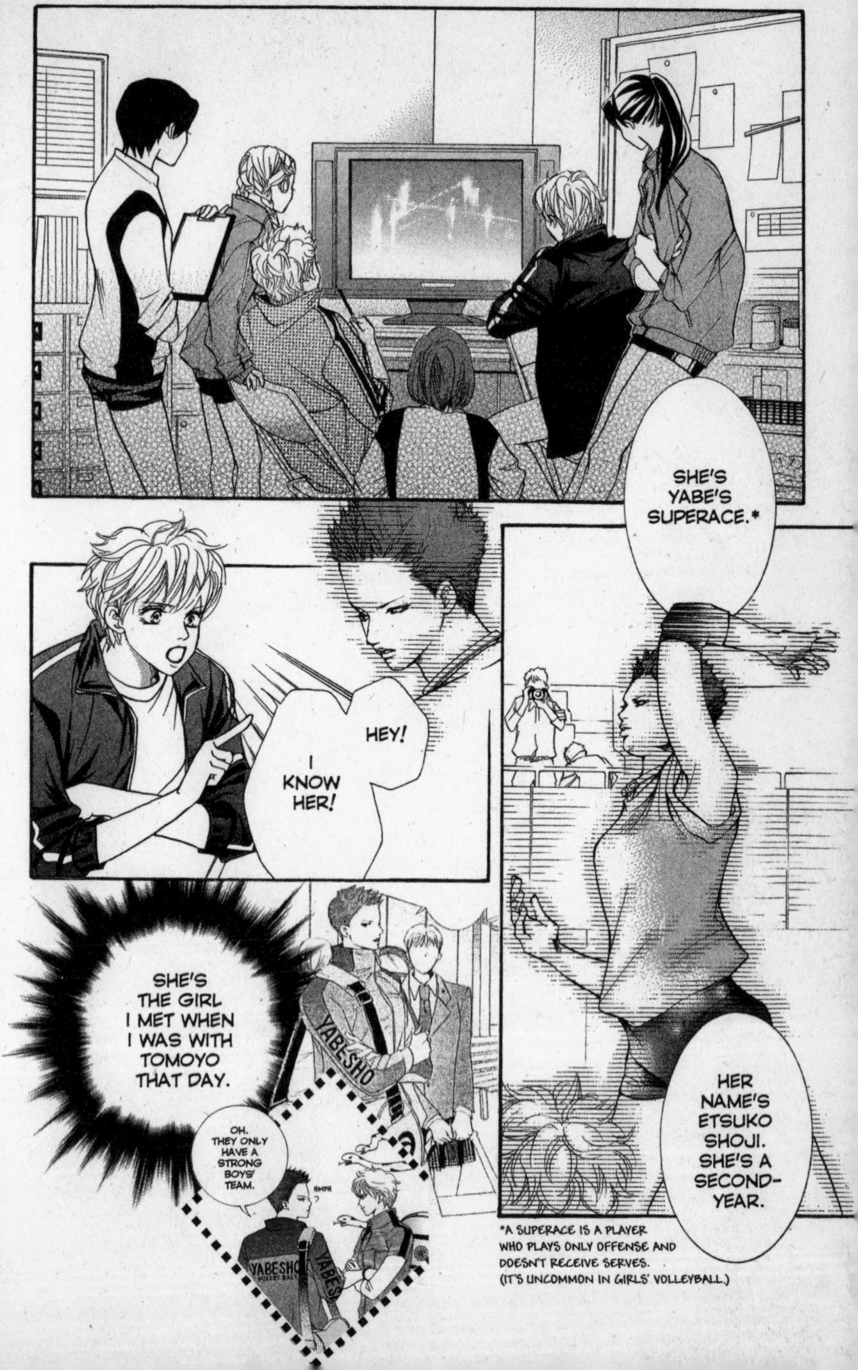
SHE'S YABE'S SUPERACE.*
HER NAME'S ETSUKO SHOJI. SHE'S A SECOND-YEAR.
HEY!
I KNOW HER!
SHE'S THE GIRL I MET WHEN I WAS WITH TOMOYO THAT DAY.
YABESHO
OH. THEY ONLY HAVE A STRONG BOYS' TEAM.
HMPH
YABESHO

*A SUPERACE IS A PLAYER WHO PLAYS ONLY OFFENSE AND DOESN'T RECEIVE SERVES. (IT'S UNCOMMON IN GIRLS' VOLLEYBALL.)

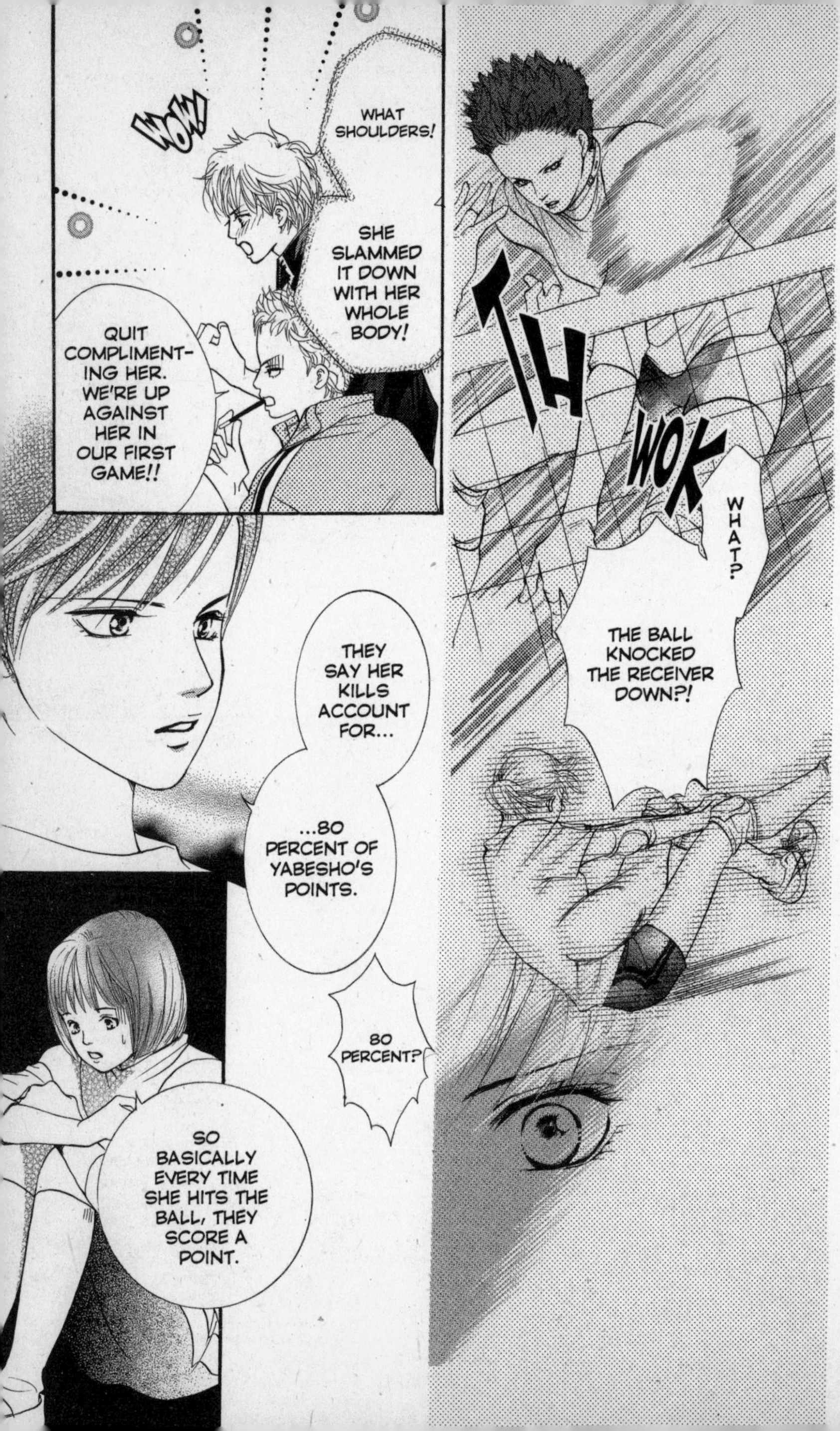
THWOK
WHAT?
THE BALL KNOCKED THE RECEIVER DOWN?!
WOW!
WHAT SHOULDERS!
SHE SLAMMED IT DOWN WITH HER WHOLE BODY!
QUIT COMPLIMENTING HER. WE'RE UP AGAINST HER IN OUR FIRST GAME!!
THEY SAY HER KILLS ACCOUNT FOR...
...80 PERCENT OF YABESHO'S POINTS.
80 PERCENT?
SO BASICALLY EVERY TIME SHE HITS THE BALL, THEY SCORE A POINT.

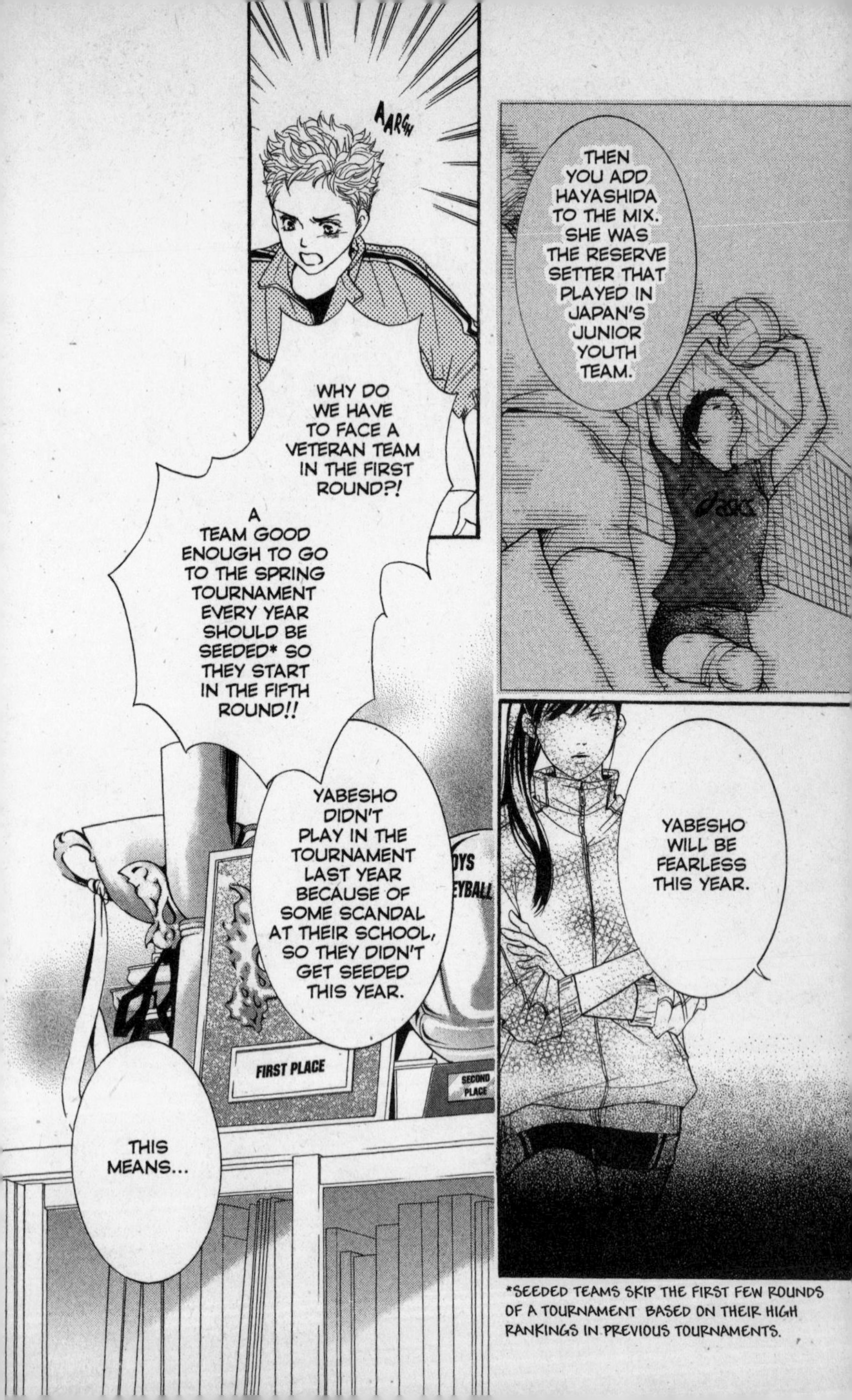
THEN YOU ADD HAYASHIDA TO THE MIX. SHE WAS THE RESERVE SETTER THAT PLAYED IN JAPAN'S JUNIOR YOUTH TEAM.
YABESHO WILL BE FEARLESS THIS YEAR.
AARGH
WHY DO WE HAVE TO FACE A VETERAN TEAM IN THE FIRST ROUND?!
A TEAM GOOD ENOUGH TO GO TO THE SPRING TOURNAMENT EVERY YEAR SHOULD BE SEEDED* SO THEY START IN THE FIFTH ROUND!!
YABESHO DIDN'T PLAY IN THE TOURNAMENT LAST YEAR BECAUSE OF SOME SCANDAL AT THEIR SCHOOL, SO THEY DIDN'T GET SEEDED THIS YEAR.
FIRST PLACE
SECOND PLACE
THIS MEANS...

*SEEDED TEAMS SKIP THE FIRST FEW ROUNDS OF A TOURNAMENT BASED ON THEIR HIGH RANKINGS IN PREVIOUS TOURNAMENTS.

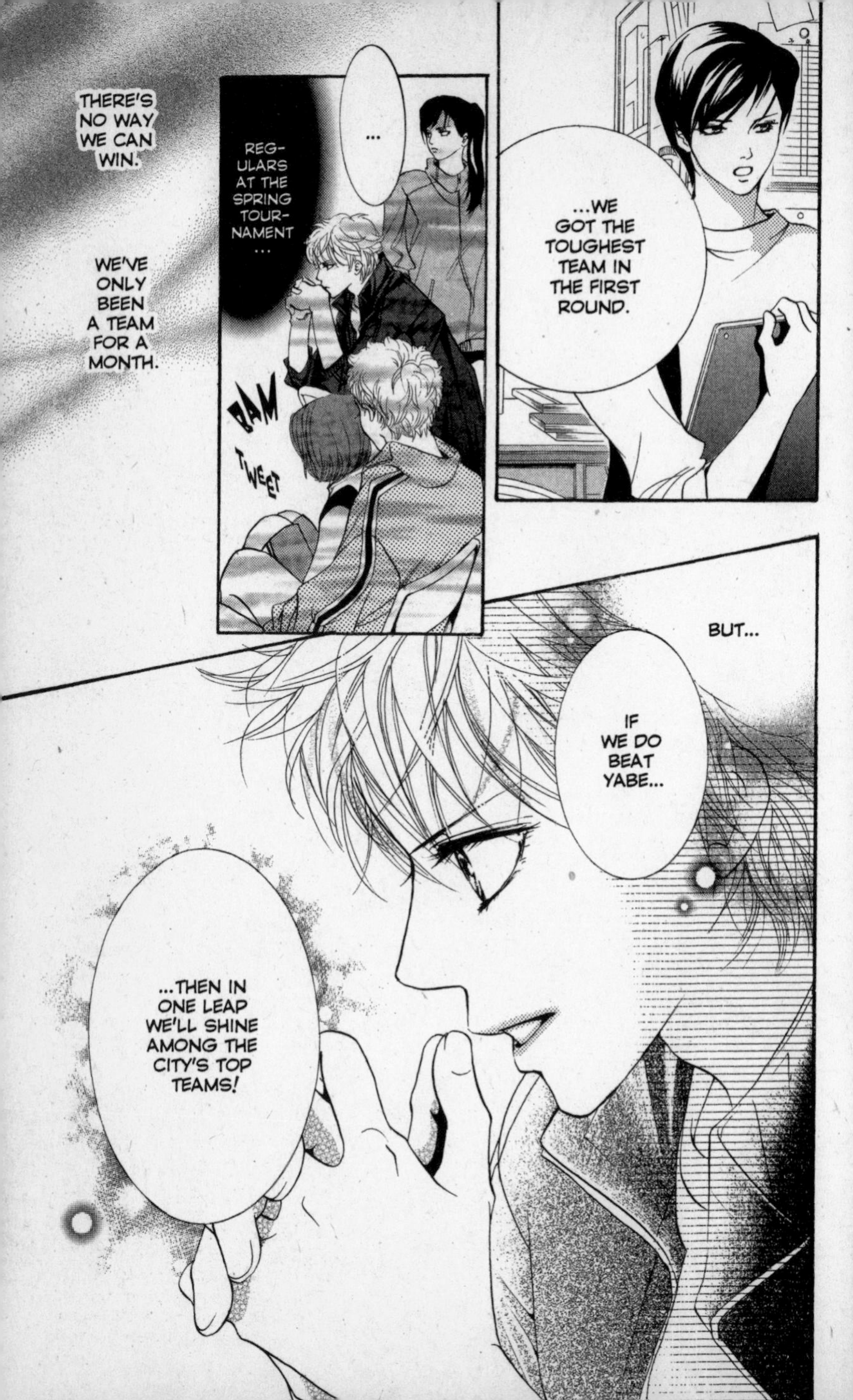
...WE GOT THE TOUGHEST TEAM IN THE FIRST ROUND.
...
REG-ULARS AT THE SPRING TOUR-NAMENT...
BAM
TWEET
THERE'S NO WAY WE CAN WIN.
WE'VE ONLY BEEN A TEAM FOR A MONTH.
BUT...
IF WE DO BEAT YABE...
...THEN IN ONE LEAP WE'LL SHINE AMONG THE CITY'S TOP TEAMS!

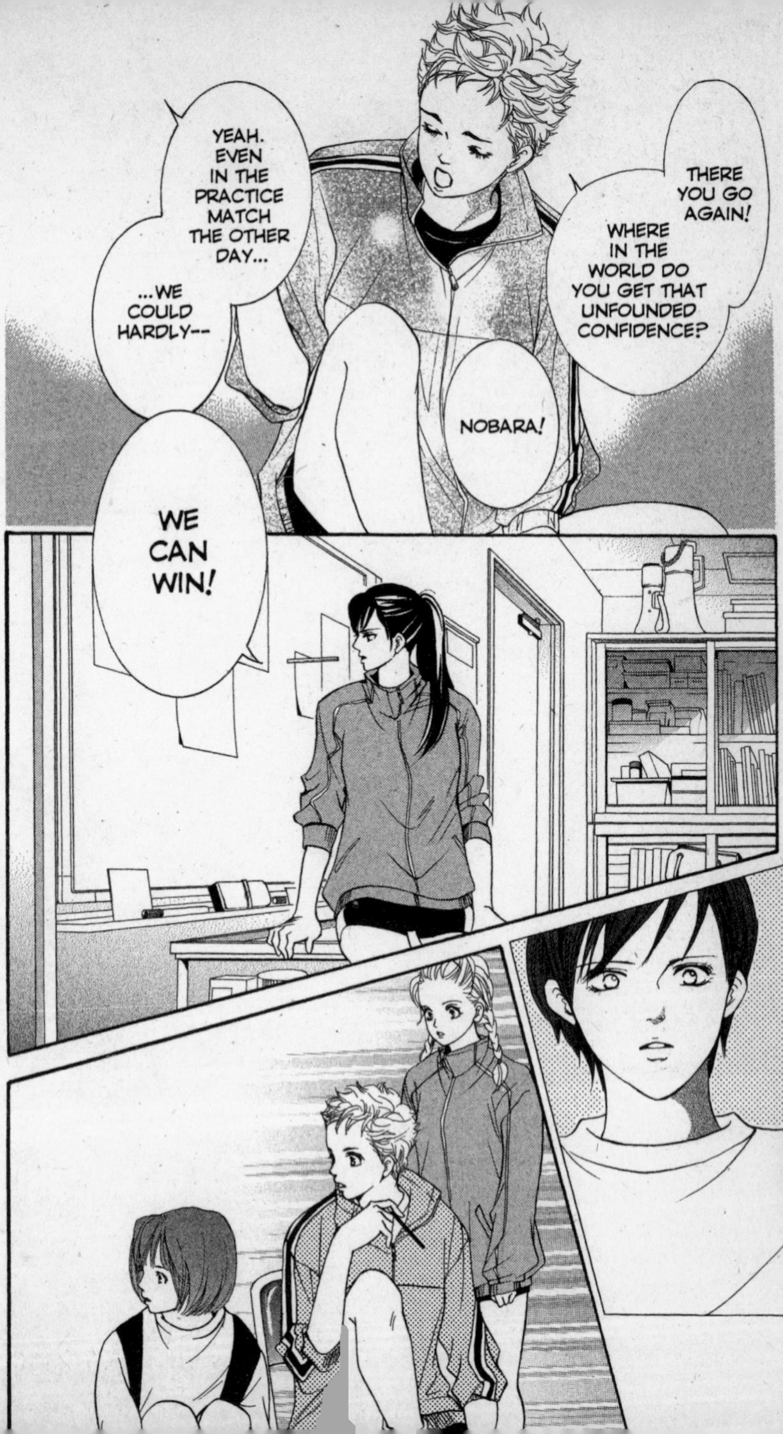

THERE YOU GO AGAIN! WHERE IN THE WORLD DO YOU GET THAT UNFOUNDED CONFIDENCE?
YEAH. EVEN IN THE PRACTICE MATCH THE OTHER DAY...
...WE COULD HARDLY--
NOBARA!
WE CAN WIN!

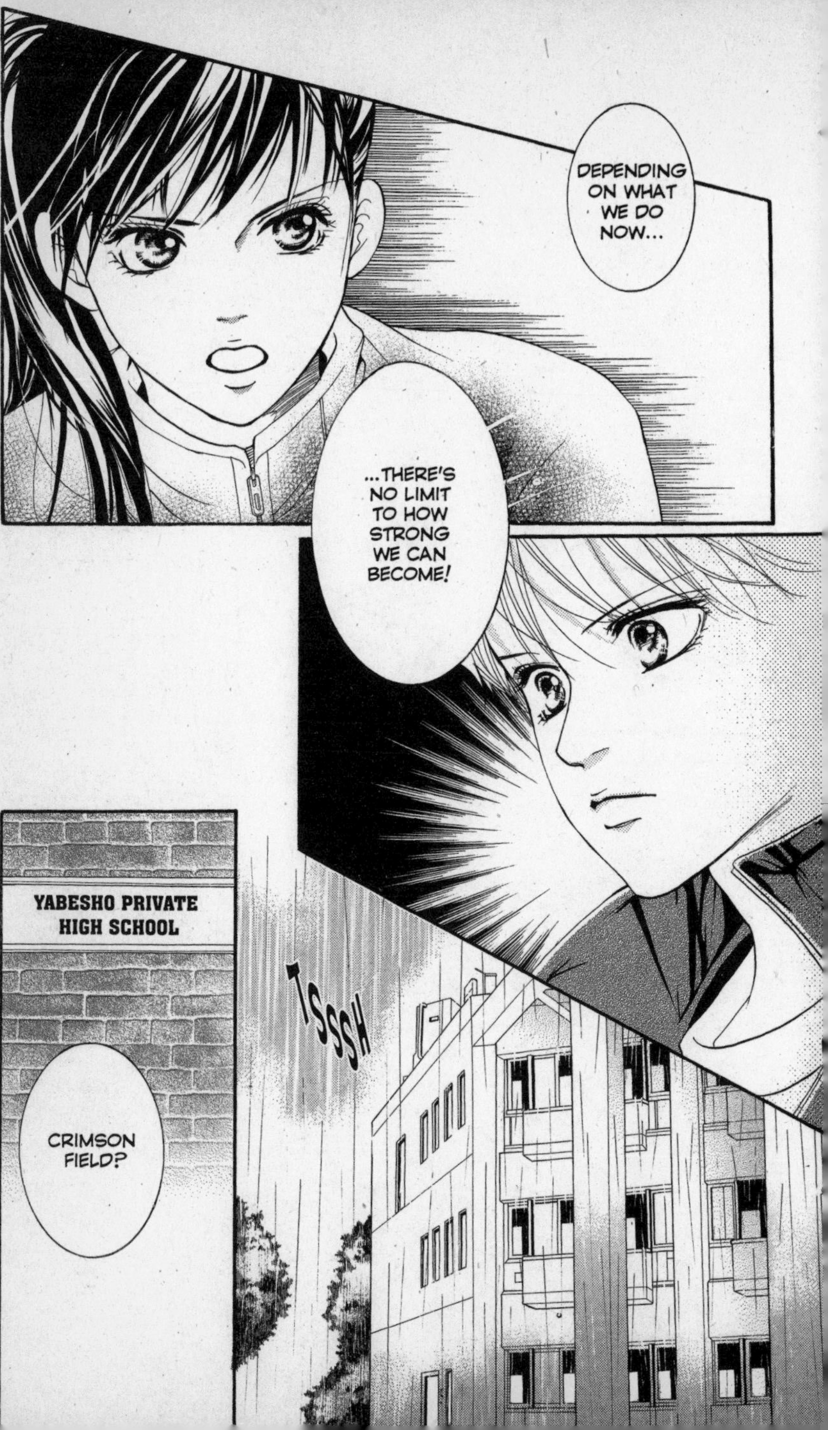
DEPENDING ON WHAT WE DO NOW...
...THERE'S NO LIMIT TO HOW STRONG WE CAN BECOME!
YABESHO PRIVATE HIGH SCHOOL
TSSSH
CRIMSON FIELD?

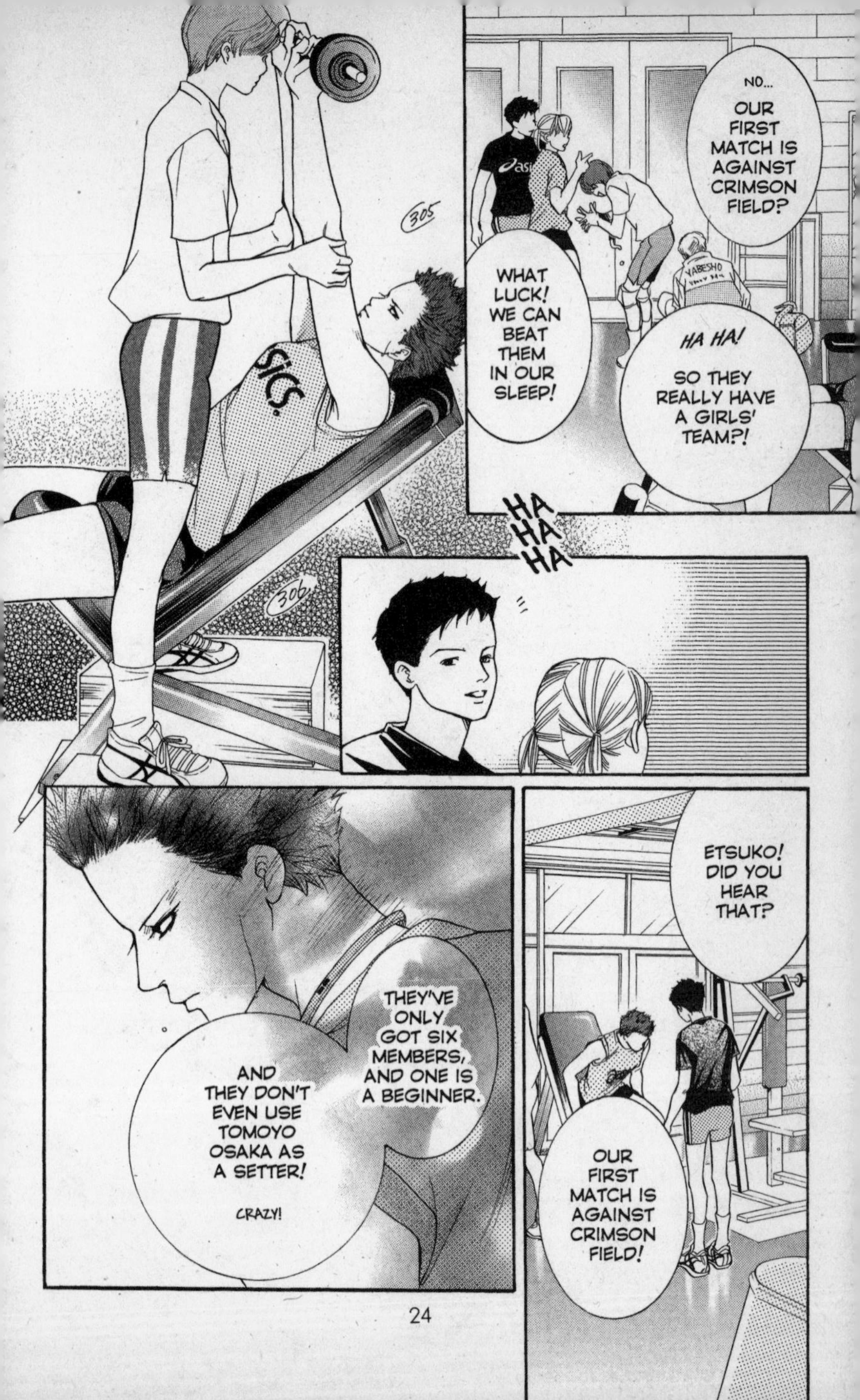
NO...
OUR FIRST MATCH IS AGAINST CRIMSON FIELD?
WHAT LUCK! WE CAN BEAT THEM IN OUR SLEEP!
HA HA!
SO THEY REALLY HAVE A GIRLS' TEAM?!
YABESHO
HA HA HA
305
306
ETSUKO! DID YOU HEAR THAT?
OUR FIRST MATCH IS AGAINST CRIMSON FIELD!
THEY'VE ONLY GOT SIX MEMBERS, AND ONE IS A BEGINNER.
AND THEY DON'T EVEN USE TOMOYO OSAKA AS A SETTER!
CRAZY!

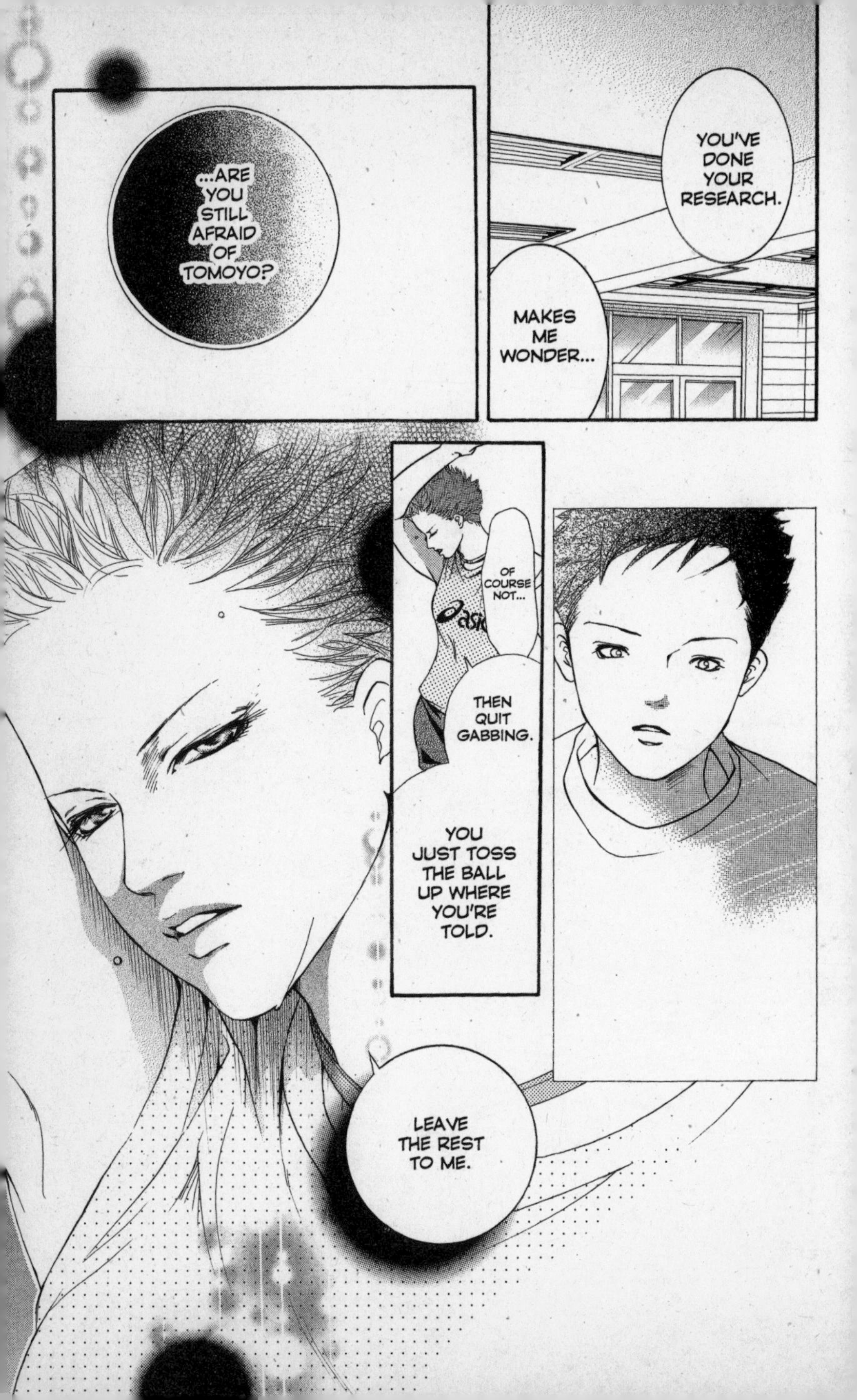
YOU'VE DONE YOUR RESEARCH.
MAKES ME WONDER...
...ARE YOU STILL AFRAID OF TOMOYO?
OF COURSE NOT...
THEN QUIT GABBING.
YOU JUST TOSS THE BALL UP WHERE YOU'RE TOLD.
LEAVE THE REST TO ME.

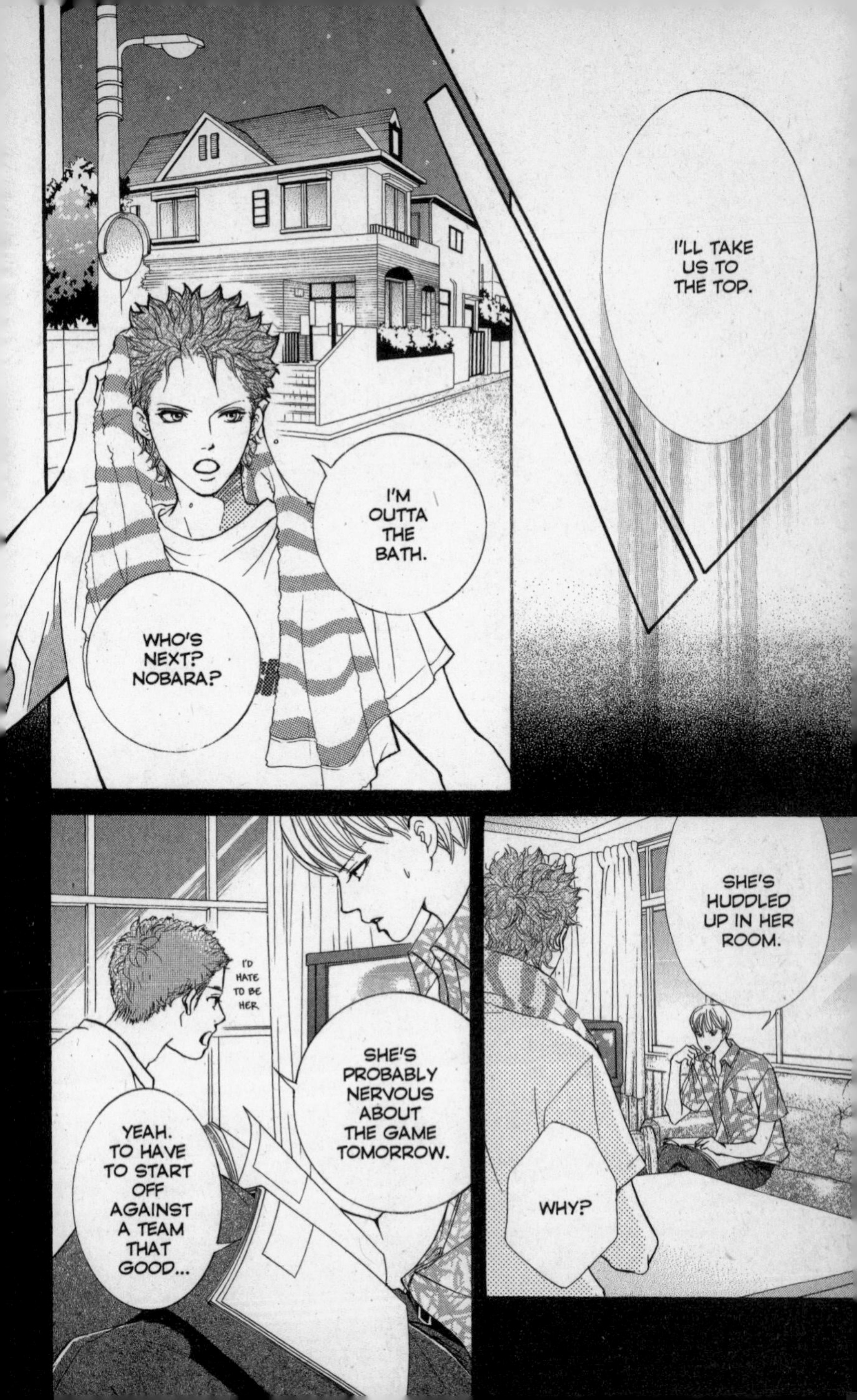
I'LL TAKE US TO THE TOP.
I'M OUTTA THE BATH.
WHO'S NEXT? NOBARA?
SHE'S HUDDLED UP IN HER ROOM.
WHY?
SHE'S PROBABLY NERVOUS ABOUT THE GAME TOMORROW.
YEAH. TO HAVE TO START OFF AGAINST A TEAM THAT GOOD...
I'D HATE TO BE HER

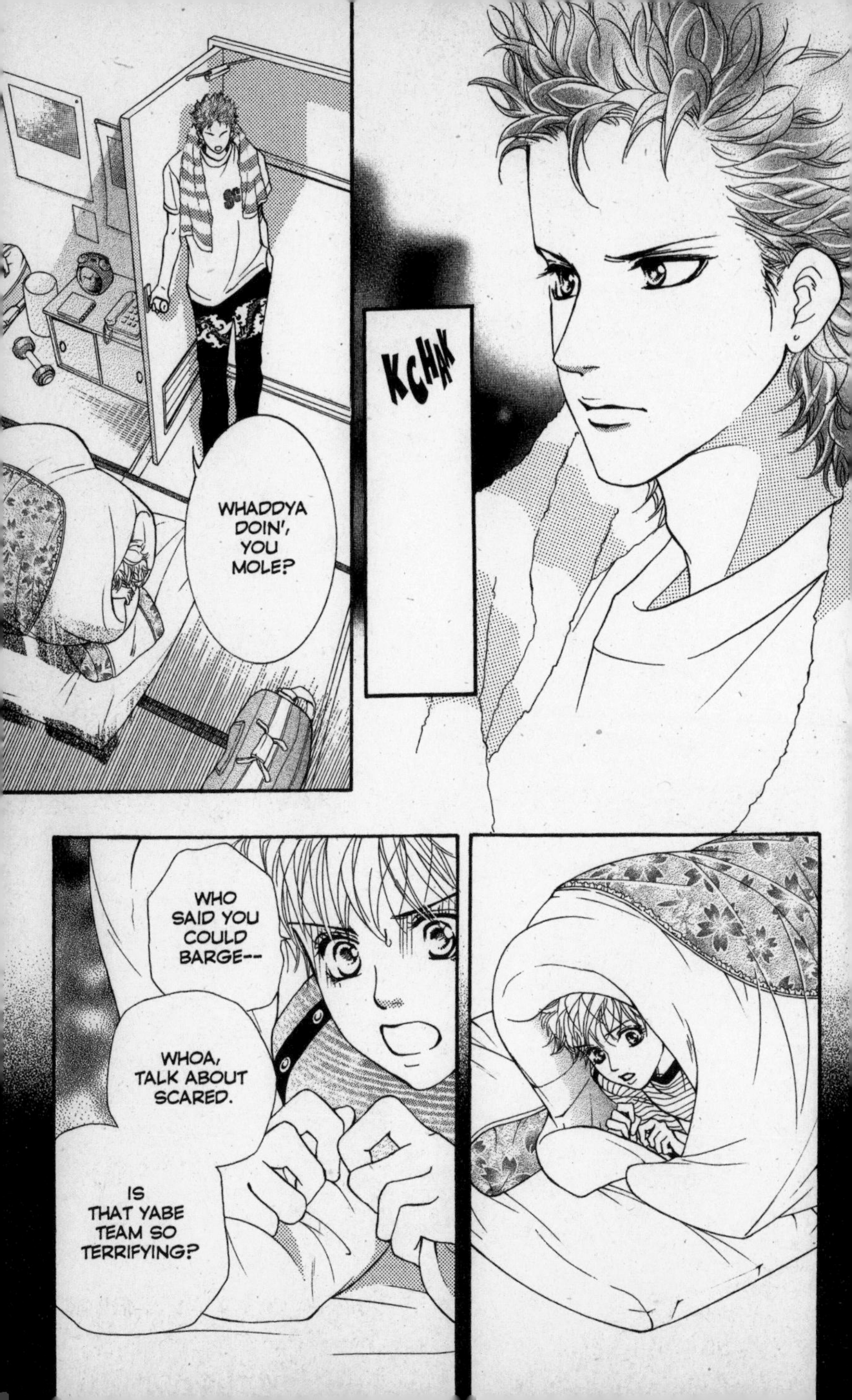
KCHAK
WHADDYA DOIN', YOU MOLE?
WHO SAID YOU COULD BARGE--
WHOA, TALK ABOUT SCARED.
IS THAT YABE TEAM SO TERRIFYING?

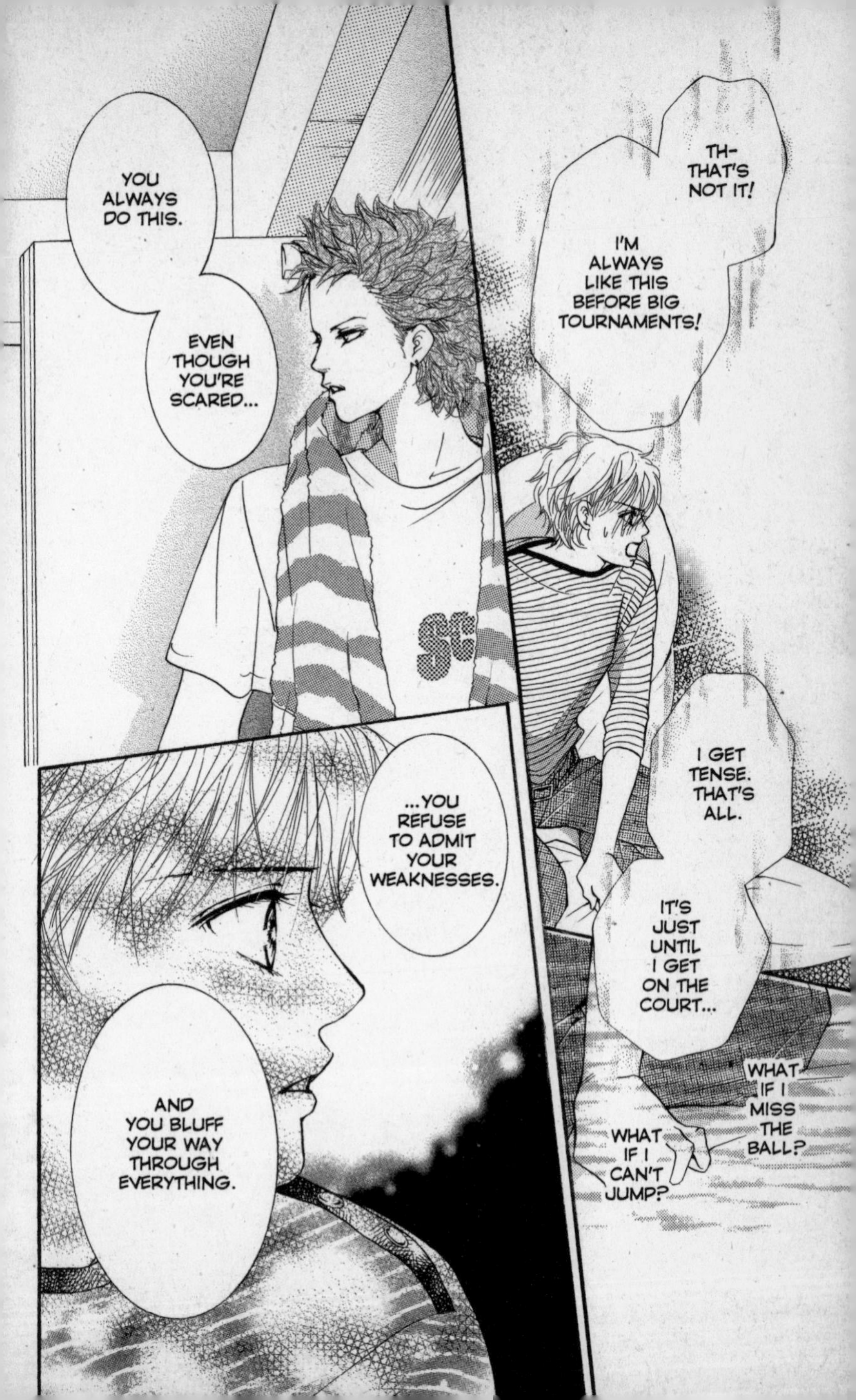
TH-THAT'S NOT IT!
I'M ALWAYS LIKE THIS BEFORE BIG TOURNAMENTS!
I GET TENSE. THAT'S ALL.
IT'S JUST UNTIL I GET ON THE COURT...
WHAT IF I MISS THE BALL?
WHAT IF I CAN'T JUMP?
YOU ALWAYS DO THIS.
EVEN THOUGH YOU'RE SCARED...
...YOU REFUSE TO ADMIT YOUR WEAKNESSES.
AND YOU BLUFF YOUR WAY THROUGH EVERYTHING.

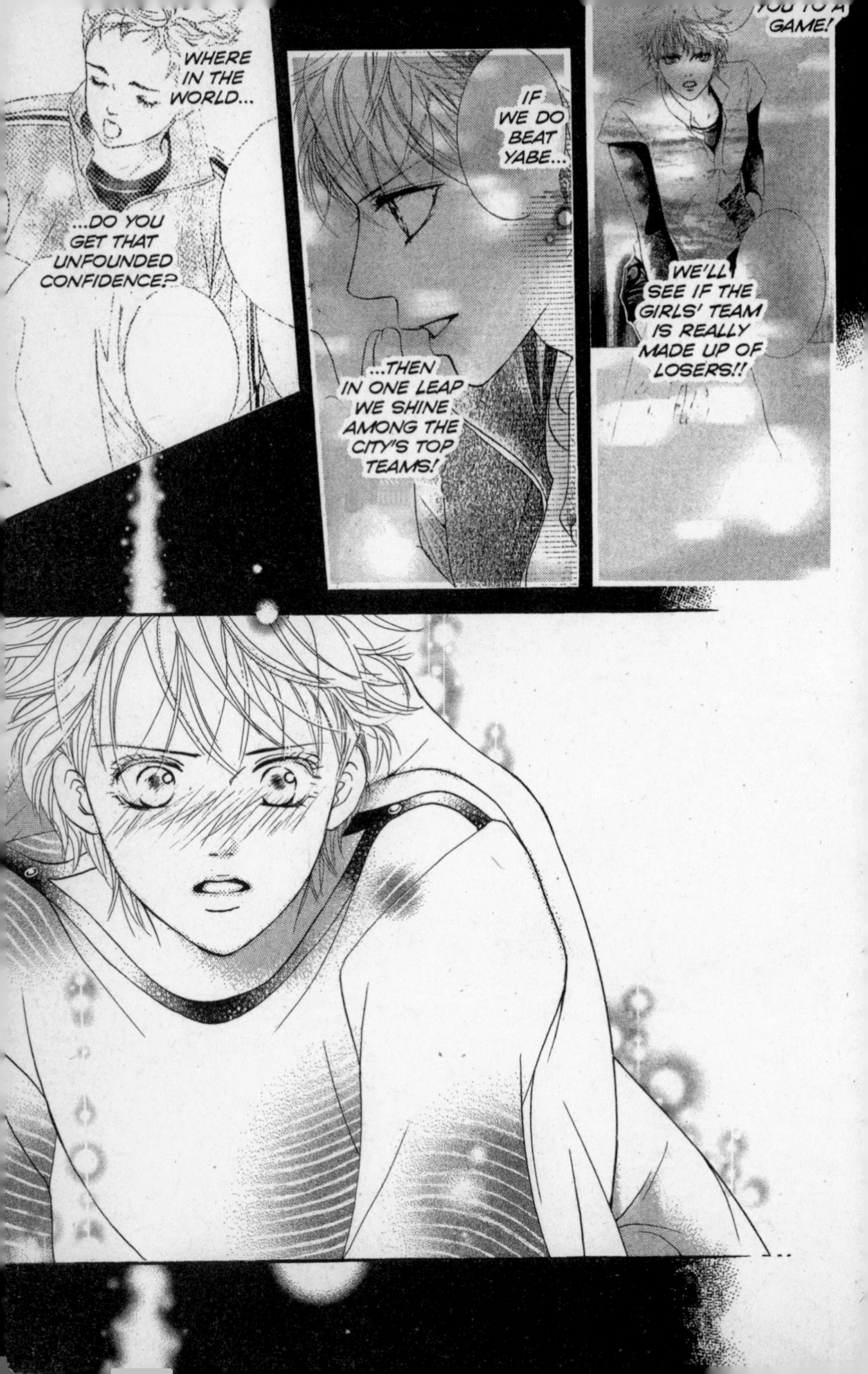
YOU TO A GAME!
WE'LL SEE IF THE GIRLS' TEAM IS REALLY MADE UP OF LOSERS!!
IF WE DO BEAT YABE...
...THEN IN ONE LEAP WE SHINE AMONG THE CITY'S TOP TEAMS!
WHERE IN THE WORLD...
...DO YOU GET THAT UNFOUNDED CONFIDENCE?

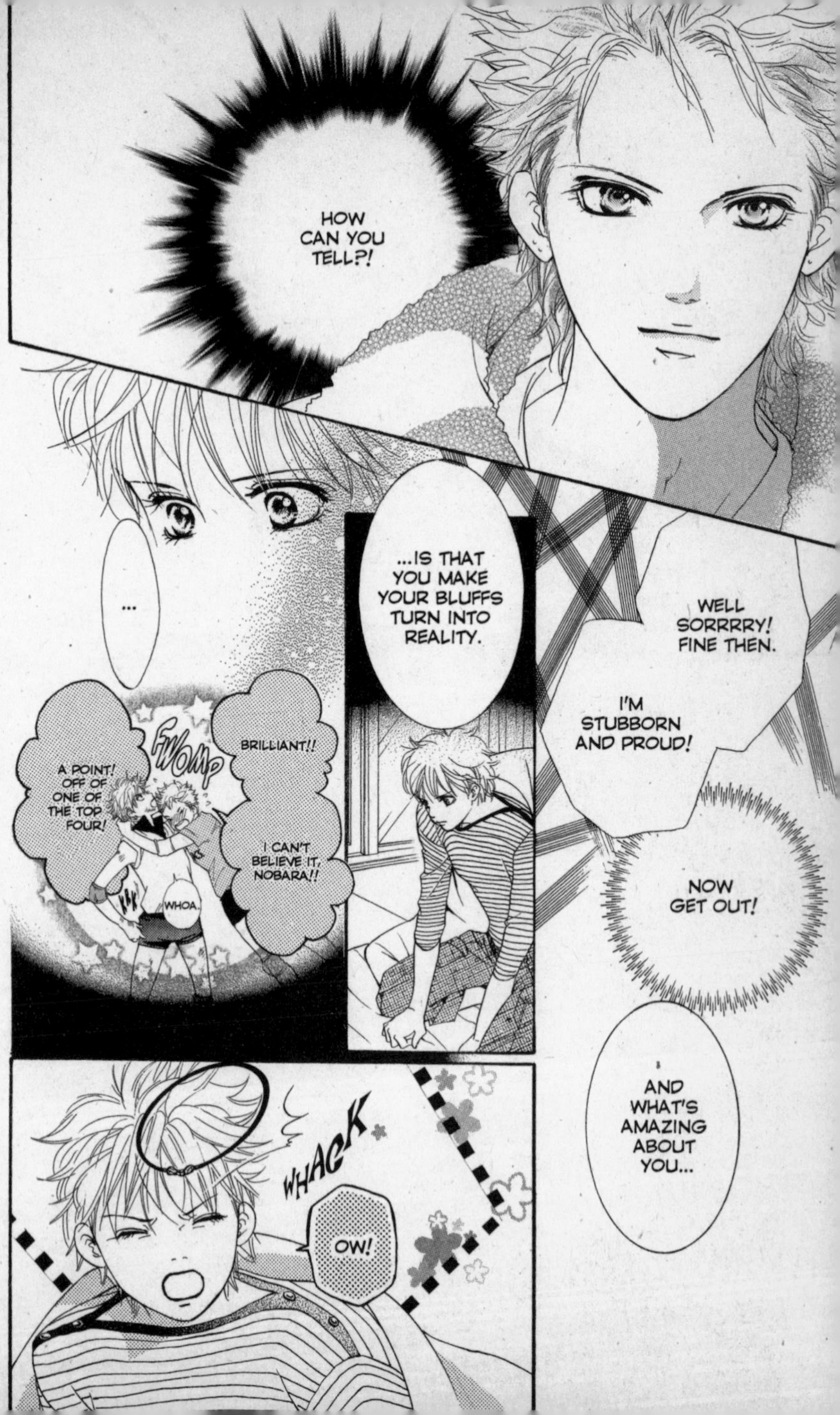
HOW CAN YOU TELL?!
WELL SORRRRY! FINE THEN.
I'M STUBBORN AND PROUD!
NOW GET OUT!
AND WHAT'S AMAZING ABOUT YOU...
...IS THAT YOU MAKE YOUR BLUFFS TURN INTO REALITY.
...
BRILLIANT!!
FWOMP
A POINT! OFF OF ONE OF THE TOP FOUR!
I CAN'T BELIEVE IT, NOBARA!!
WHOA.
WHACK
OW!

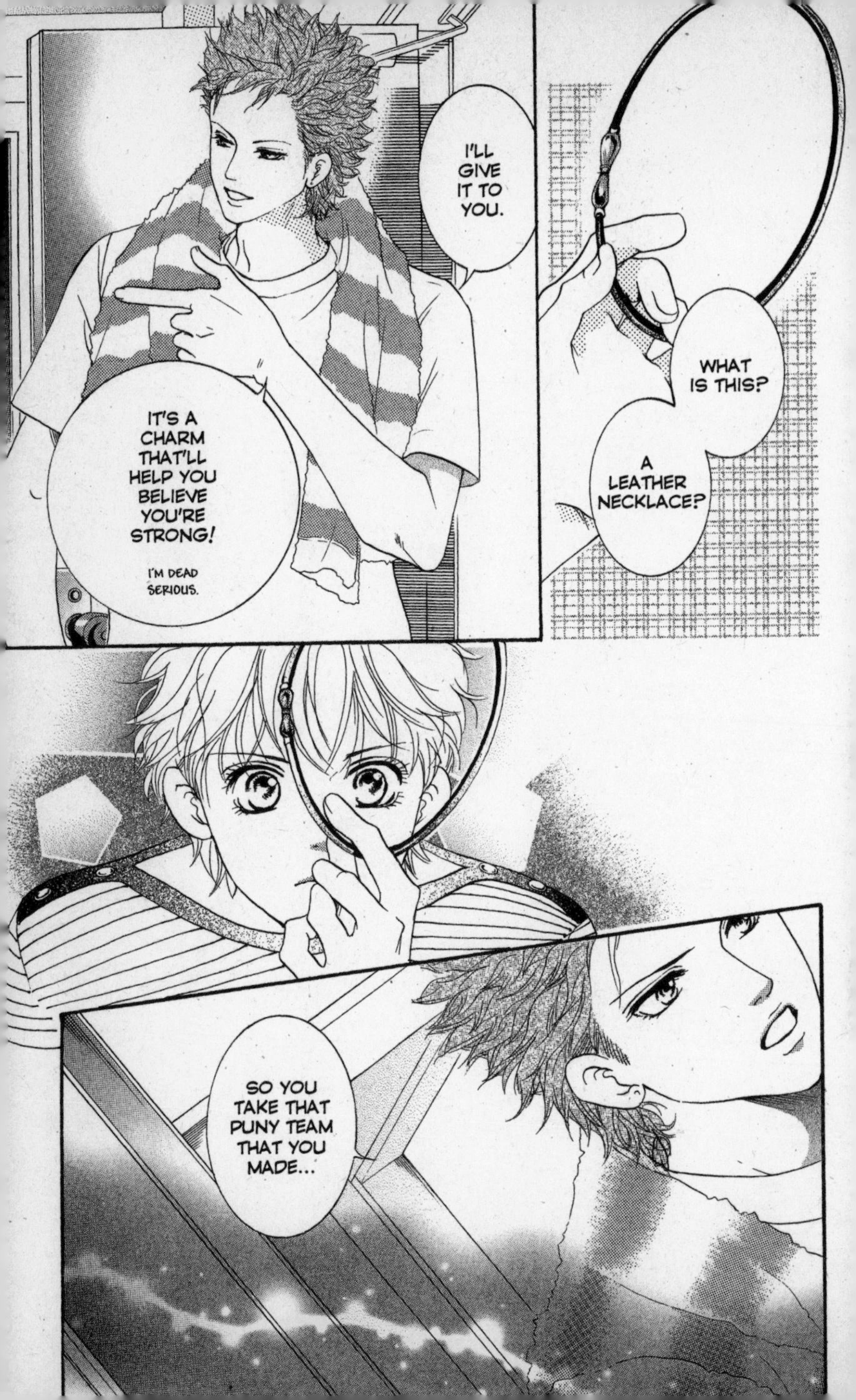
WHAT IS THIS?
A LEATHER NECKLACE?
I'LL GIVE IT TO YOU.
IT'S A CHARM THAT'LL HELP YOU BELIEVE YOU'RE STRONG!
I'M DEAD SERIOUS.
SO YOU TAKE THAT PUNY TEAM THAT YOU MADE...

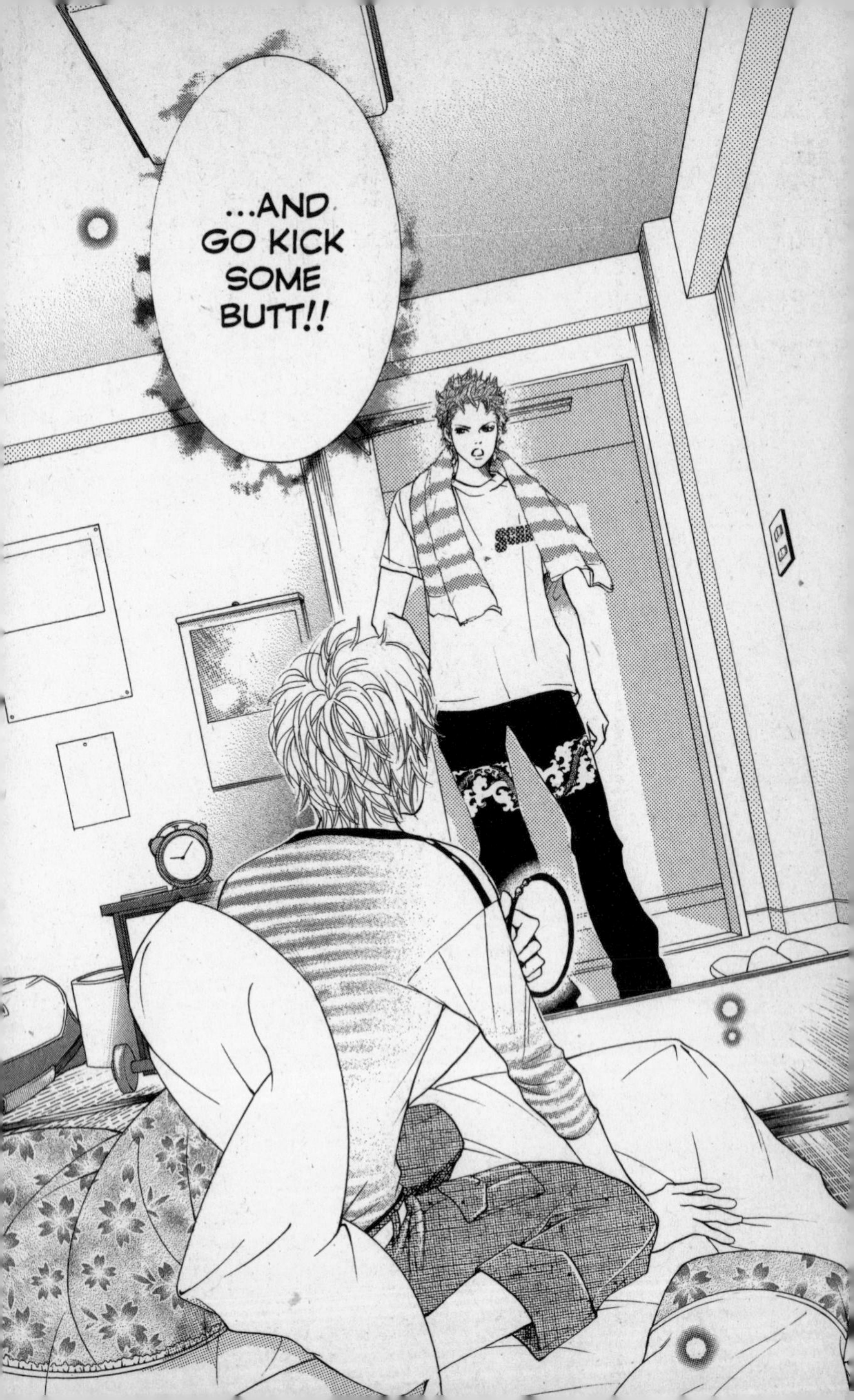
...AND GO KICK SOME BUTT!!

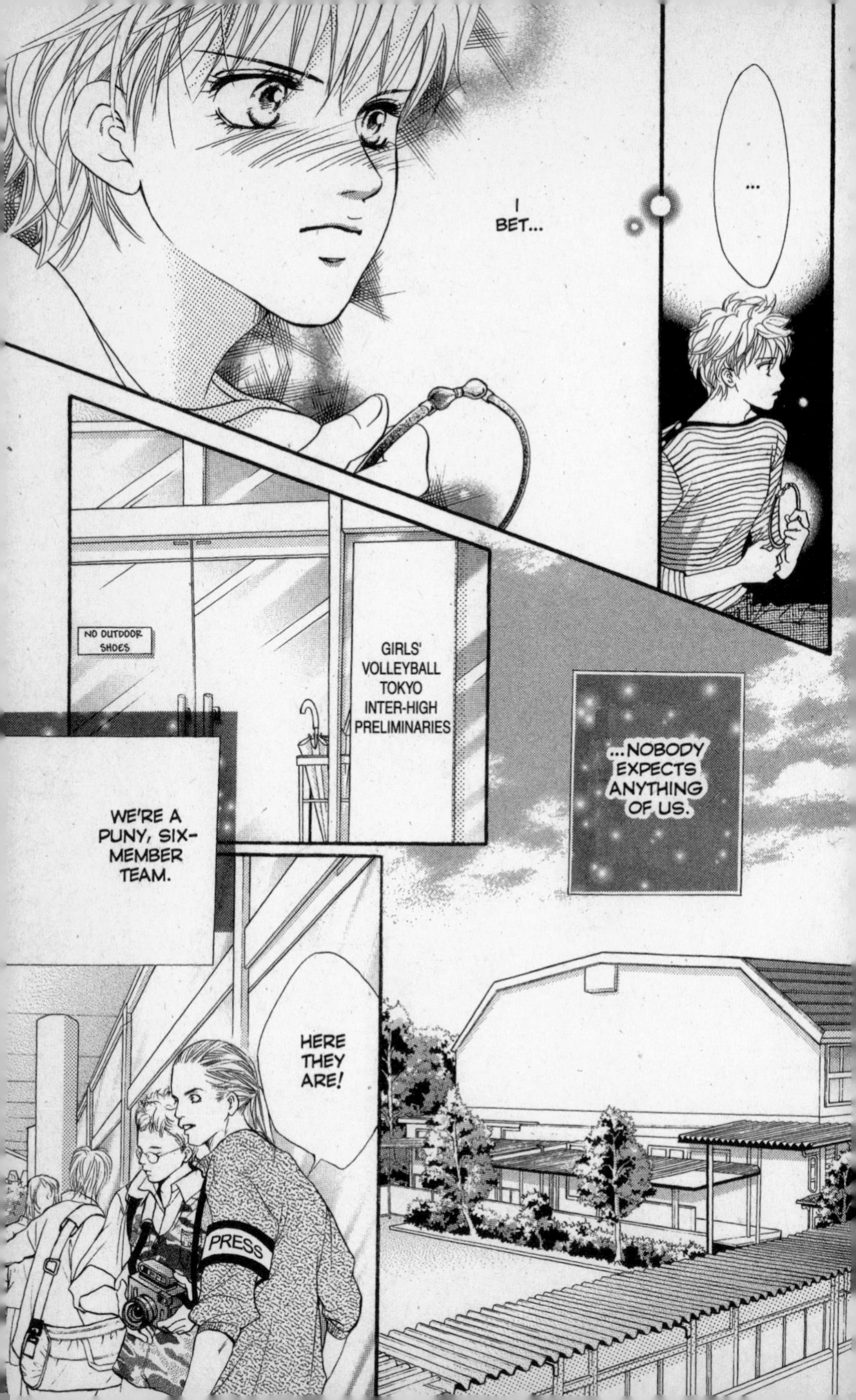
...
I BET...
...NOBODY EXPECTS ANYTHING OF US.
GIRLS' VOLLEYBALL TOKYO INTER-HIGH PRELIMINARIES
NO OUTDOOR SHOES
WE'RE A PUNY, SIX-MEMBER TEAM.
HERE THEY ARE!
PRESS

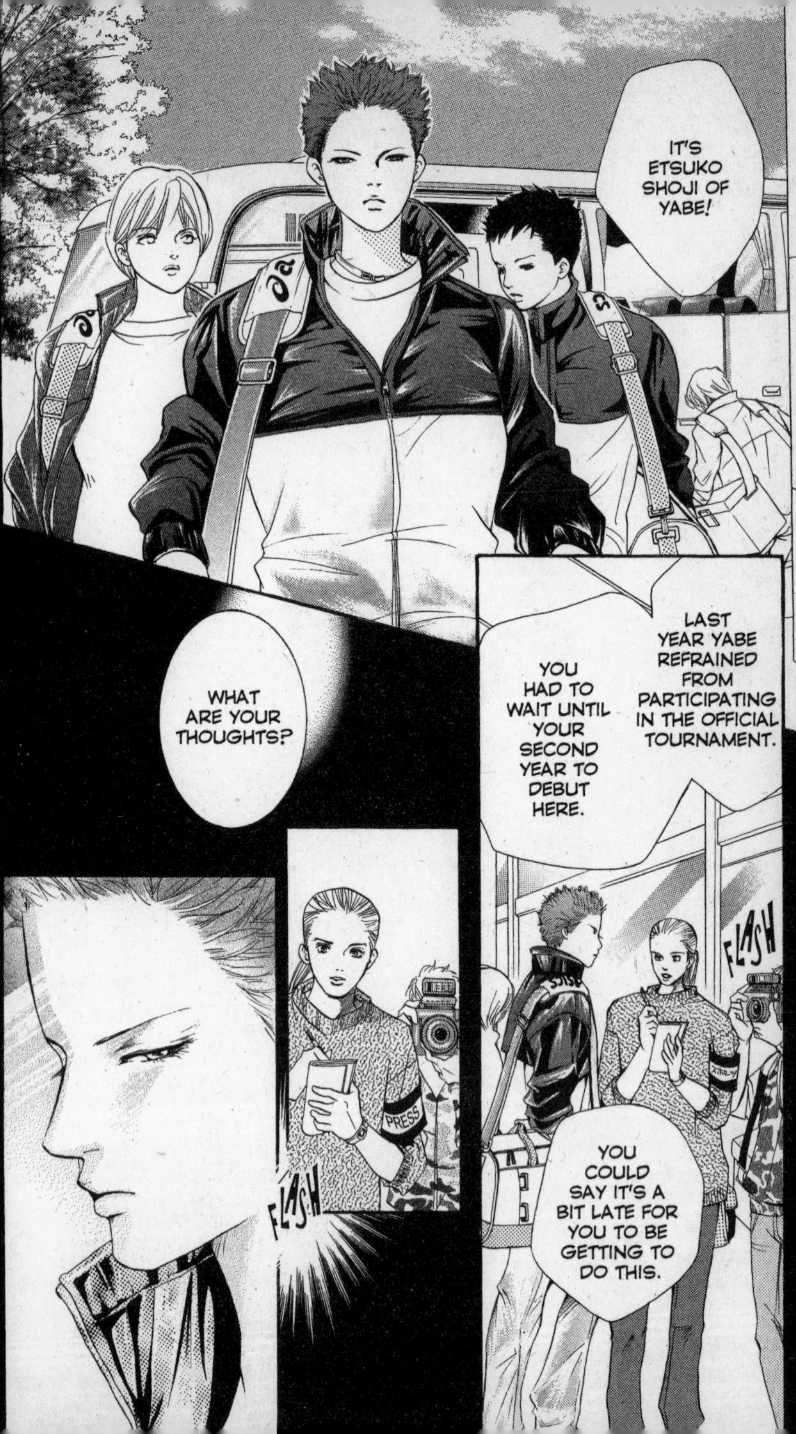
IT'S ETSUKO SHOJI OF YABE!
LAST YEAR YABE REFRAINED FROM PARTICIPATING IN THE OFFICIAL TOURNAMENT.
YOU HAD TO WAIT UNTIL YOUR SECOND YEAR TO DEBUT HERE.
FLASH
YOU COULD SAY IT'S A BIT LATE FOR YOU TO BE GETTING TO DO THIS.
PRESS
FLASH
WHAT ARE YOUR THOUGHTS?

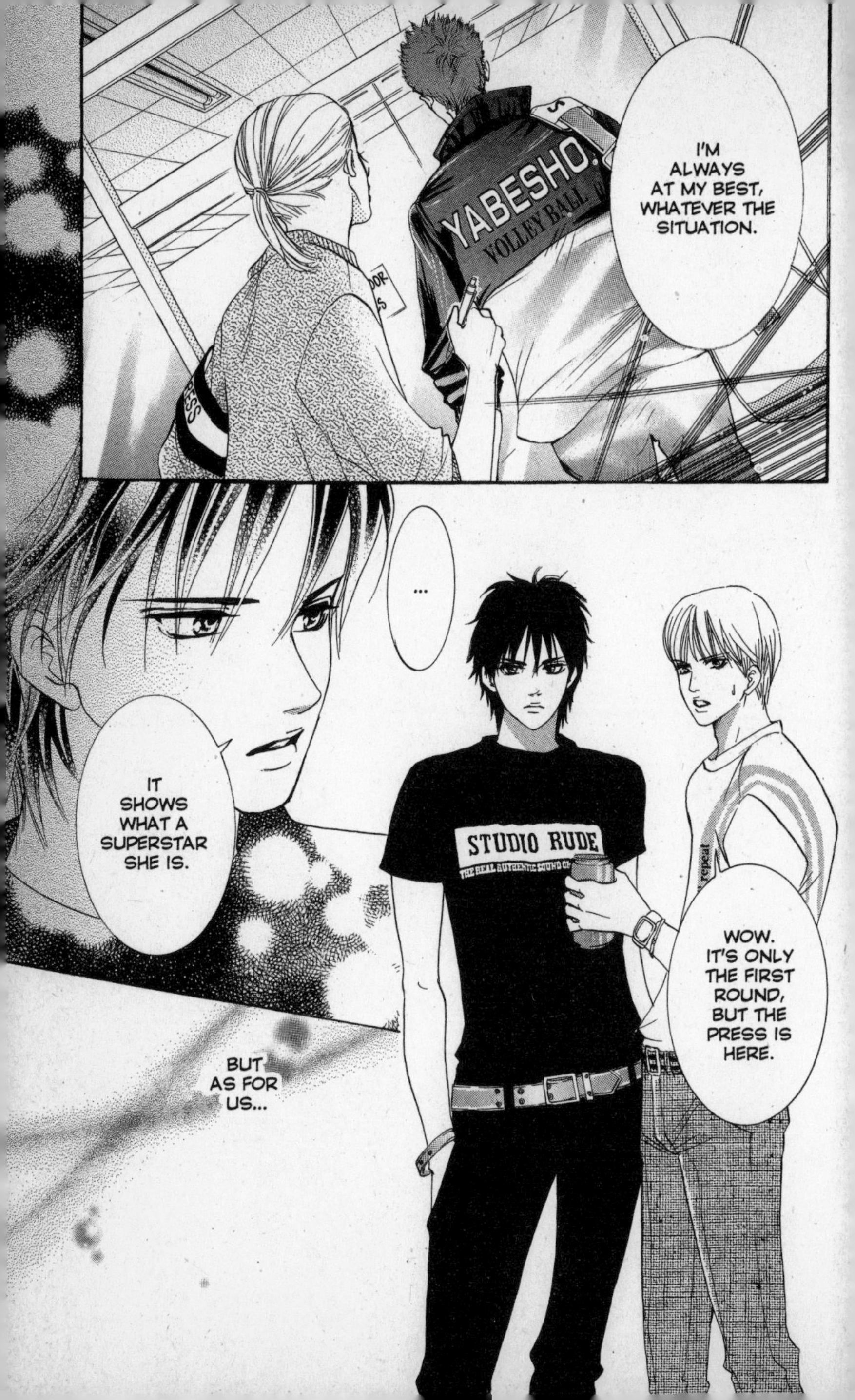
YABESHO
VOLLEY BALL
I'M ALWAYS AT MY BEST, WHATEVER THE SITUATION.
WOW. IT'S ONLY THE FIRST ROUND, BUT THE PRESS IS HERE.
STUDIO RUDE
...
IT SHOWS WHAT A SUPERSTAR SHE IS.
BUT AS FOR US...

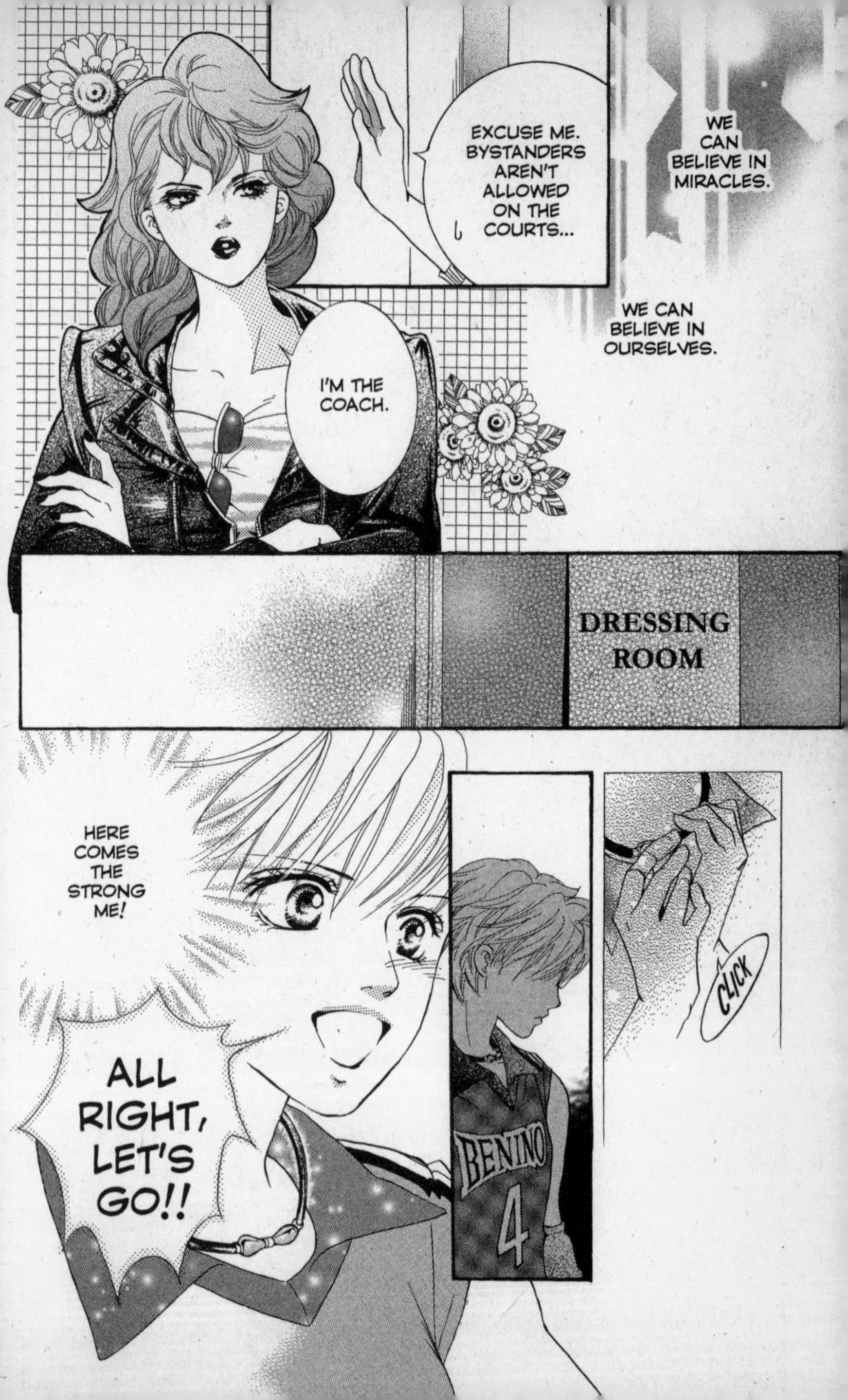
WE CAN BELIEVE IN MIRACLES.
WE CAN BELIEVE IN OURSELVES.
EXCUSE ME. BYSTANDERS AREN'T ALLOWED ON THE COURTS...
I'M THE COACH.
DRESSING ROOM
CLICK
BENINO 4
HERE COMES THE STRONG ME!
ALL RIGHT, LET'S GO!!

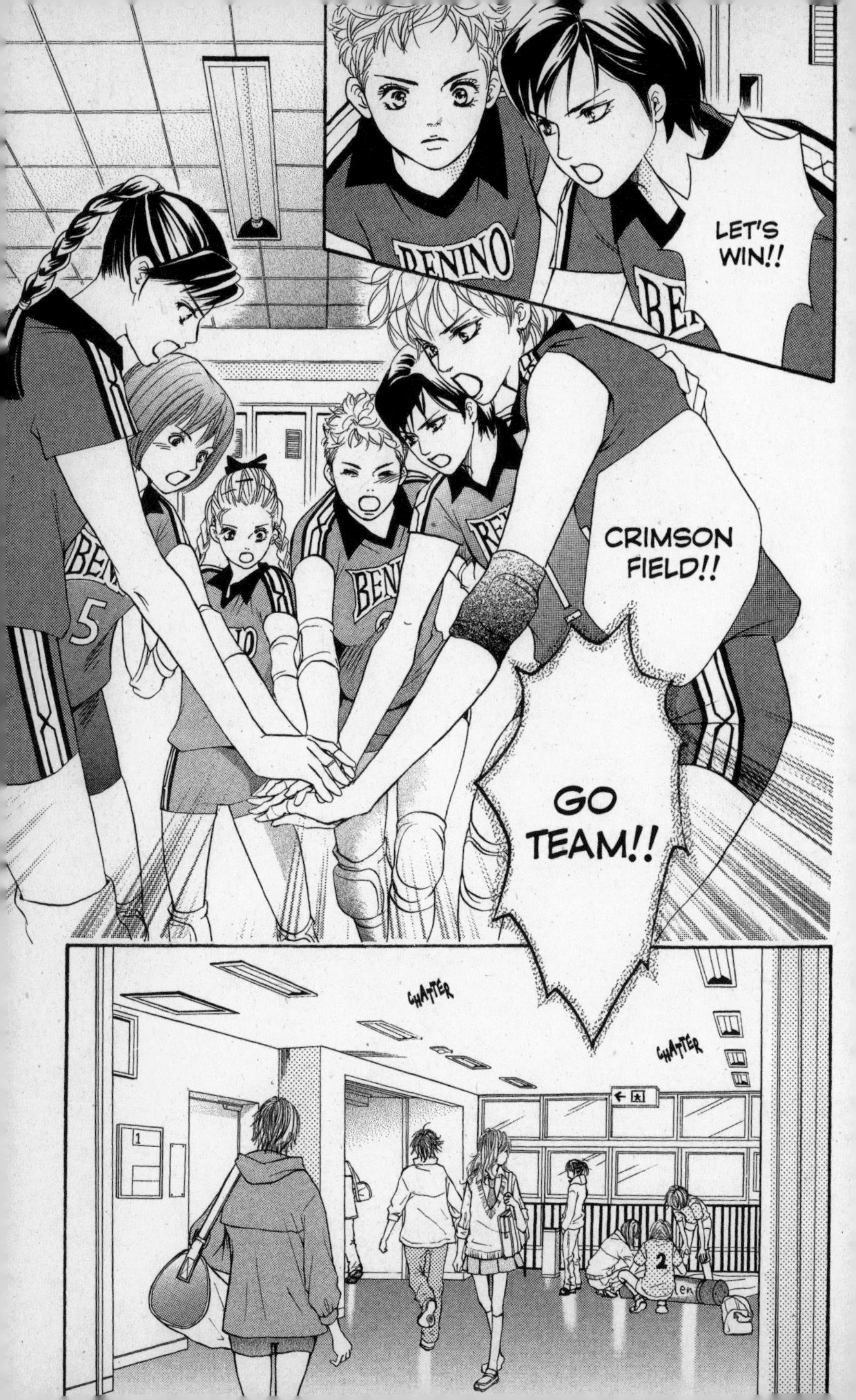
LET'S WIN!!
CRIMSON FIELD!!
GO TEAM!!
BENINO
CHATTER
CHATTER

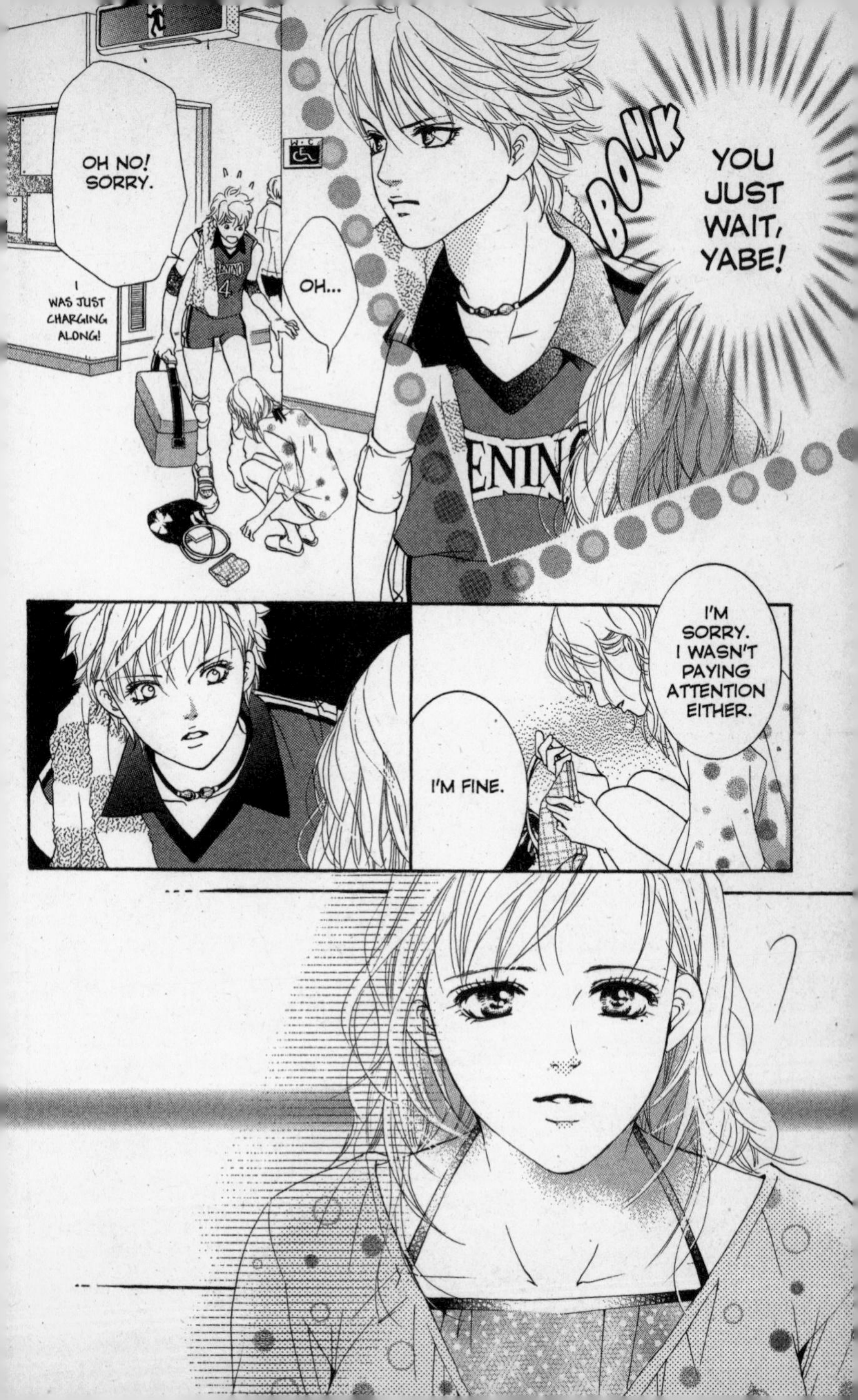
YOU JUST WAIT, YABE!
BONK
OH...
OH NO! SORRY.
I WAS JUST CHARGING ALONG!
I'M SORRY. I WASN'T PAYING ATTENTION EITHER.
I'M FINE.

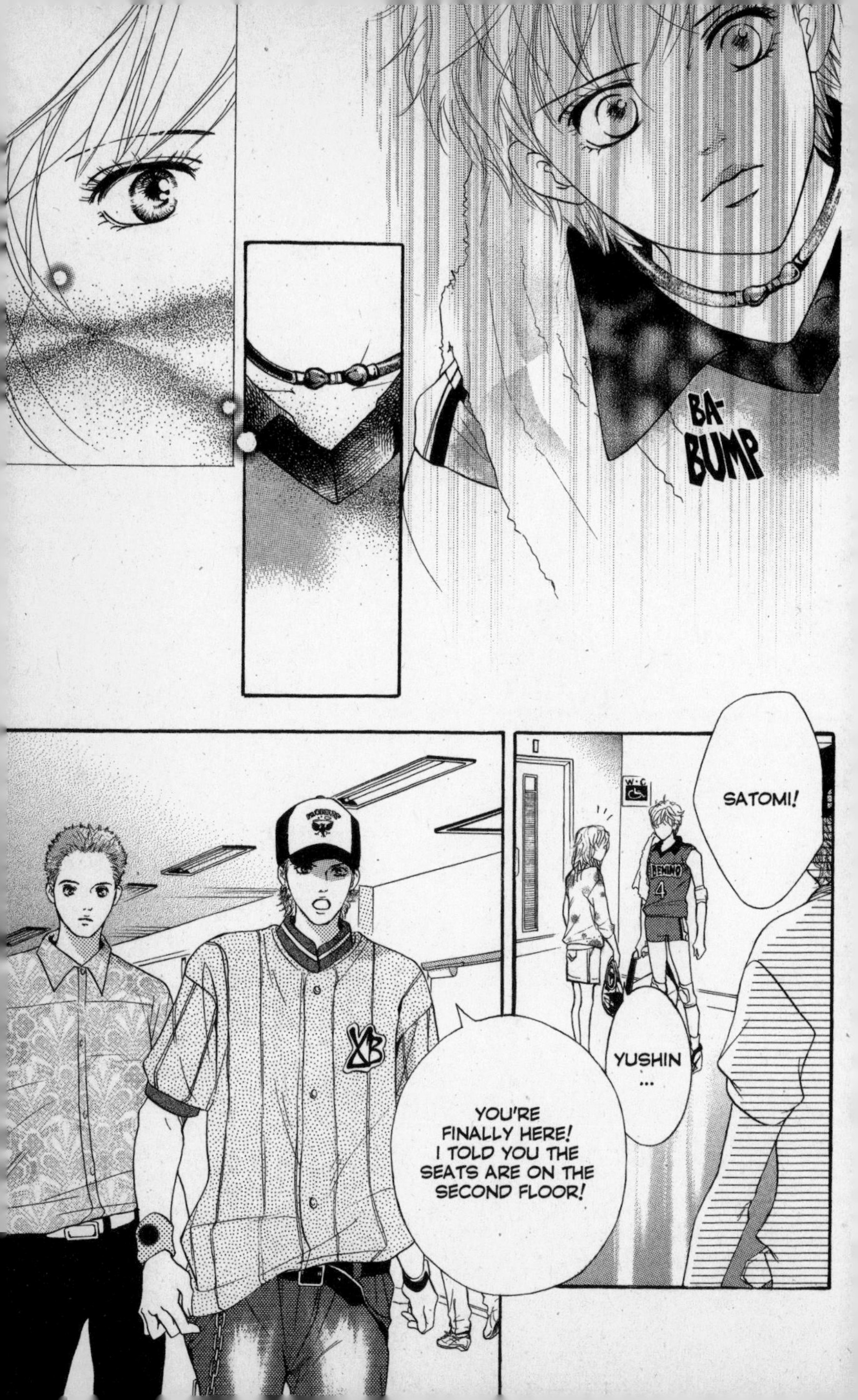
BA-BUMP
SATOMI!
YUSHIN ...
YOU'RE FINALLY HERE! I TOLD YOU THE SEATS ARE ON THE SECOND FLOOR!

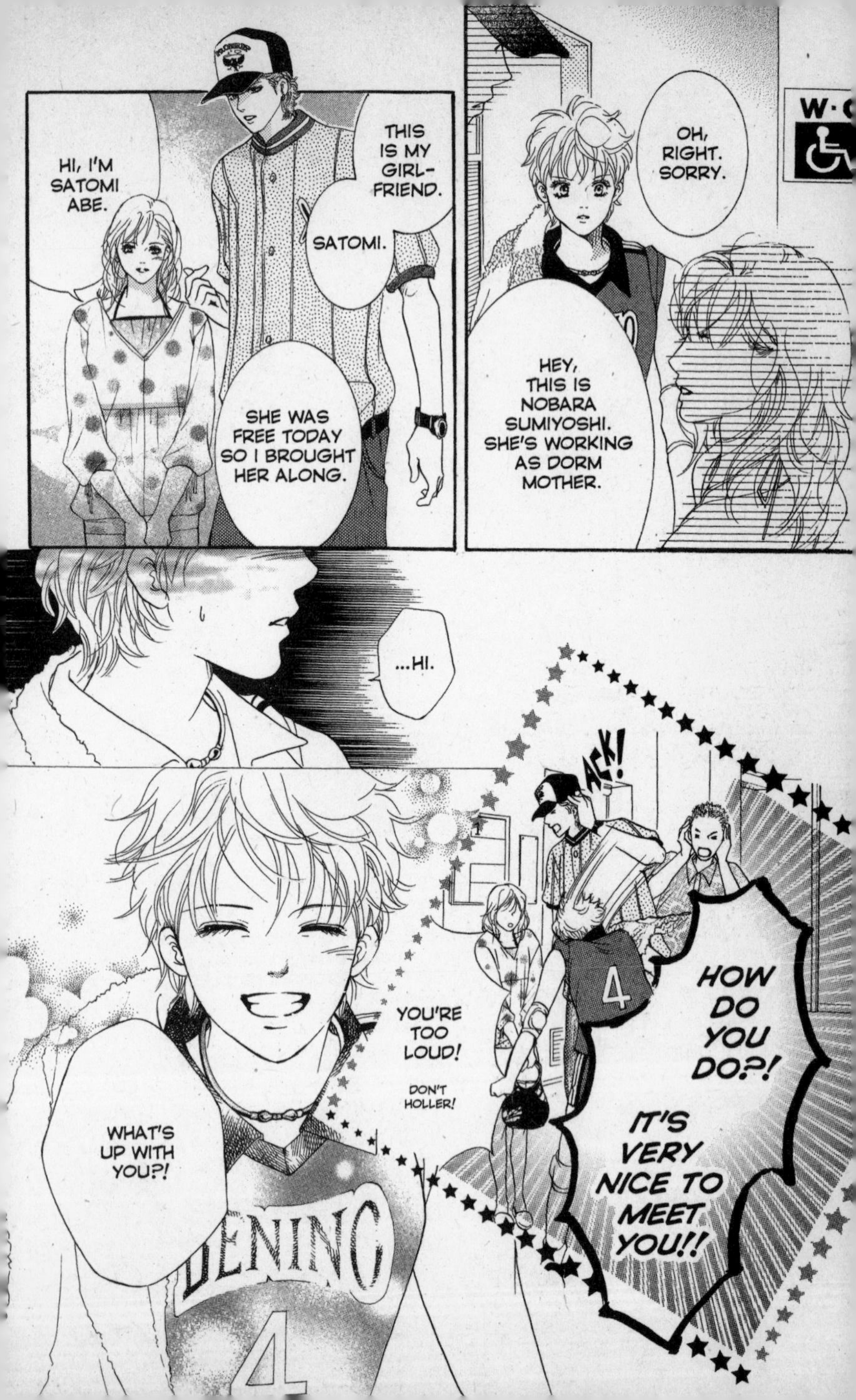
W·C
OH, RIGHT. SORRY.
HEY, THIS IS NOBARA SUMIYOSHI. SHE'S WORKING AS DORM MOTHER.
THIS IS MY GIRL-FRIEND.
SATOMI.
HI, I'M SATOMI ABE.
SHE WAS FREE TODAY SO I BROUGHT HER ALONG.
...HI.
HOW DO YOU DO?!
IT'S VERY NICE TO MEET YOU!!
ACK!
YOU'RE TOO LOUD!
DON'T HOLLER!
WHAT'S UP WITH YOU?!

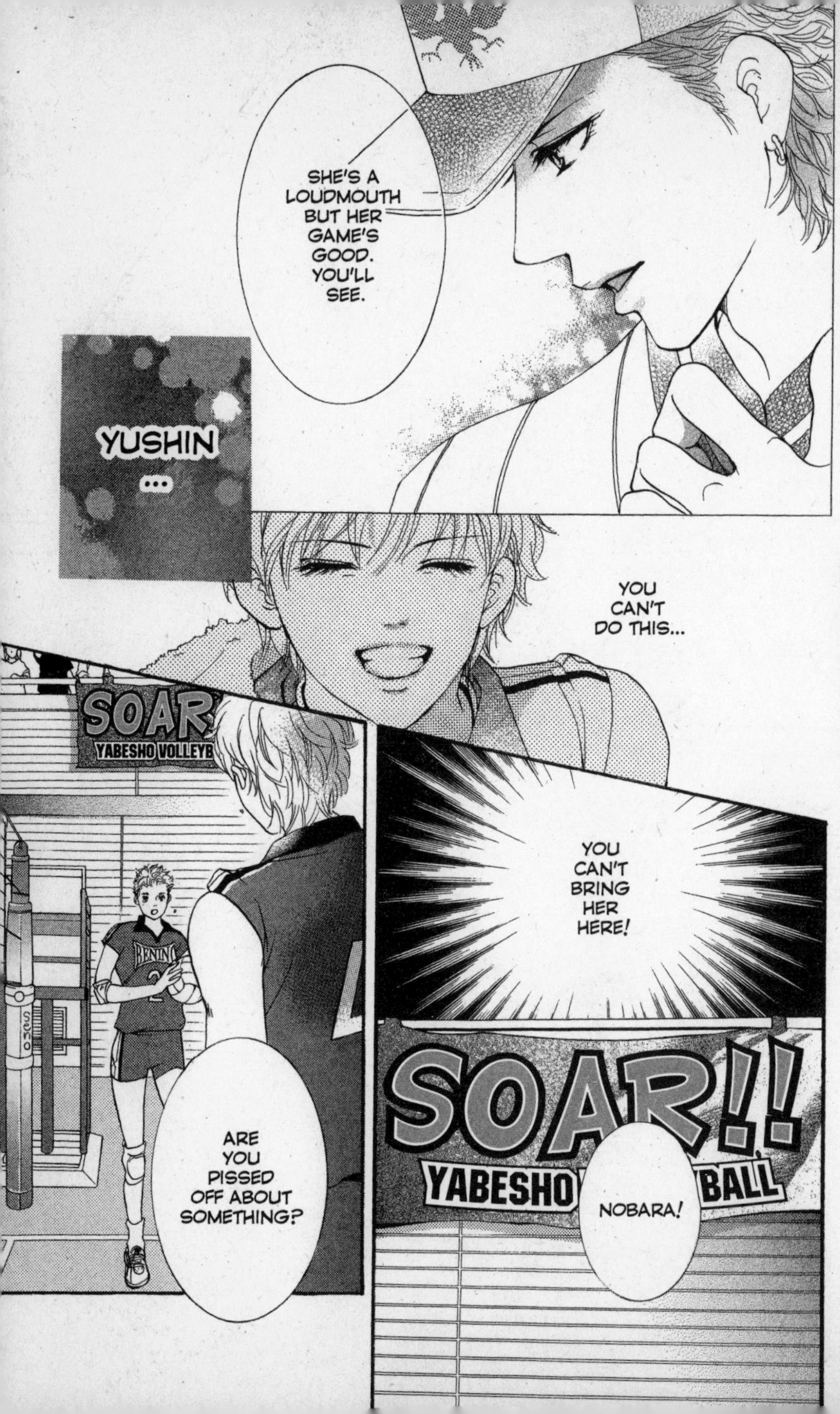
SHE'S A LOUDMOUTH BUT HER GAME'S GOOD. YOU'LL SEE.
YUSHIN ...
YOU CAN'T DO THIS...
YOU CAN'T BRING HER HERE!
SOAR!!
YABESHO
BALL
NOBARA!
SOAR
YABESHO VOLLEYB
ARE YOU PISSED OFF ABOUT SOMETHING?

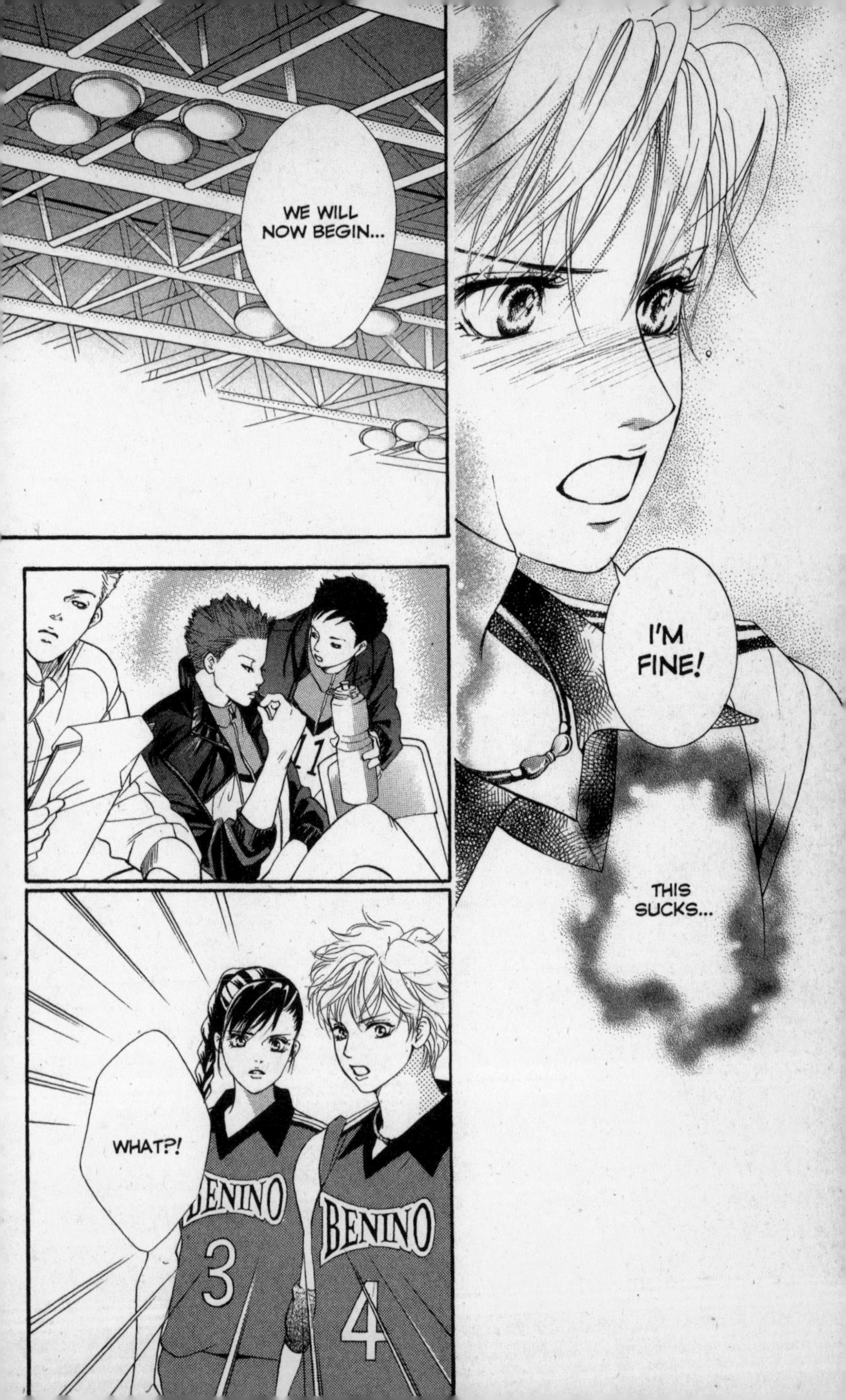
I'M FINE!
THIS SUCKS...
WE WILL NOW BEGIN...
WHAT?!
BENINO
3
BENINO
4

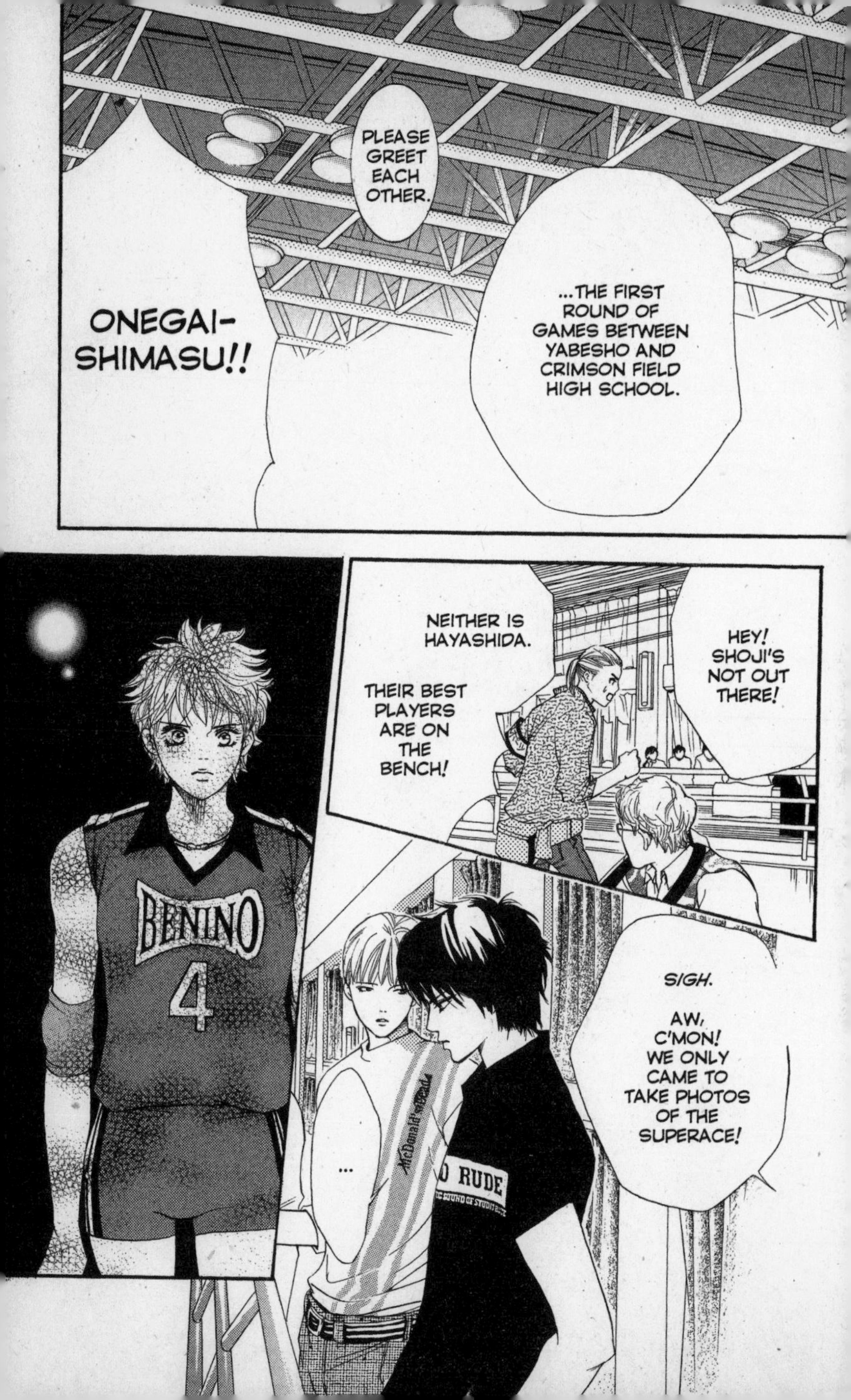
...THE FIRST ROUND OF GAMES BETWEEN YABESHO AND CRIMSON FIELD HIGH SCHOOL.
PLEASE GREET EACH OTHER.
ONEGAI-SHIMASU!!
HEY! SHOJI'S NOT OUT THERE!
NEITHER IS HAYASHIDA.
THEIR BEST PLAYERS ARE ON THE BENCH!
SIGH.
AW, C'MON! WE ONLY CAME TO TAKE PHOTOS OF THE SUPERACE!
...

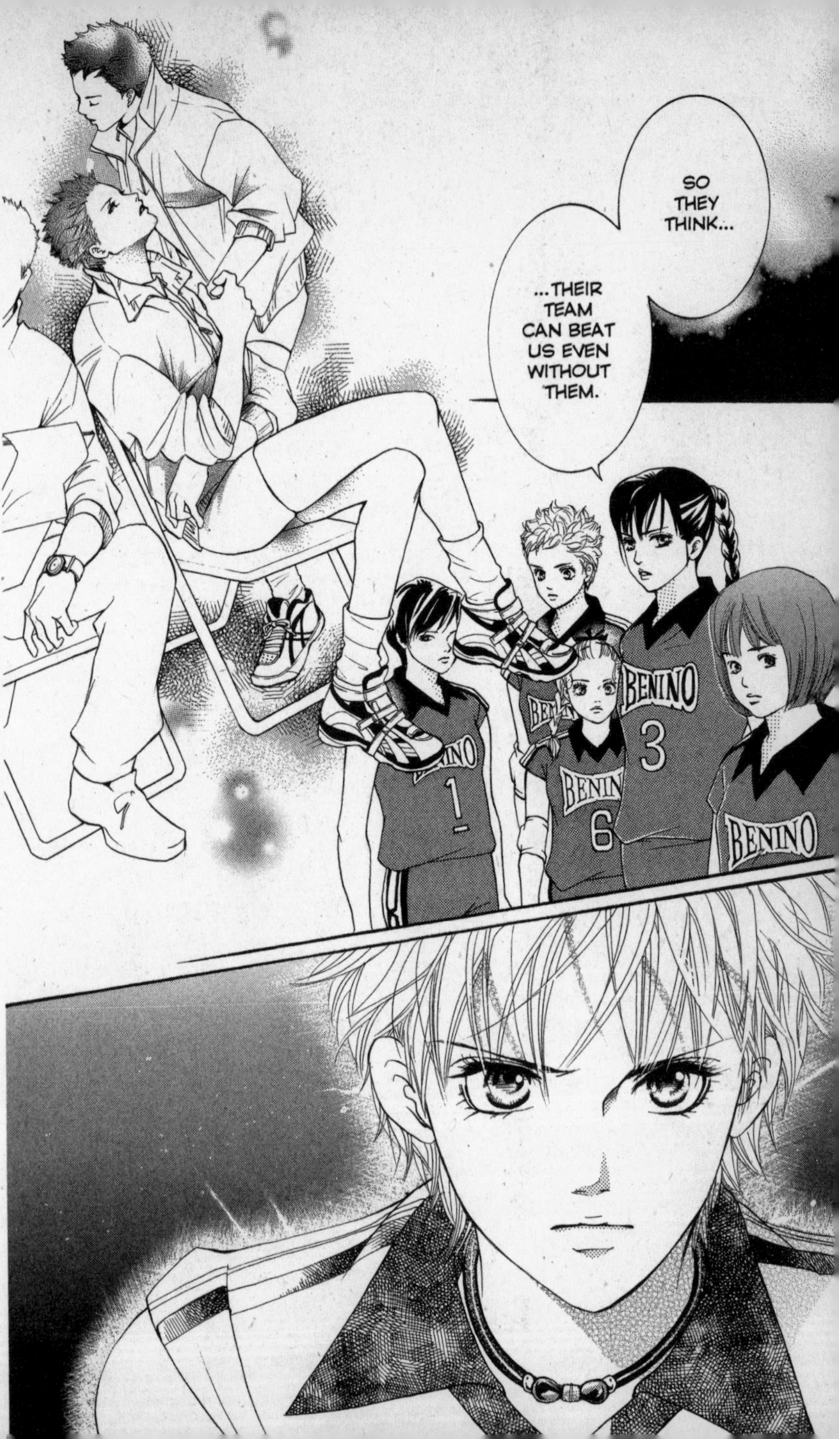
SO THEY THINK...
...THEIR TEAM CAN BEAT US EVEN WITHOUT THEM.
BENINO
1
BENINO
BENINO
6
BENINO
3
BENINO

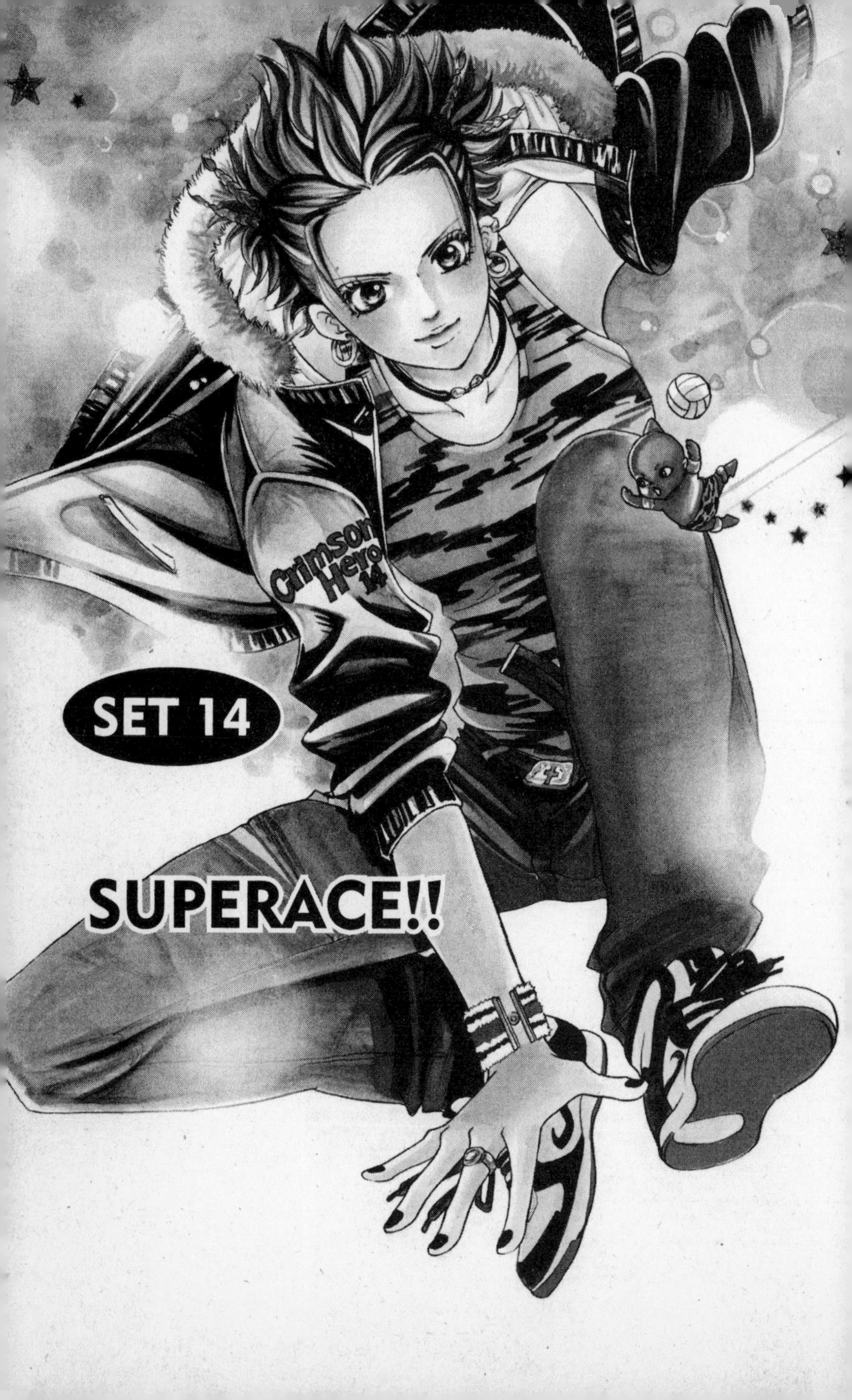
Crimson Hero 14
SET 14
SUPERACE!!

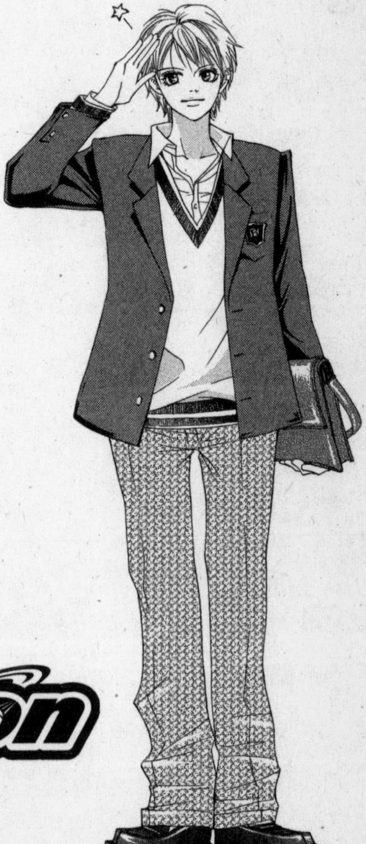

Crimson Hero

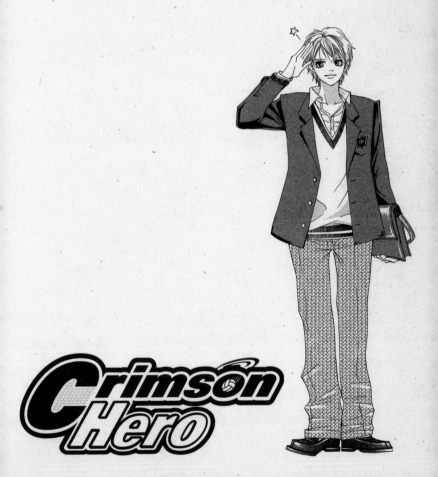

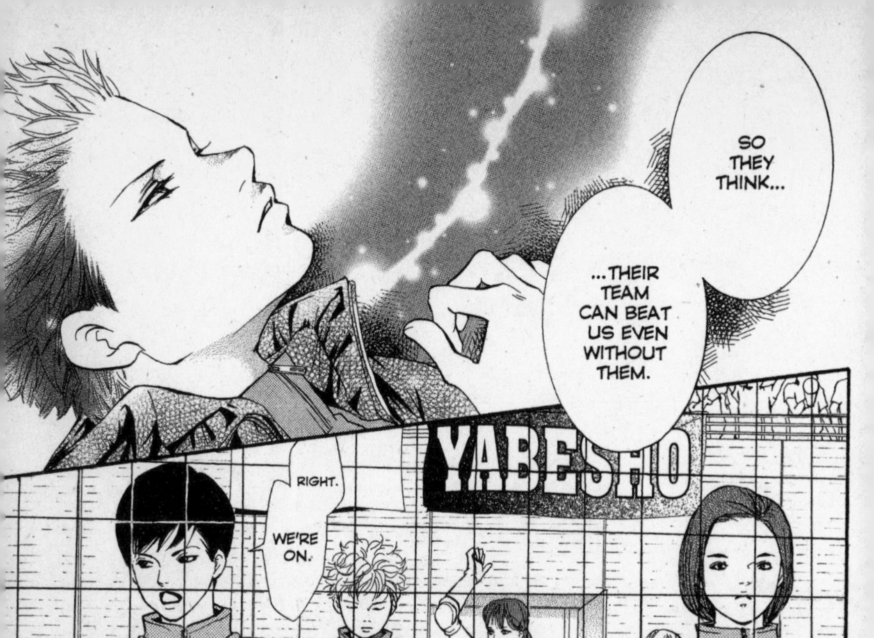
SO THEY THINK...
...THEIR TEAM CAN BEAT US EVEN WITHOUT THEM.
YABESHO
RIGHT.
WE'RE ON.

THE MAKING OF CRIMSON HERO

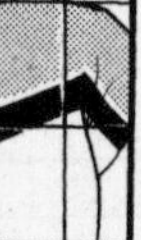

DORM RESIDENTS, PART 1:
YOU GUYS SMELL LIKE SWEAT.

YUSHIN KUMAGAI

MY THEME FOR THIS GUY IS...THE MAN!! HE'S A TYPE I HAVEN'T DRAWN MUCH BEFORE SO IT'S A NEW DISCOVERY FOR ME, BUT I FEEL LIKE I NEED TO HAVE HIM MAKE BOLDER MOVES. HE SEEMS LIKE THE TYPE TO DRY HIS HAIR REALLY VIGOROUSLY WITH A TOWEL AFTER SHAMPOOING IT.

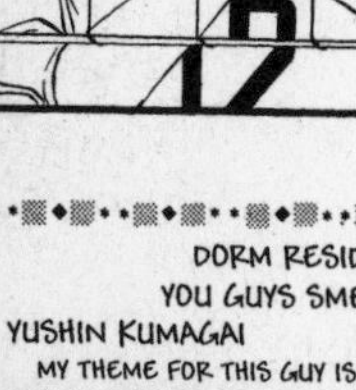

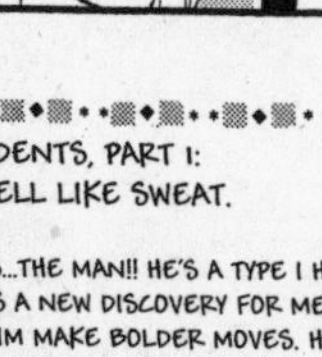
RUB
CHOMP

OH, HE ALSO SCARFS DOWN PUDDING CUPS...

...WITH A SCOWL.

BECAUSE HE'S ONLY 15.

NAOTO TSUCHIYA Vol. 2

THIS GUY WENT TO THE SAME JUNIOR HIGH AS YUSHIN. THEY GET ALONG WELL. HE'S PRETTY QUICK TO VOICE HIS COMPLAINTS, ISN'T HE? THE MENTAL IMAGE I HAVE AS I DRAW HIM IS OF A REGULAR HIGH SCHOOL BOY WHO LIKES VIDEO GAMES AND MANGA.

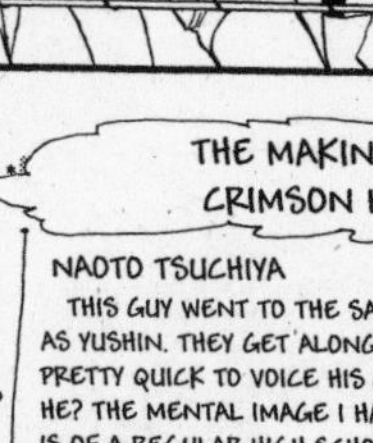
...BEFORE TELLING HIS GIRLFRIEND HOW HE FELT ABOUT HER.
SHE WAS THE TEAM MANAGER, SEE.

I CREATED HIM AND EVEN I ALMOST FORGET HIS NAME SOMETIMES. BUT AS A V-BALL SCHOLARSHIP STUDENT, HE MUST BE A PRETTY SKILLED PLAYER. UNFORTUNATELY, I DON'T KNOW IF I'LL HAVE A CHANCE TO FEATURE HIM IN ACTION FOR THE TIME BEING ANYWAY.

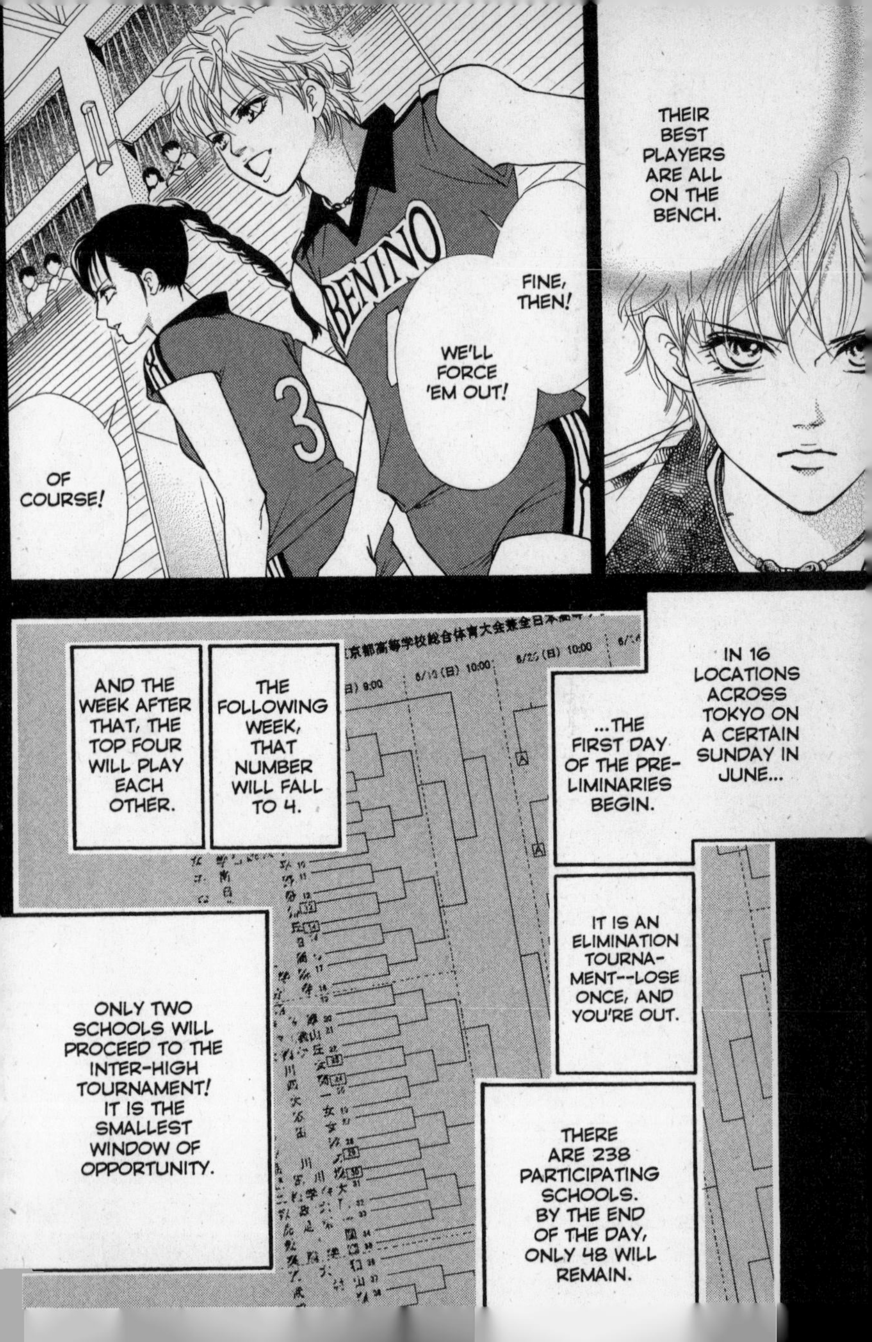
THEIR BEST PLAYERS ARE ALL ON THE BENCH.
FINE, THEN!
WE'LL FORCE 'EM OUT!
OF COURSE!
BENINO
IN 16 LOCATIONS ACROSS TOKYO ON A CERTAIN SUNDAY IN JUNE...
...THE FIRST DAY OF THE PRE-LIMINARIES BEGIN.
IT IS AN ELIMINATION TOURNA-MENT--LOSE ONCE, AND YOU'RE OUT.
THERE ARE 238 PARTICIPATING SCHOOLS. BY THE END OF THE DAY, ONLY 48 WILL REMAIN.
THE FOLLOWING WEEK, THAT NUMBER WILL FALL TO 4.
AND THE WEEK AFTER THAT, THE TOP FOUR WILL PLAY EACH OTHER.
ONLY TWO SCHOOLS WILL PROCEED TO THE INTER-HIGH TOURNAMENT! IT IS THE SMALLEST WINDOW OF OPPORTUNITY.

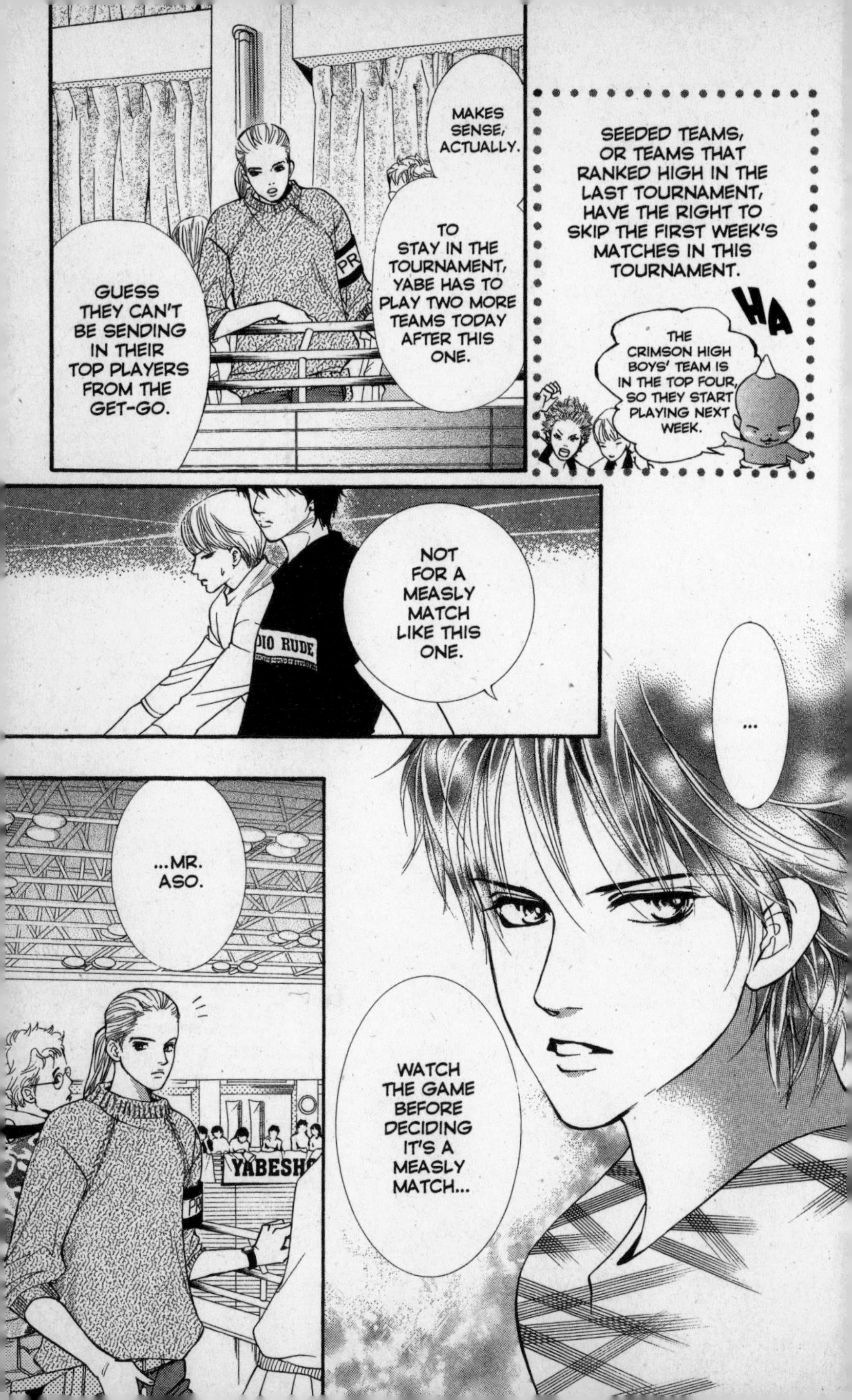
SEEDED TEAMS, OR TEAMS THAT RANKED HIGH IN THE LAST TOURNAMENT, HAVE THE RIGHT TO SKIP THE FIRST WEEK'S MATCHES IN THIS TOURNAMENT.
HA
THE CRIMSON HIGH BOYS' TEAM IS IN THE TOP FOUR, SO THEY START PLAYING NEXT WEEK.
MAKES SENSE, ACTUALLY.
TO STAY IN THE TOURNAMENT, YABE HAS TO PLAY TWO MORE TEAMS TODAY AFTER THIS ONE.
GUESS THEY CAN'T BE SENDING IN THEIR TOP PLAYERS FROM THE GET-GO.
...
WATCH THE GAME BEFORE DECIDING IT'S A MEASLY MATCH...
NOT FOR A MEASLY MATCH LIKE THIS ONE.
...MR. ASO.

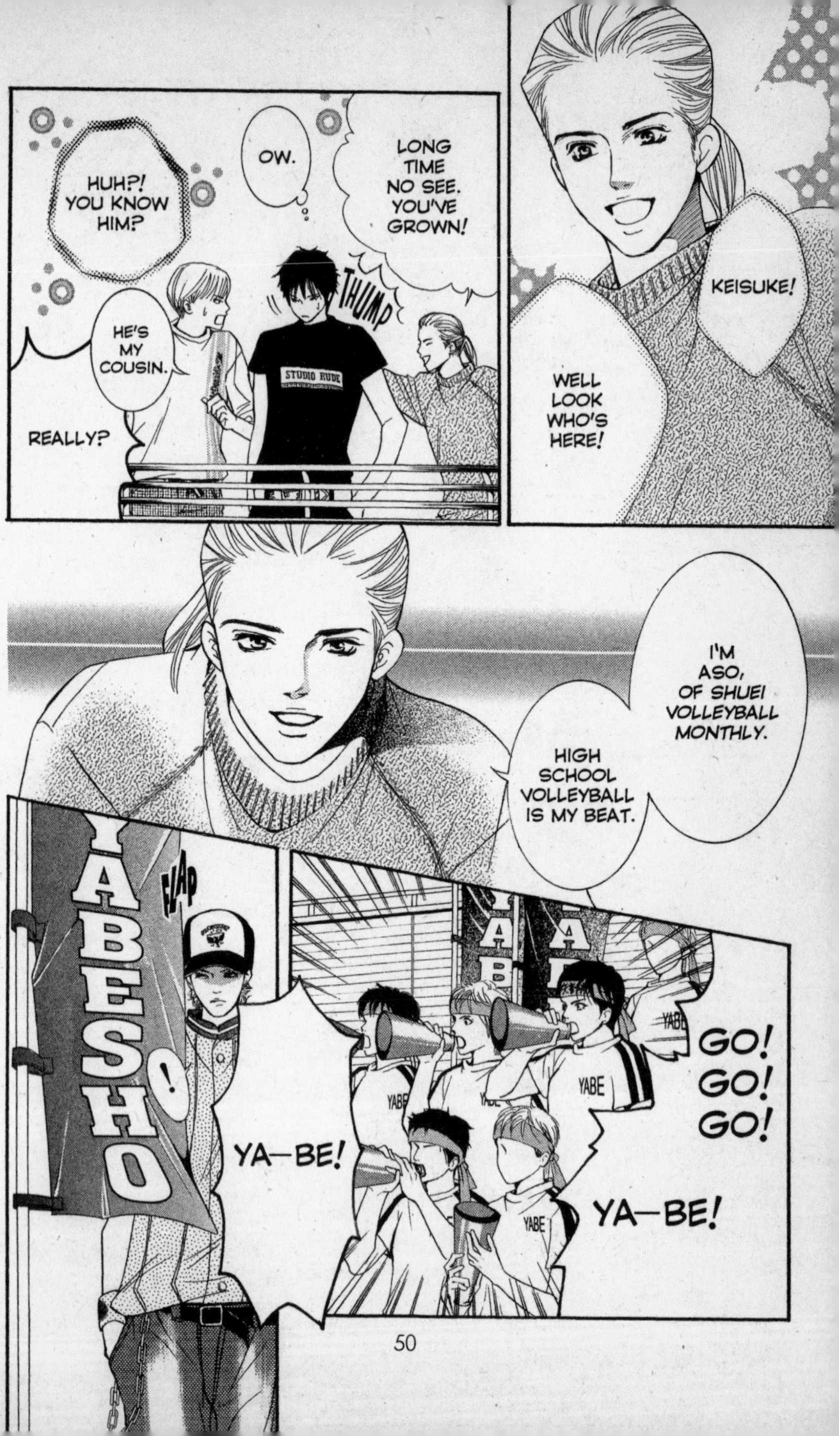
KEISUKE!
WELL LOOK WHO'S HERE!
LONG TIME NO SEE. YOU'VE GROWN!
THUMP
OW.
HUH?! YOU KNOW HIM?
HE'S MY COUSIN.
REALLY?
STUDIO RUDE
I'M ASO, OF SHUEI VOLLEYBALL MONTHLY.
HIGH SCHOOL VOLLEYBALL IS MY BEAT.
GO! GO! GO!
YA-BE!
YABE
YA-BE!
YABE SHO
FLAP
!

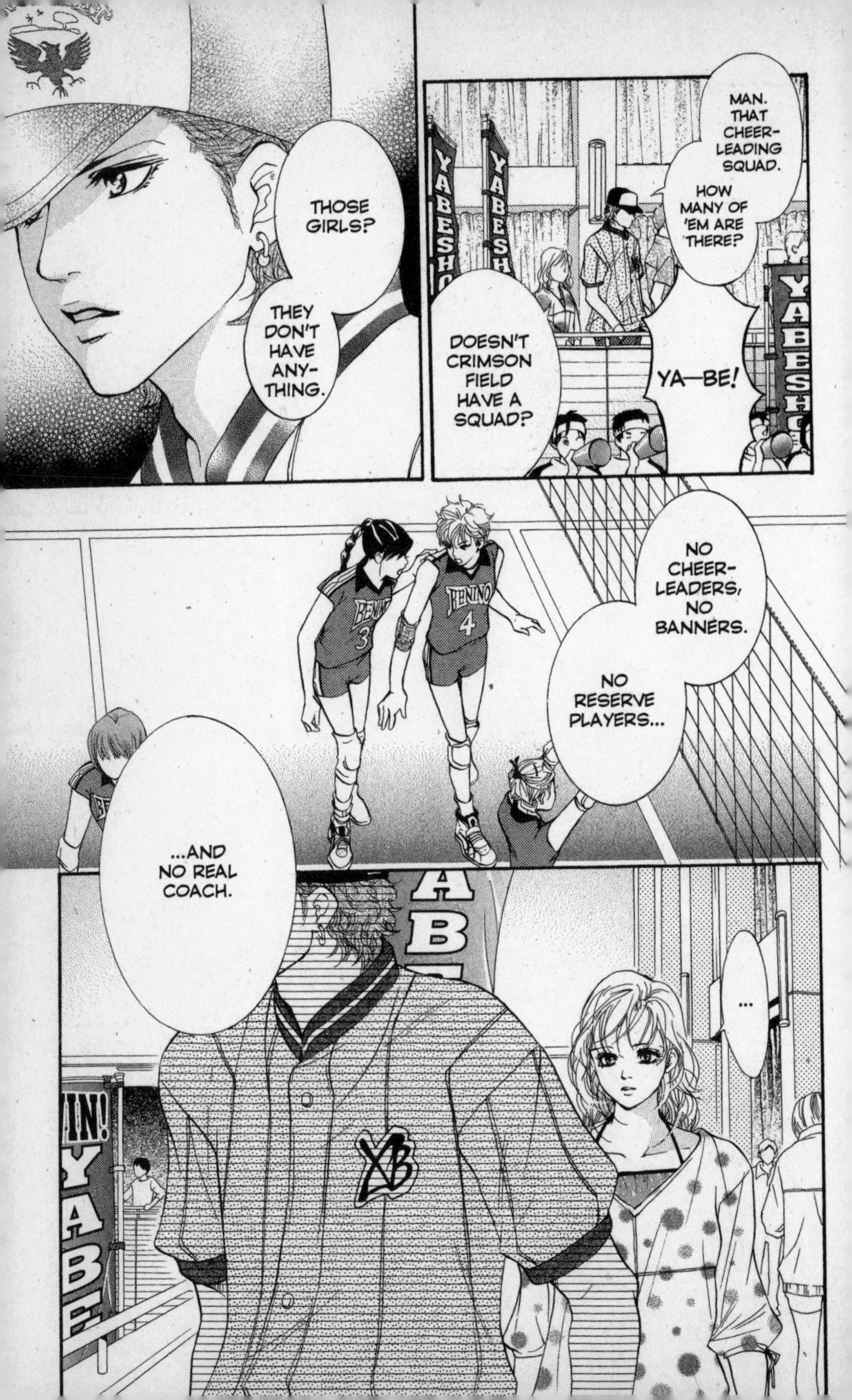
MAN. THAT CHEER-LEADING SQUAD.
HOW MANY OF 'EM ARE THERE?
YABESHO
YA—BE!
DOESN'T CRIMSON FIELD HAVE A SQUAD?
THOSE GIRLS?
THEY DON'T HAVE ANY-THING.
NO CHEER-LEADERS, NO BANNERS.
NO RESERVE PLAYERS...
...AND NO REAL COACH.
...

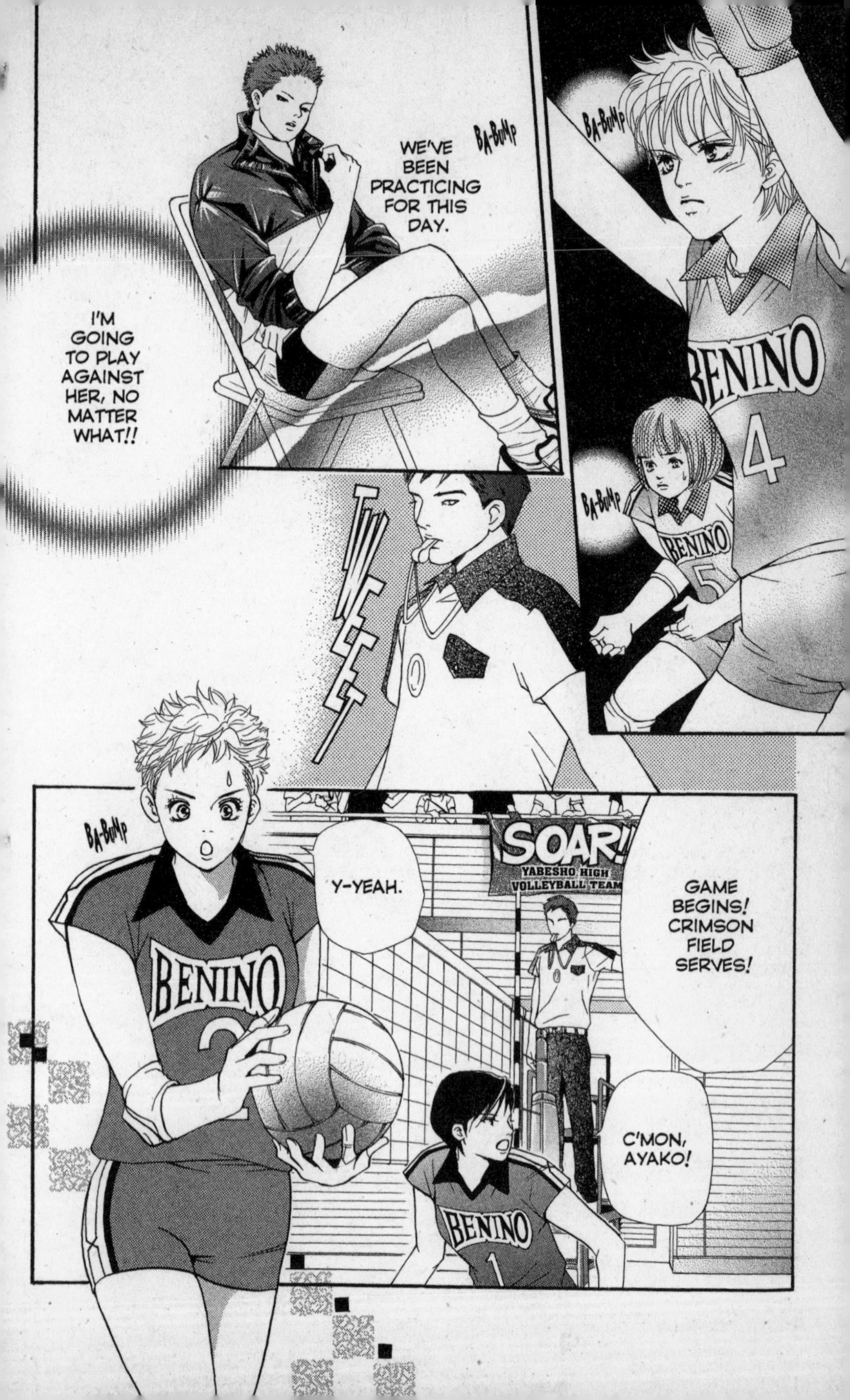

BA-BUMP
BA-BUMP
BA-BUMP
WE'VE BEEN PRACTICING FOR THIS DAY.
I'M GOING TO PLAY AGAINST HER, NO MATTER WHAT!!
TWEET
GAME BEGINS! CRIMSON FIELD SERVES!
C'MON, AYAKO!
SOAR!
YABESHO HIGH VOLLEYBALL TEAM
Y-YEAH.
BA-BUMP

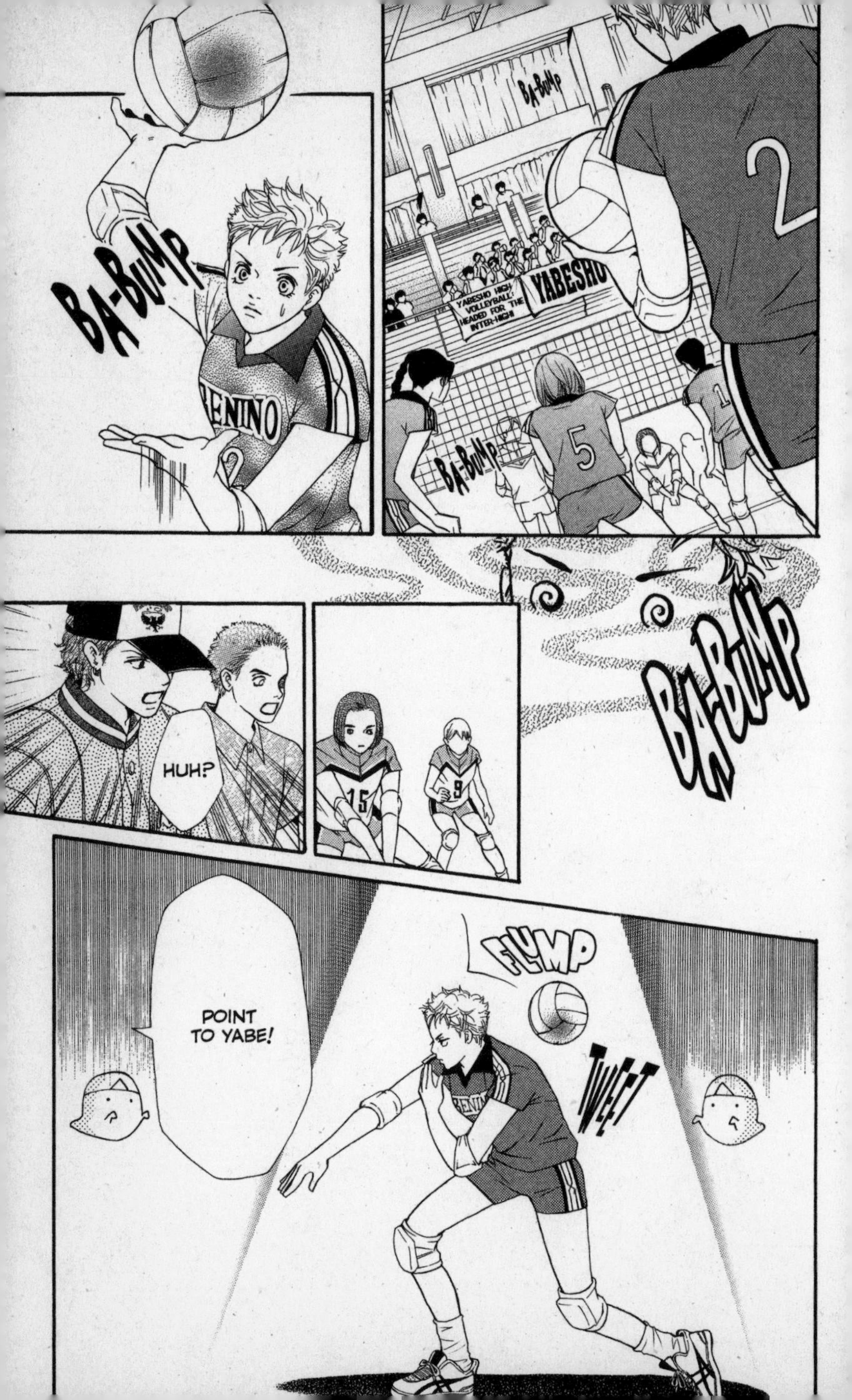
BA-BUMP
YABESHO HIGH VOLLEYBALL! HEADED FOR THE INTER-HIGH
YABESHO
BA-BUMP
BENINO
BA-BUMP
BA-BUMP
HUH?
FLUMP
POINT TO YABE!
TWEET

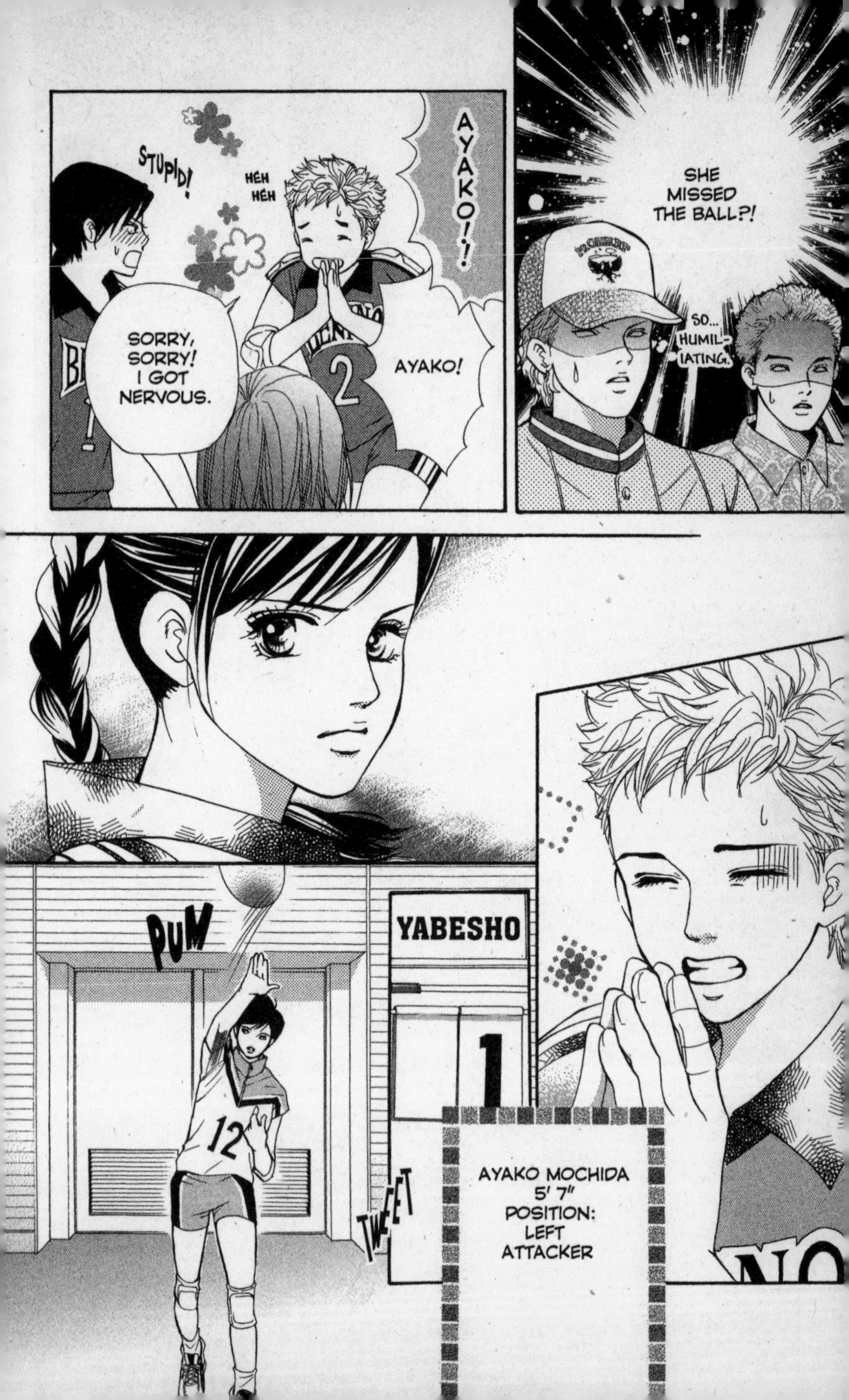
SHE MISSED THE BALL?!
SO... HUMIL-IATING.
AYAKO!!
HEH HEH
STUPID!
AYAKO!
SORRY, SORRY! I GOT NERVOUS.
YABESHO
1
PUM
TWEET
AYAKO MOCHIDA
5' 7"
POSITION:
LEFT
ATTACKER

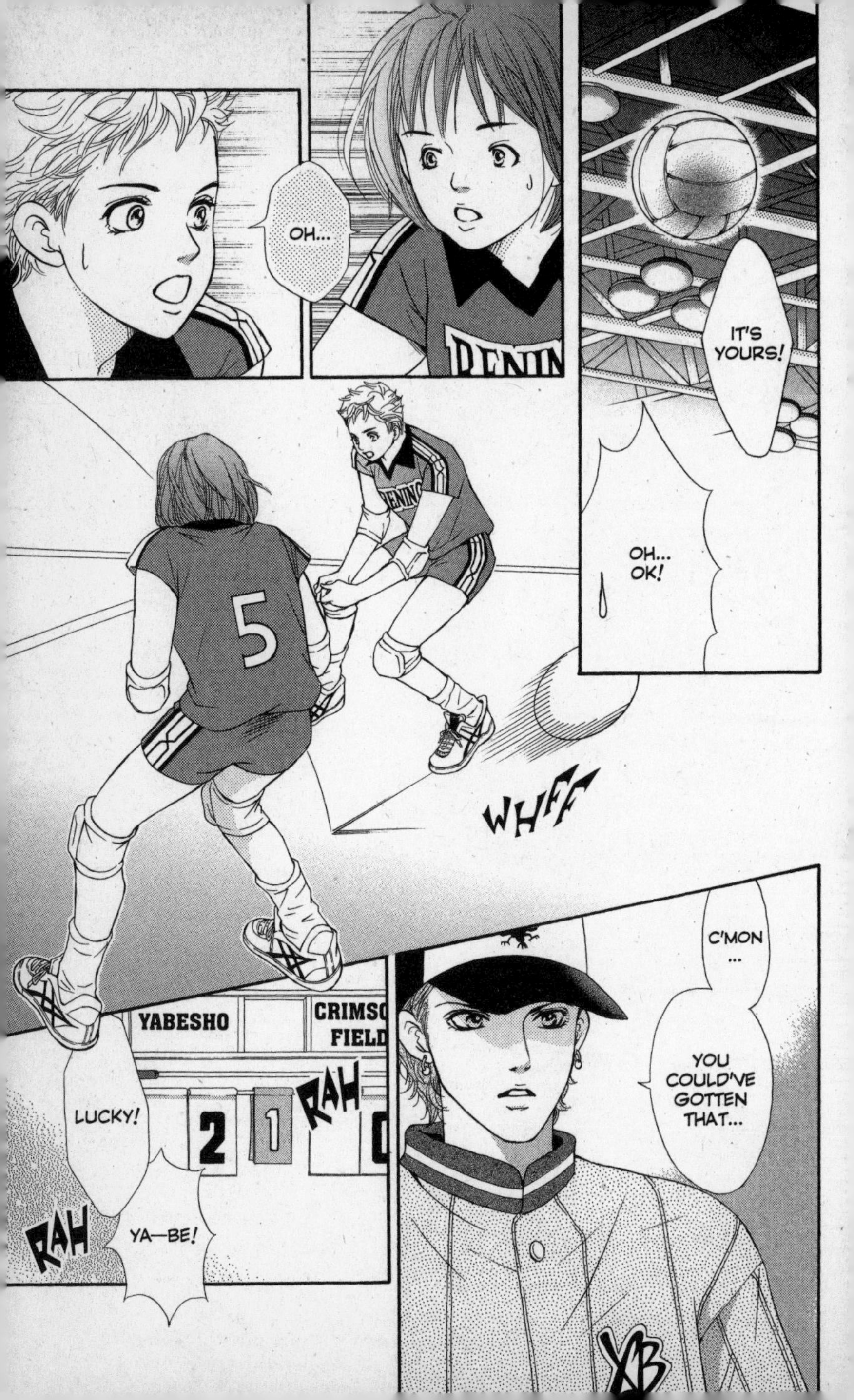
IT'S YOURS!
OH... OK!
OH...
WHFF
C'MON ...
YOU COULD'VE GOTTEN THAT...
YABESHO
RAH
LUCKY!
RAH
YA—BE!

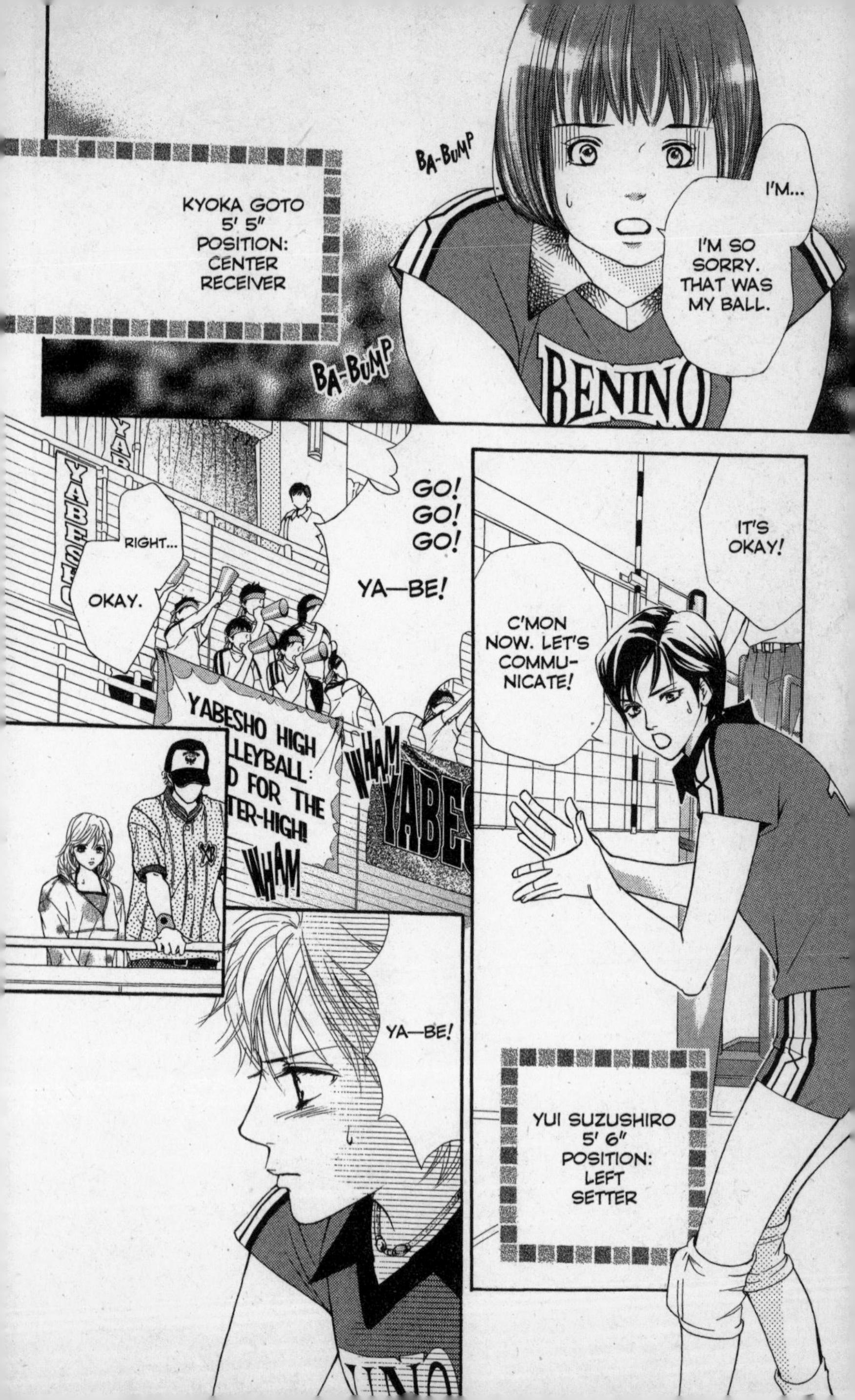
I'M...
I'M SO SORRY. THAT WAS MY BALL.
BA-BUMP
KYOKA GOTO 5' 5" POSITION: CENTER RECEIVER
BA-BUMP
BENINO
IT'S OKAY!
C'MON NOW. LET'S COMMUNICATE!
YUI SUZUSHIRO 5' 6" POSITION: LEFT SETTER
GO! GO! GO!
YA—BE!
RIGHT...
OKAY.
YABESHO HIGH
LLEYBALL:
D FOR THE
TER-HIGH!
WHAM
WHAM
YA—BE!

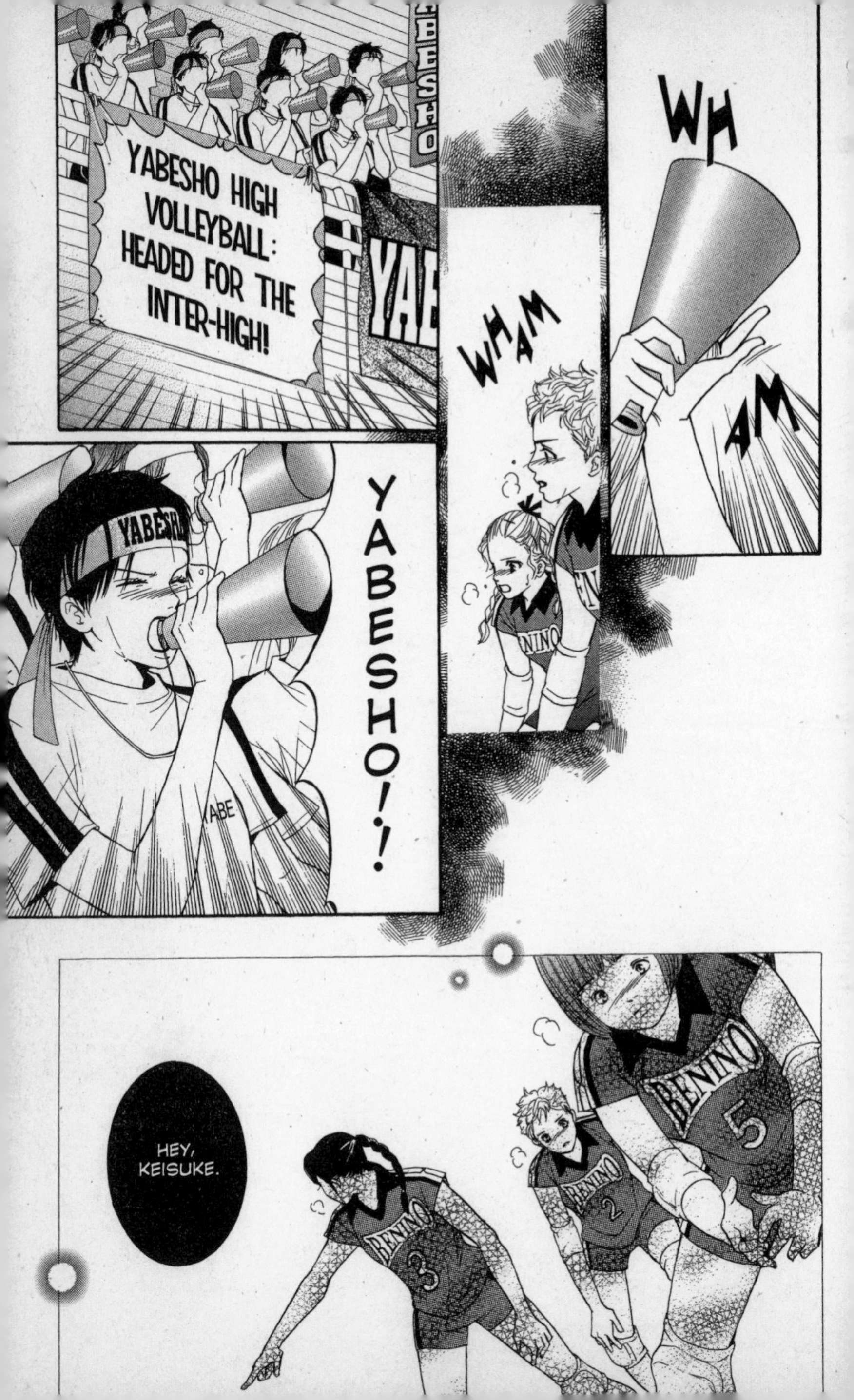
WH
AM
WHAM
YABESHO HIGH VOLLEYBALL: HEADED FOR THE INTER-HIGH!
YABESHO
YABESHO!!
ABE
BENINO
HEY, KEISUKE.

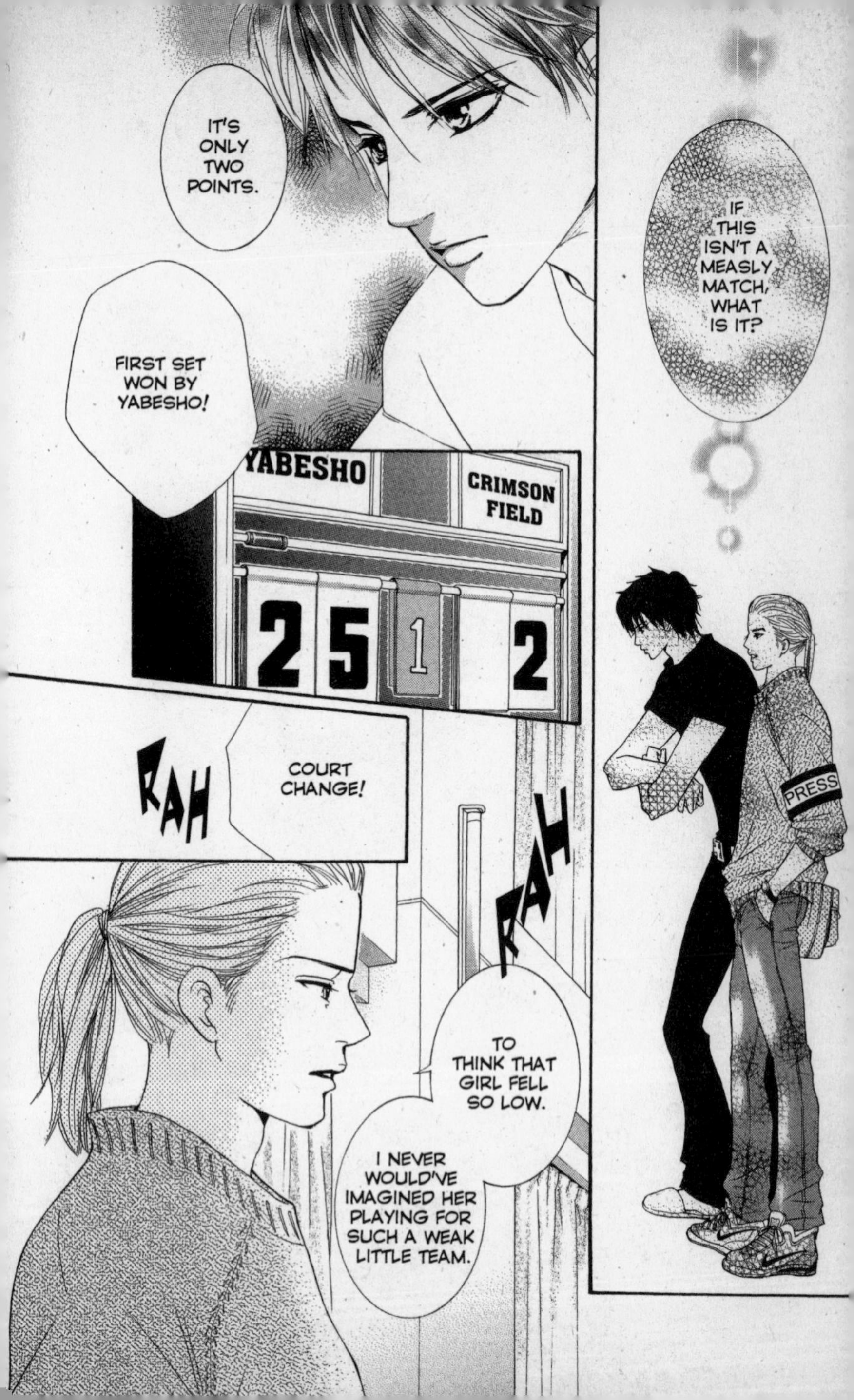
IF THIS ISN'T A MEASLY MATCH, WHAT IS IT?
PRESS
IT'S ONLY TWO POINTS.
FIRST SET WON BY YABESHO!
YABESHO
CRIMSON FIELD
25 1 2
COURT CHANGE!
RAH
RAH
TO THINK THAT GIRL FELL SO LOW.
I NEVER WOULD'VE IMAGINED HER PLAYING FOR SUCH A WEAK LITTLE TEAM.

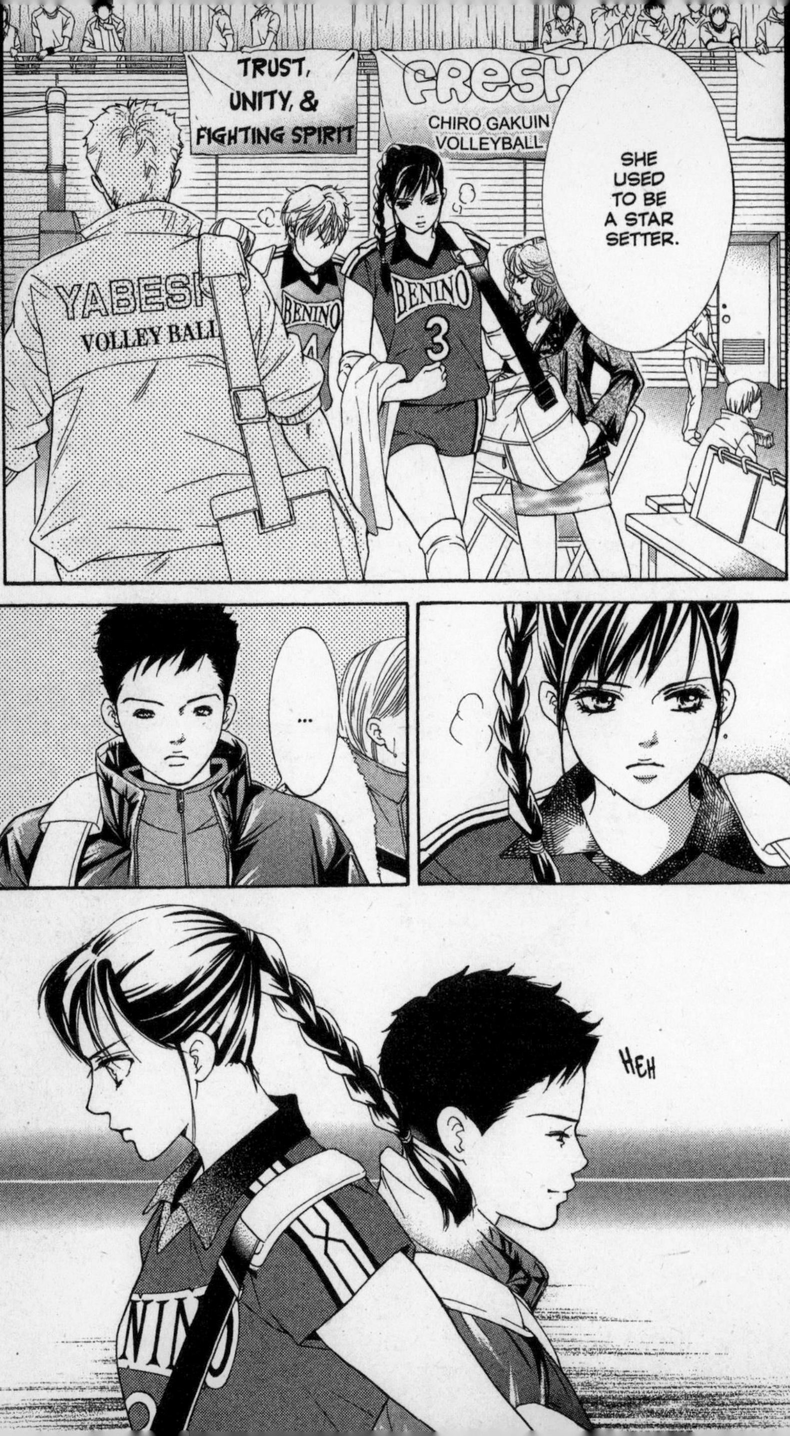
SHE USED TO BE A STAR SETTER.
FRESH
CHIRO GAKUIN VOLLEYBALL
TRUST, UNITY, & FIGHTING SPIRIT
BENINO
3
...
HEH

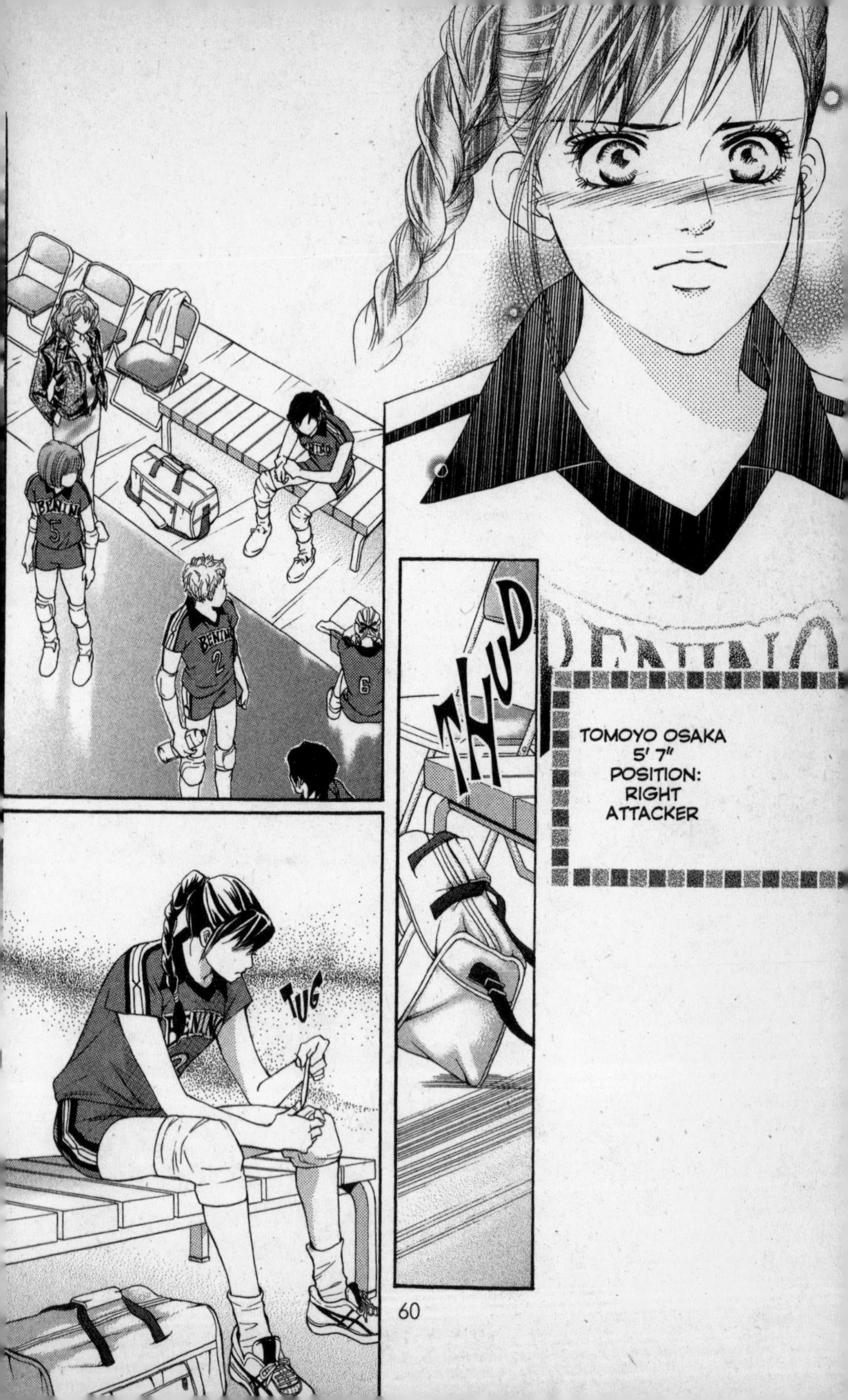
TOMOYO OSAKA
5' 7"
POSITION:
RIGHT
ATTACKER
THUD
TUG

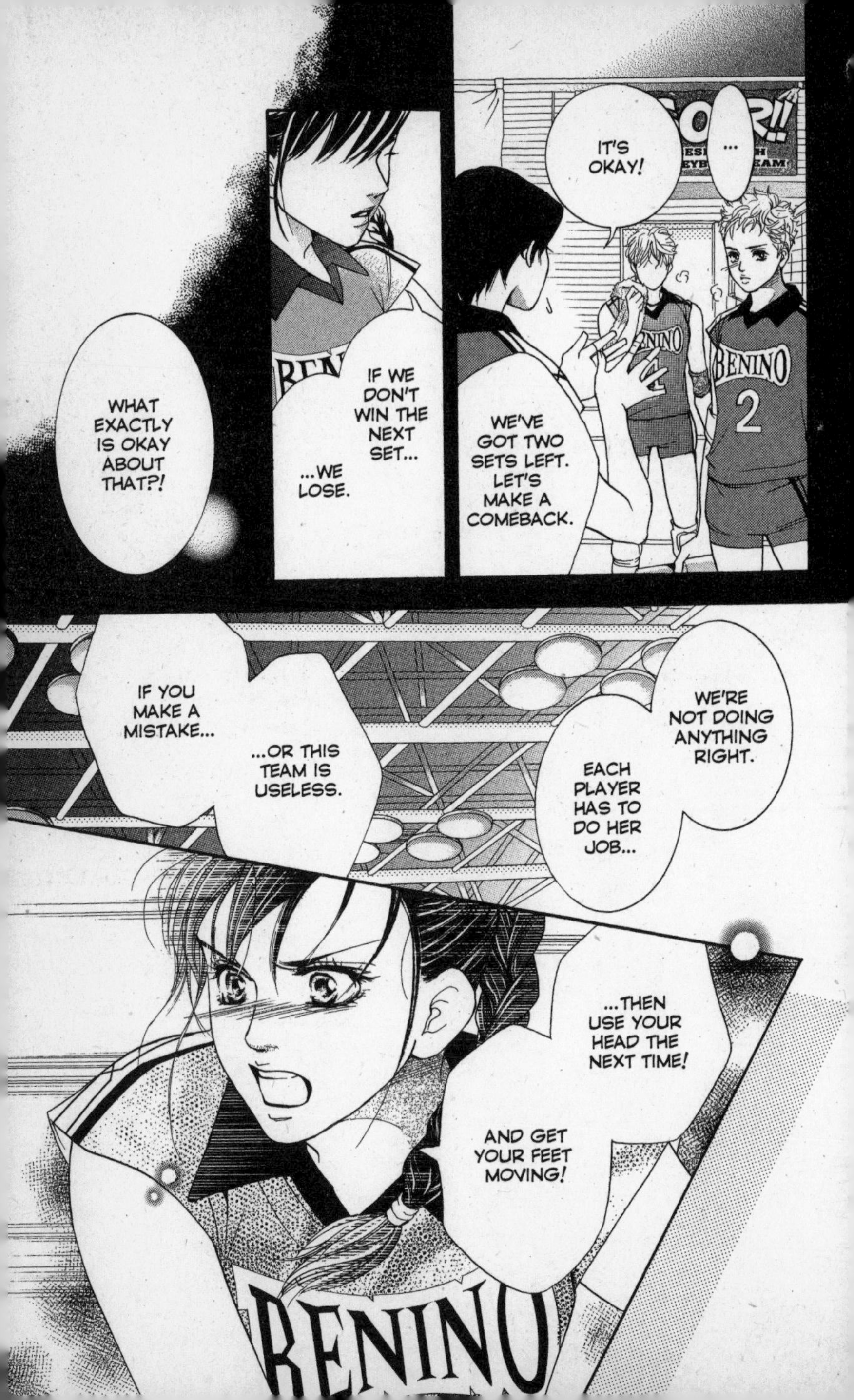
...
IT'S OKAY!
WE'VE GOT TWO SETS LEFT. LET'S MAKE A COMEBACK.
IF WE DON'T WIN THE NEXT SET...
...WE LOSE.
WHAT EXACTLY IS OKAY ABOUT THAT?!
WE'RE NOT DOING ANYTHING RIGHT.
EACH PLAYER HAS TO DO HER JOB...
...OR THIS TEAM IS USELESS.
IF YOU MAKE A MISTAKE...
...THEN USE YOUR HEAD THE NEXT TIME!
AND GET YOUR FEET MOVING!

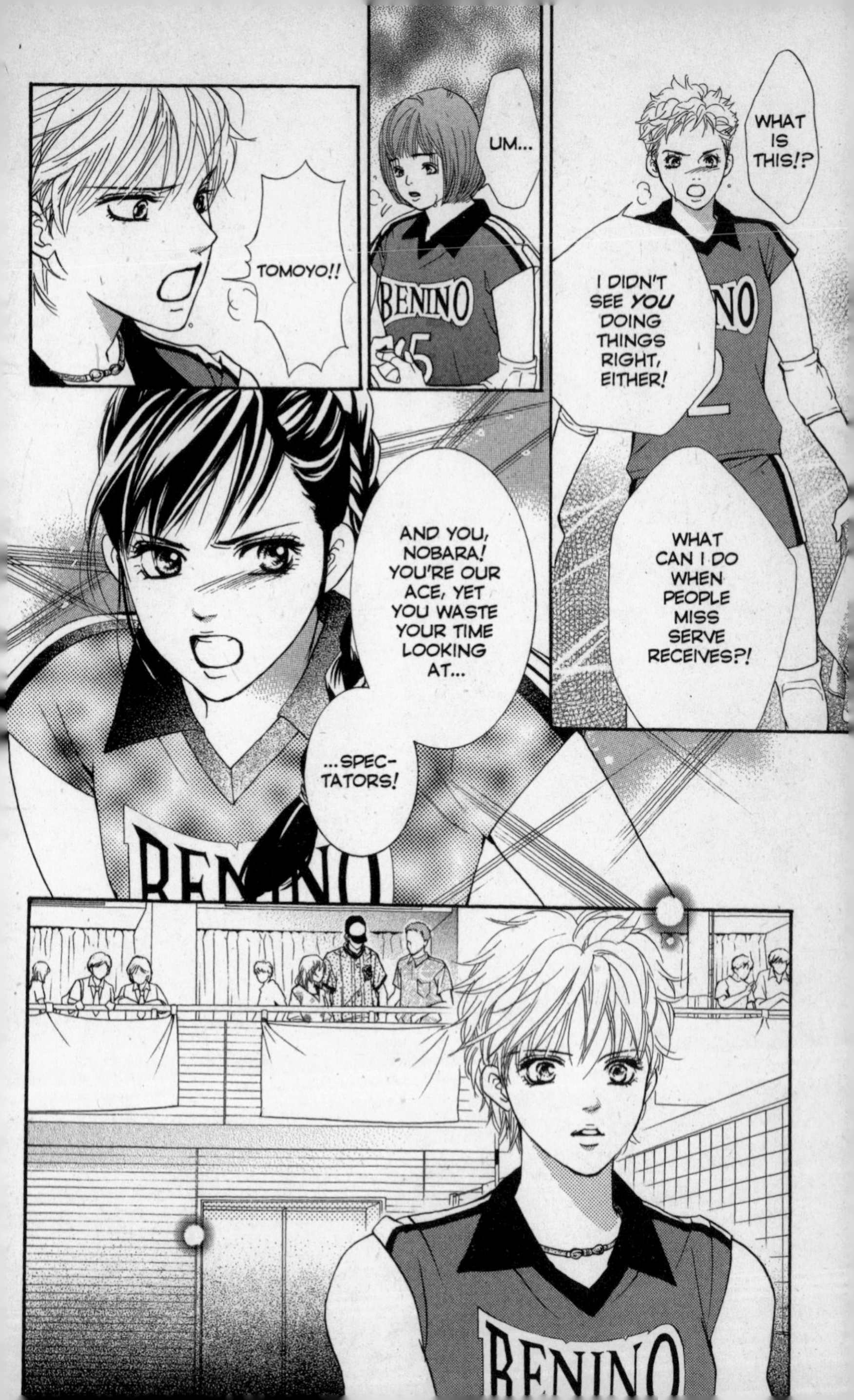
WHAT IS THIS!?
I DIDN'T SEE *YOU* DOING THINGS RIGHT, EITHER!
WHAT CAN I DO WHEN PEOPLE MISS SERVE RECEIVES?!
UM...
TOMOYO!!
AND YOU, NOBARA! YOU'RE OUR ACE, YET YOU WASTE YOUR TIME LOOKING AT...
...SPECTATORS!

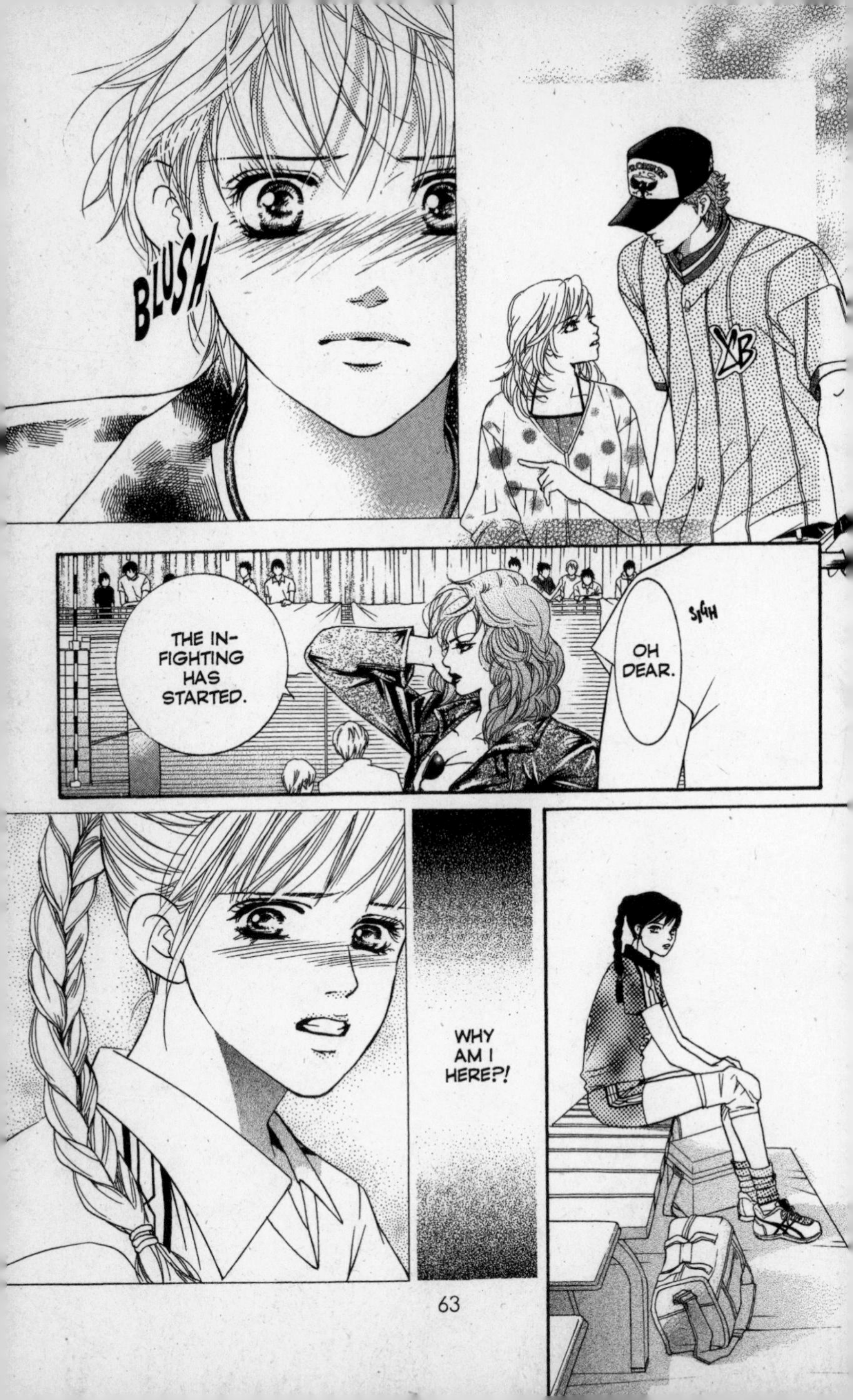
BLUSH
OH DEAR.
SIGH
THE IN-FIGHTING HAS STARTED.
WHY AM I HERE?!

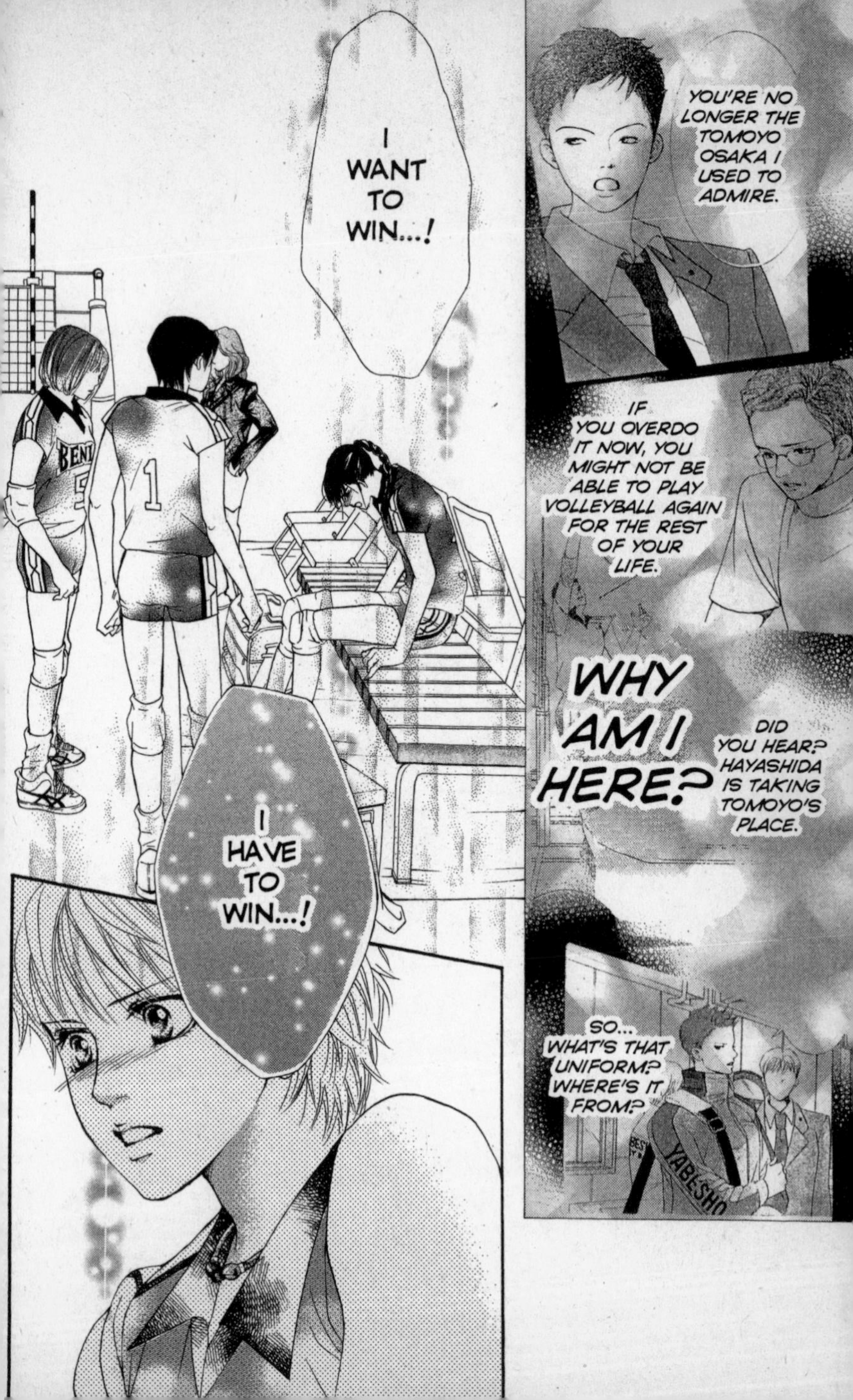
YOU'RE NO LONGER THE TOMOYO OSAKA I USED TO ADMIRE.
IF YOU OVERDO IT NOW, YOU MIGHT NOT BE ABLE TO PLAY VOLLEYBALL AGAIN FOR THE REST OF YOUR LIFE.
DID YOU HEAR? HAYASHIDA IS TAKING TOMOYO'S PLACE.
WHY AM I HERE?
SO... WHAT'S THAT UNIFORM? WHERE'S IT FROM?
I WANT TO WIN...!
I HAVE TO WIN...!

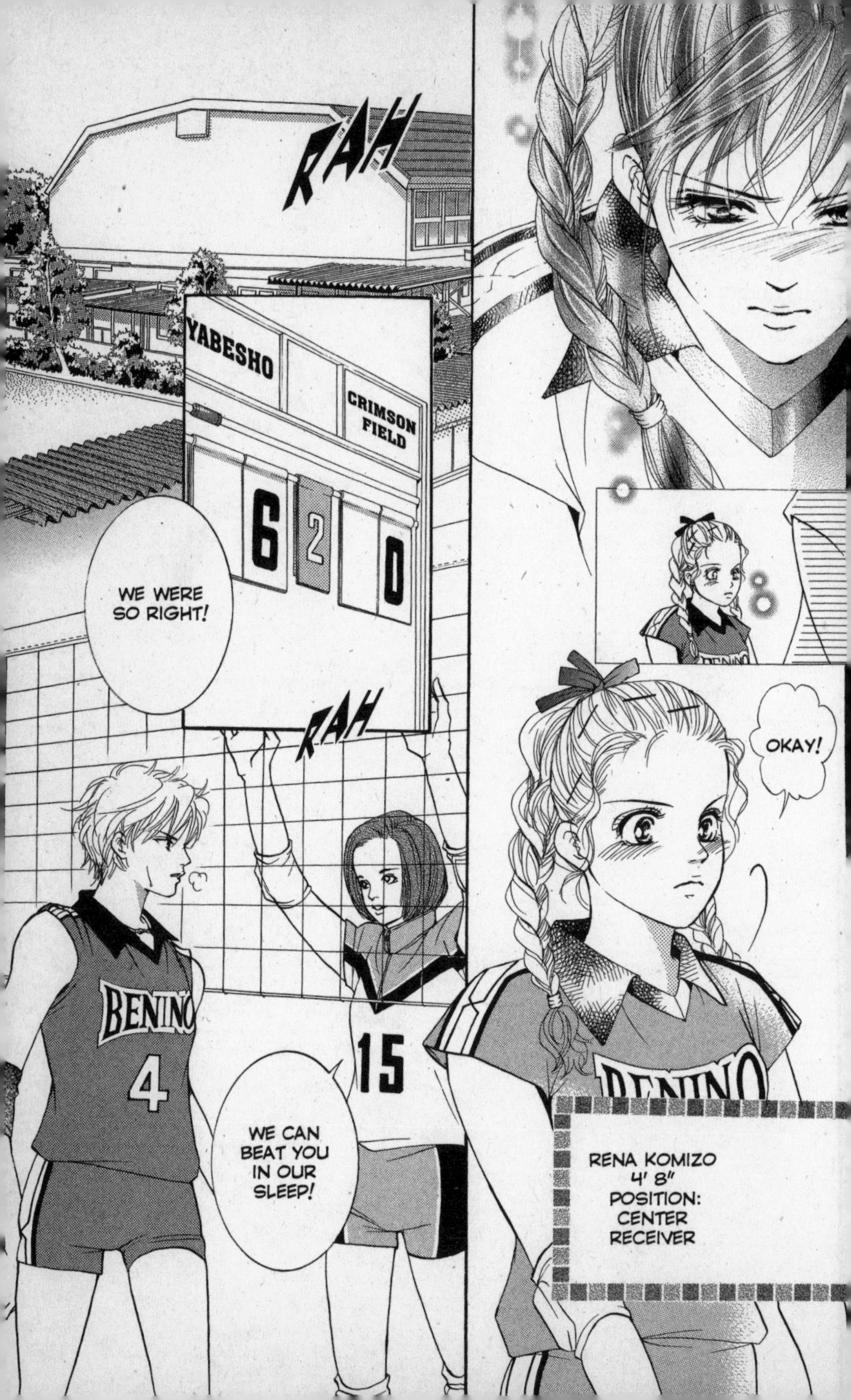
OKAY!
RENA KOMIZO
4' 8"
POSITION:
CENTER
RECEIVER
RAH
YABESHO
CRIMSON FIELD
6 2 0
WE WERE SO RIGHT!
RAH
BENINO
4
15
WE CAN BEAT YOU IN OUR SLEEP!

AND YOU, NOBARA! YOU'RE OUR ACE, YET YOU WASTE YOUR TIME LOOKING AT SPECTATORS!

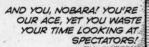

WHAT WAS I DOING IN THE FIRST SET?

THIS ONE WAS A SHALLOW SERVE!

BAM

TWEE

SHOOT.

OUT AGAIN.

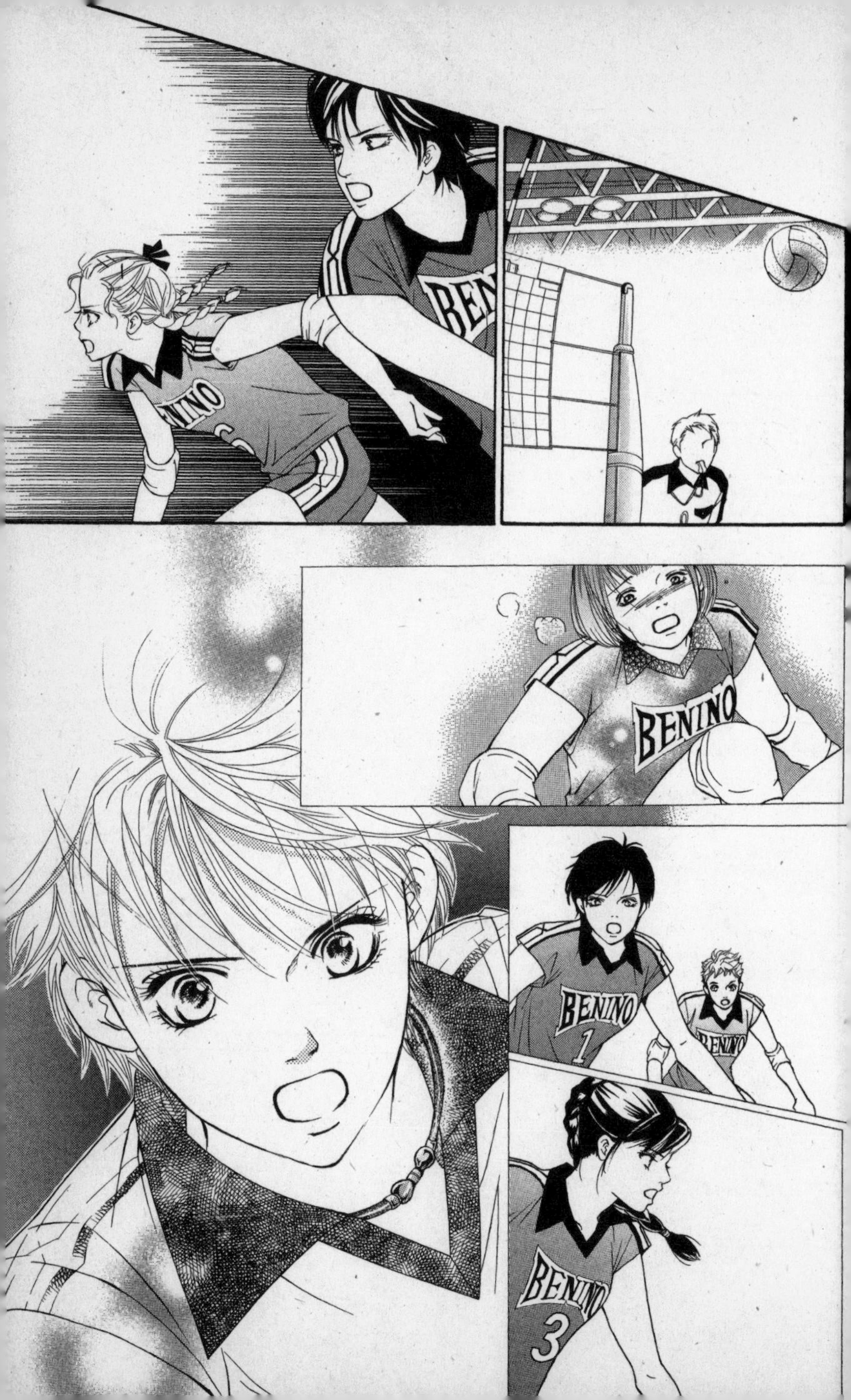
BENINO
BENINO
BENINO
1
BENINO
BENINO
3

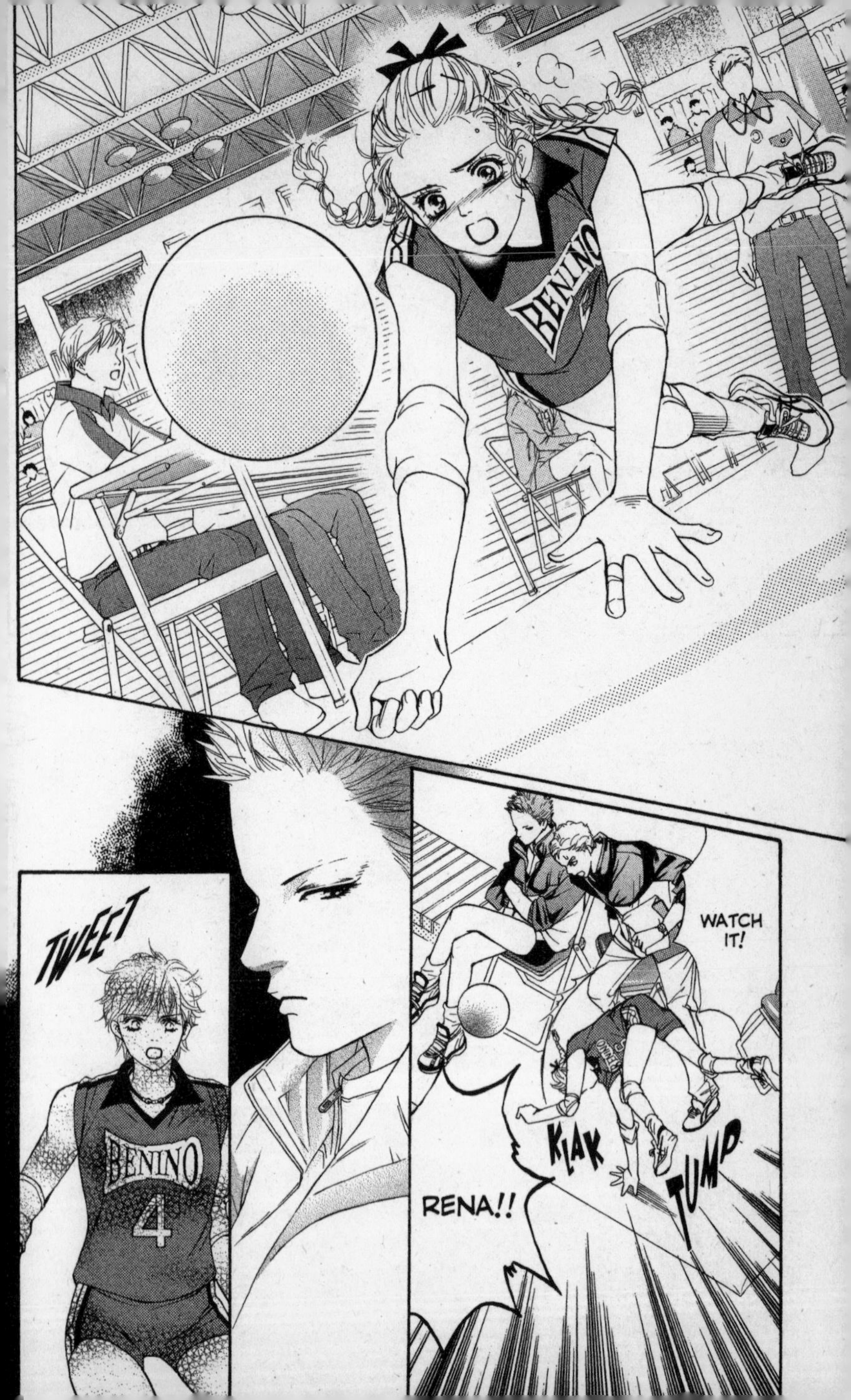
WATCH IT!
KLAK
TUMP
RENA!!
TWEET

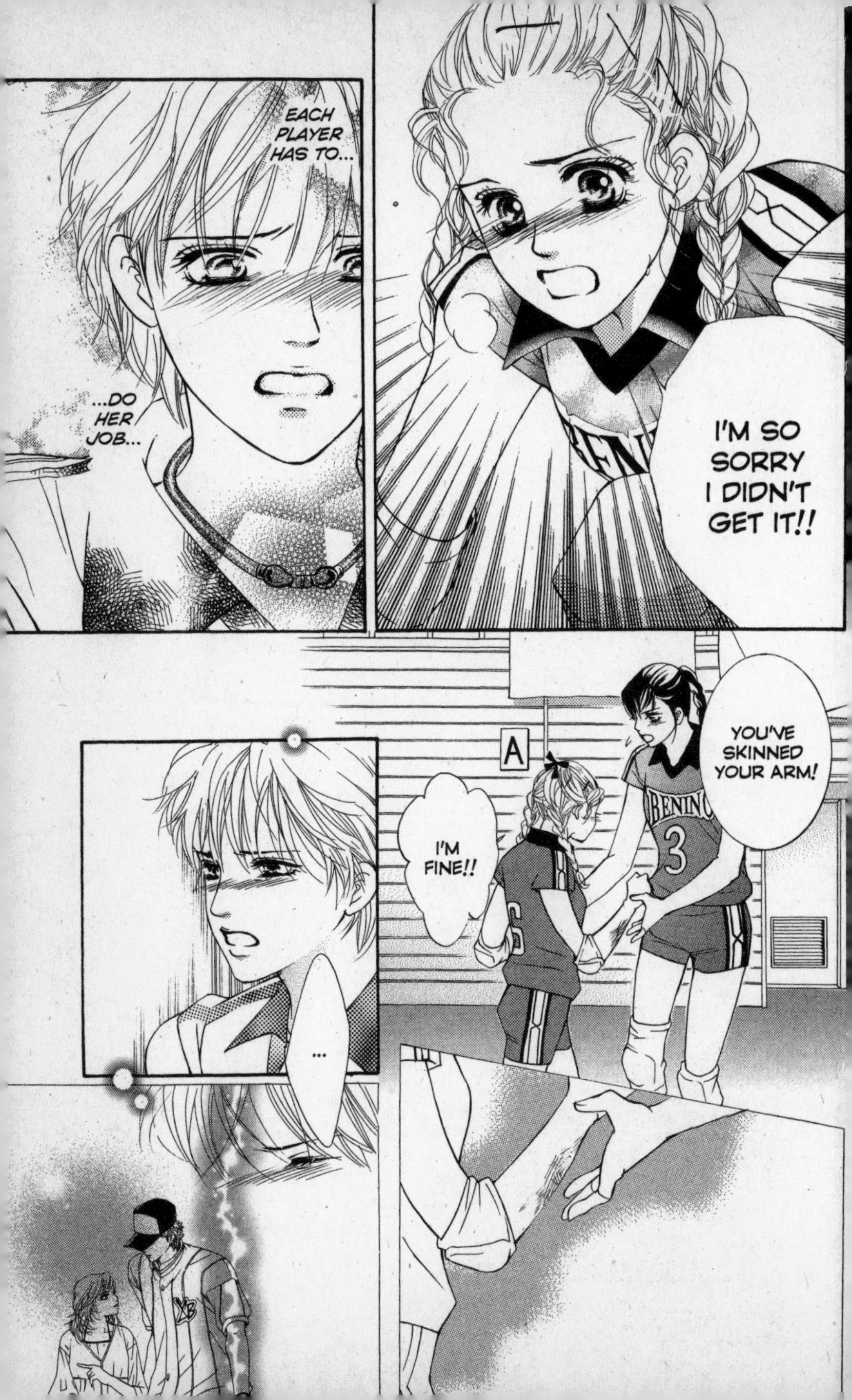
I'M SO SORRY I DIDN'T GET IT!!
EACH PLAYER HAS TO...
...DO HER JOB...
YOU'VE SKINNED YOUR ARM!
I'M FINE!!
A
BENING
3
...

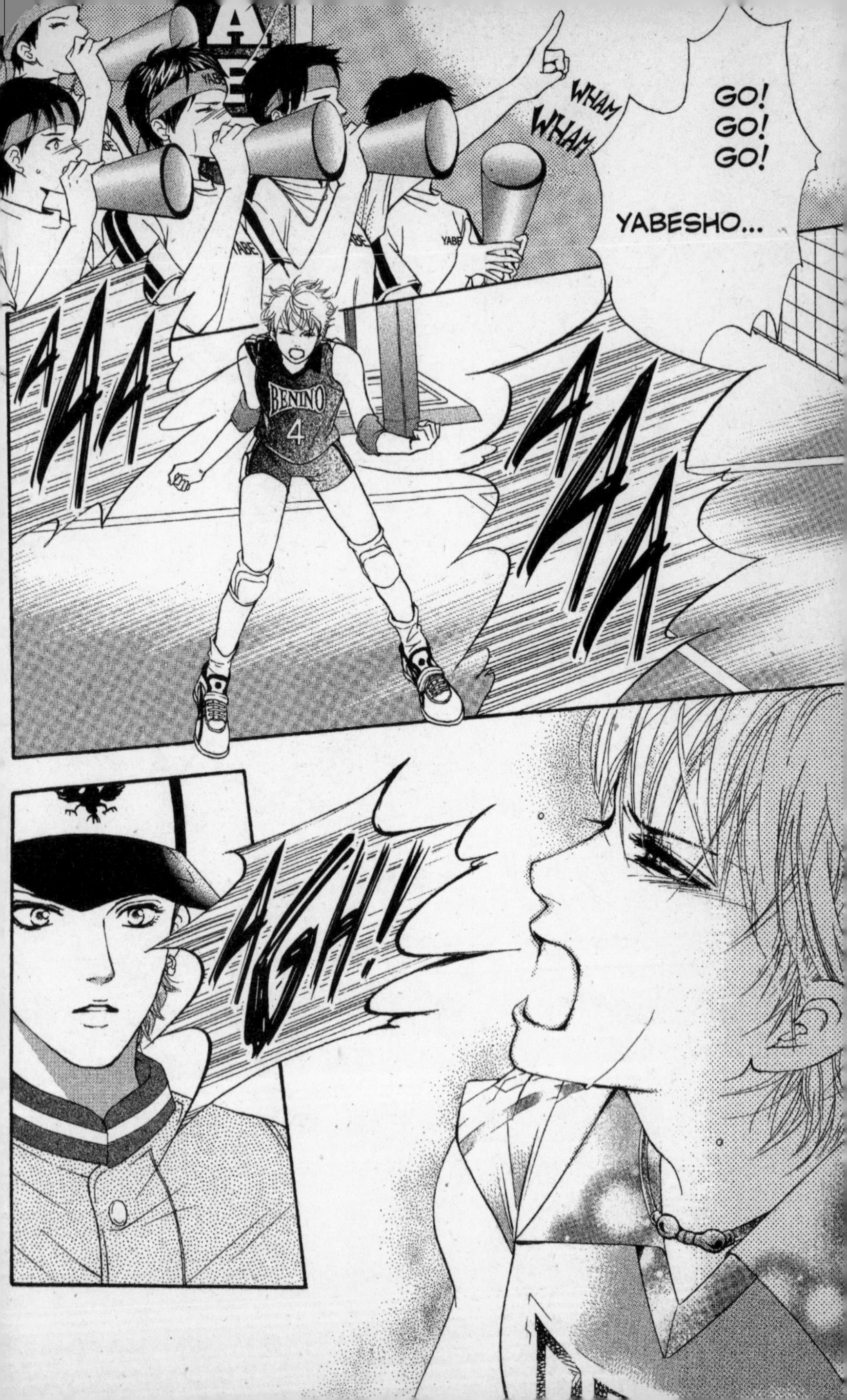
GO! GO! GO!
YABESHO...
WHAM
WHAM
AAAA
AAA
AGH!

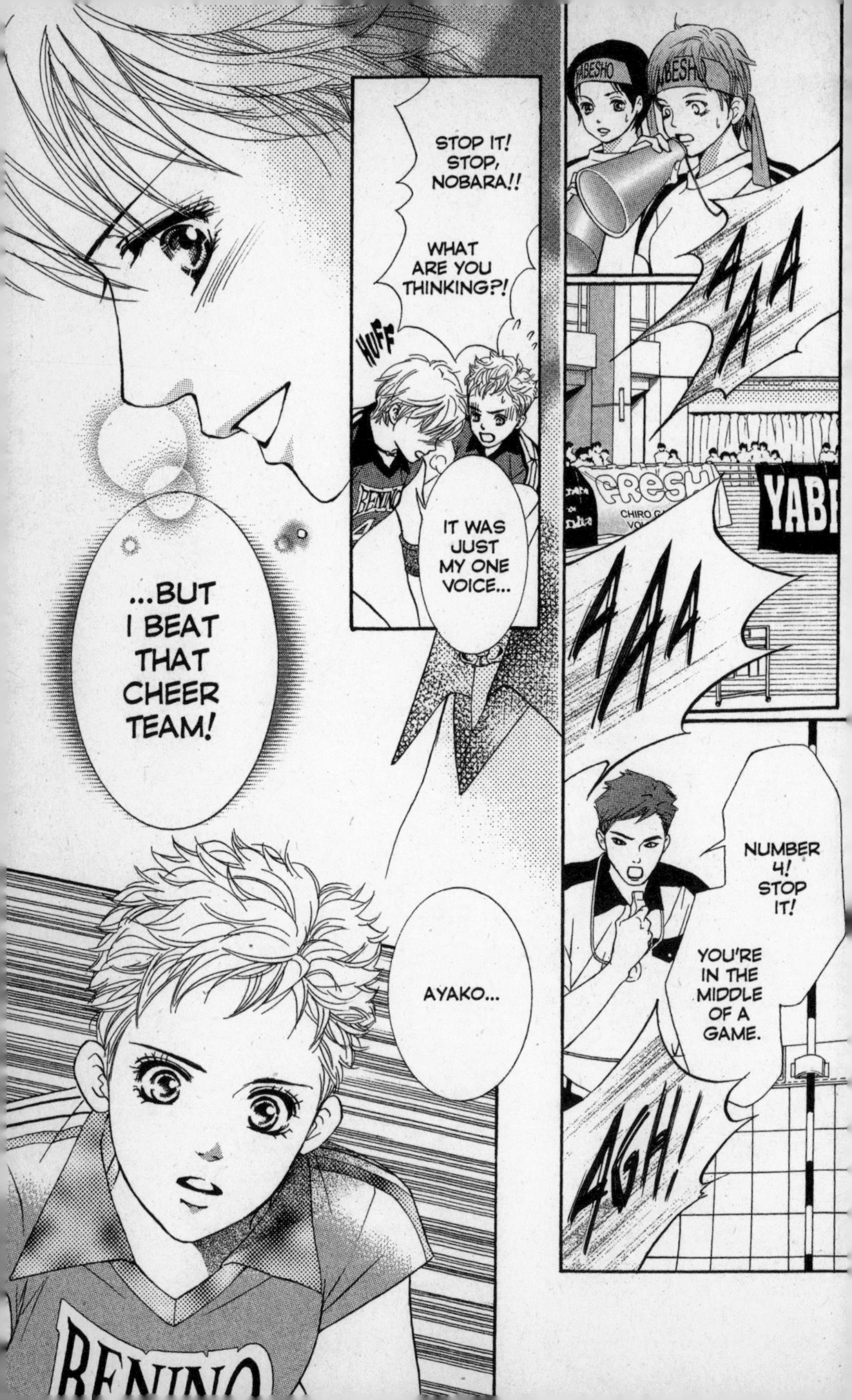
YABESHO
YABESHO
AAA
FRESH
YAB
AAA
NUMBER 4! STOP IT!
YOU'RE IN THE MIDDLE OF A GAME.
AGH!
STOP IT! STOP, NOBARA!!
WHAT ARE YOU THINKING?!
HUFF
IT WAS JUST MY ONE VOICE...
...BUT I BEAT THAT CHEER TEAM!
AYAKO...
BENINO

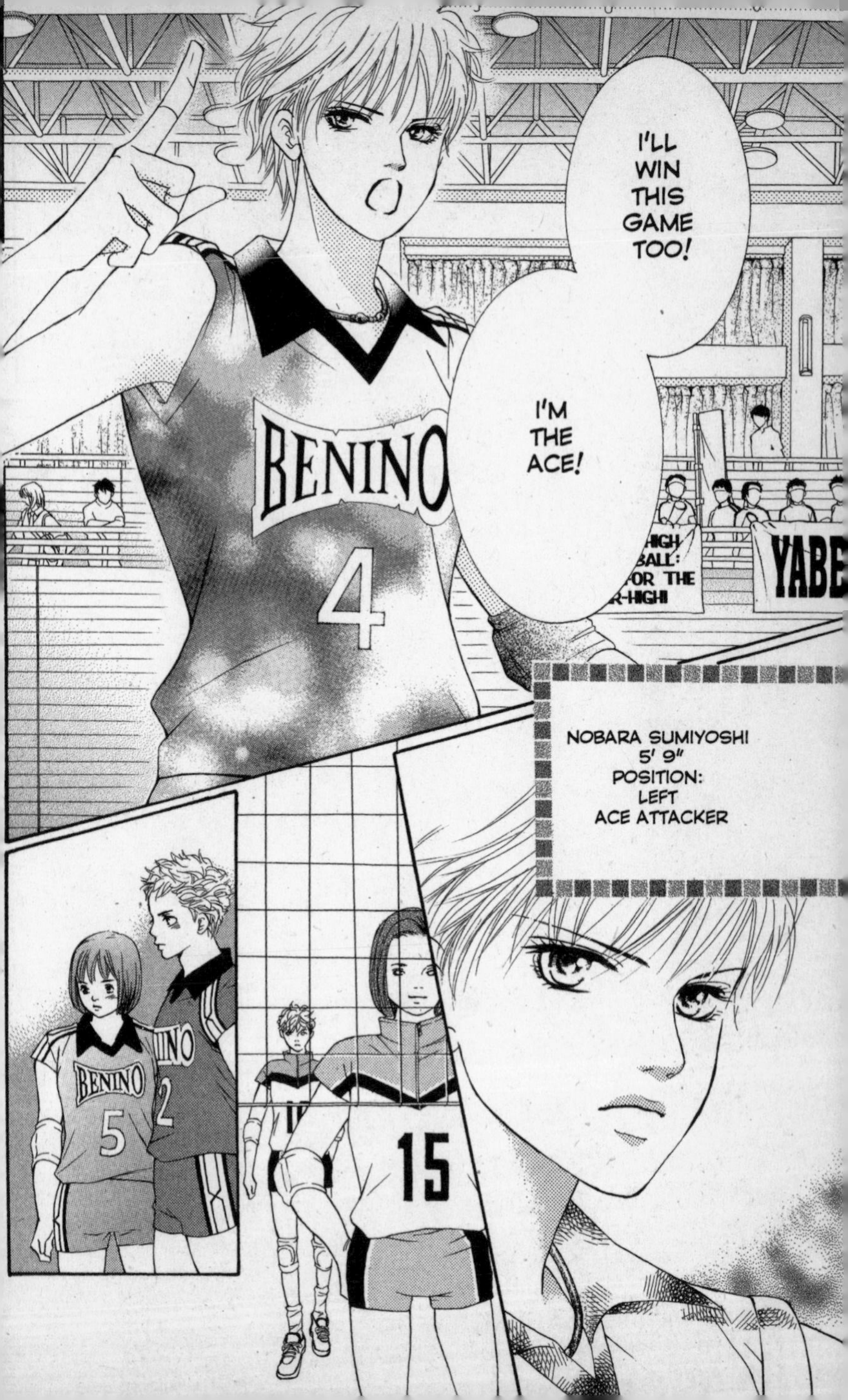
I'LL WIN THIS GAME TOO!
I'M THE ACE!
NOBARA SUMIYOSHI 5' 9" POSITION: LEFT ACE ATTACKER

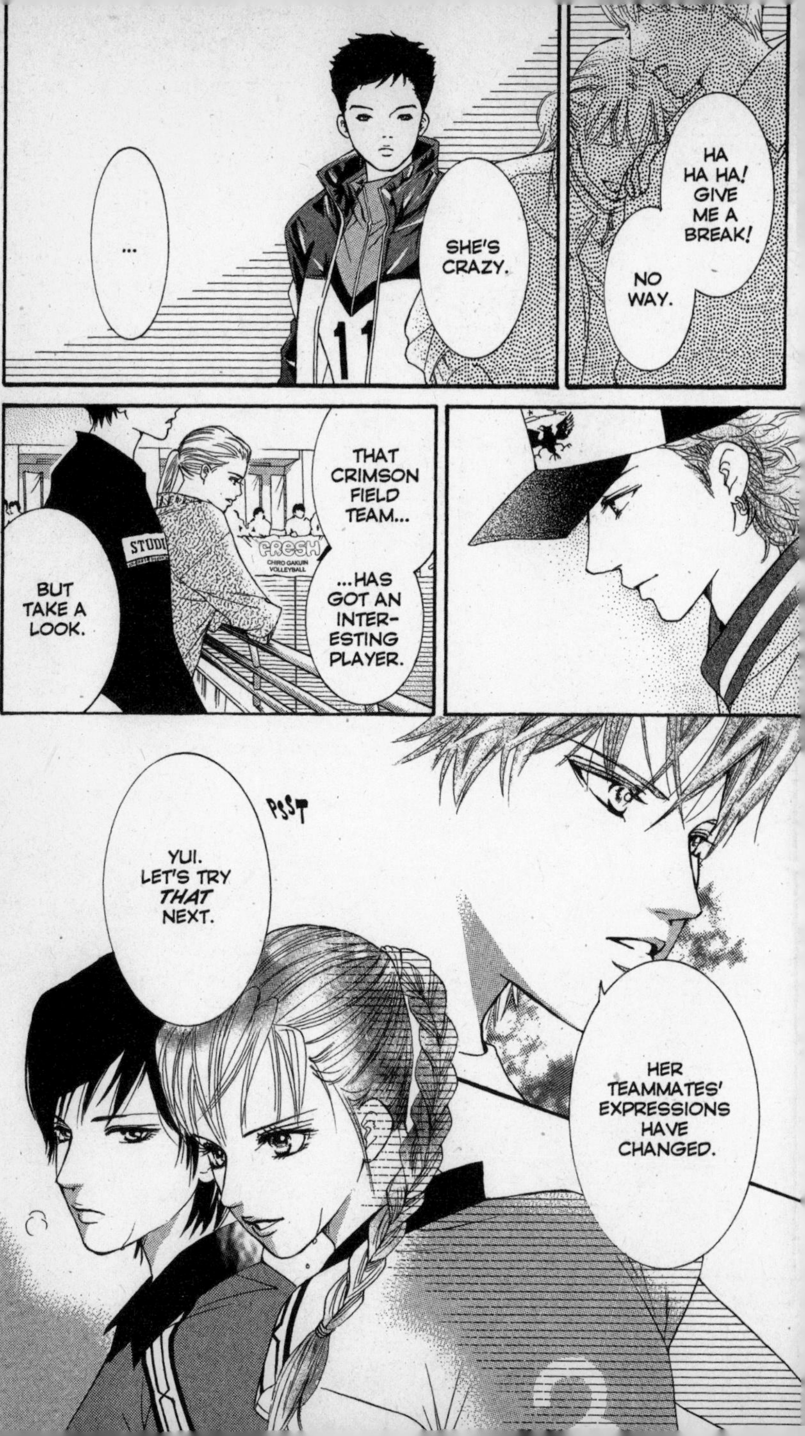
HA HA HA! GIVE ME A BREAK!
NO WAY.
SHE'S CRAZY.
...
THAT CRIMSON FIELD TEAM...
...HAS GOT AN INTERESTING PLAYER.
FRESH
CHIRO GAKUIN VOLLEYBALL
BUT TAKE A LOOK.
PSST
YUI. LET'S TRY *THAT* NEXT.
HER TEAMMATES' EXPRESSIONS HAVE CHANGED.

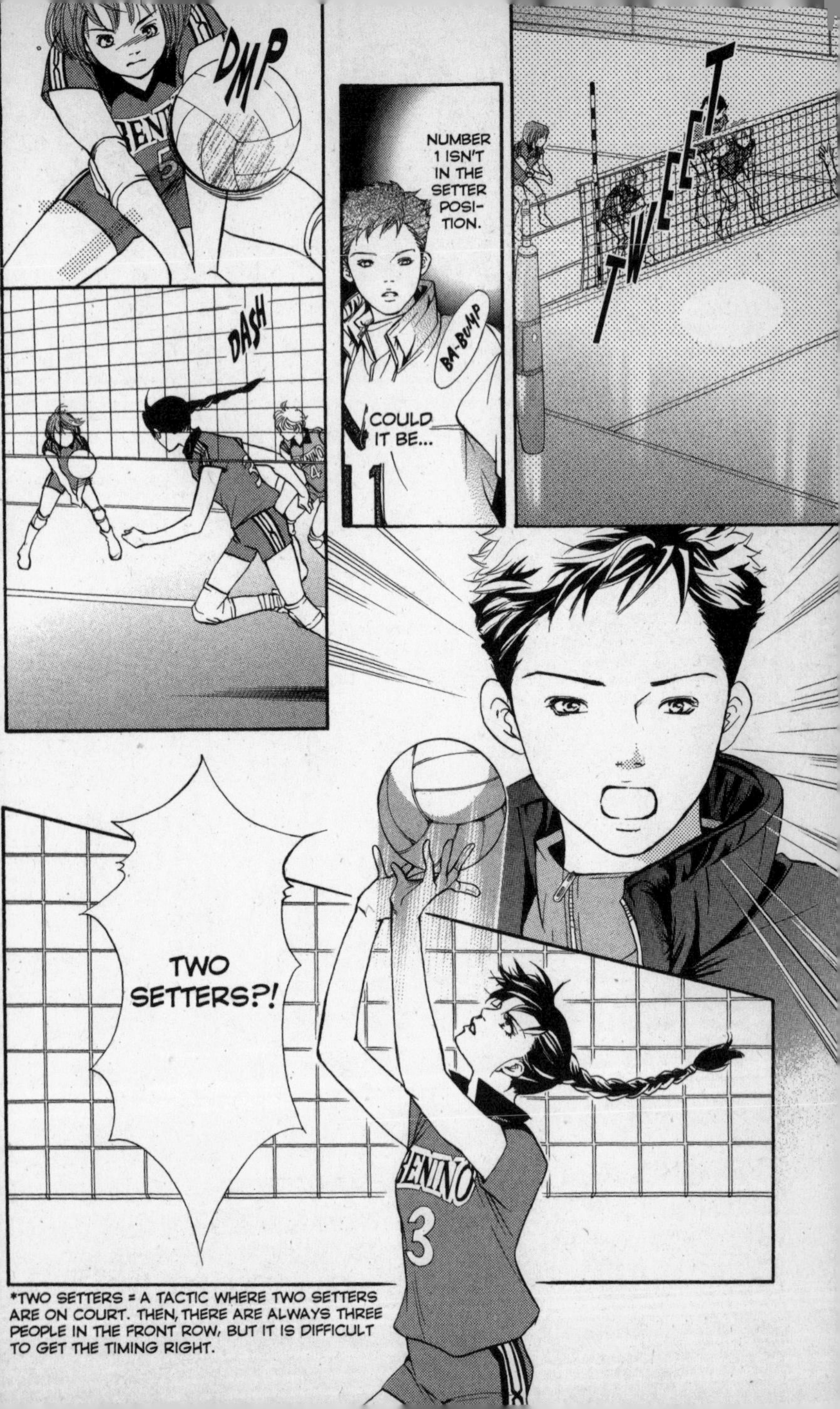
TWEEET
NUMBER 1 ISN'T IN THE SETTER POSITION.
BA-BUMP
COULD IT BE...
DMP
DASH
TWO SETTERS?!

*TWO SETTERS = A TACTIC WHERE TWO SETTERS ARE ON COURT. THEN, THERE ARE ALWAYS THREE PEOPLE IN THE FRONT ROW, BUT IT IS DIFFICULT TO GET THE TIMING RIGHT.

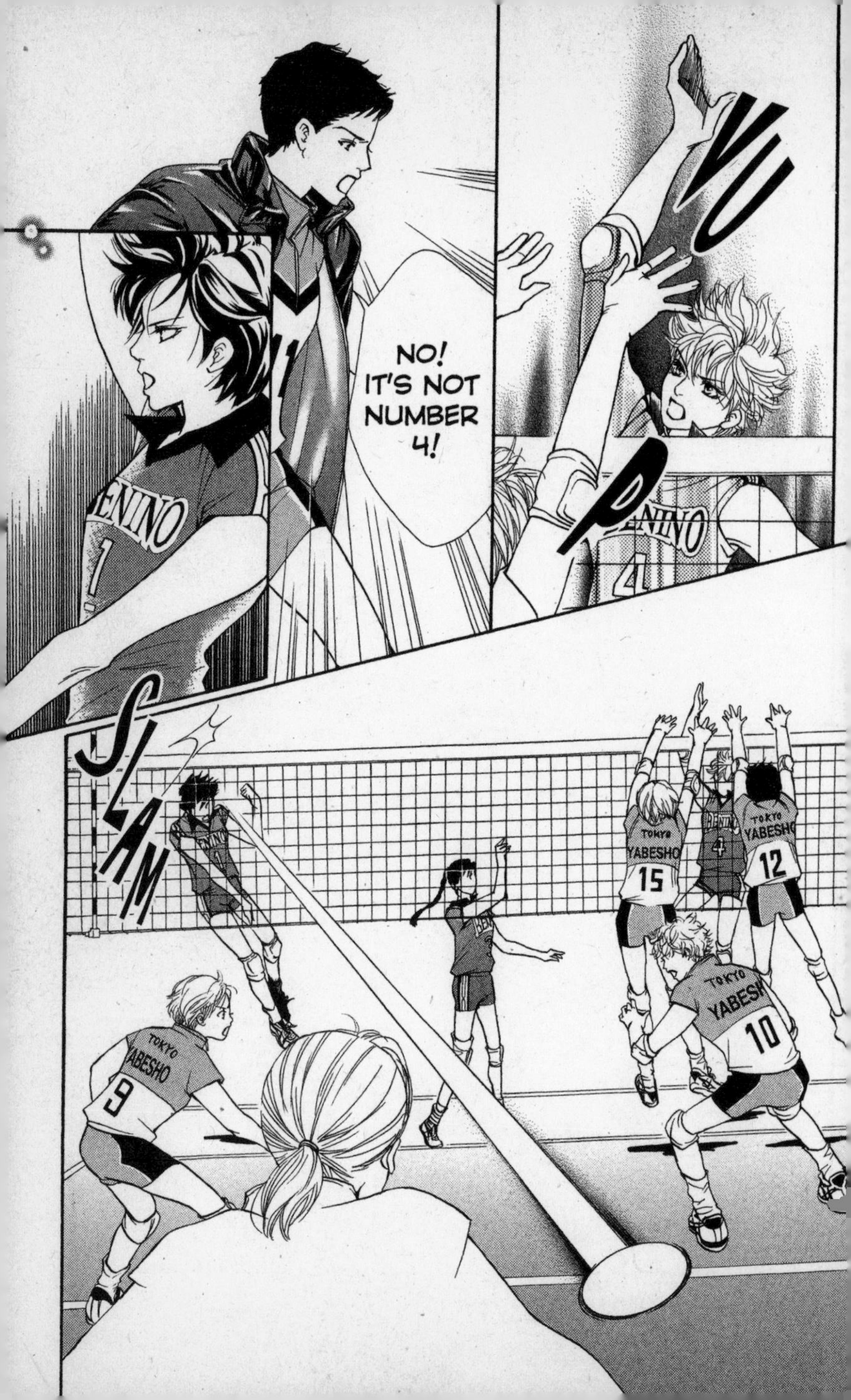
VU
P
NO! IT'S NOT NUMBER 4!
SLAM

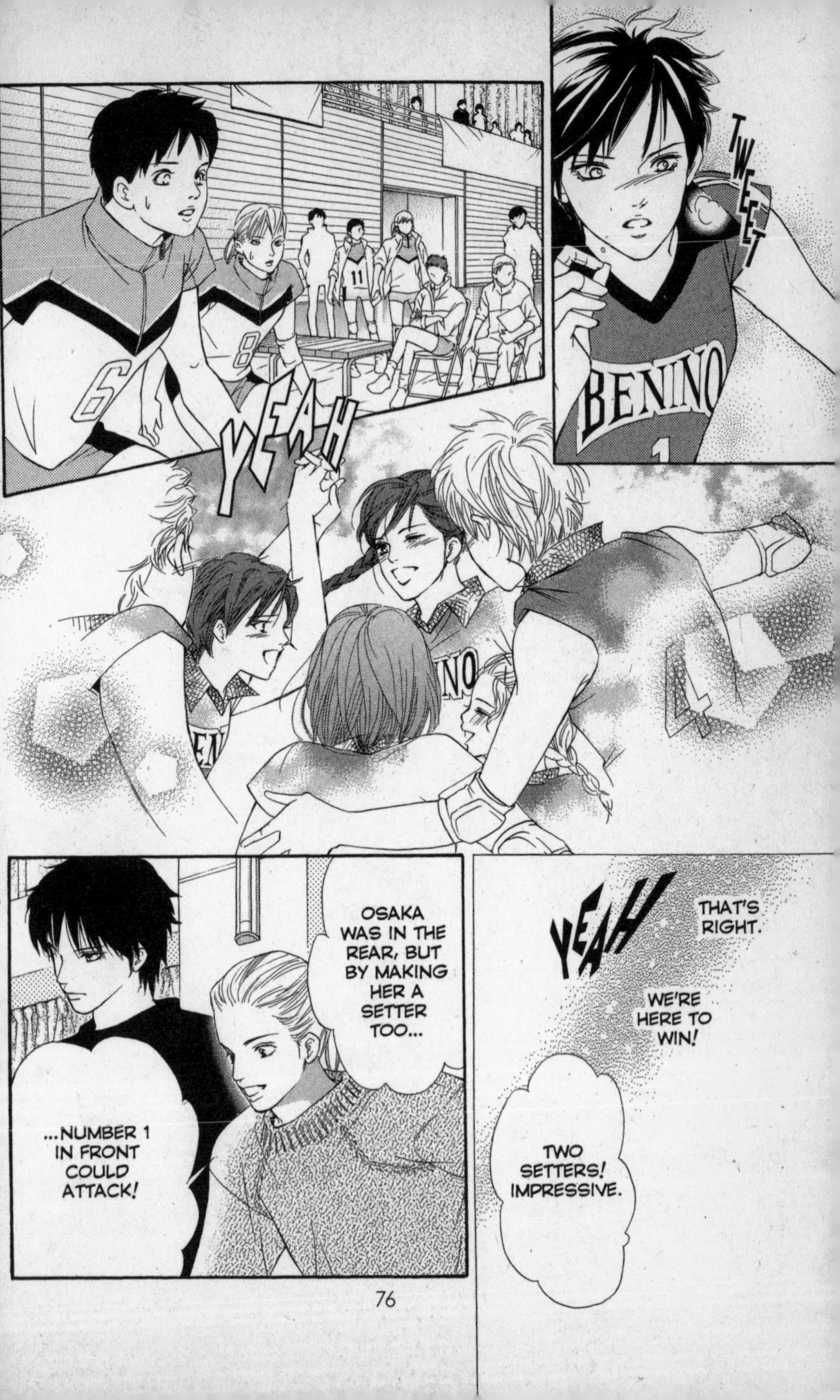
TWEET
BENINO
YEAH
YEAH
THAT'S RIGHT.
WE'RE HERE TO WIN!
TWO SETTERS! IMPRESSIVE.
OSAKA WAS IN THE REAR, BUT BY MAKING HER A SETTER TOO...
...NUMBER 1 IN FRONT COULD ATTACK!

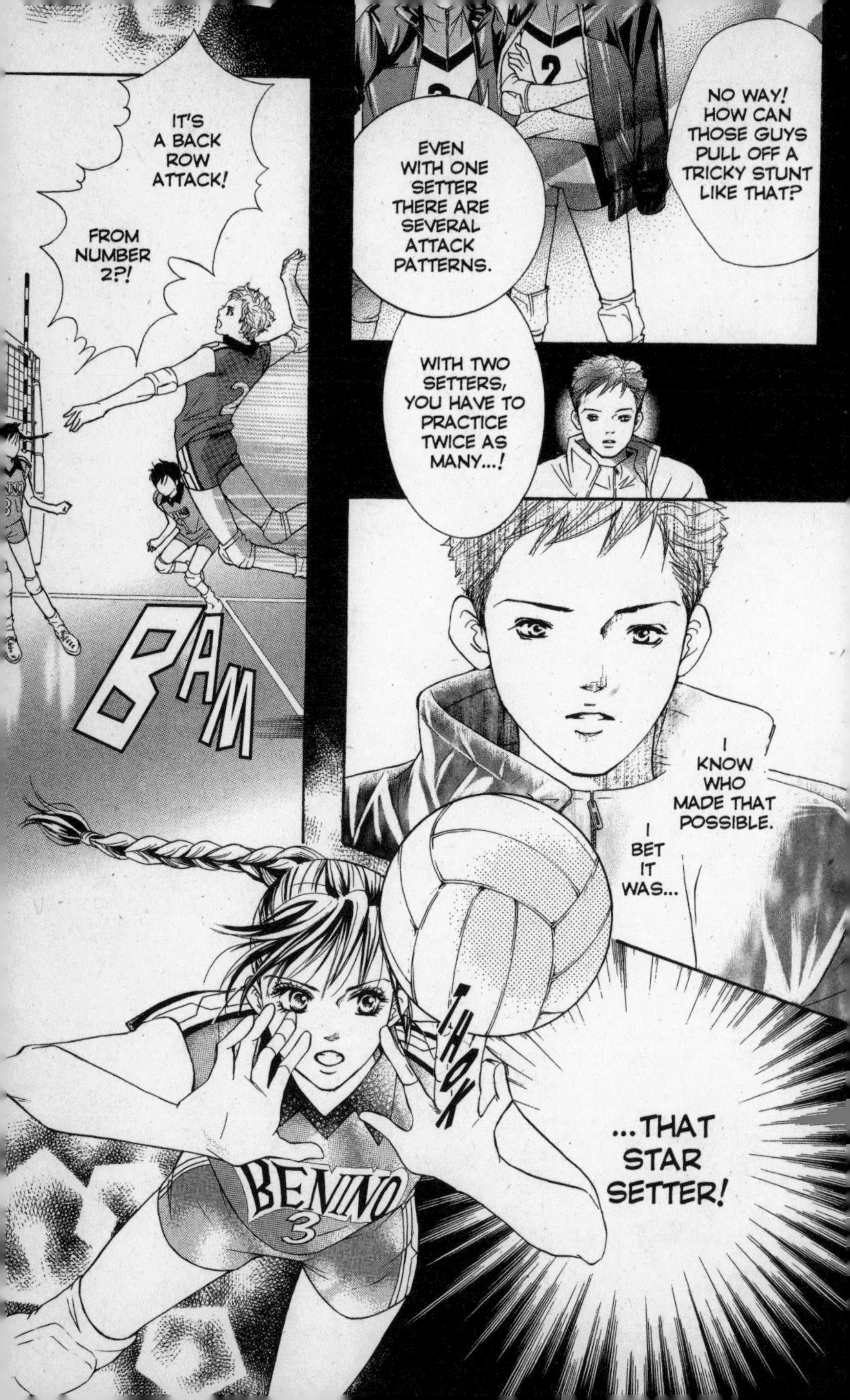
IT'S A BACK ROW ATTACK!
FROM NUMBER 2?!
BAM
NO WAY! HOW CAN THOSE GUYS PULL OFF A TRICKY STUNT LIKE THAT?
EVEN WITH ONE SETTER THERE ARE SEVERAL ATTACK PATTERNS.
WITH TWO SETTERS, YOU HAVE TO PRACTICE TWICE AS MANY...!
I KNOW WHO MADE THAT POSSIBLE.
I BET IT WAS...
THOK
...THAT STAR SETTER!
BENINO
3

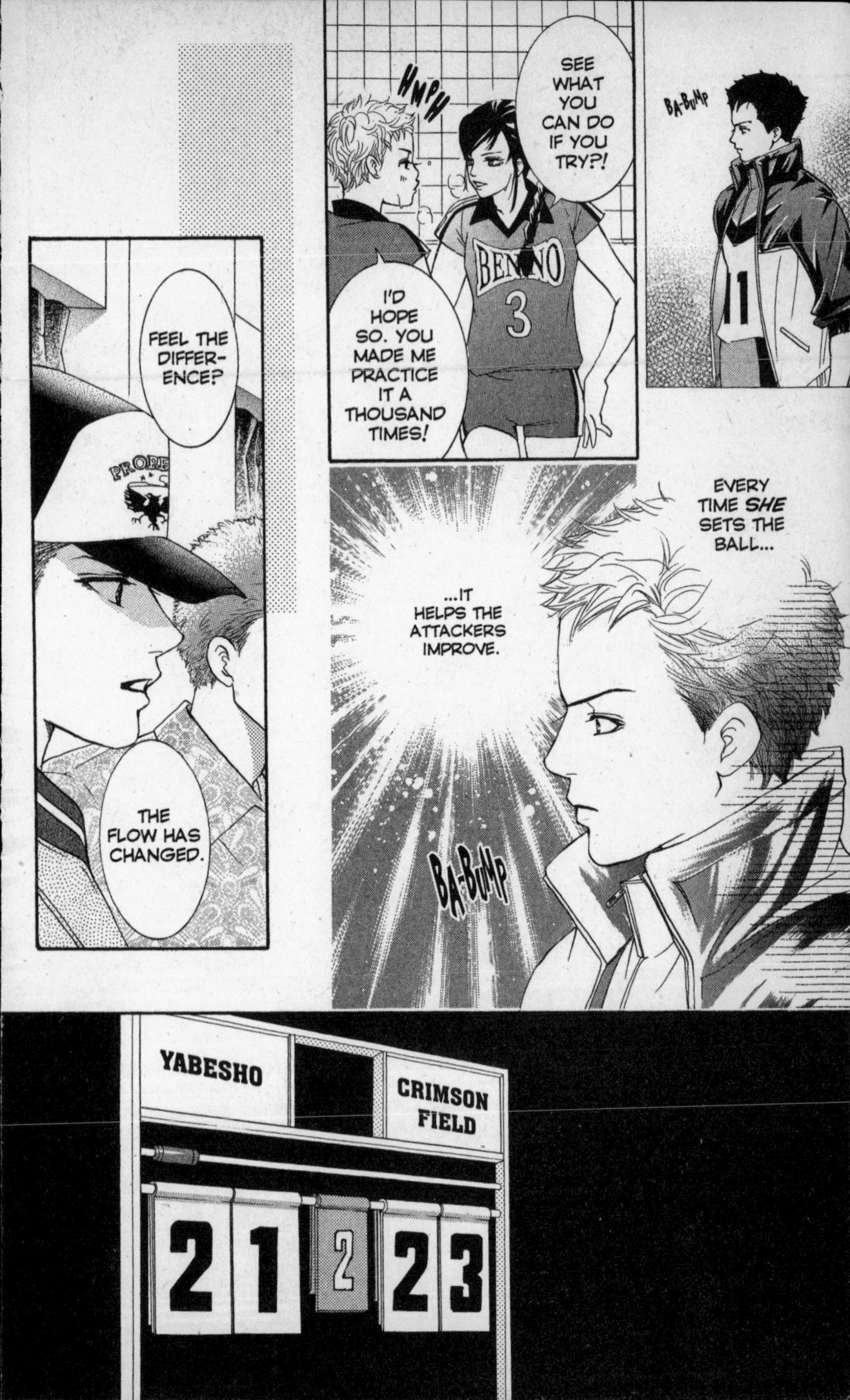
BA-BUMP
SEE WHAT YOU CAN DO IF YOU TRY?!
HMPH
I'D HOPE SO. YOU MADE ME PRACTICE IT A THOUSAND TIMES!
BENNO 3
11
EVERY TIME *SHE* SETS THE BALL...
...IT HELPS THE ATTACKERS IMPROVE.
BA-BUMP
FEEL THE DIFFER-ENCE?
THE FLOW HAS CHANGED.
YABESHO
CRIMSON FIELD
21 2 23

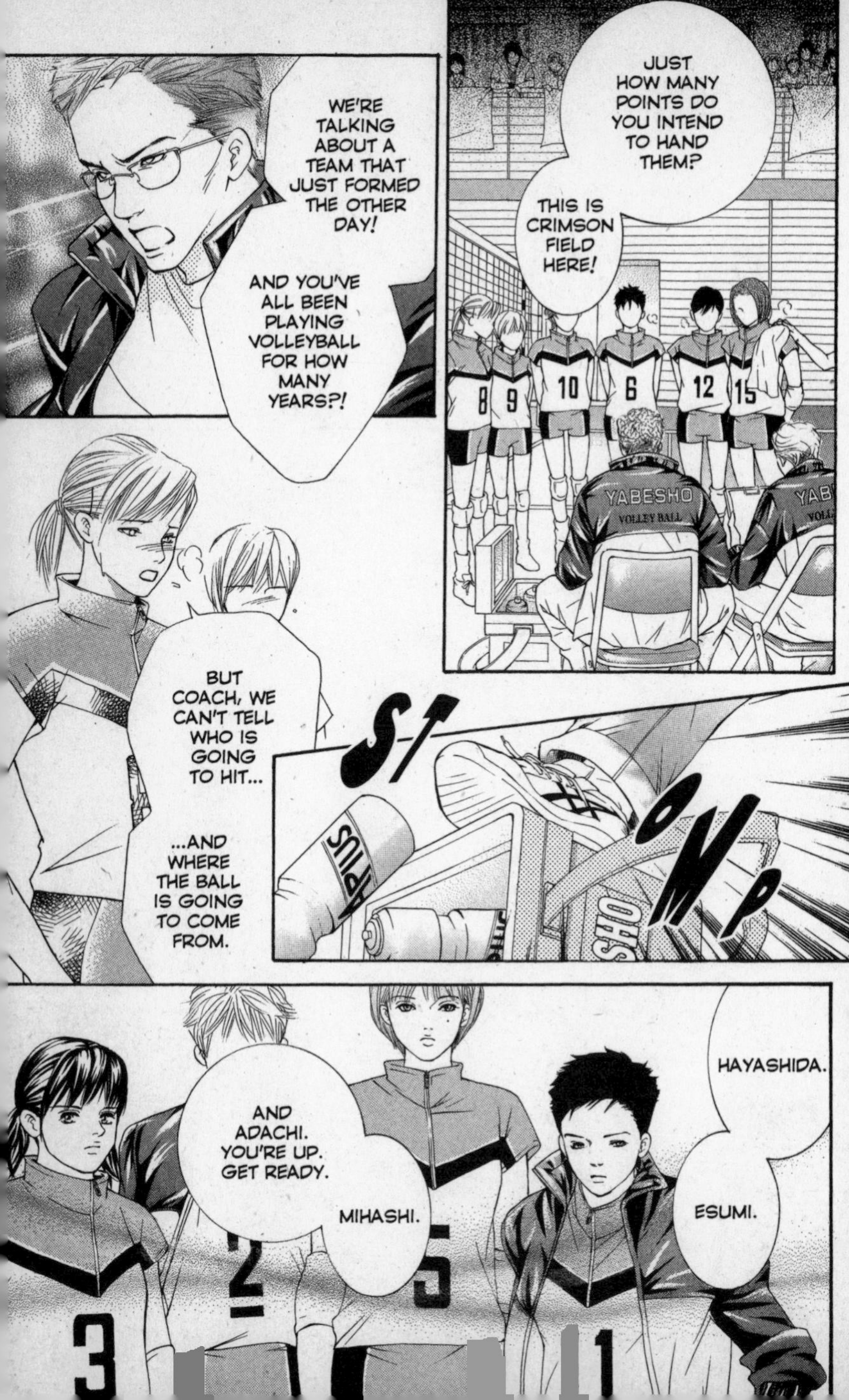
JUST HOW MANY POINTS DO YOU INTEND TO HAND THEM?
THIS IS CRIMSON FIELD HERE!
YABESHO VOLLEY BALL
WE'RE TALKING ABOUT A TEAM THAT JUST FORMED THE OTHER DAY!
AND YOU'VE ALL BEEN PLAYING VOLLEYBALL FOR HOW MANY YEARS?!
STOMP
BUT COACH, WE CAN'T TELL WHO IS GOING TO HIT...
...AND WHERE THE BALL IS GOING TO COME FROM.
HAYASHIDA.
ESUMI.
MIHASHI.
AND ADACHI. YOU'RE UP. GET READY.

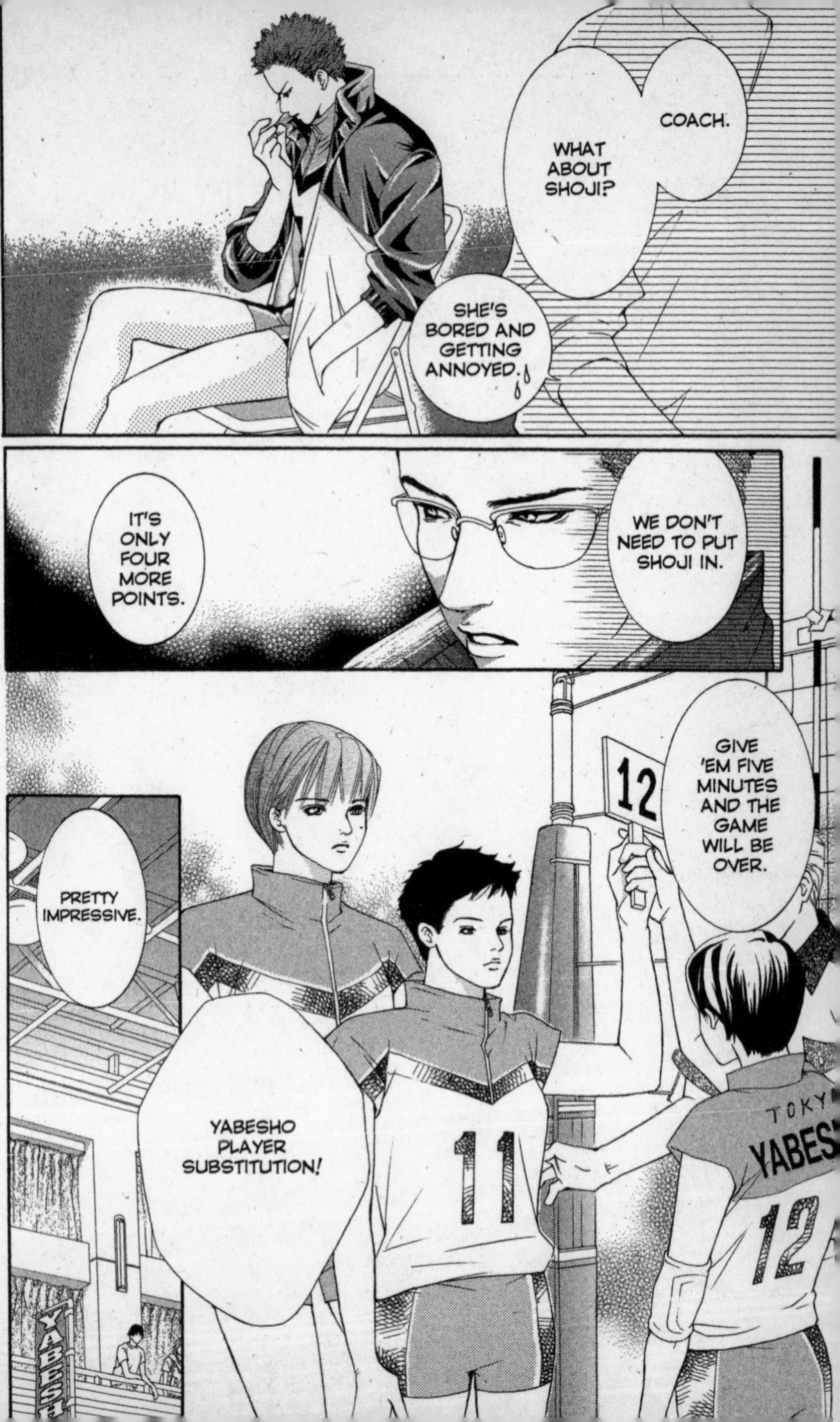
COACH.
WHAT ABOUT SHOJI?
SHE'S BORED AND GETTING ANNOYED.
WE DON'T NEED TO PUT SHOJI IN.
IT'S ONLY FOUR MORE POINTS.
GIVE 'EM FIVE MINUTES AND THE GAME WILL BE OVER.
12
PRETTY IMPRESSIVE.
YABESHO PLAYER SUBSTITUTION!
11
TOKY
YABES
12
YABESH

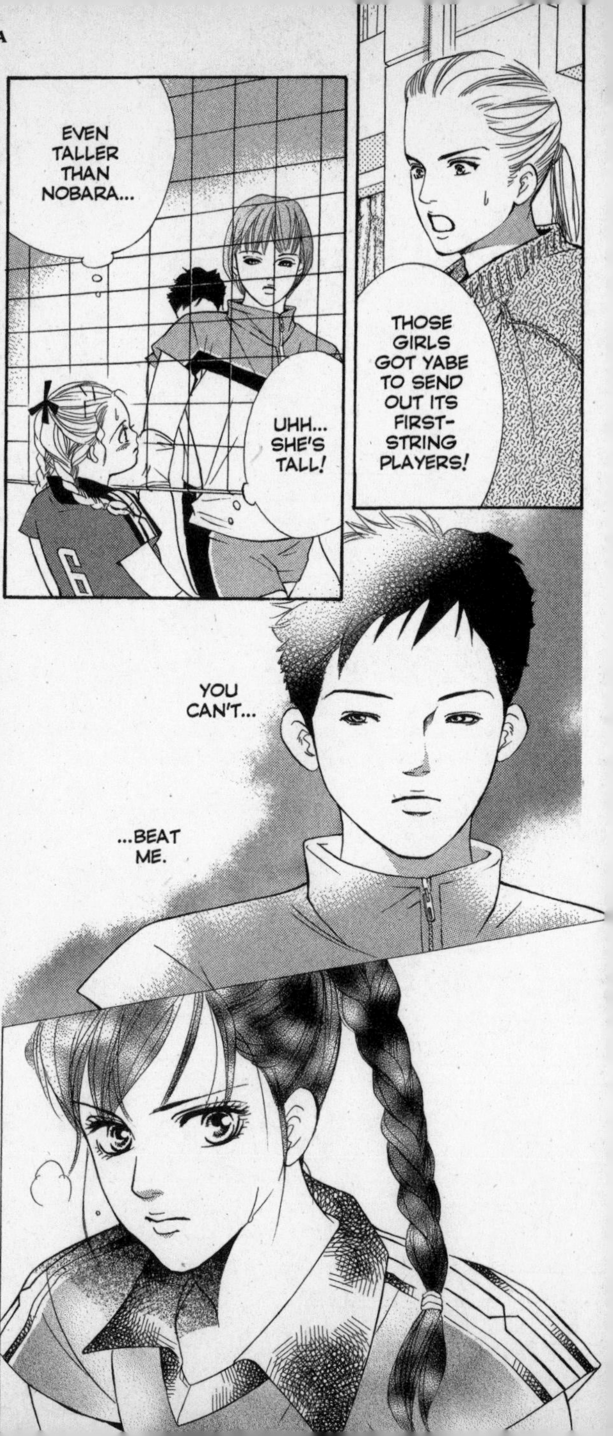
THOSE GIRLS GOT YABE TO SEND OUT ITS FIRST-STRING PLAYERS!
EVEN TALLER THAN NOBARA...
UHH... SHE'S TALL!
YOU CAN'T...
...BEAT ME.

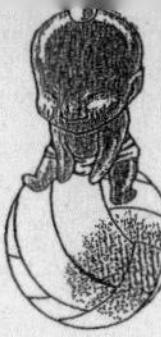

MITSUBA CLUB

Vol. 2

LAKE BIWA

BACK WHEN I STILL LIVED IN KYOTO, I WENT TO LAKE BIWA TO SWIM. THE AMERICAN CAR I BORROWED FROM A FRIEND WAS A CLUNKER AND KEPT STALLING. THE AIR CONDITIONER DIDN'T WORK EITHER SO IT WAS A HECK OF A TRIP. THEN AT THE BEACH, A BABY PREYING MANTIS CRAWLED ON SOMEONE'S SHIN. IT GOT ALL TANGLED UP IN HIS LEG HAIR!!! IT WAS SO HILARIOUS. WHERE IN THE WORLD DID THAT PREYING MANTIS COME FROM?! WAS THIS, LIKE, NAUSICAA?!

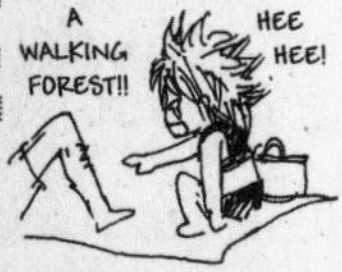
A WALKING FOREST!!
HEE HEE!

AFTERWARDS WE FREED THE PREYING MANTIS.

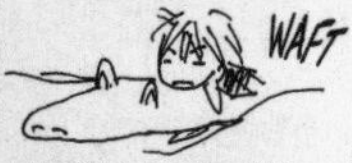
WAFT

WE'D BROUGHT A HUGE INFLATABLE CROCODILE WITH US.
ITS NAME WAS GAULTIER. WE ENDED UP LENDING IT TO SOME KID WHO WAS TERRIBLY ENVIOUS OF IT. NOW THAT I'M THIS AGE, I'M TOO SCARED OF GETTING SUNBURN TO GO TO THE BEACH ANYMORE, AND I WOULDN'T HAVE THE ENERGY ANYWAY. BUT WHEN I THINK BACK, THOSE WERE SOME FUN SUMMER DAYS. BOY, THIS YEAR MY SCHEDULE IS SO JAMMED THERE'S NO WAY I'LL BE ABLE TO TAKE OFF ANYWHERE...

WATERMELON

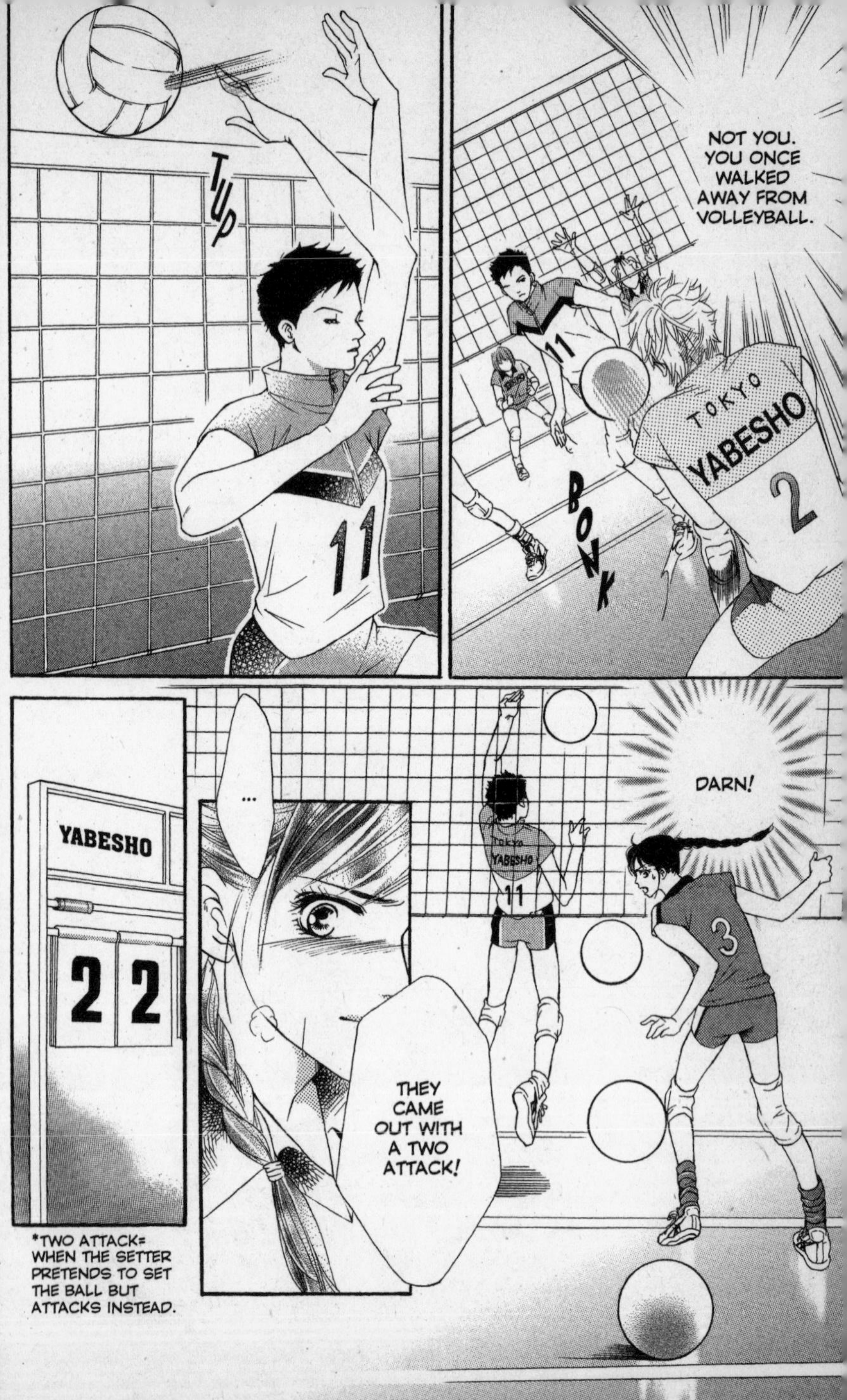
NOT YOU. YOU ONCE WALKED AWAY FROM VOLLEYBALL.
TOKYO YABESHO 2
11
BONK
TUP
11
DARN!
TOKYO YABESHO 11
3
...
THEY CAME OUT WITH A TWO ATTACK!
YABESHO
2 2
*TWO ATTACK= WHEN THE SETTER PRETENDS TO SET THE BALL BUT ATTACKS INSTEAD.

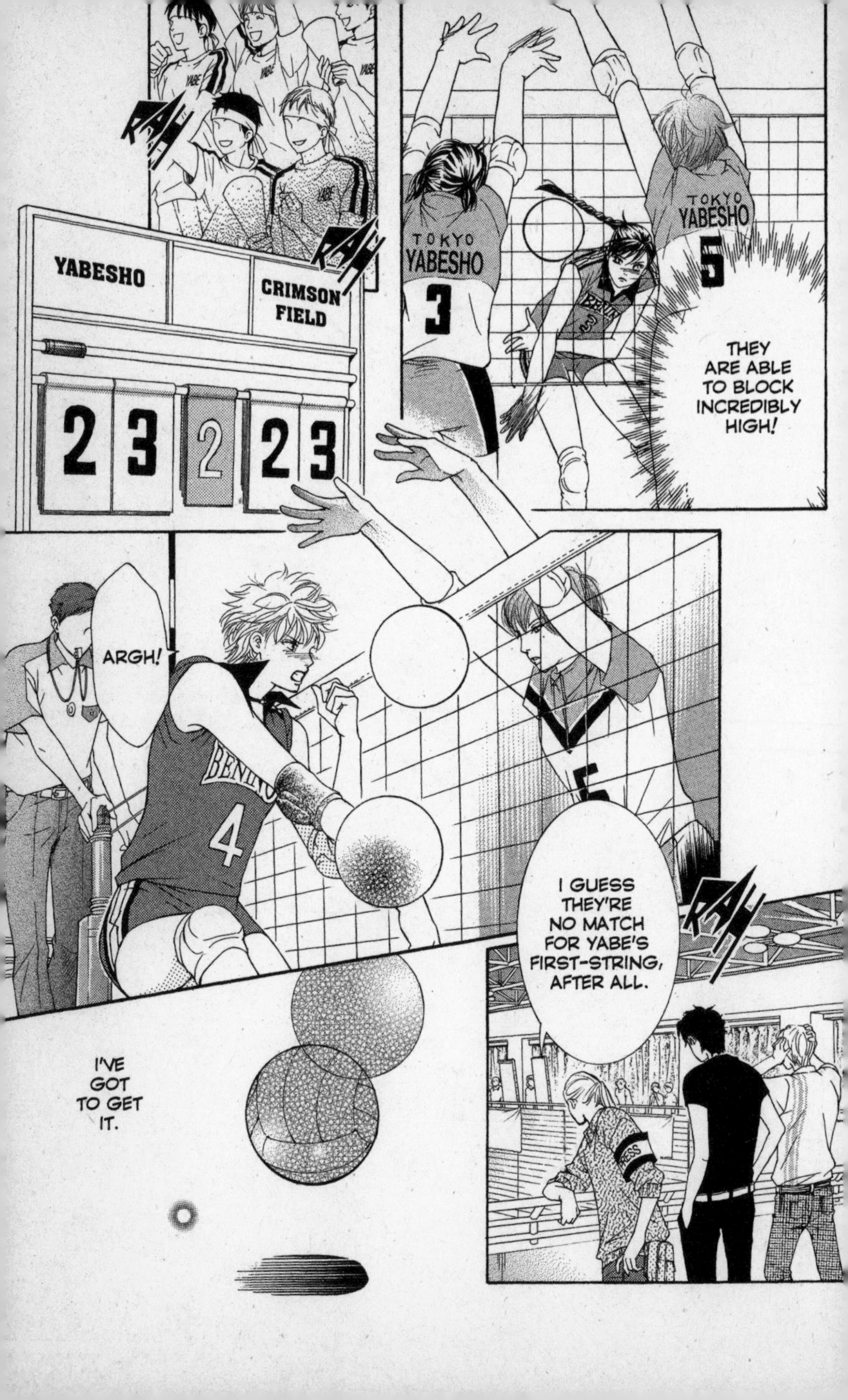
THEY ARE ABLE TO BLOCK INCREDIBLY HIGH!
RAH
RAH
YABESHO
CRIMSON FIELD
23 2 23
ARGH!
RAH
I GUESS THEY'RE NO MATCH FOR YABE'S FIRST-STRING, AFTER ALL.
I'VE GOT TO GET IT.

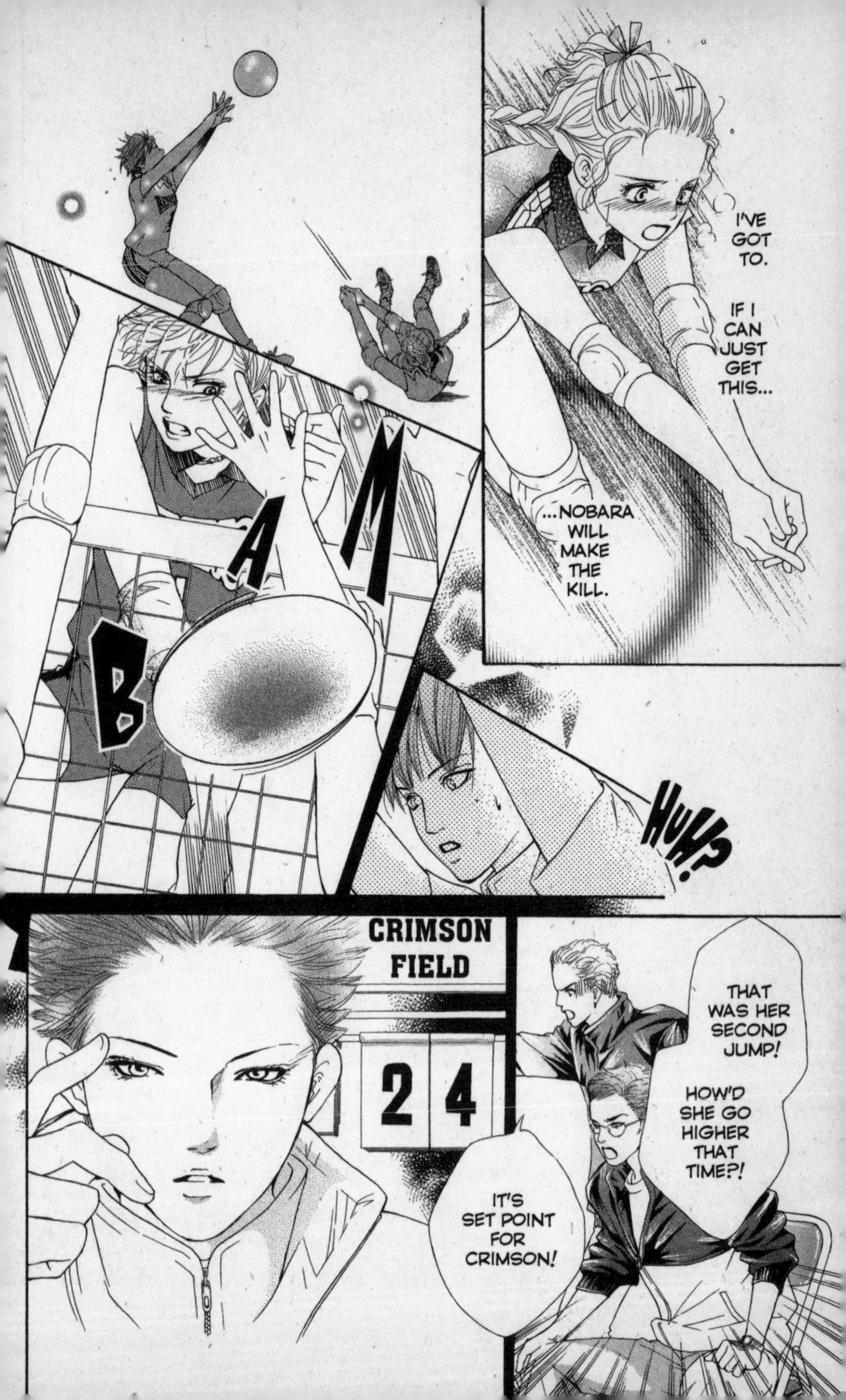
I'VE GOT TO.
IF I CAN JUST GET THIS...
...NOBARA WILL MAKE THE KILL.
HUH?
BAM
THAT WAS HER SECOND JUMP!
HOW'D SHE GO HIGHER THAT TIME?!
IT'S SET POINT FOR CRIMSON!
CRIMSON FIELD
24

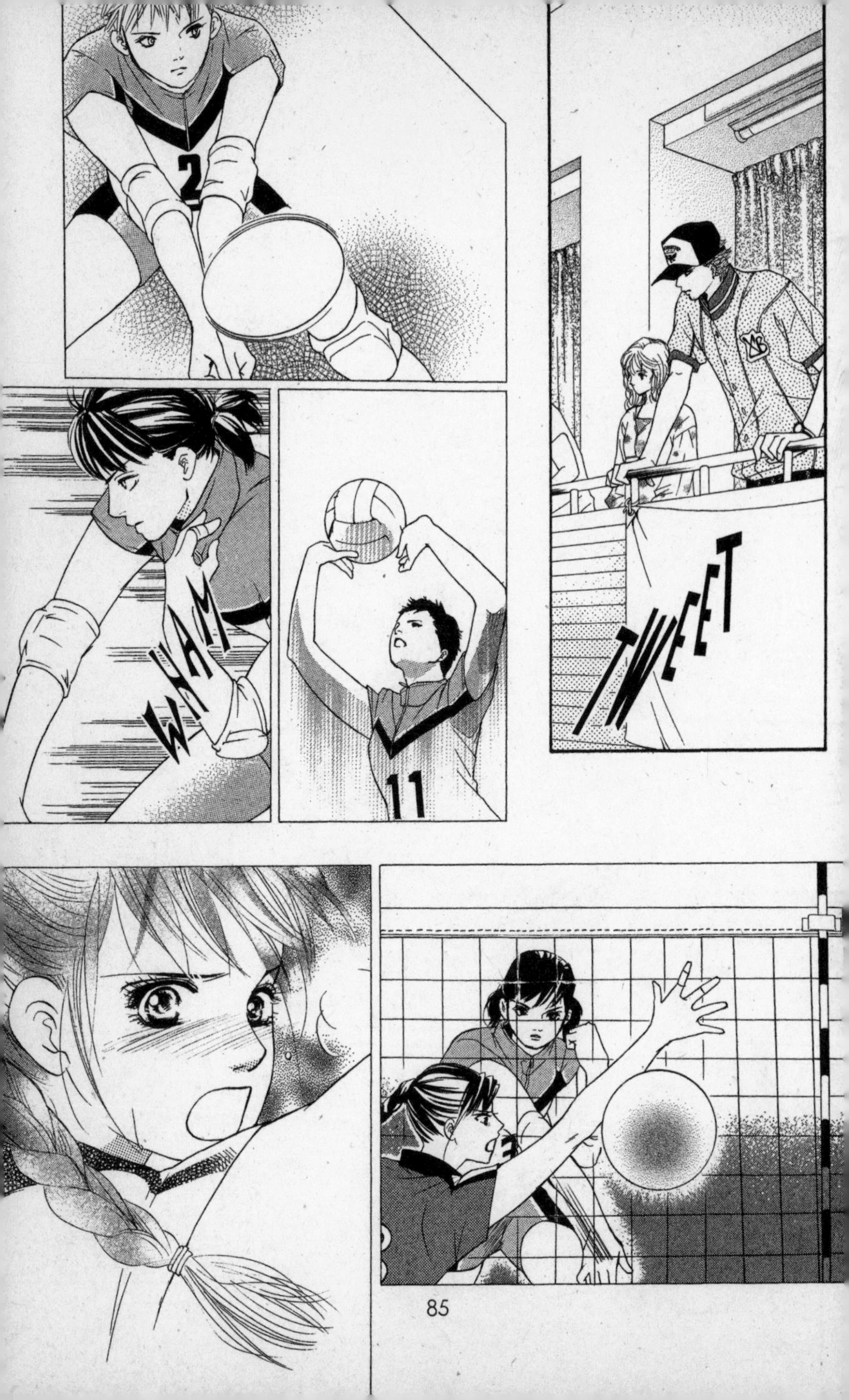
TWEEET
WHAM

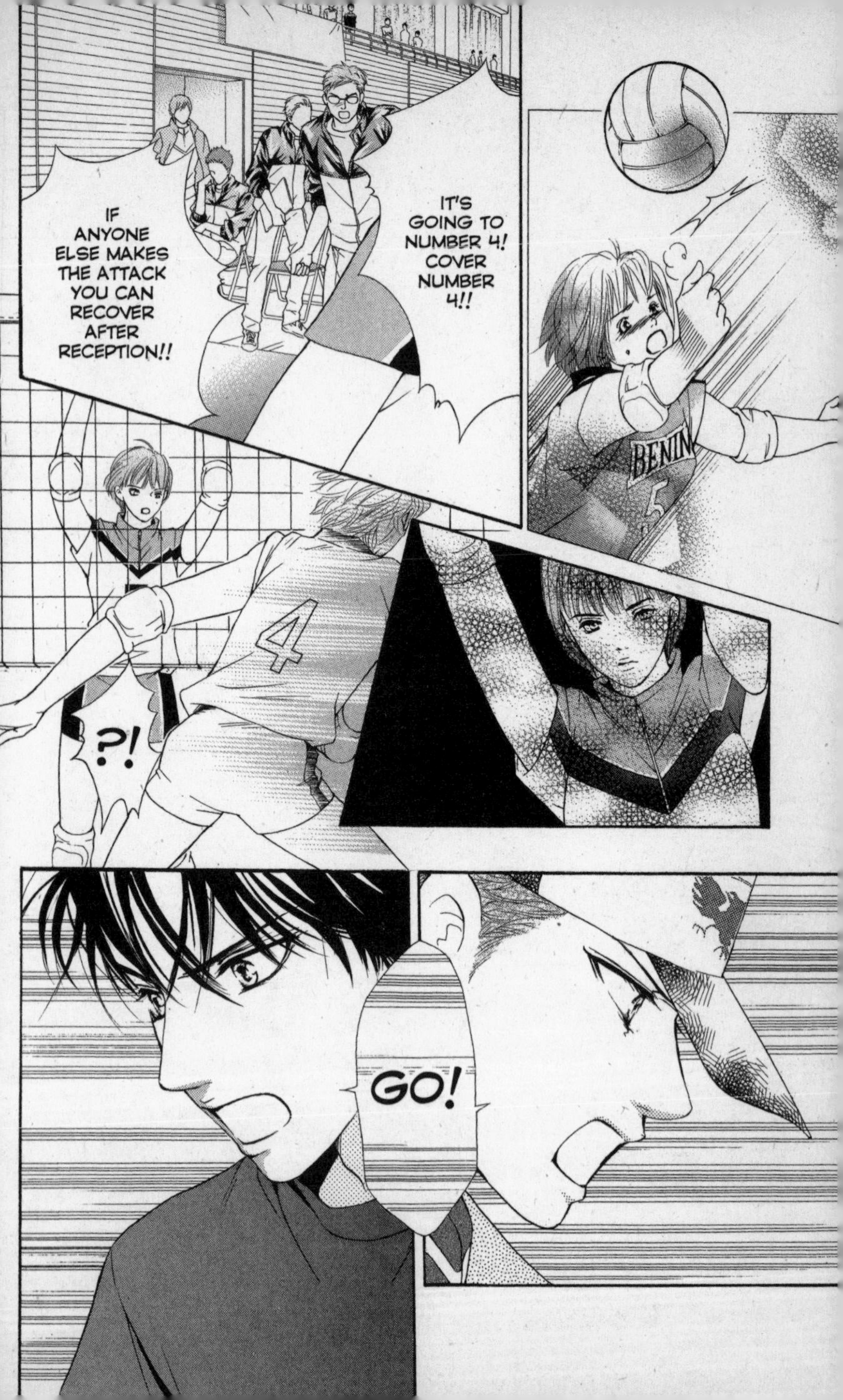
IT'S GOING TO NUMBER 4! COVER NUMBER 4!!
IF ANYONE ELSE MAKES THE ATTACK YOU CAN RECOVER AFTER RECEPTION!!
?!
GO!

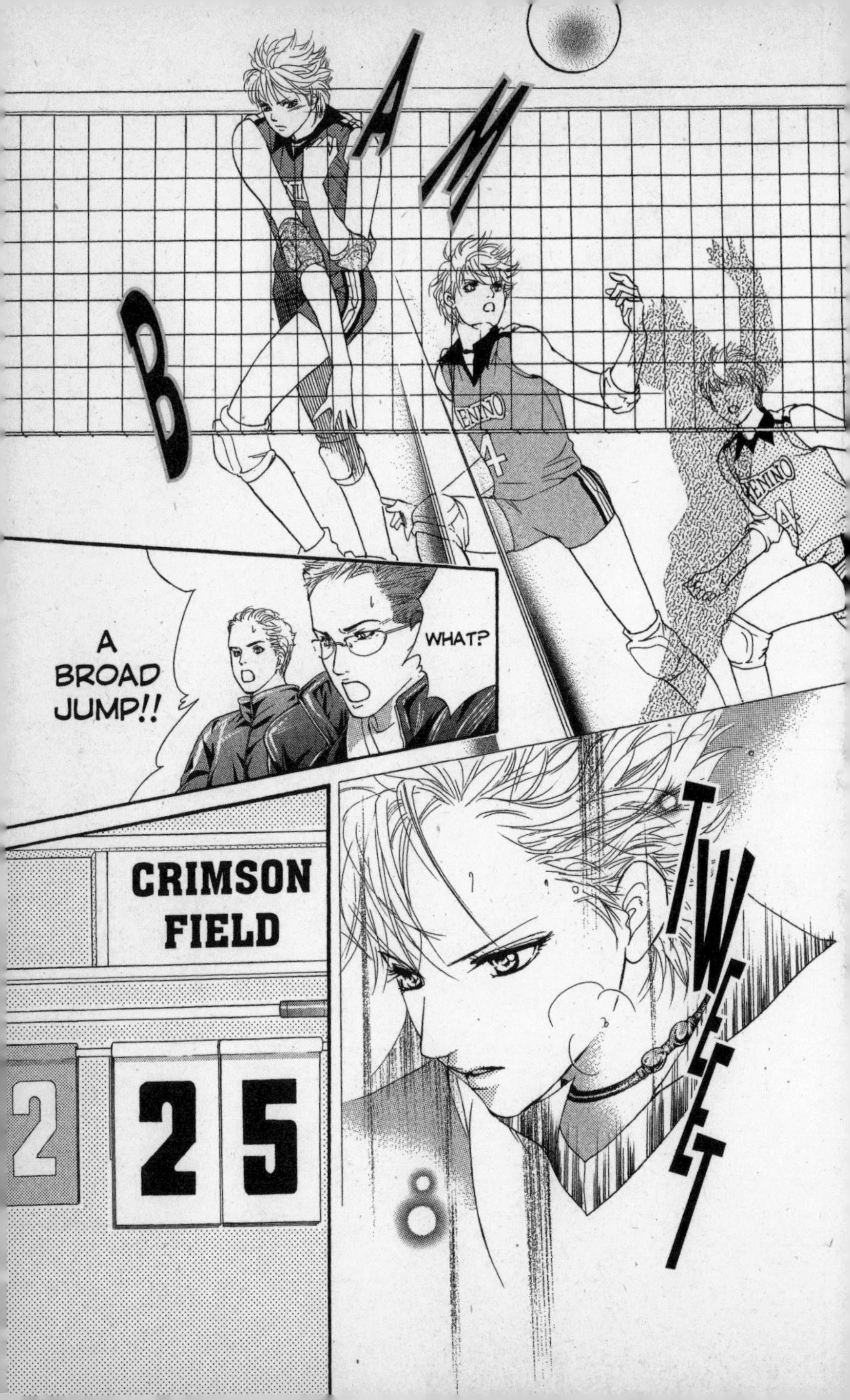
BAM
WHAT?
A BROAD JUMP!!
TWEET
CRIMSON FIELD
2
25

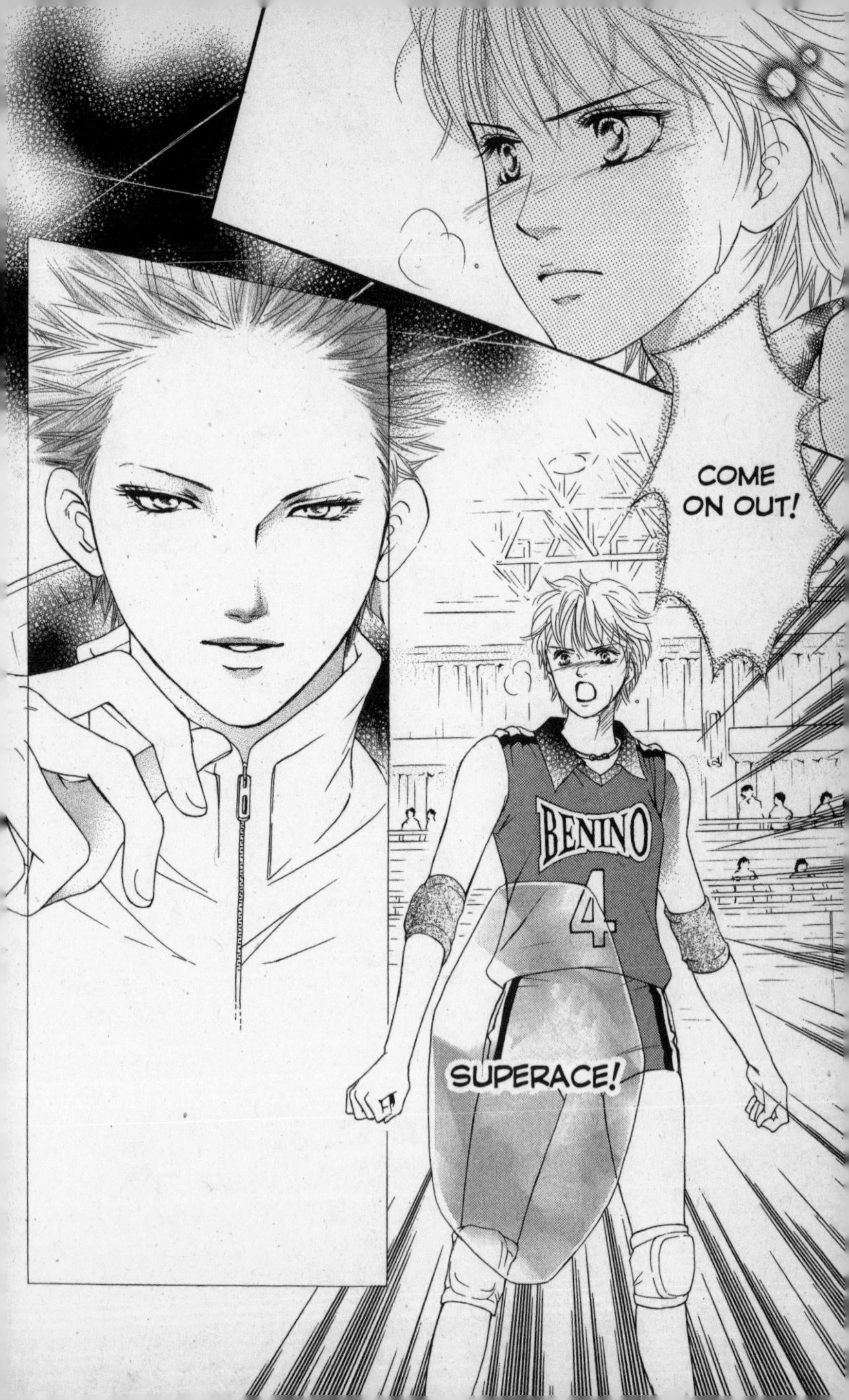
COME ON OUT!
BENINO
4
SUPERACE!

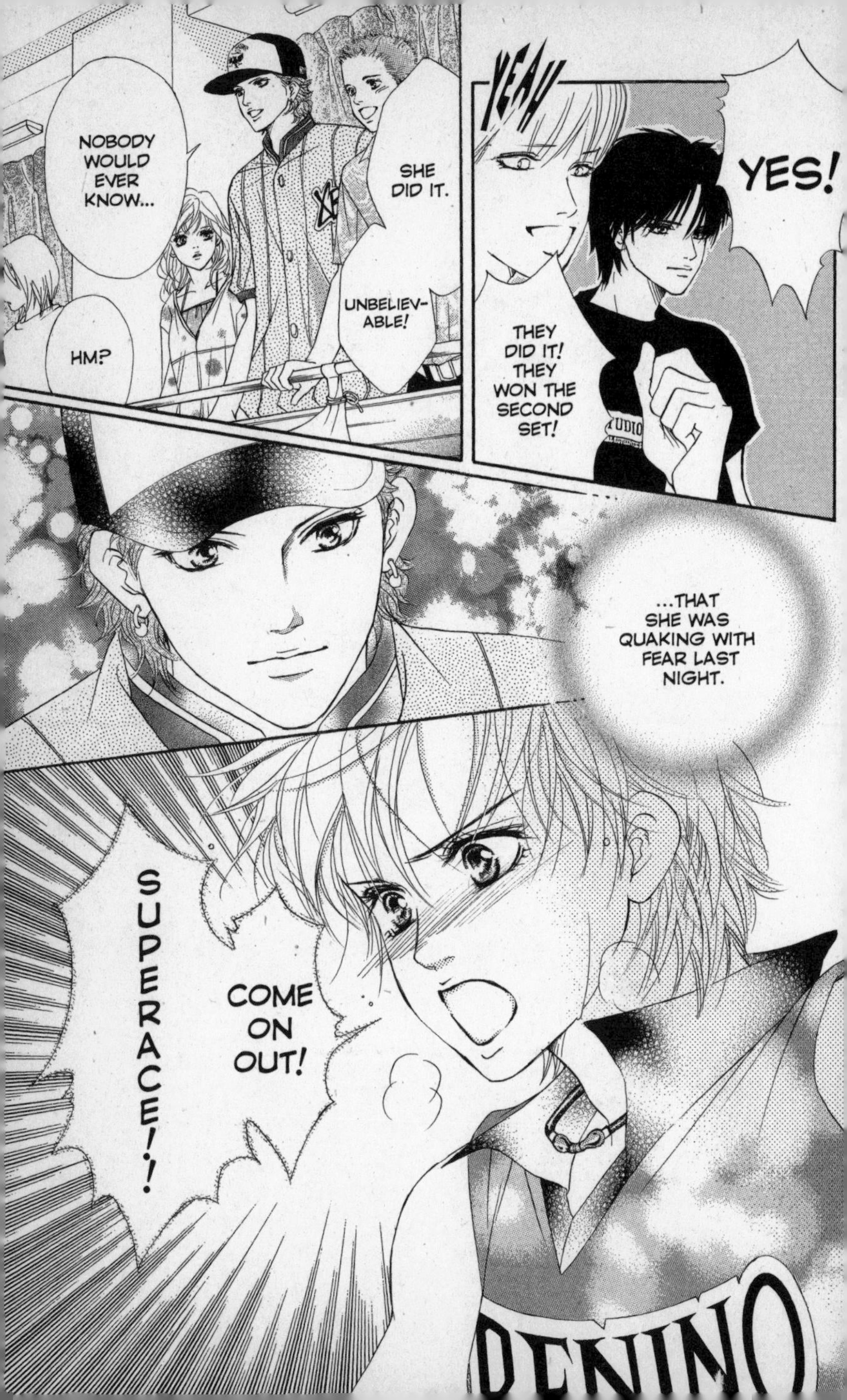
YEAH
YES!
THEY DID IT! THEY WON THE SECOND SET!
SHE DID IT.
NOBODY WOULD EVER KNOW...
UNBELIEVABLE!
HM?
...THAT SHE WAS QUAKING WITH FEAR LAST NIGHT.
COME ON OUT!
SUPERACE!!

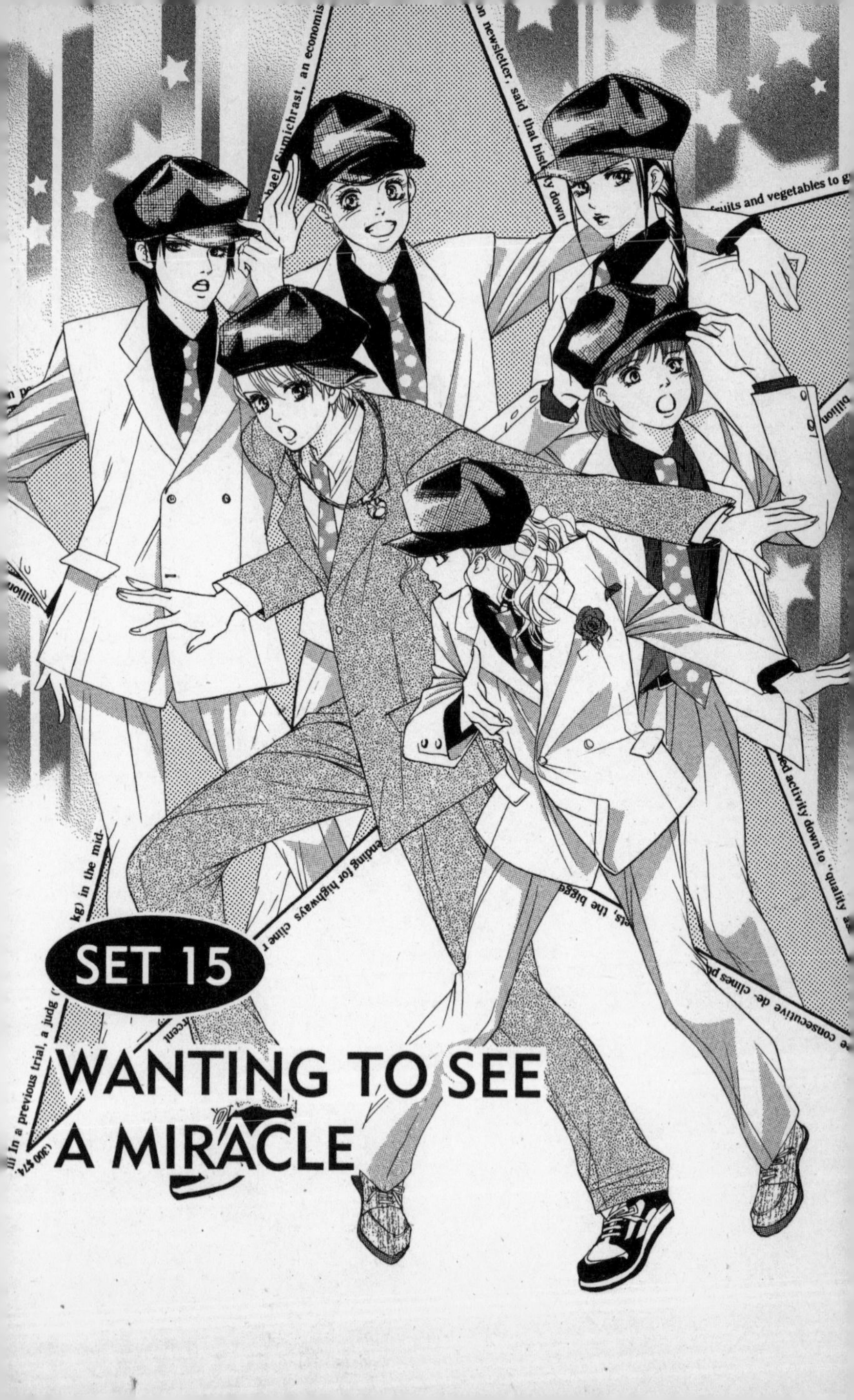
SET 15
WANTING TO SEE A MIRACLE

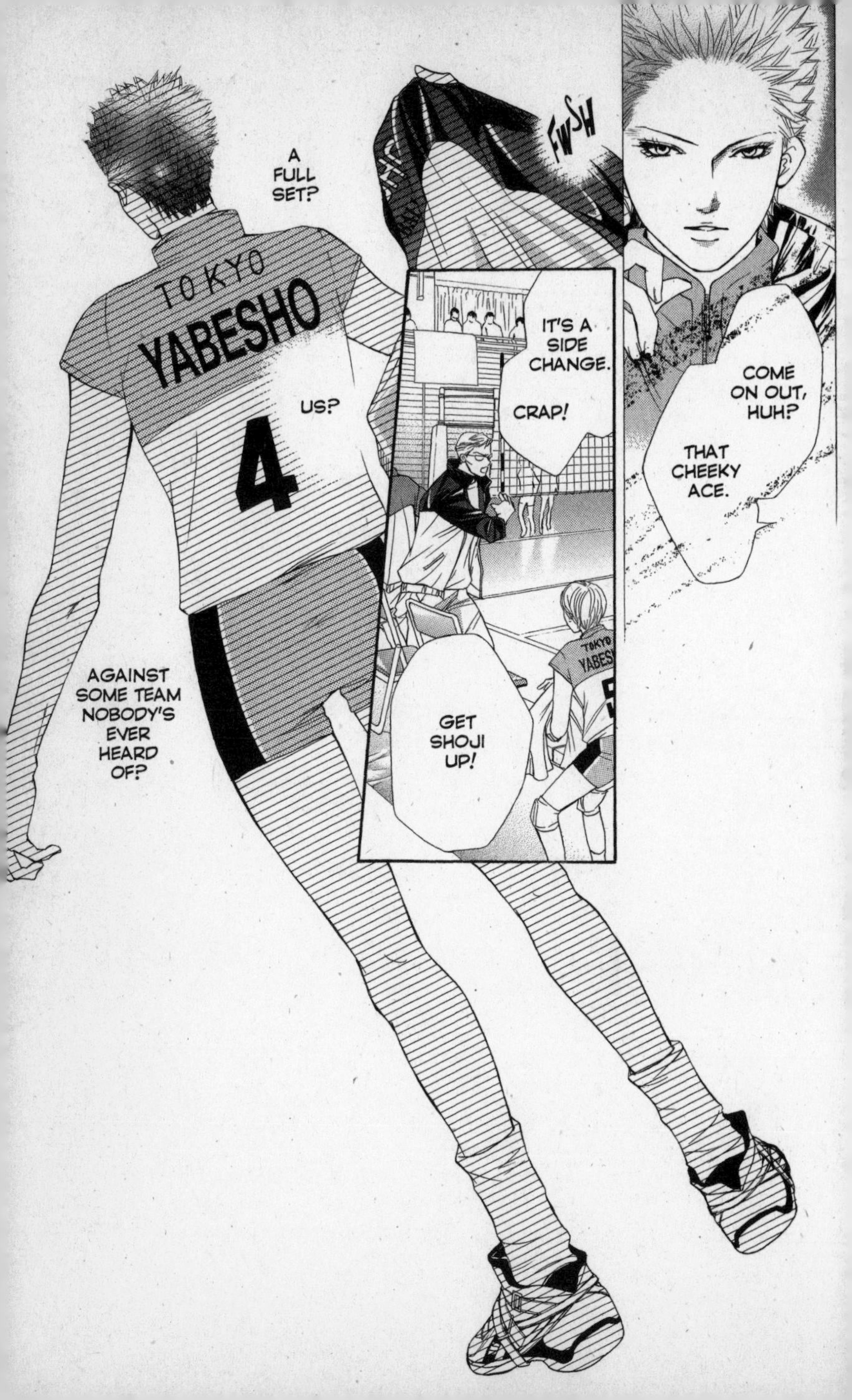
FWSH
COME ON OUT, HUH?
THAT CHEEKY ACE.
IT'S A SIDE CHANGE.
CRAP!
GET SHOJI UP!
A FULL SET?
US?
AGAINST SOME TEAM NOBODY'S EVER HEARD OF?
TOKYO YABESHO 4

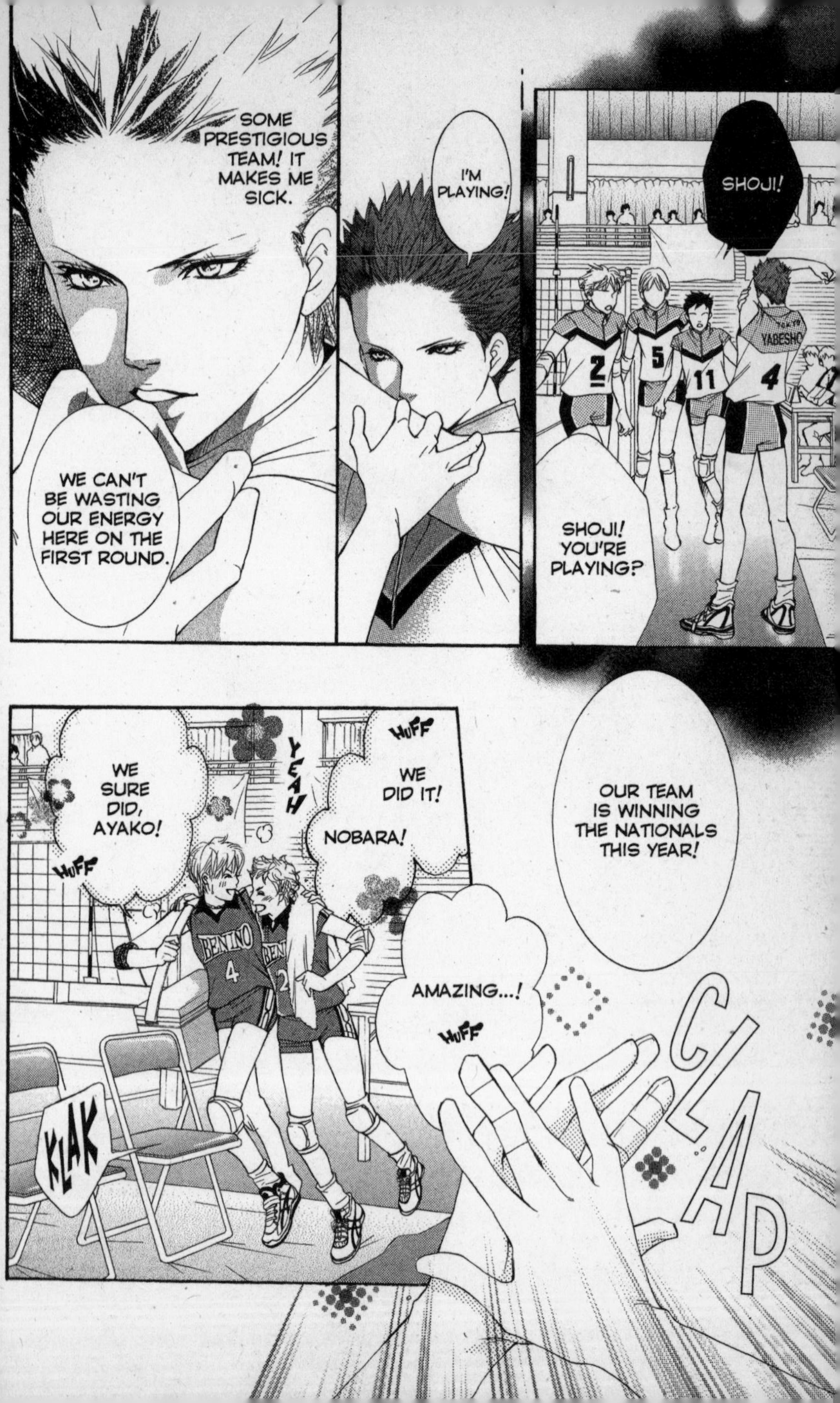
SHOJI!
SHOJI! YOU'RE PLAYING?
YABESHO
I'M PLAYING!
SOME PRESTIGIOUS TEAM! IT MAKES ME SICK.
WE CAN'T BE WASTING OUR ENERGY HERE ON THE FIRST ROUND.
OUR TEAM IS WINNING THE NATIONALS THIS YEAR!
AMAZING...!
HUFF
CLAP
HUFF
WE DID IT!
NOBARA!
YEAH
WE SURE DID, AYAKO!
HUFF
BENINO
KLAK

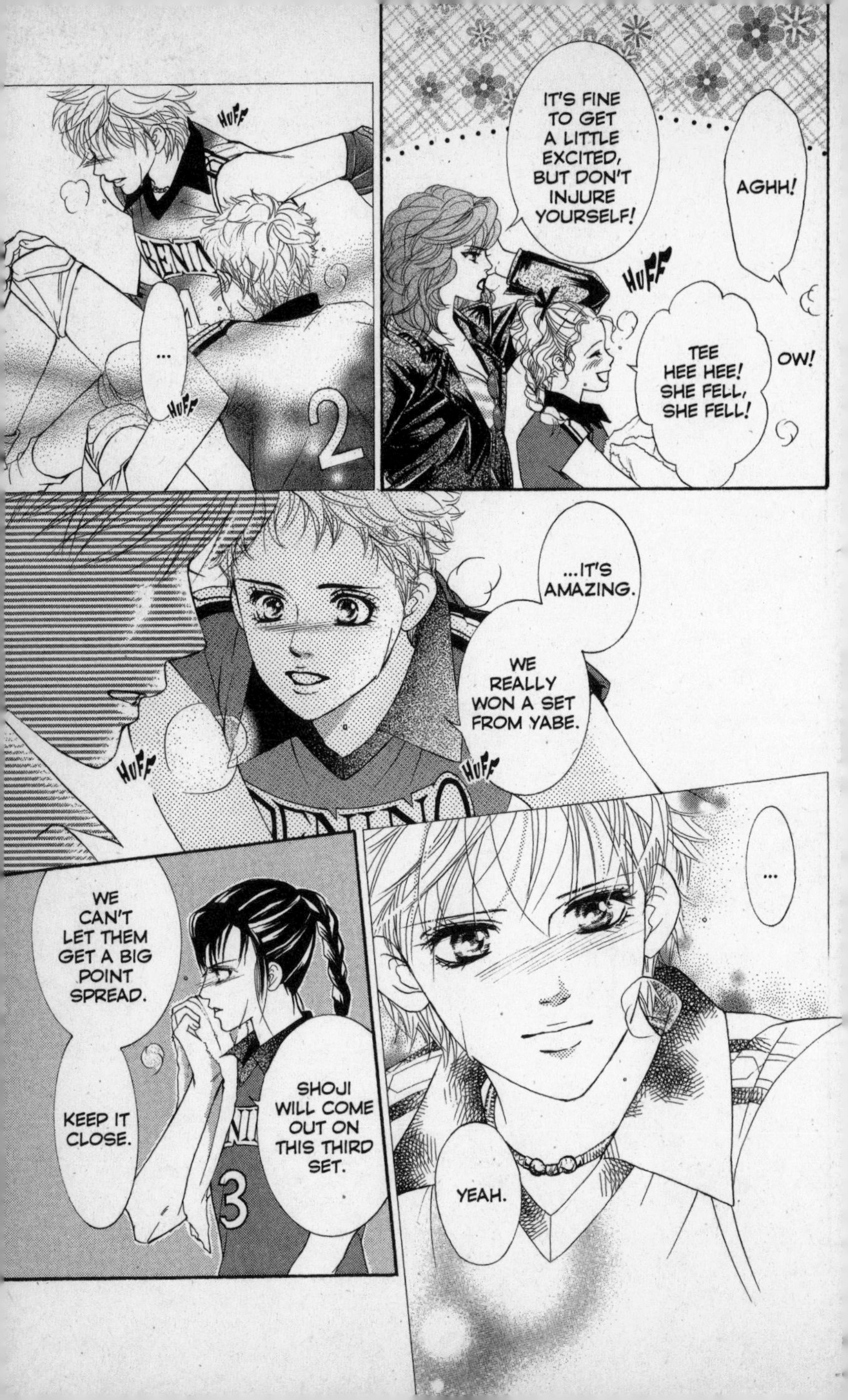
AGHH!
OW!
IT'S FINE TO GET A LITTLE EXCITED, BUT DON'T INJURE YOURSELF!
HUFF
TEE HEE HEE! SHE FELL, SHE FELL!
HUFF
...
HUFF
...IT'S AMAZING.
WE REALLY WON A SET FROM YABE.
HUFF
HUFF
...
YEAH.
WE CAN'T LET THEM GET A BIG POINT SPREAD.
SHOJI WILL COME OUT ON THIS THIRD SET.
KEEP IT CLOSE.

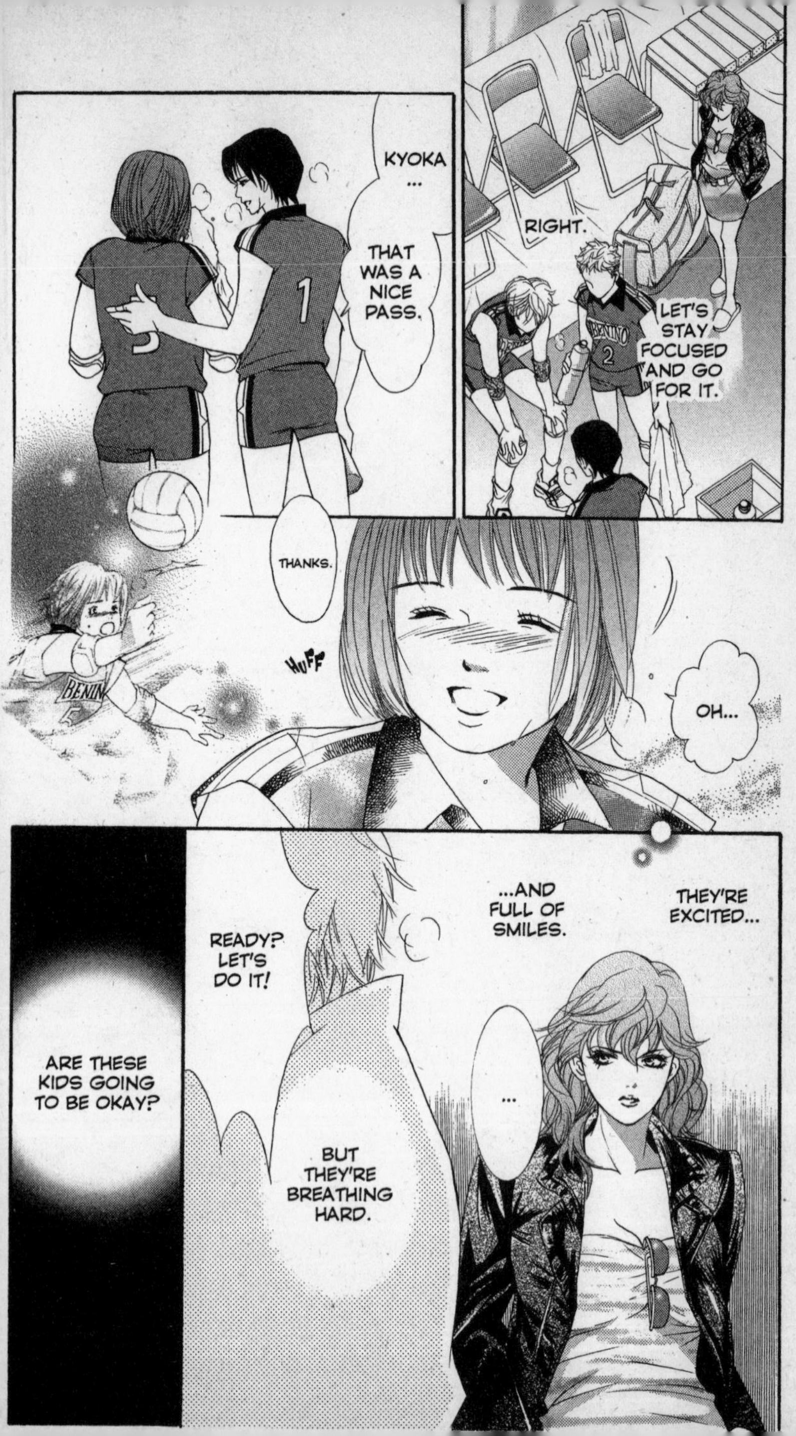
LET'S STAY FOCUSED AND GO FOR IT.
RIGHT.
KYOKA...
THAT WAS A NICE PASS.
OH...
THANKS.
HUFF
THEY'RE EXCITED...
...AND FULL OF SMILES.
...
READY? LET'S DO IT!
BUT THEY'RE BREATHING HARD.
ARE THESE KIDS GOING TO BE OKAY?

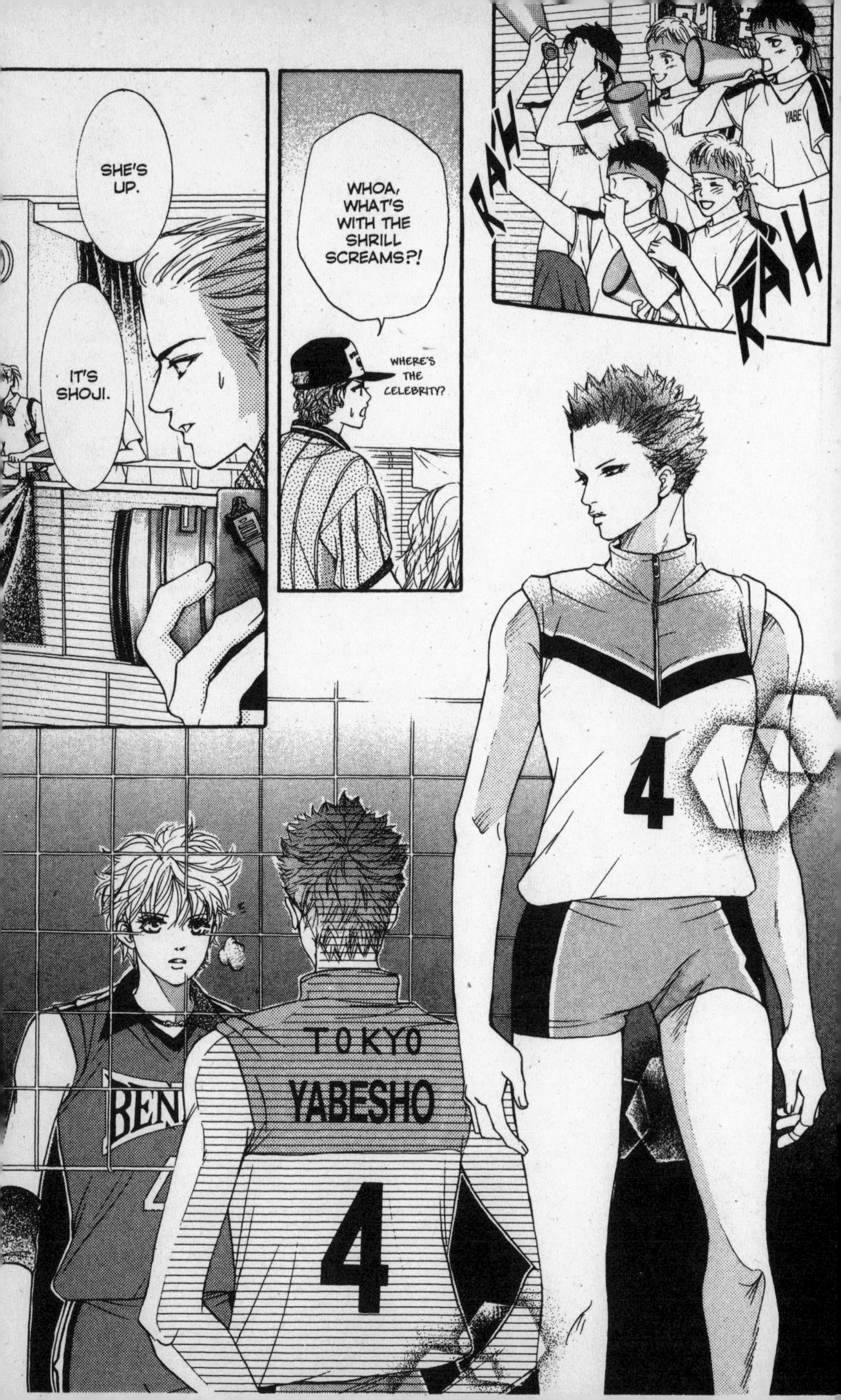
RAH
RAH
WHOA, WHAT'S WITH THE SHRILL SCREAMS?!
WHERE'S THE CELEBRITY?
SHE'S UP.
IT'S SHOJI.
TOKYO
YABESHO
4

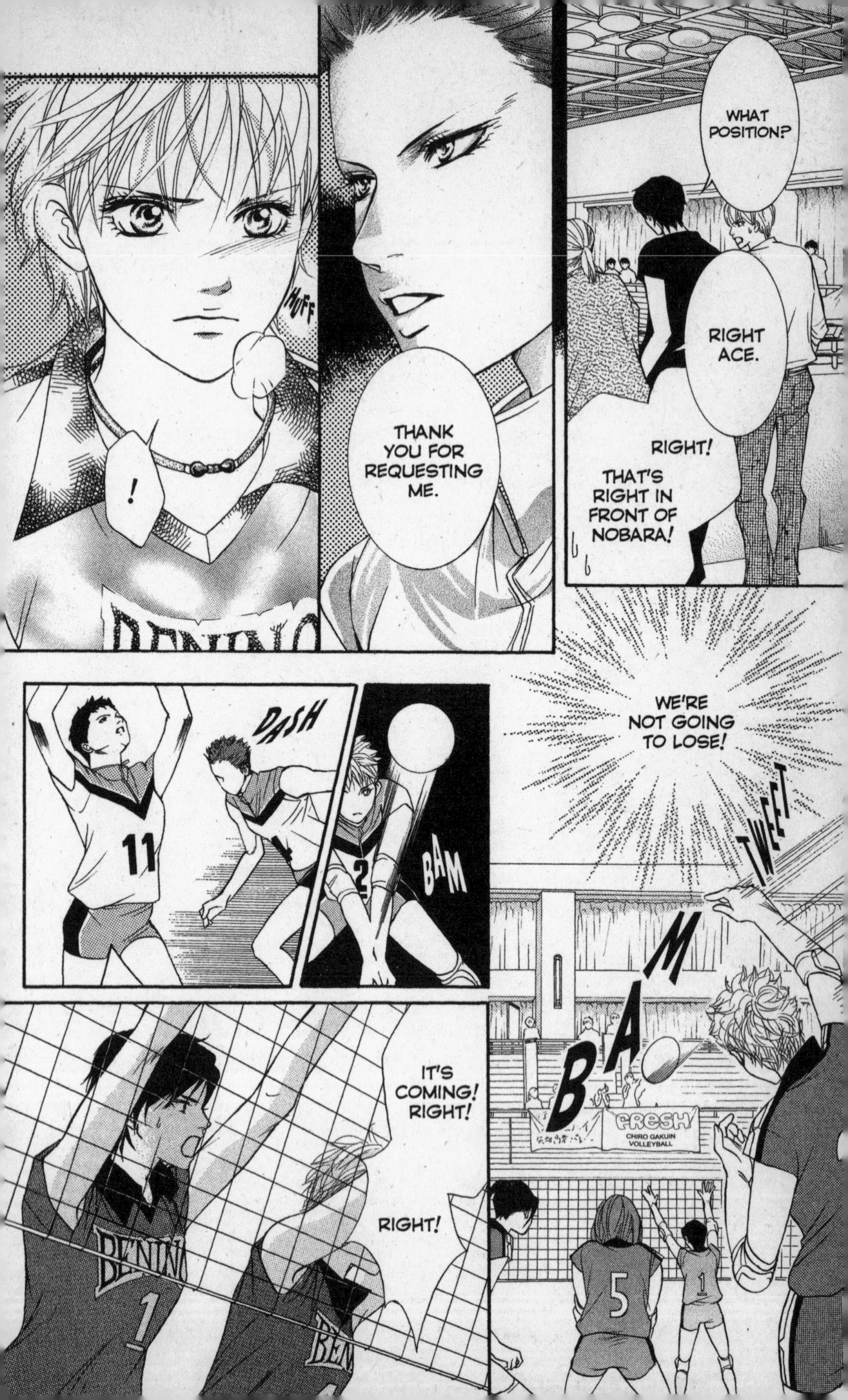
WHAT POSITION?
RIGHT ACE.
RIGHT!
THAT'S RIGHT IN FRONT OF NOBARA!
THANK YOU FOR REQUESTING ME.
HUFF
!
WE'RE NOT GOING TO LOSE!
TWEET
BAM
FRESH
CHIRO GAKUIN VOLLEYBALL
BAM
DASH
IT'S COMING! RIGHT!
RIGHT!

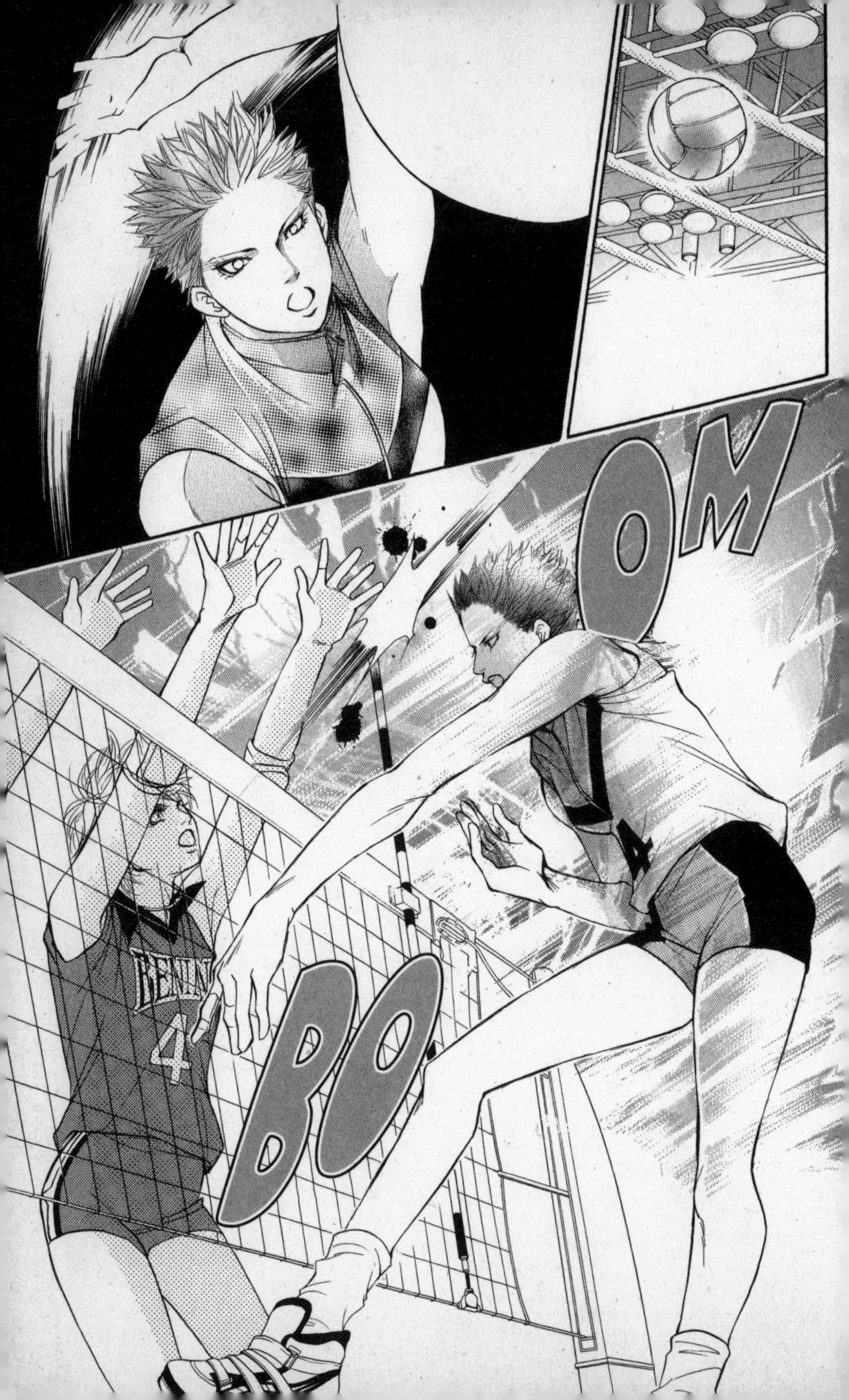
BO
OM

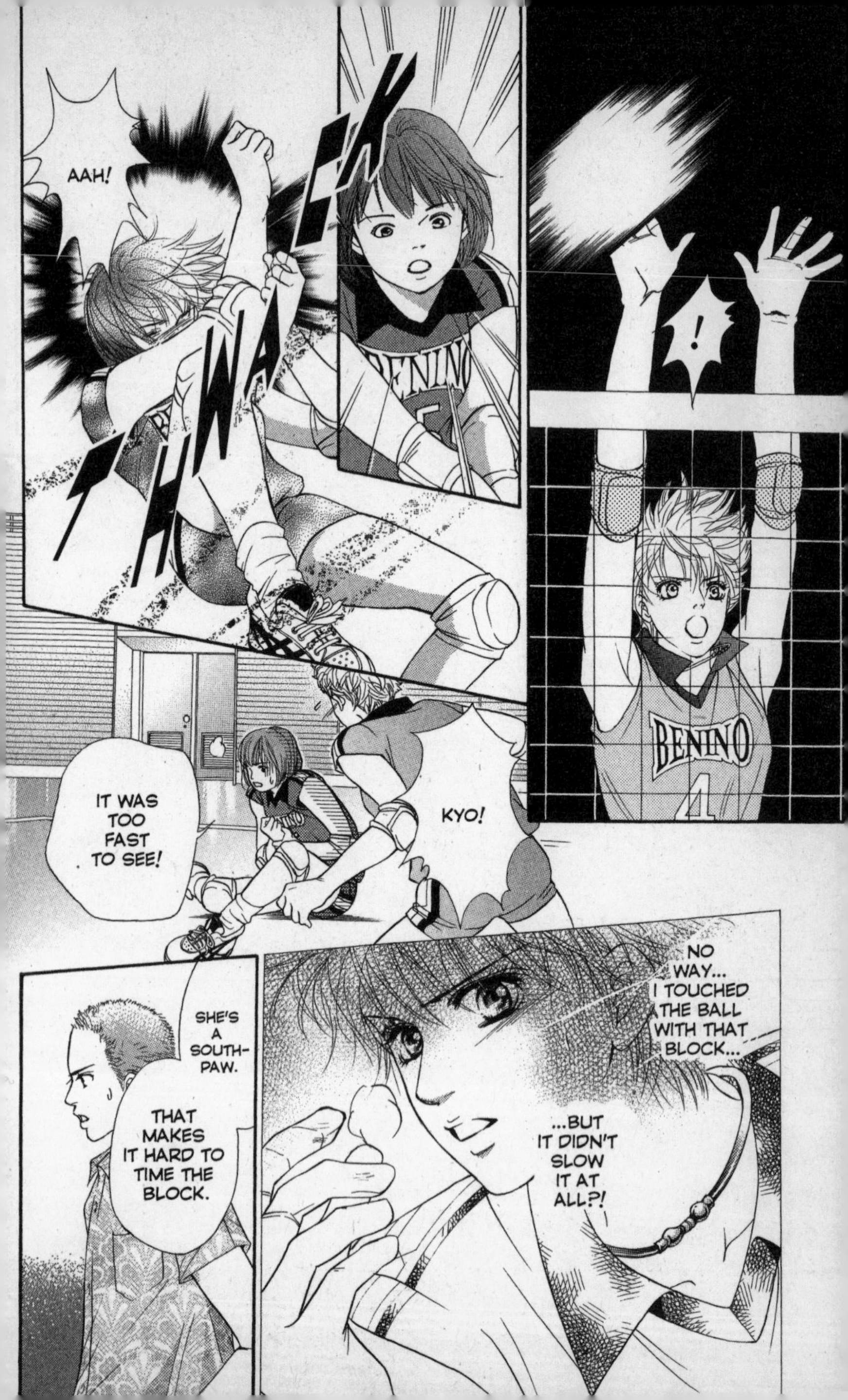
!
THWACK
AAH!
KYO!
IT WAS TOO FAST TO SEE!
NO WAY... I TOUCHED THE BALL WITH THAT BLOCK...
...BUT IT DIDN'T SLOW IT AT ALL?!
SHE'S A SOUTHPAW.
THAT MAKES IT HARD TO TIME THE BLOCK.

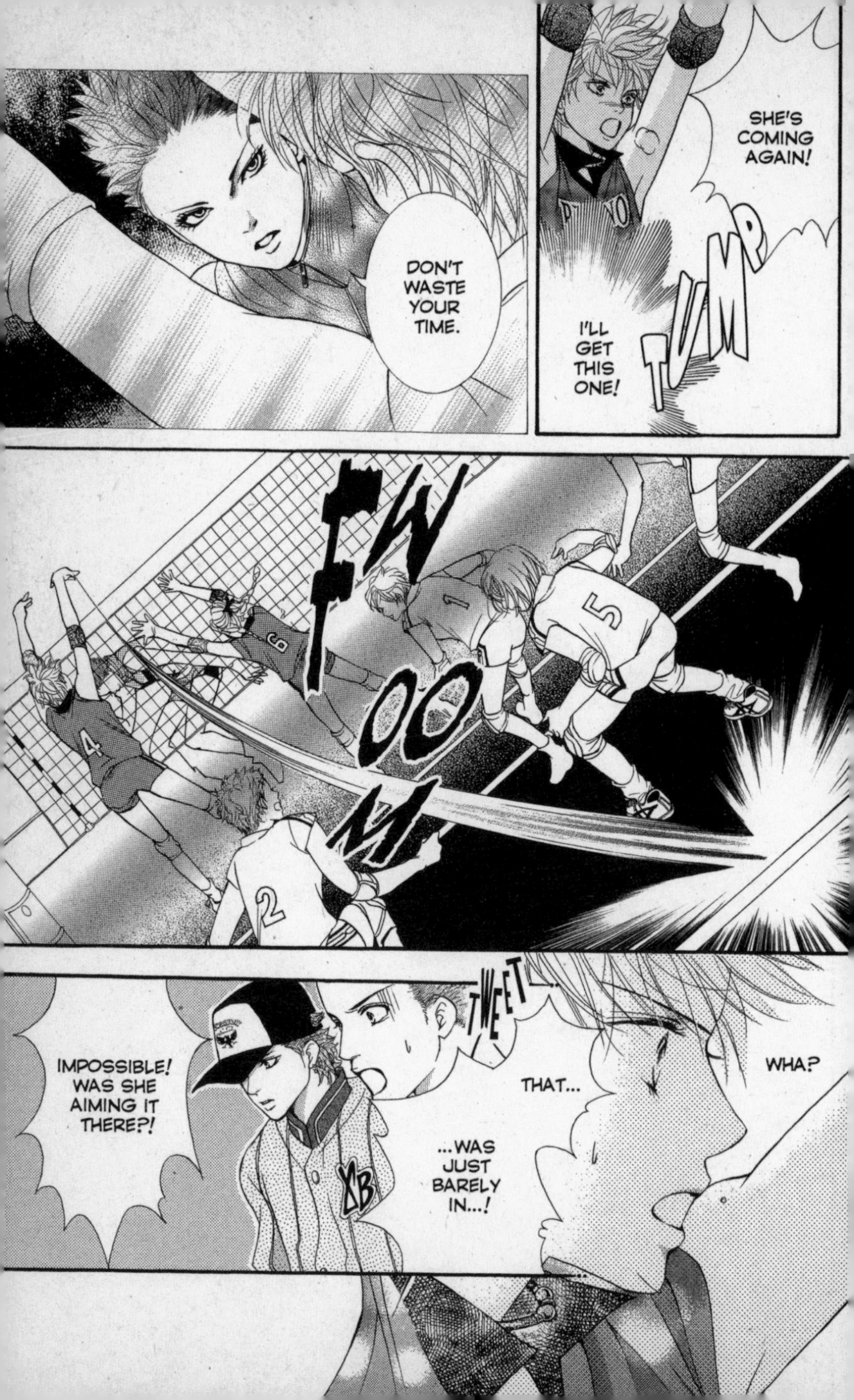
SHE'S COMING AGAIN!
TUMP
I'LL GET THIS ONE!
DON'T WASTE YOUR TIME.
FWOOM
WHA?
TWEET...
THAT...
...WAS JUST BARELY IN...!
IMPOSSIBLE! WAS SHE AIMING IT THERE?!

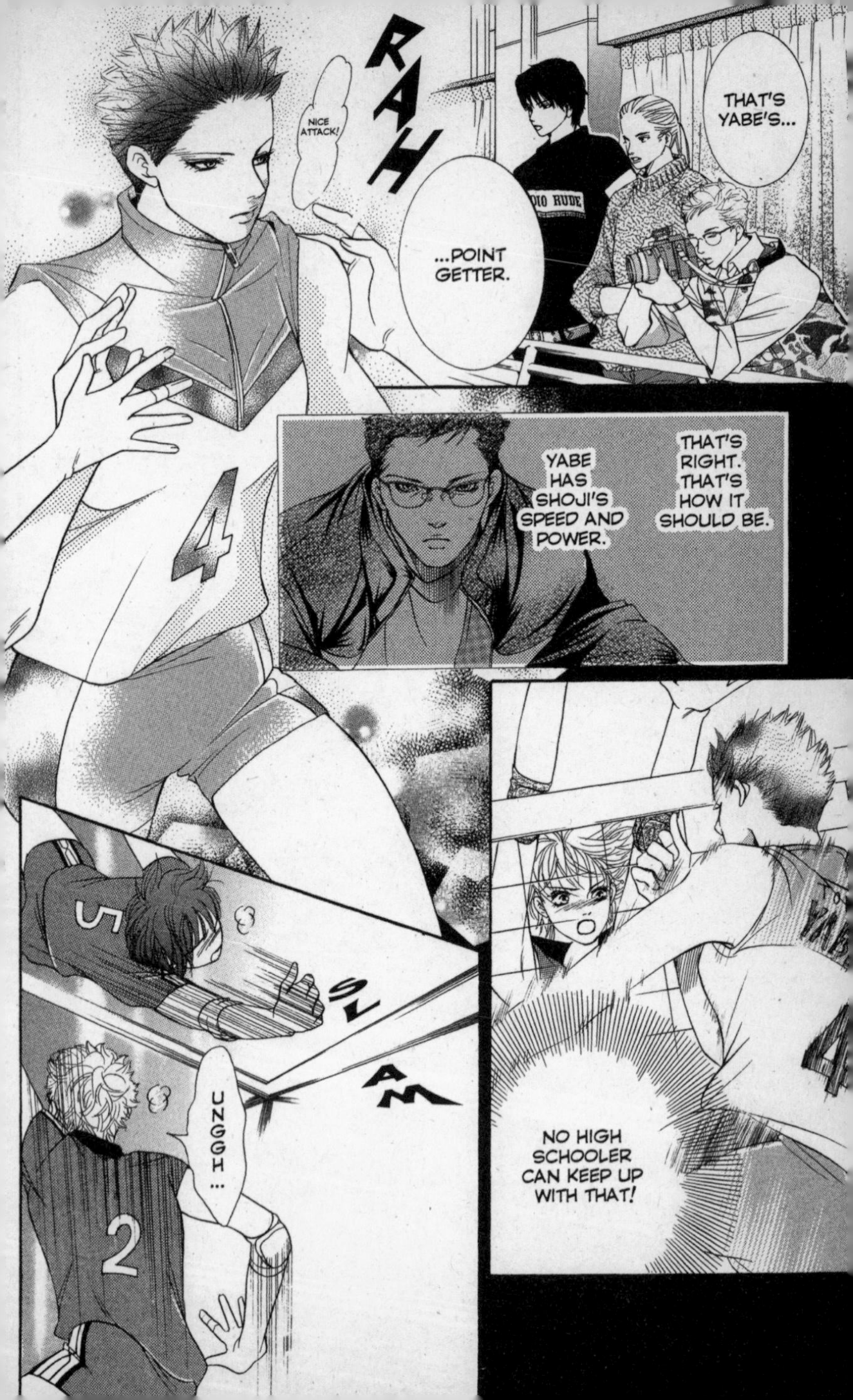
THAT'S YABE'S...
...POINT GETTER.
RAH
NICE ATTACK!
THAT'S RIGHT. THAT'S HOW IT SHOULD BE.
YABE HAS SHOJI'S SPEED AND POWER.
NO HIGH SCHOOLER CAN KEEP UP WITH THAT!
SLAM
UNGGH...

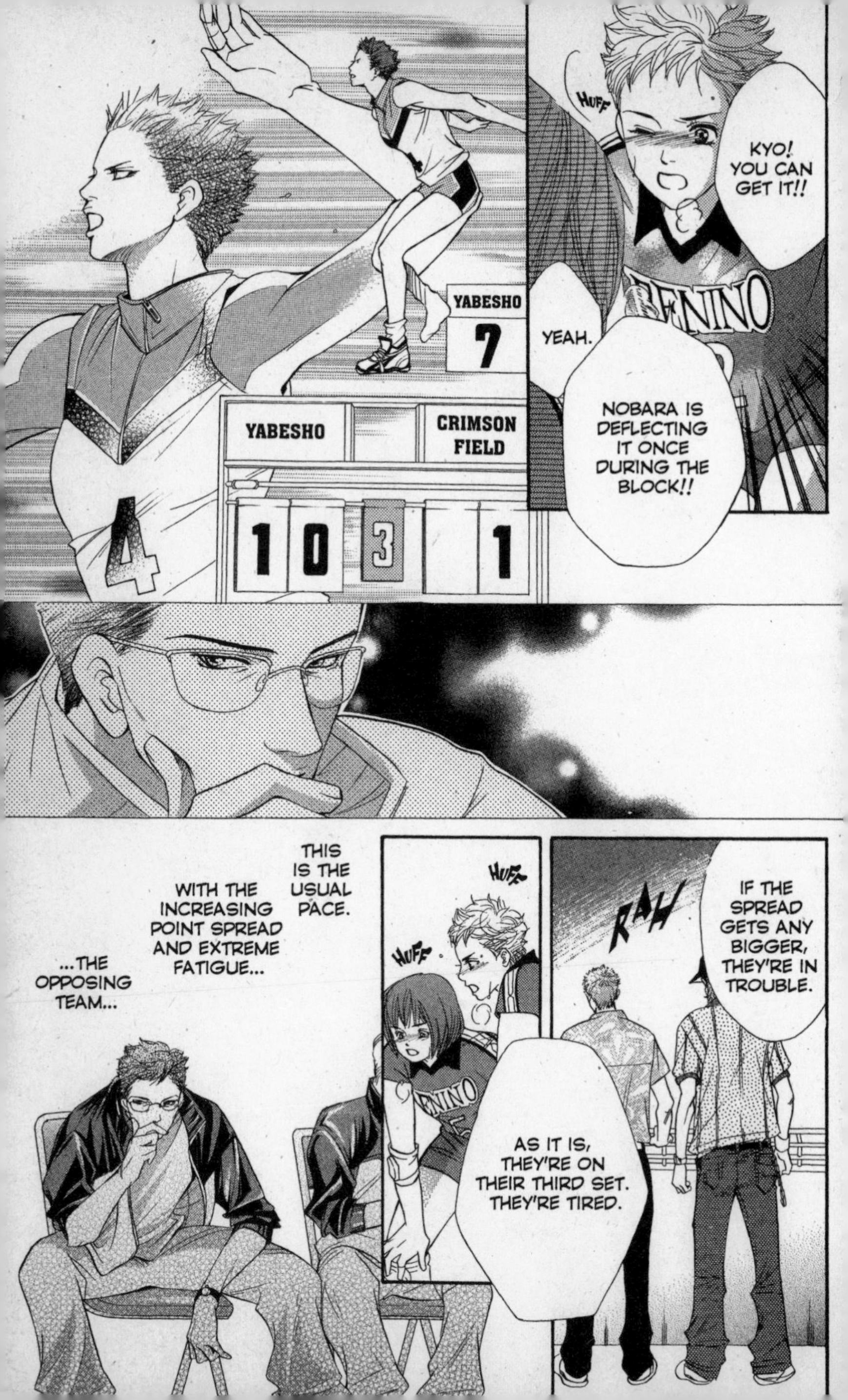
HUFF
KYO! YOU CAN GET IT!!
YEAH.
NOBARA IS DEFLECTING IT ONCE DURING THE BLOCK!!
YABESHO
7
YABESHO
CRIMSON FIELD
10
3
1
IF THE SPREAD GETS ANY BIGGER, THEY'RE IN TROUBLE.
RAH
AS IT IS, THEY'RE ON THEIR THIRD SET. THEY'RE TIRED.
HUFF
HUFF
THIS IS THE USUAL PACE.
WITH THE INCREASING POINT SPREAD AND EXTREME FATIGUE...
...THE OPPOSING TEAM...

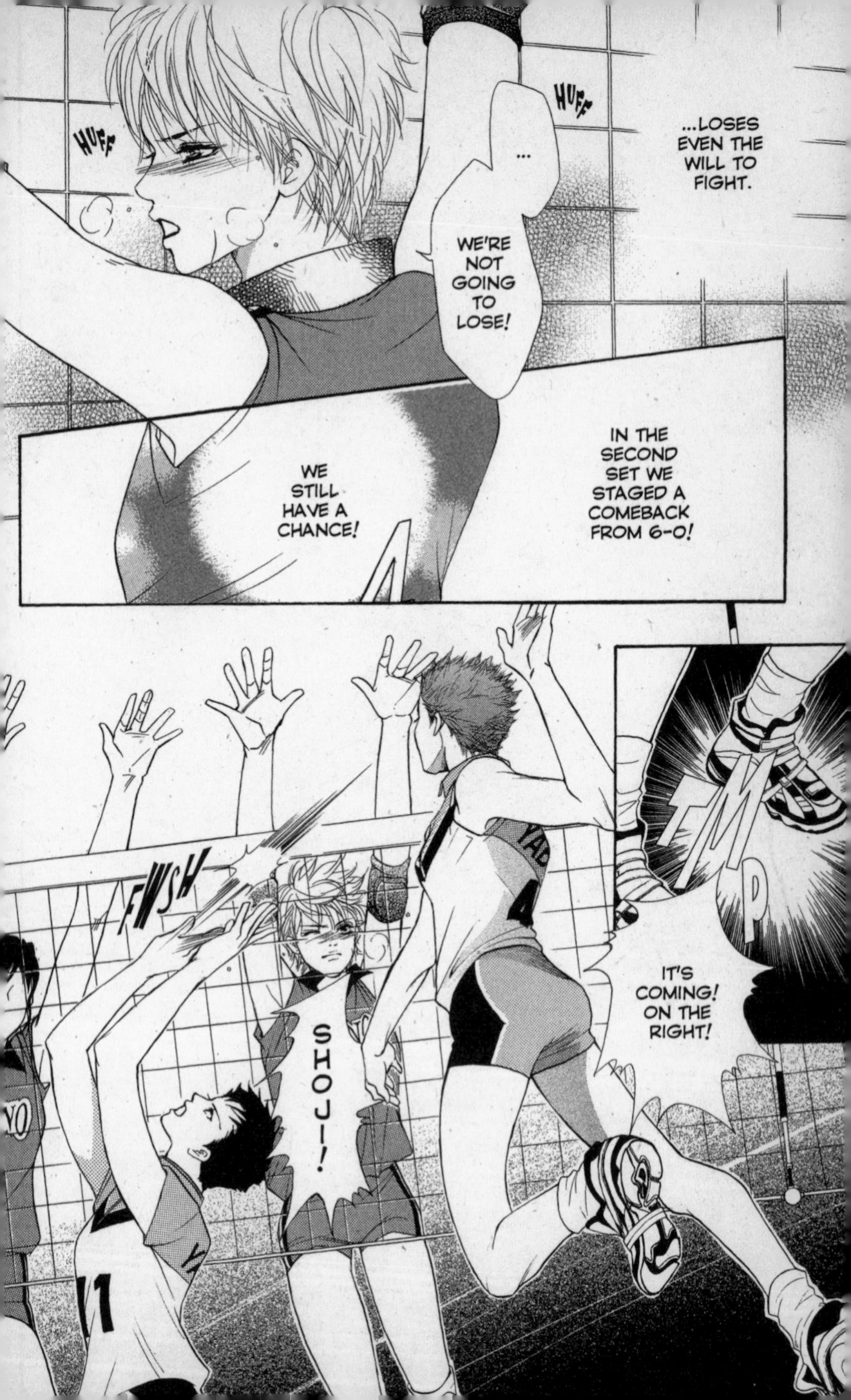
...LOSES EVEN THE WILL TO FIGHT.
HUFF
...
WE'RE NOT GOING TO LOSE!
HUFF
IN THE SECOND SET WE STAGED A COMEBACK FROM 6-0!
WE STILL HAVE A CHANCE!
TMP
IT'S COMING! ON THE RIGHT!
SHOJI!
FWSH

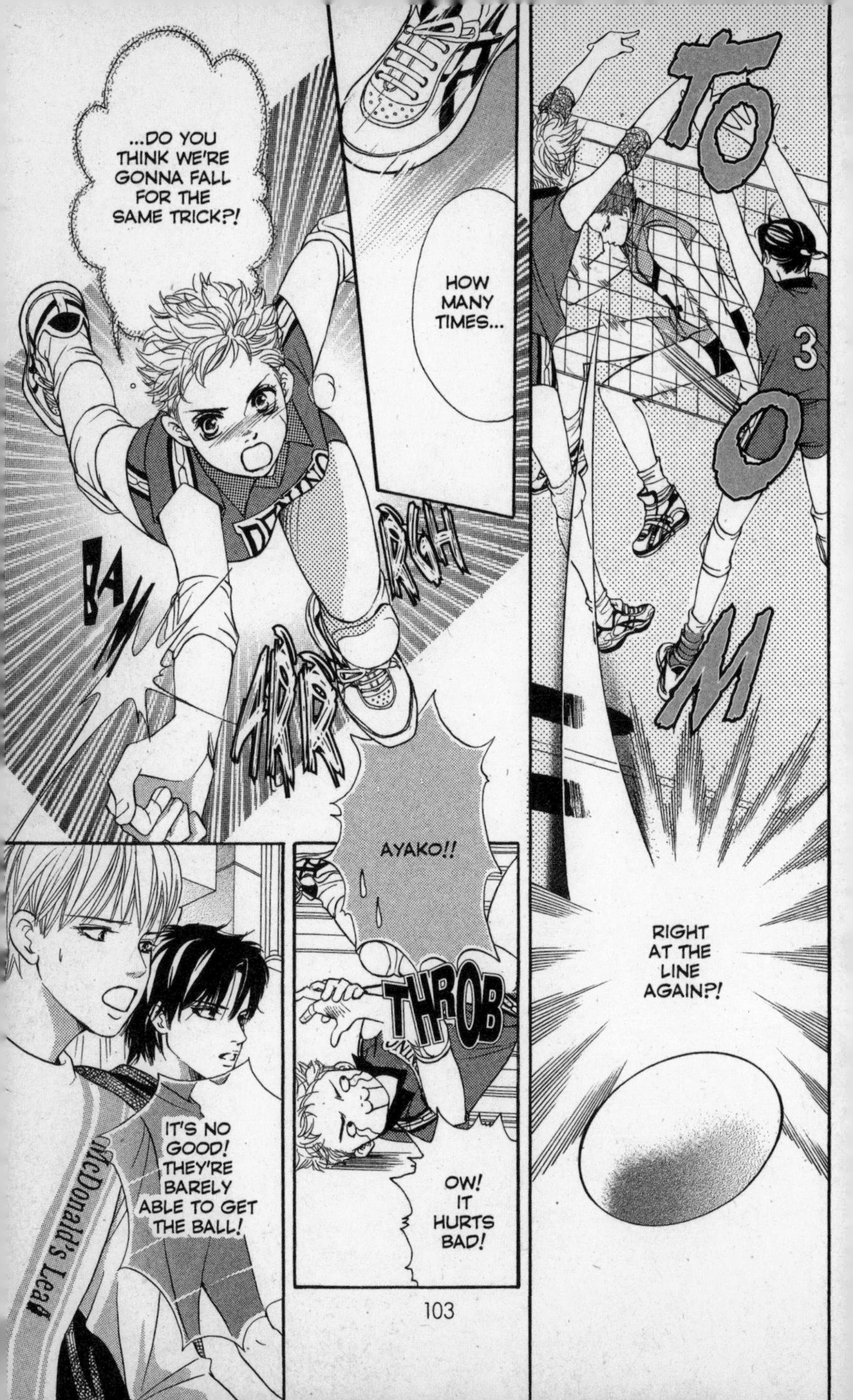
TOOM
RIGHT AT THE LINE AGAIN?!
HOW MANY TIMES...
...DO YOU THINK WE'RE GONNA FALL FOR THE SAME TRICK?!
ARRRGH
BAM
AYAKO!!
THROB
OW! IT HURTS BAD!
IT'S NO GOOD! THEY'RE BARELY ABLE TO GET THE BALL!
McDonald's Lead

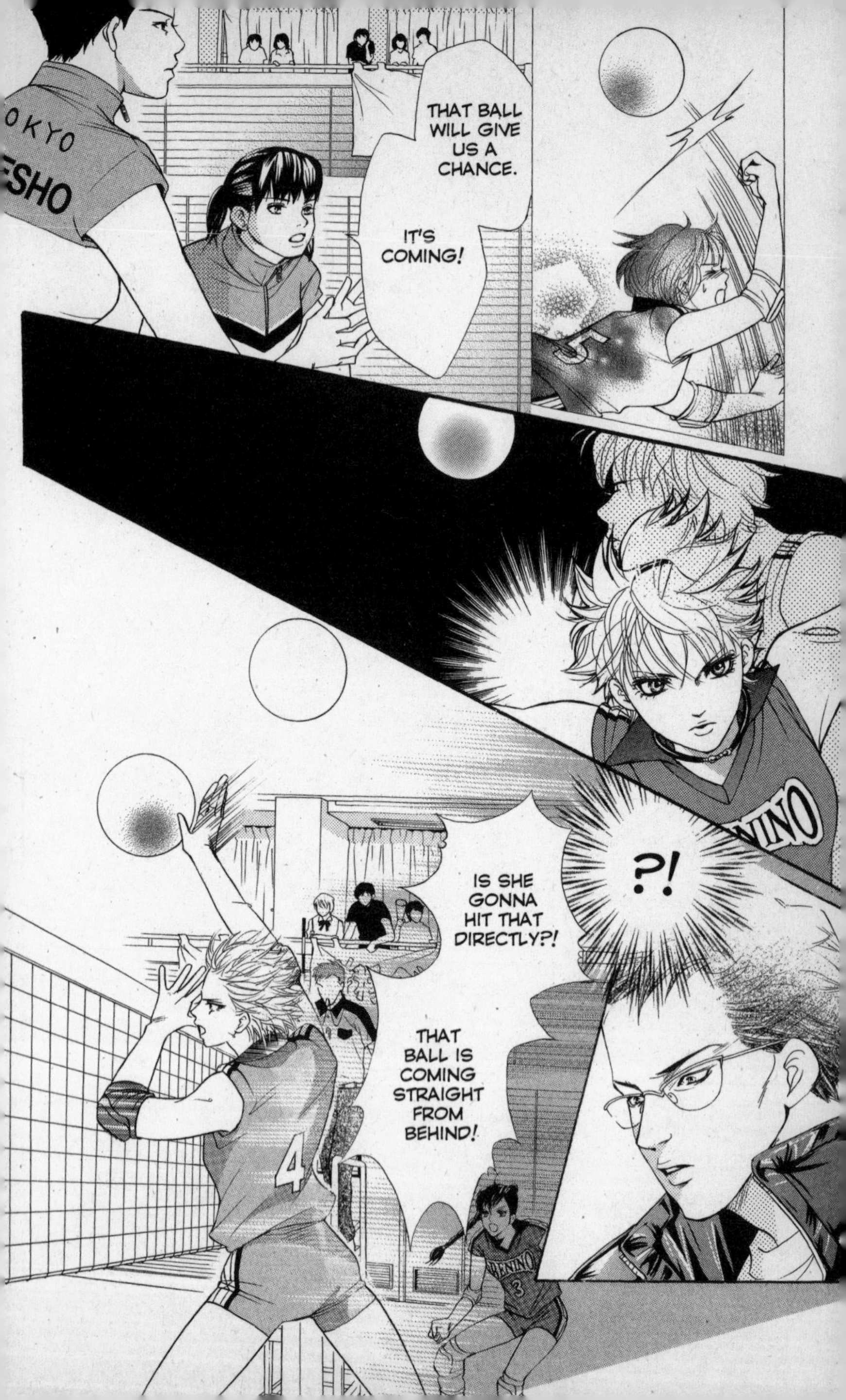
THAT BALL WILL GIVE US A CHANCE.
IT'S COMING!
?!
IS SHE GONNA HIT THAT DIRECTLY?!
THAT BALL IS COMING STRAIGHT FROM BEHIND!

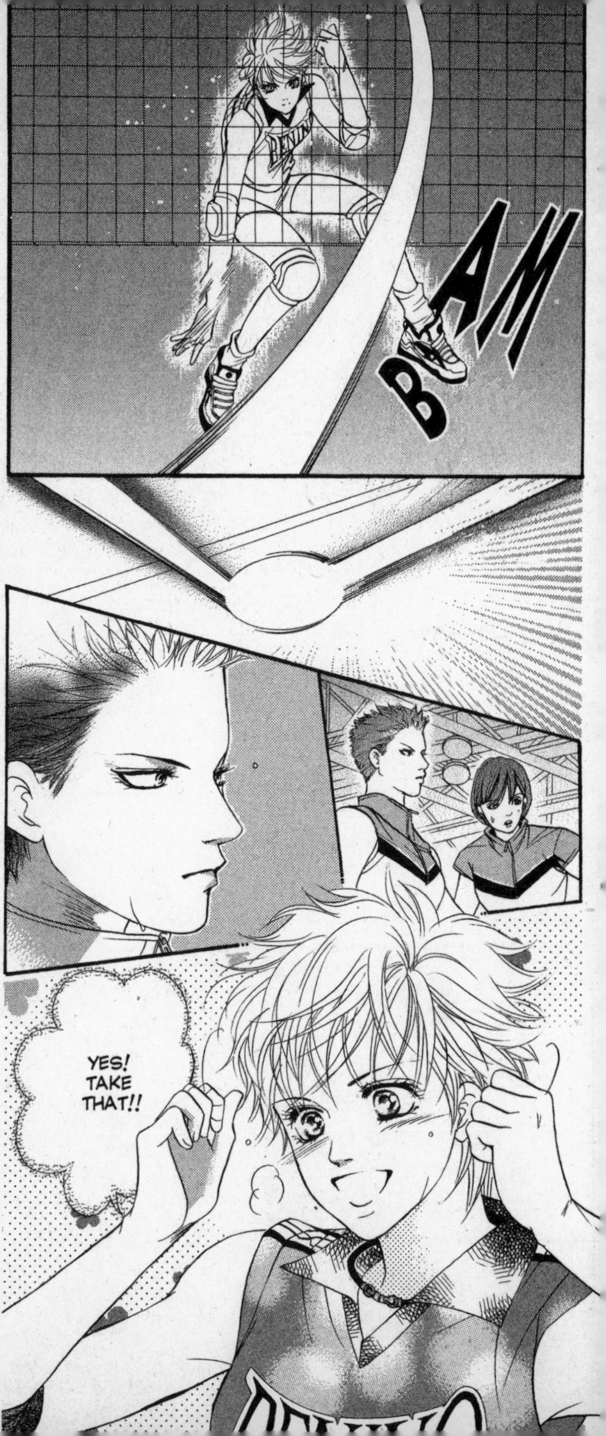
BAM
YES! TAKE THAT!!

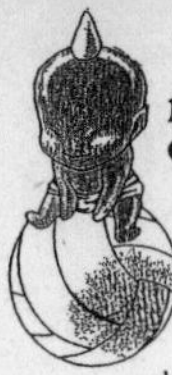

MITSUBA CLUB

Vol.3

ANNOUNCEMENT: ASSISTANT WANTED

DO YOU WANT TO DRAW MANGA WITH ME?! THAT IS TO SAY, I'M LOOKING FOR AN ASSISTANT. TO BE HONEST, WE WORK PEOPLE PRETTY HARD. I'M LOOKING FOR PEOPLE WHO'D BE INTERESTED ANYWAY. AGE 18 AND OVER. SOMEONE WHO LIVES NEAR TOKYO AND CAN COME IN FOR FOUR DAYS AT THE END OF EACH MONTH. SEND A COPY OF A BACKGROUND SCENE YOU DREW YOURSELF (NO TRACING ALLOWED) AND A RESUME TO THE ADDRESS BELOW. WE WILL ONLY CONTACT YOU IF WE WISH TO HIRE YOU. AND PLEASE UNDERSTAND THAT NO SUBMISSIONS WILL BE RETURNED.

PEOPLE WHO HAVE ALREADY DEBUTED ARE VERY WELCOME ALSO!!

ADDRESS:
MITSUBA TAKANASHI
BESSATSU MARGARET
EDITORIAL DEPT.
SHUEISHA
2-5-10 HITOTSUBASHI
CHIYODA-KU, TOKYO
101-8050

ATTN:
ASSISTANT SEARCH

THANK YOU VERY MUCH.

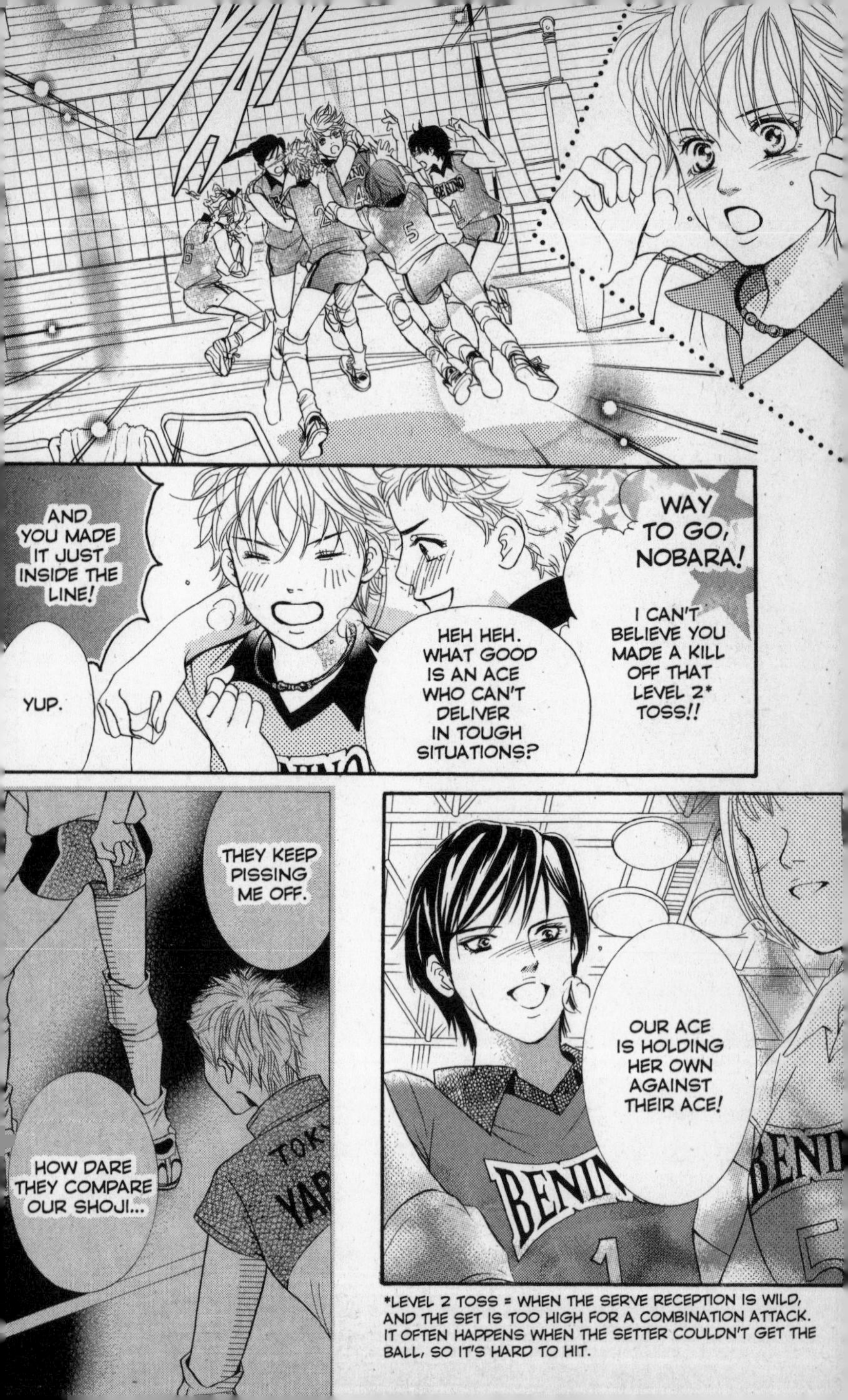
YAY
WAY TO GO, NOBARA!
I CAN'T BELIEVE YOU MADE A KILL OFF THAT LEVEL 2* TOSS!!
HEH HEH. WHAT GOOD IS AN ACE WHO CAN'T DELIVER IN TOUGH SITUATIONS?
AND YOU MADE IT JUST INSIDE THE LINE!
YUP.
OUR ACE IS HOLDING HER OWN AGAINST THEIR ACE!
THEY KEEP PISSING ME OFF.
HOW DARE THEY COMPARE OUR SHOJI...

*LEVEL 2 TOSS = WHEN THE SERVE RECEPTION IS WILD, AND THE SET IS TOO HIGH FOR A COMBINATION ATTACK. IT OFTEN HAPPENS WHEN THE SETTER COULDN'T GET THE BALL, SO IT'S HARD TO HIT.

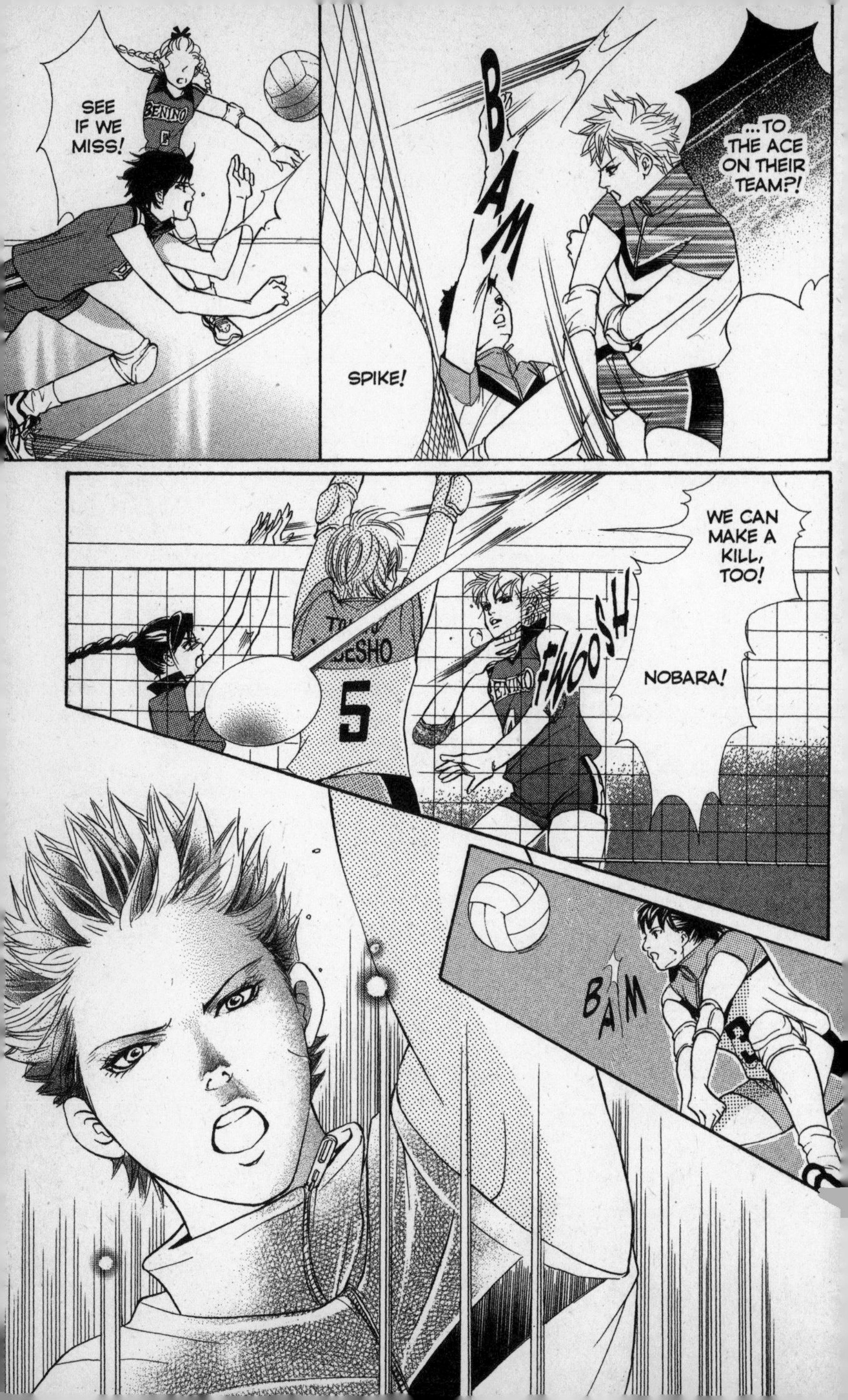
...TO THE ACE ON THEIR TEAM?!
BAM
SPIKE!
SEE IF WE MISS!
WE CAN MAKE A KILL, TOO!
FWOOSH
NOBARA!
BAM

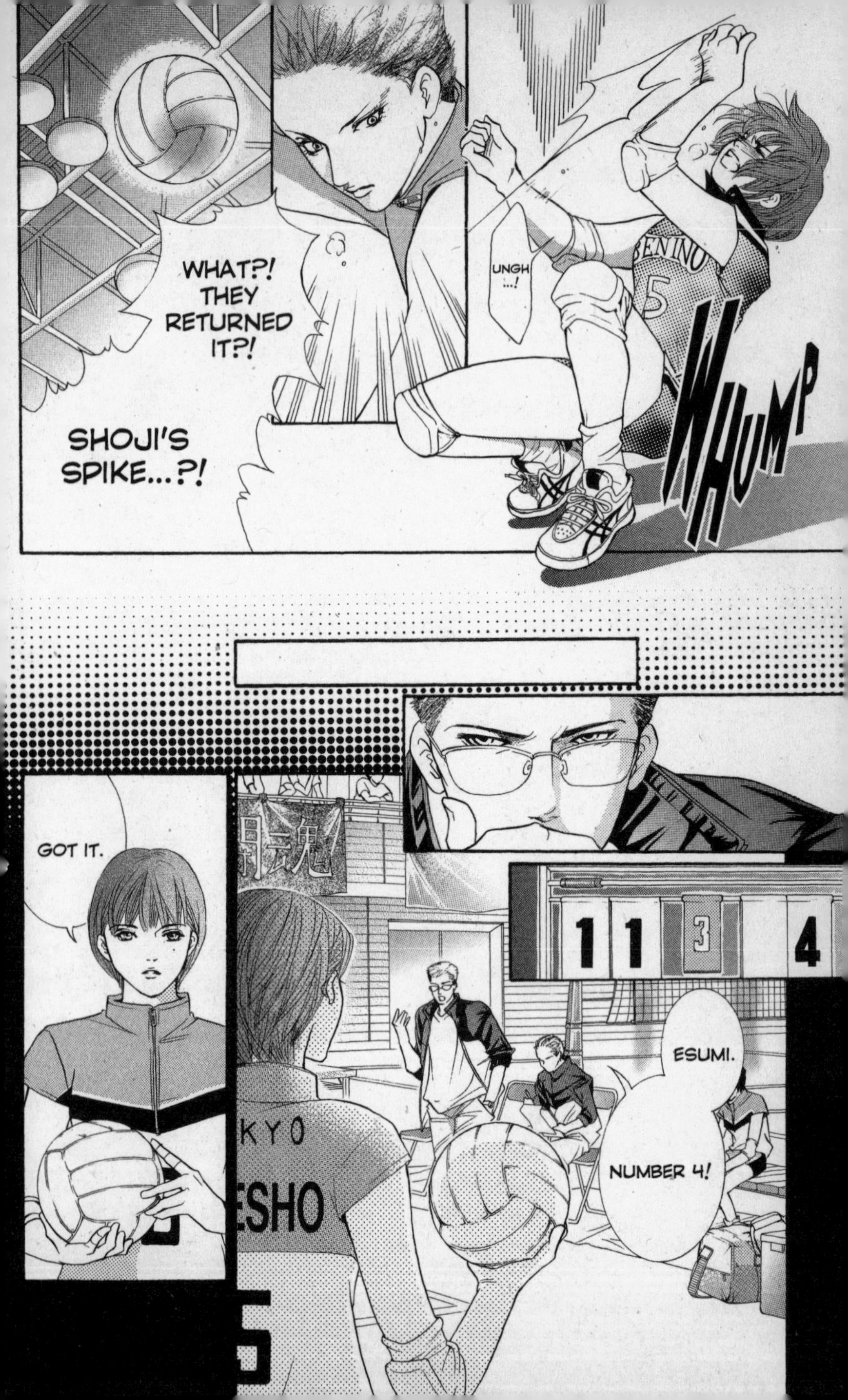
UNGH ...!
WHUMP
WHAT?! THEY RETURNED IT?!
SHOJI'S SPIKE...?!
11 3 4
ESUMI.
NUMBER 4!
GOT IT.

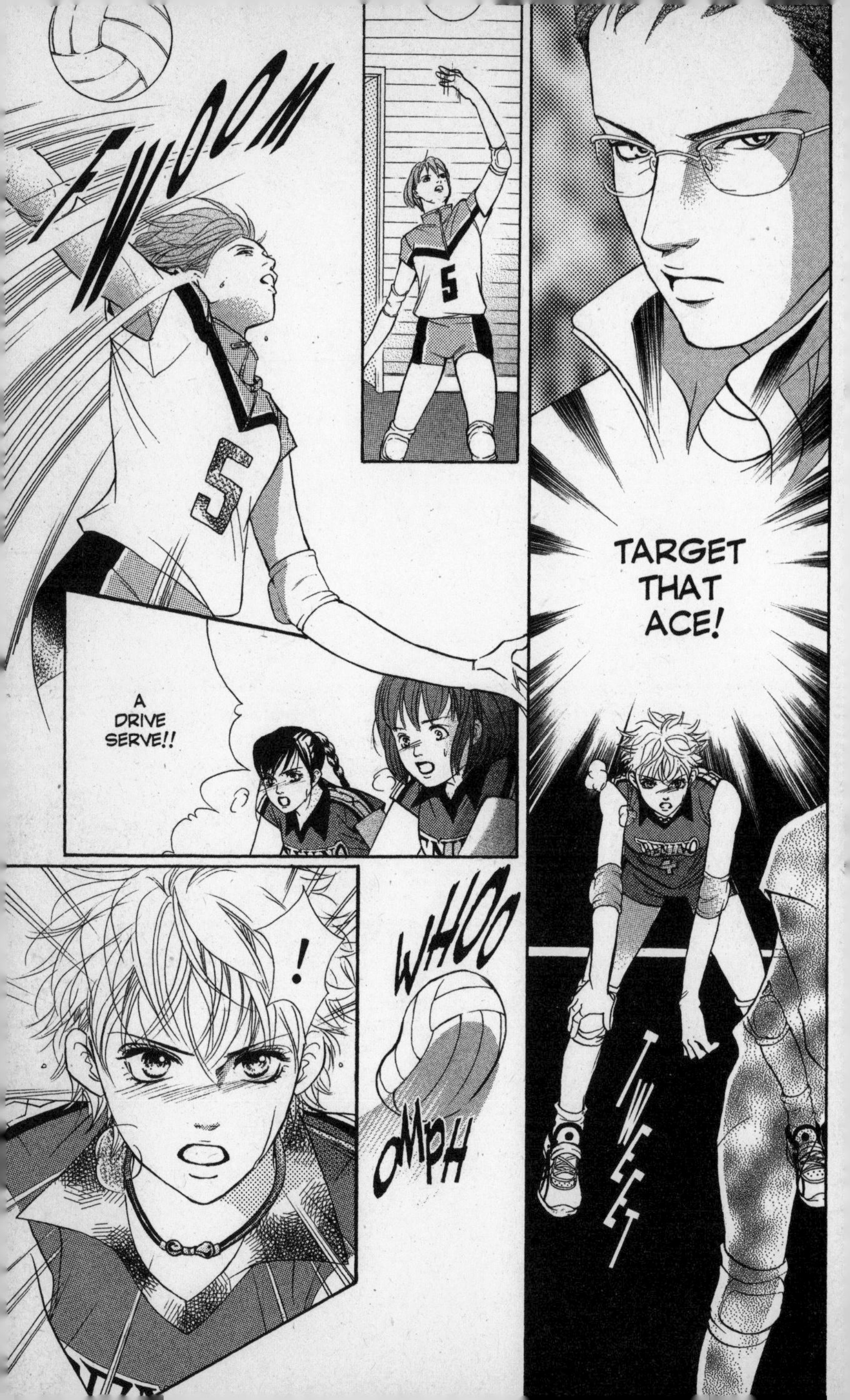
TARGET THAT ACE!
TWEEET
FWOOM
A DRIVE SERVE!!
WHOO
OMPH
!

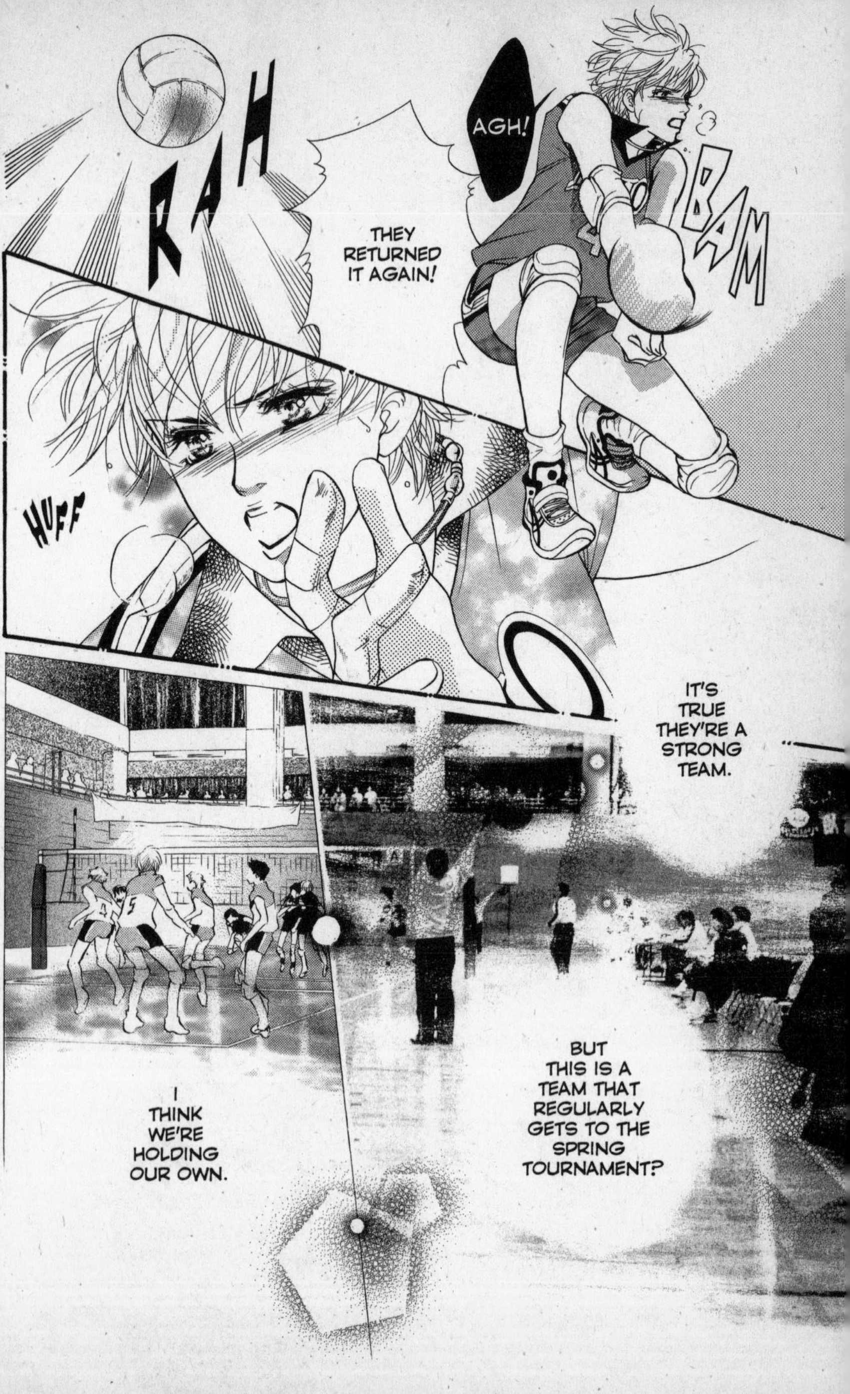
AGH!
BAM
RAH
THEY RETURNED IT AGAIN!
HUFF
IT'S TRUE THEY'RE A STRONG TEAM.
BUT THIS IS A TEAM THAT REGULARLY GETS TO THE SPRING TOURNAMENT?
I THINK WE'RE HOLDING OUR OWN.

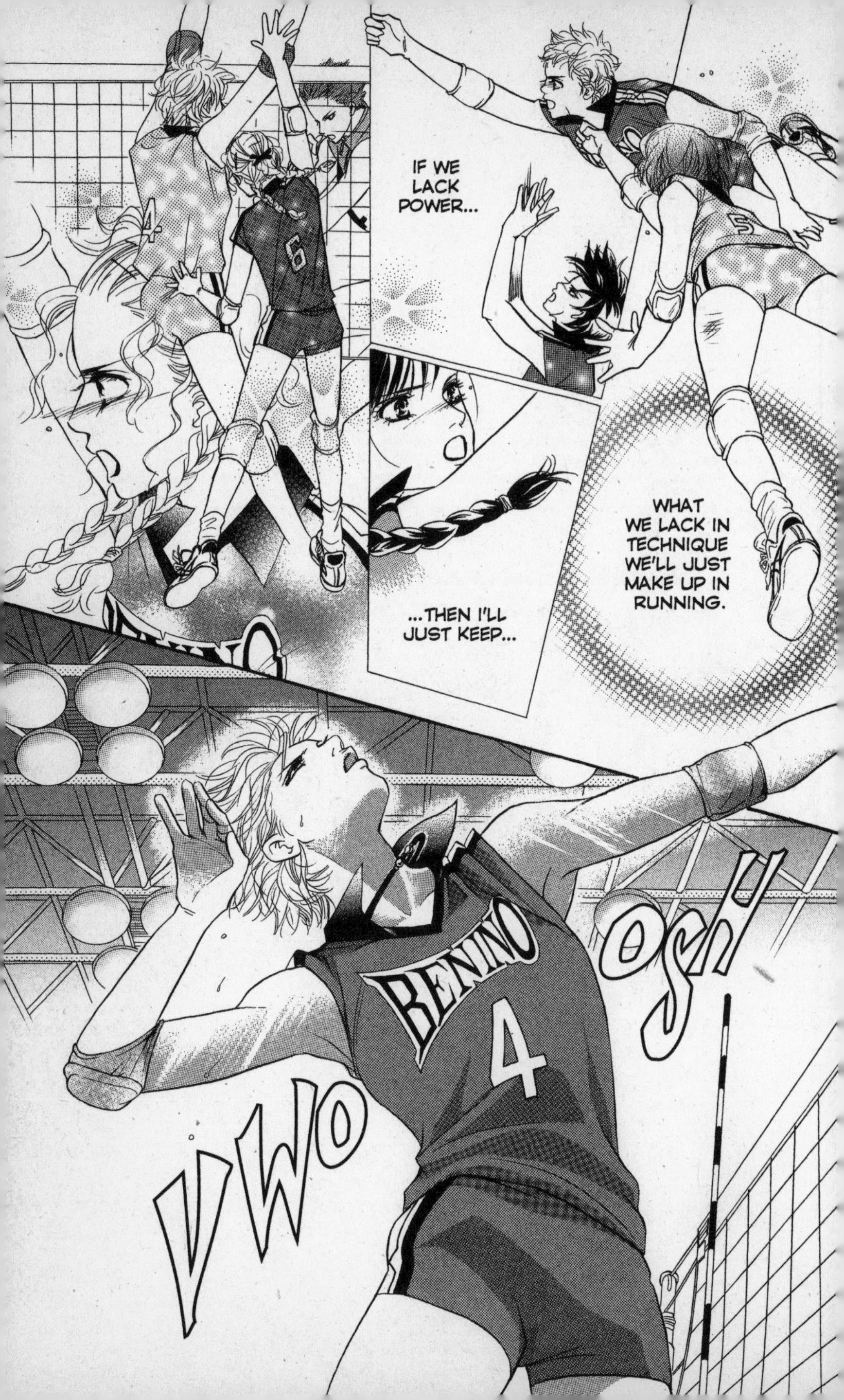
IF WE LACK POWER...
...THEN I'LL JUST KEEP...
WHAT WE LACK IN TECHNIQUE WE'LL JUST MAKE UP IN RUNNING.
BENINO
4
VWOOSH

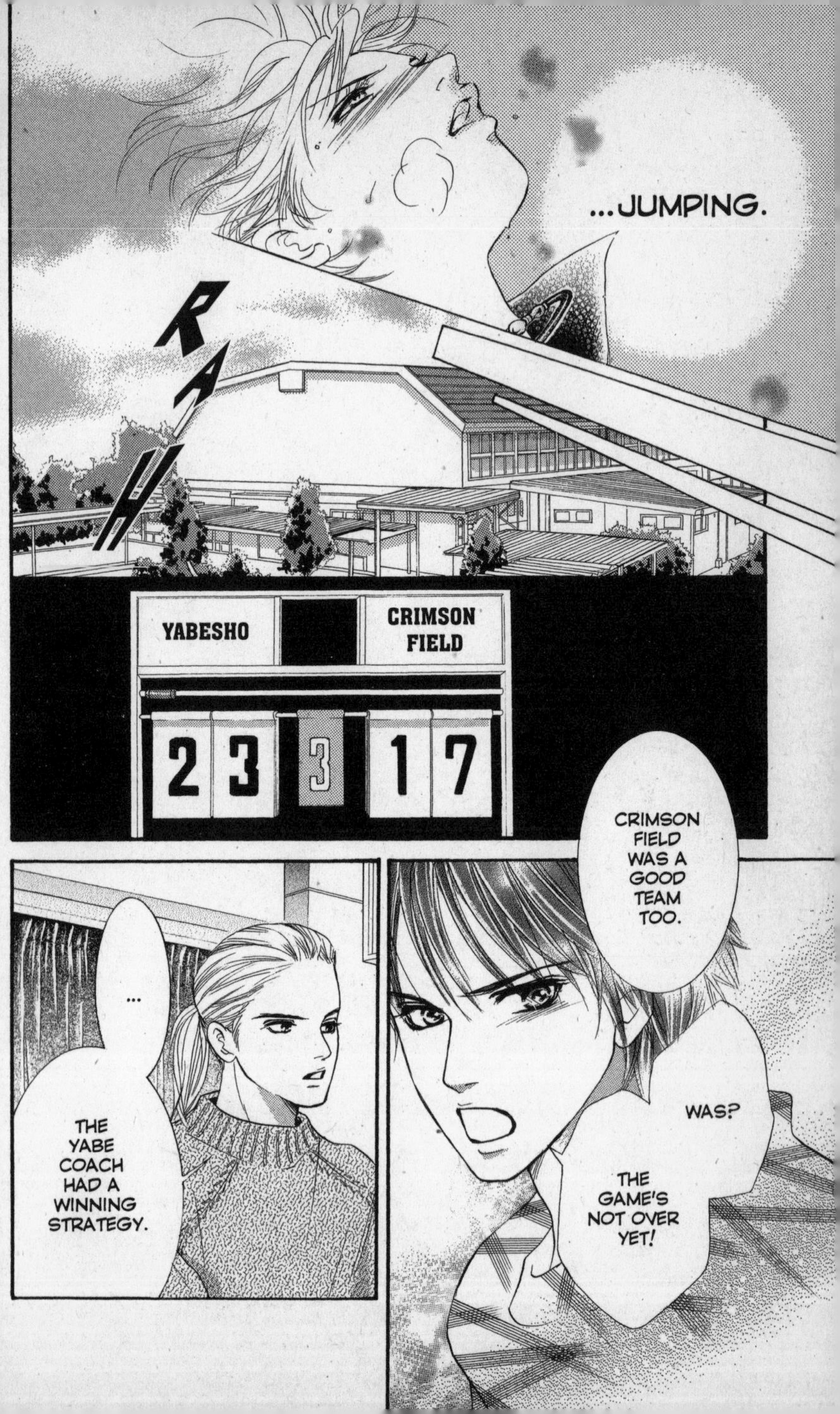
...JUMPING.
RAH
YABESHO
CRIMSON FIELD
23
3
17
CRIMSON FIELD WAS A GOOD TEAM TOO.
WAS?
THE GAME'S NOT OVER YET!
...
THE YABE COACH HAD A WINNING STRATEGY.

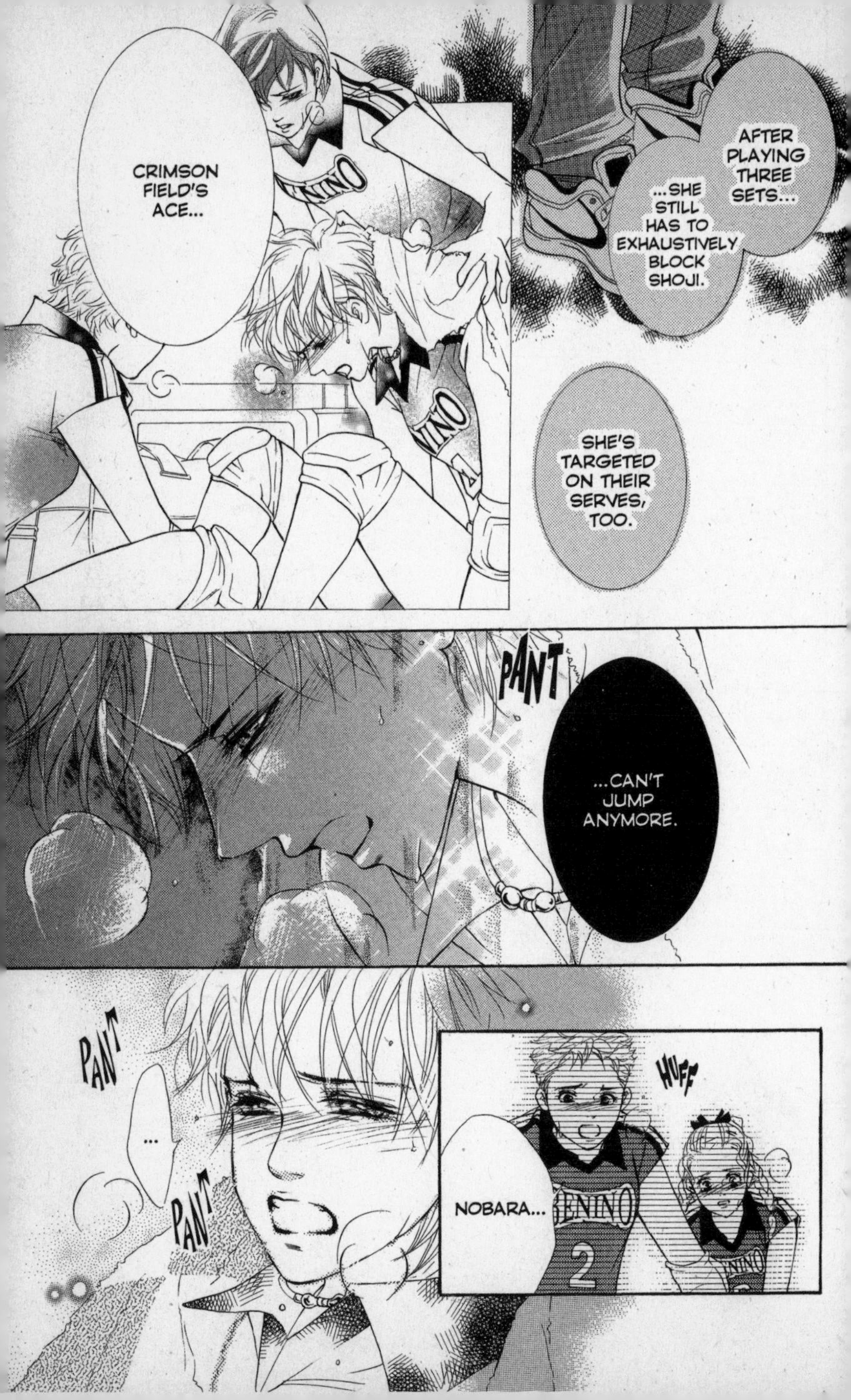
AFTER PLAYING THREE SETS...
...SHE STILL HAS TO EXHAUSTIVELY BLOCK SHOJI.
SHE'S TARGETED ON THEIR SERVES, TOO.
CRIMSON FIELD'S ACE...
PANT
...CAN'T JUMP ANYMORE.
HUFF
NOBARA...
PANT
...
PANT

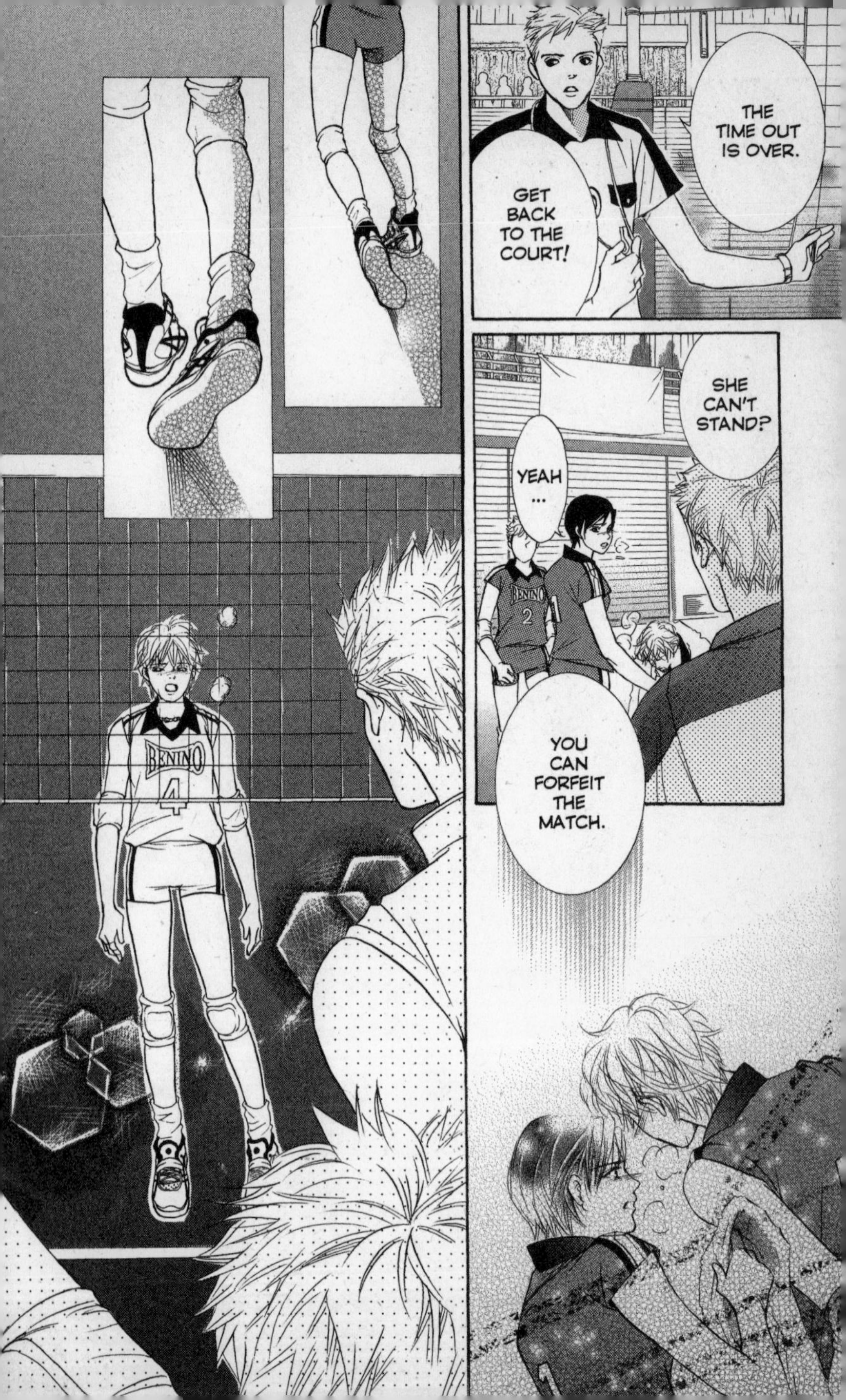
THE TIME OUT IS OVER.
GET BACK TO THE COURT!
SHE CAN'T STAND?
YEAH ...
YOU CAN FORFEIT THE MATCH.

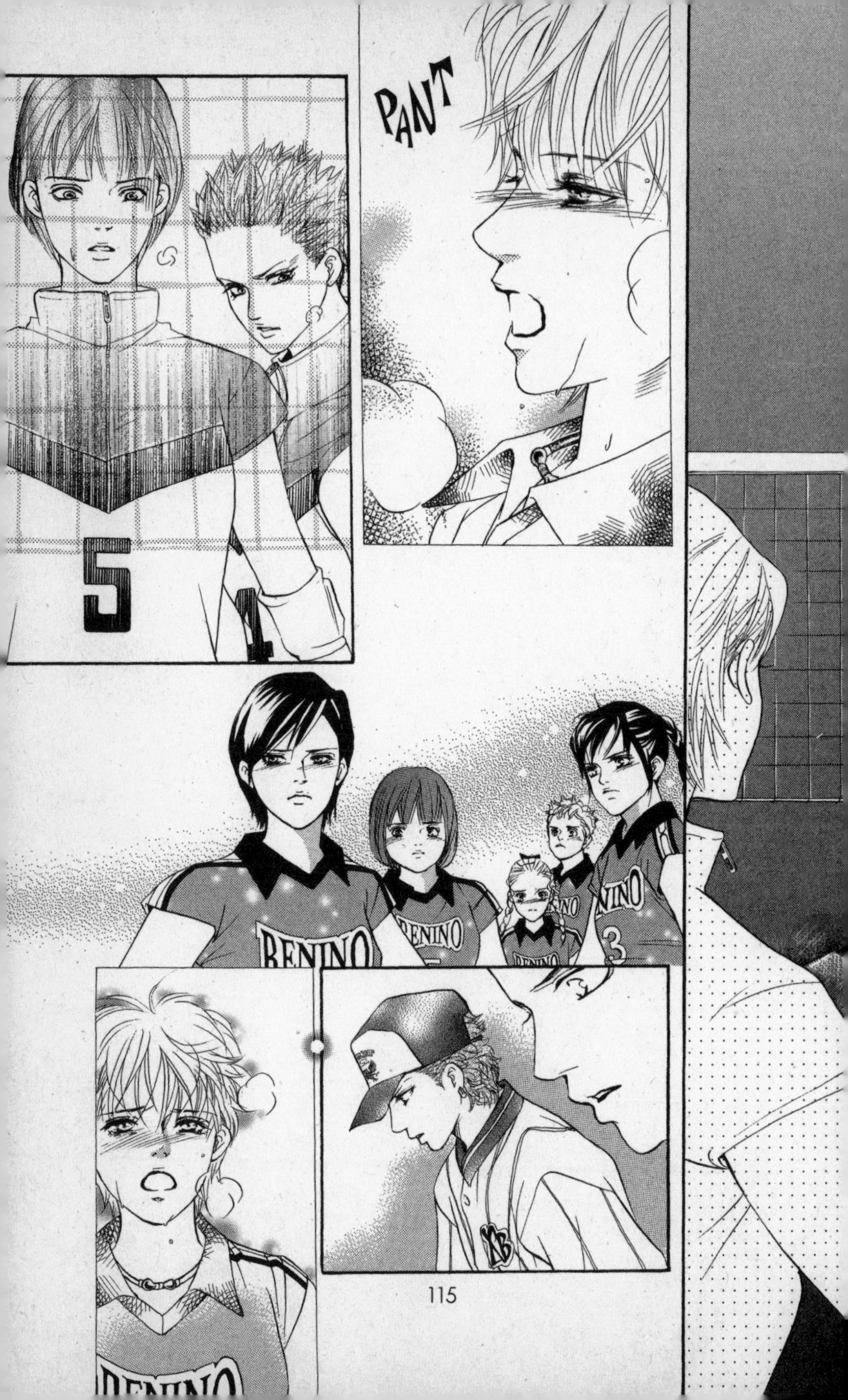
PANT

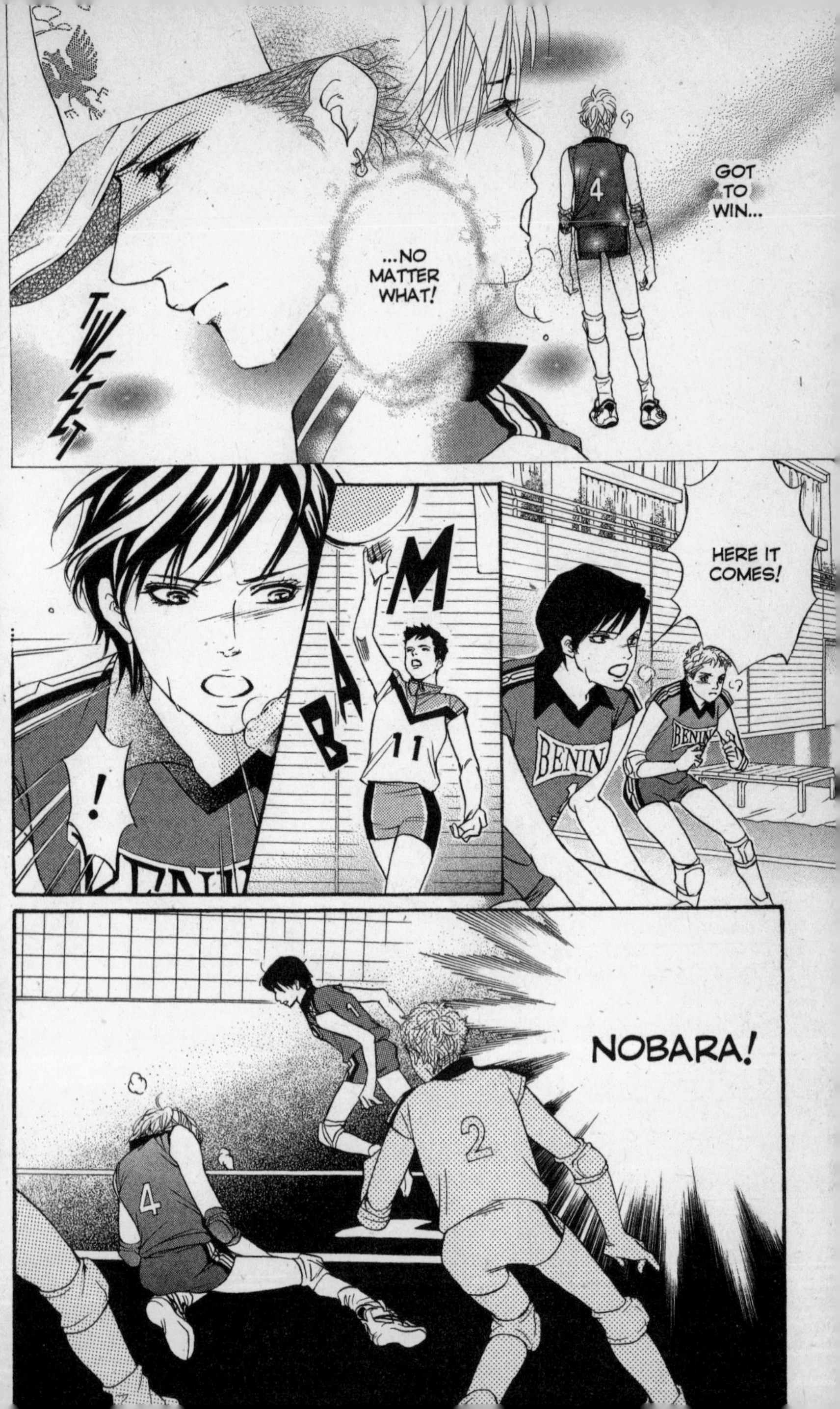
GOT TO WIN...
...NO MATTER WHAT!
TWEET
HERE IT COMES!
BENIN
BENIN
BAM
11
!
NOBARA!

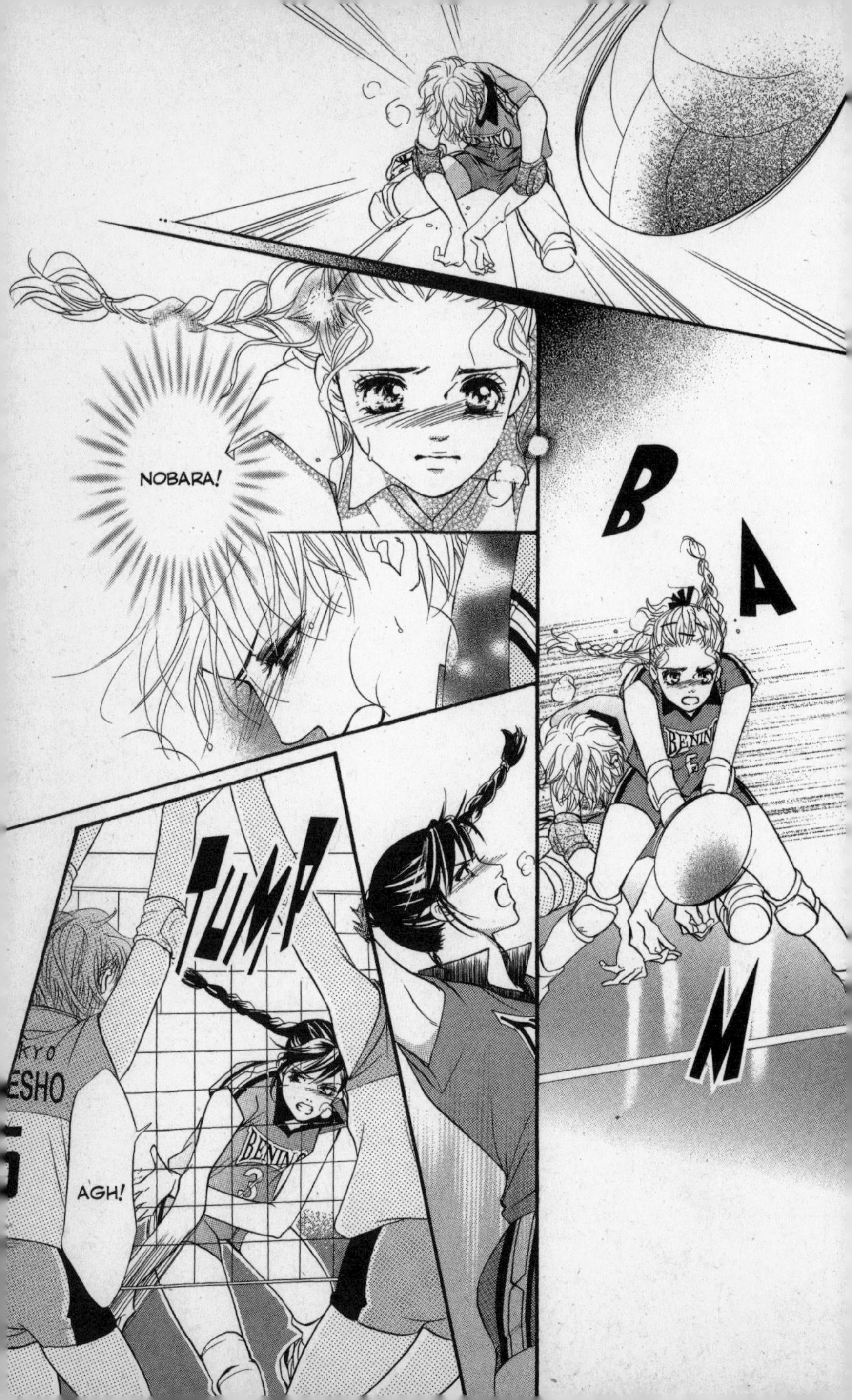
B
A
M
NOBARA!
TUMP
AGH!

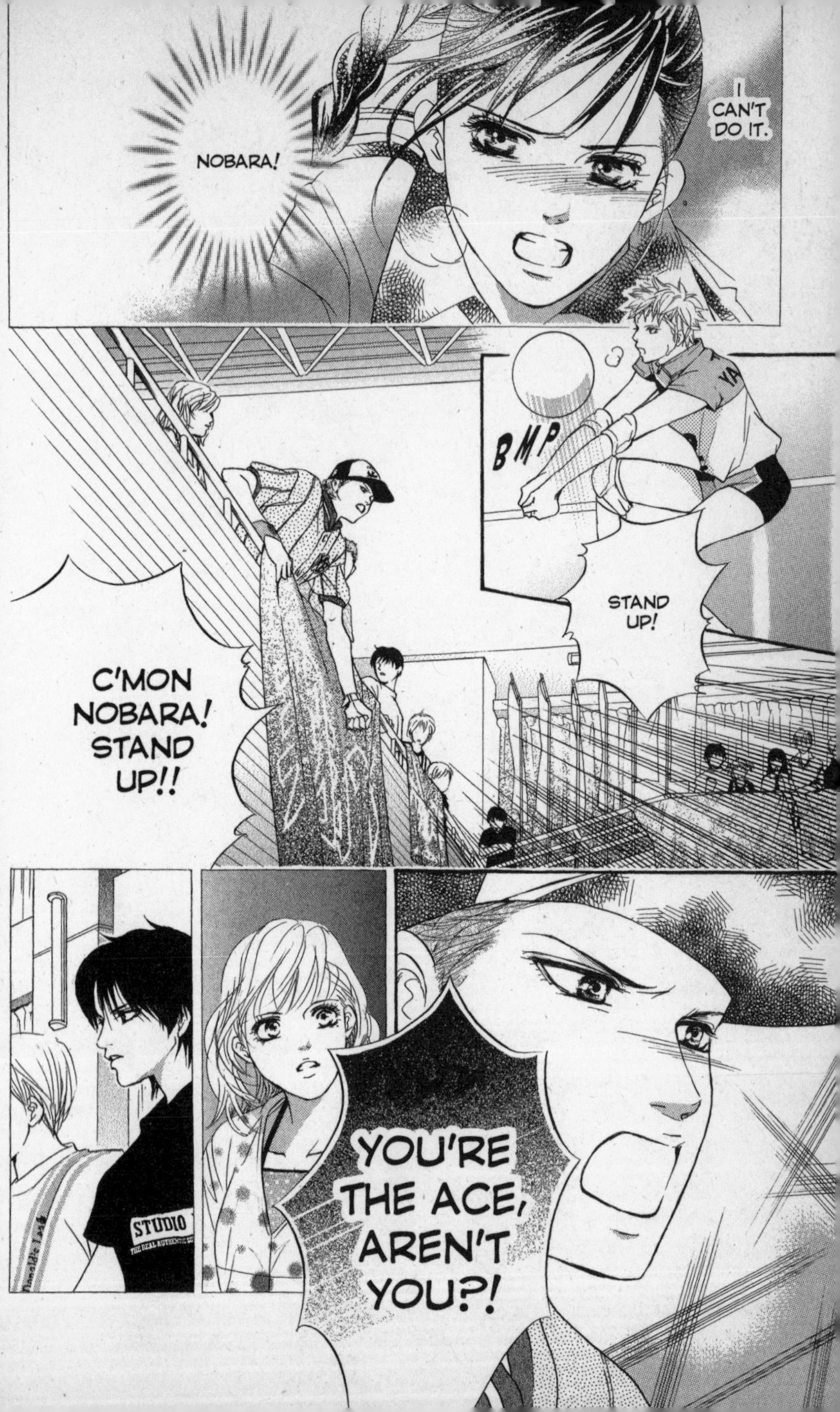
I CAN'T DO IT.
NOBARA!
BMP
STAND UP!
C'MON NOBARA! STAND UP!!
YOU'RE THE ACE, AREN'T YOU?!
STUDIO

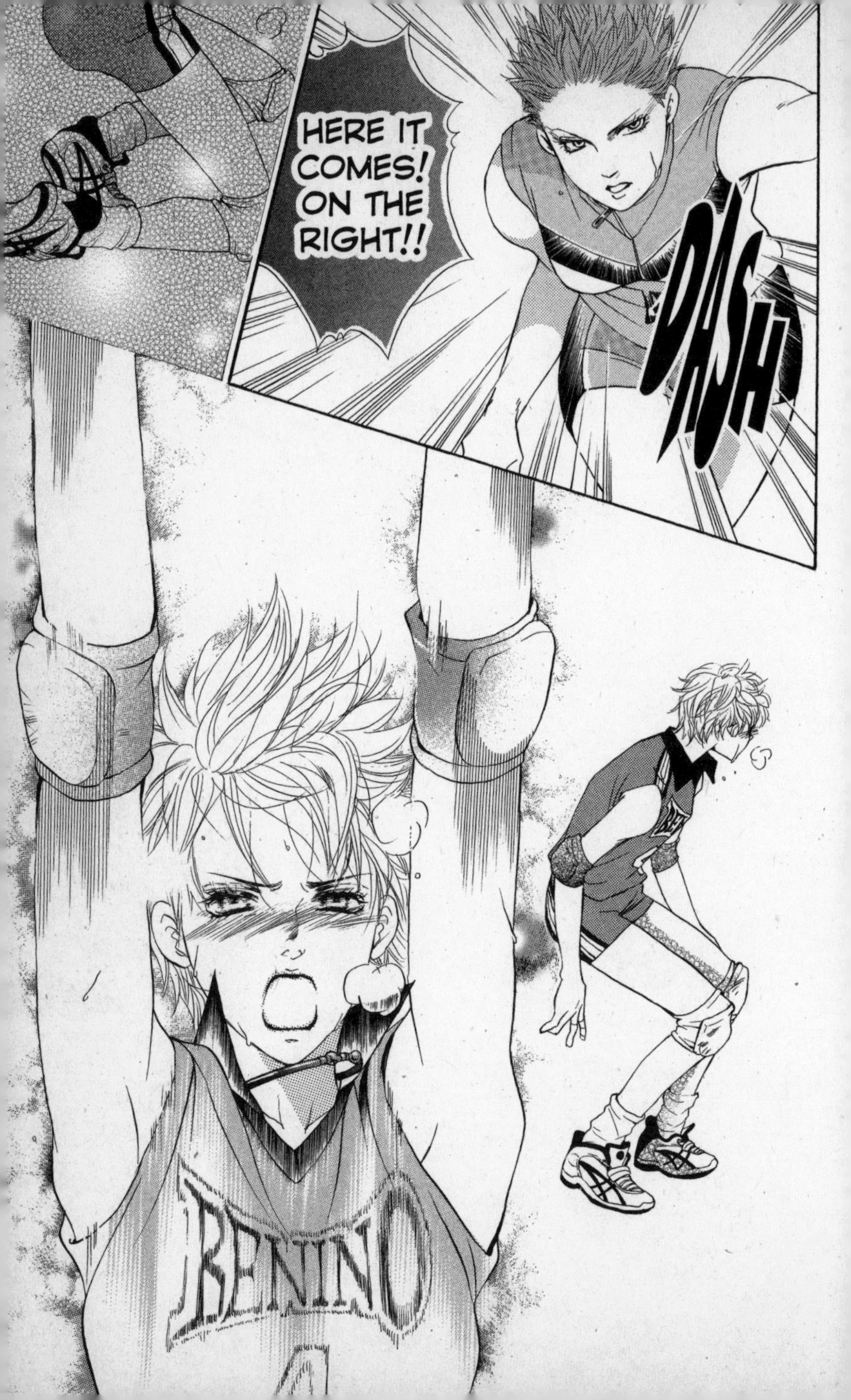
HERE IT COMES! ON THE RIGHT!!
DASH
BENINO

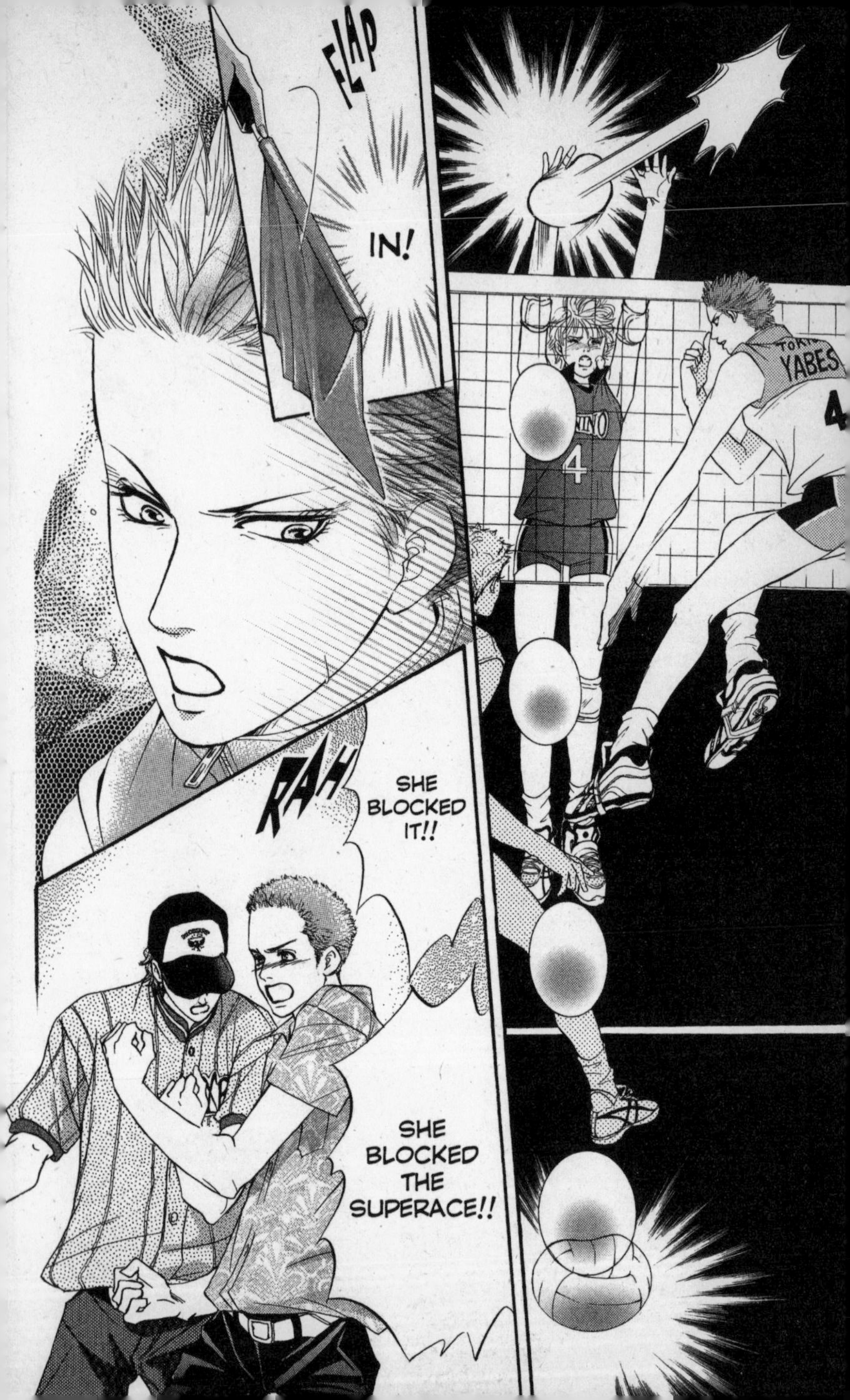
YABES
FLAP
IN!
RAH
SHE BLOCKED IT!!
SHE BLOCKED THE SUPERACE!!

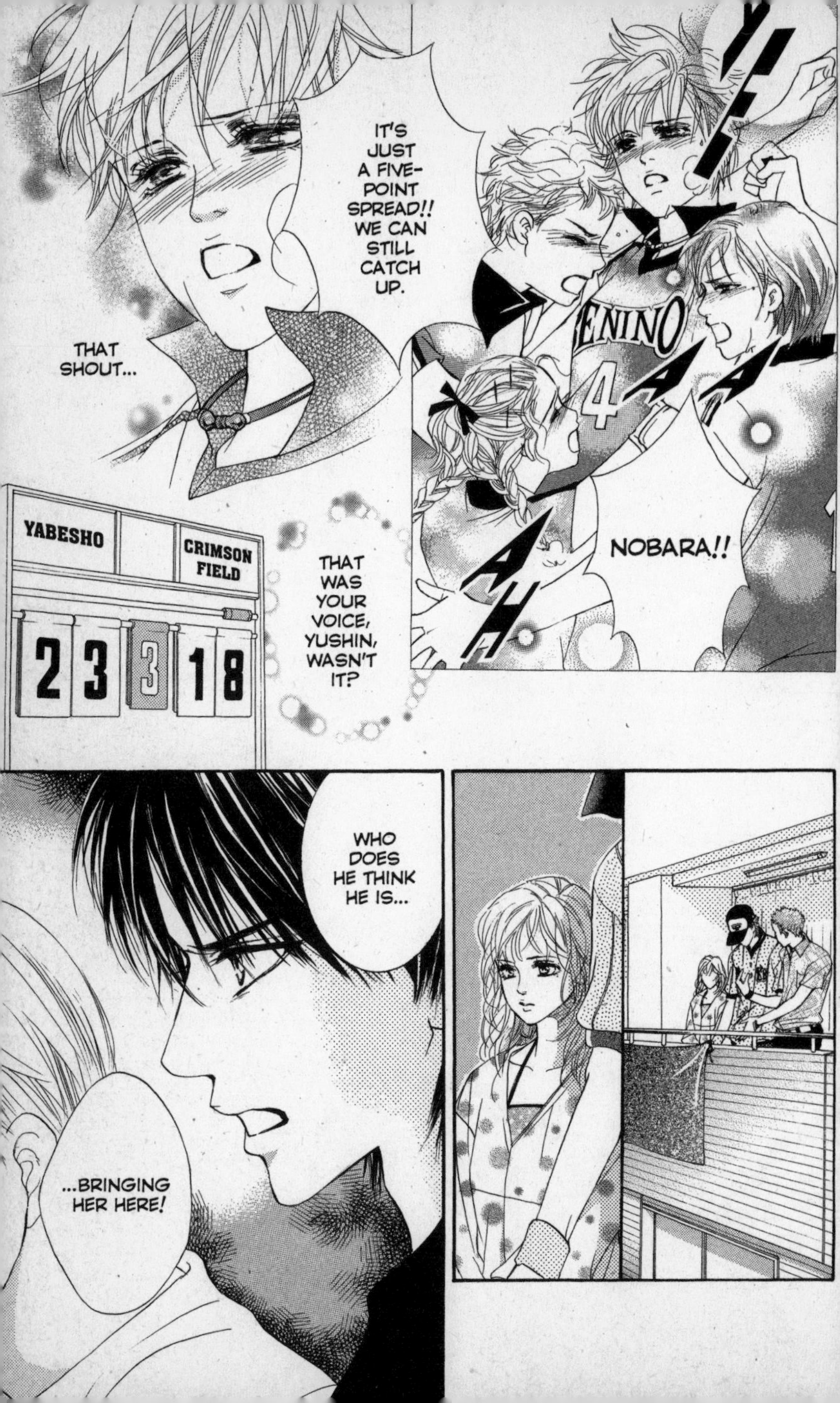
IT'S JUST A FIVE-POINT SPREAD!! WE CAN STILL CATCH UP.
NOBARA!!
THAT SHOUT...
YABESHO
CRIMSON FIELD
23 3 18
THAT WAS YOUR VOICE, YUSHIN, WASN'T IT?
WHO DOES HE THINK HE IS...
...BRINGING HER HERE!

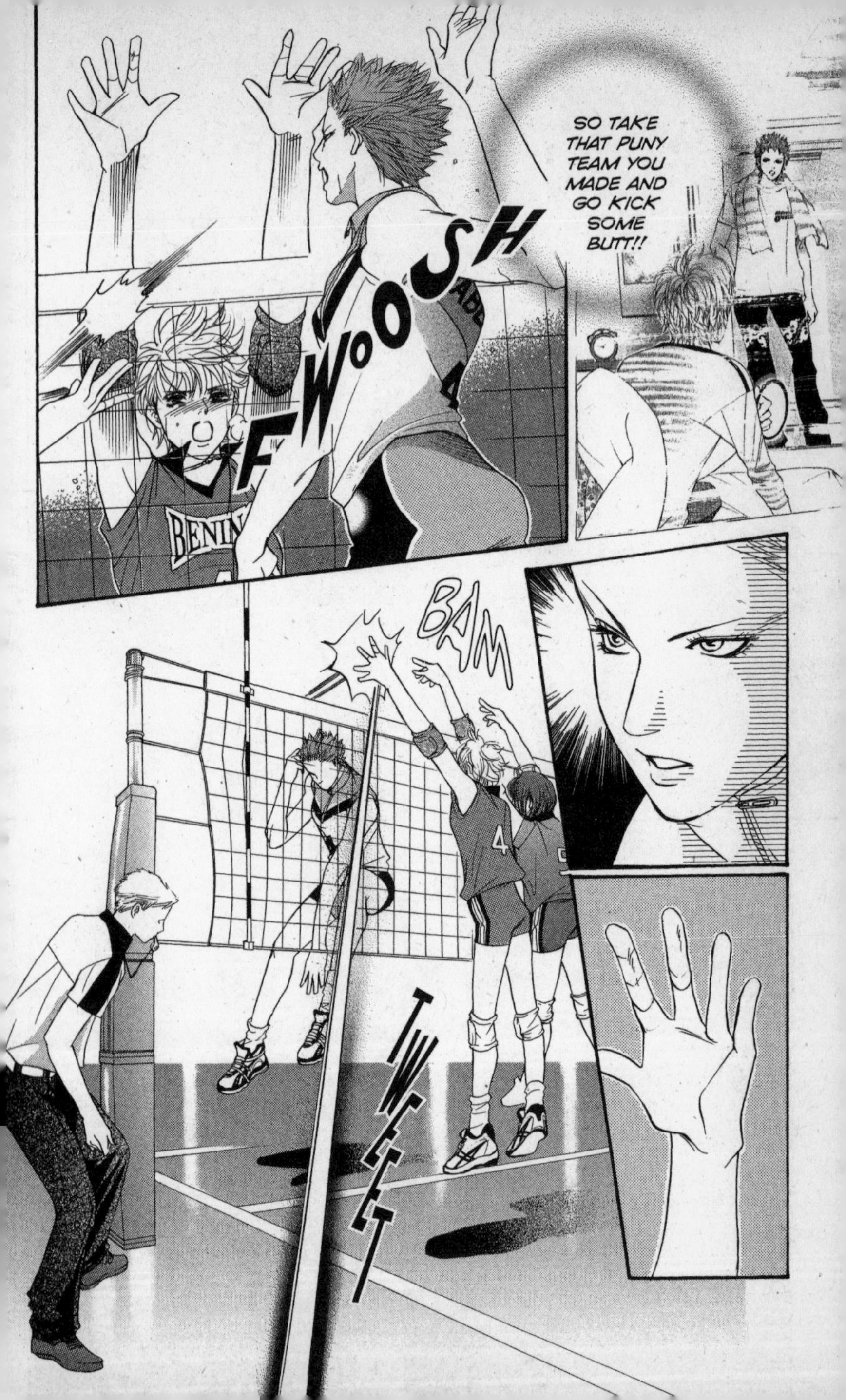
SO TAKE THAT PUNY TEAM YOU MADE AND GO KICK SOME BUTT!!
FWOOSH
BAM
TWEEET

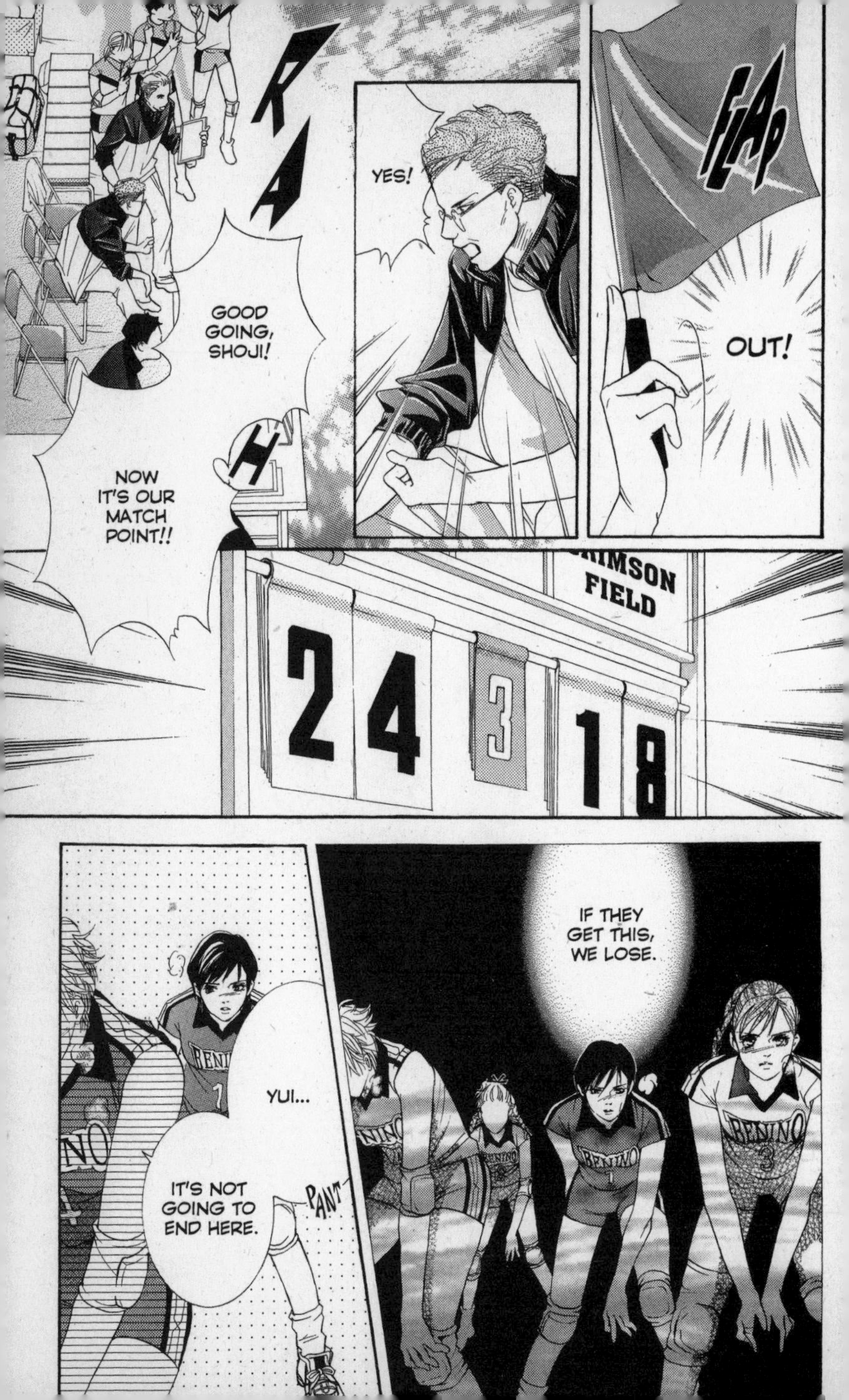
FLAP
OUT!
YES!
RAH
GOOD GOING, SHOJI!
NOW IT'S OUR MATCH POINT!!
CRIMSON FIELD
24
3
18
IF THEY GET THIS, WE LOSE.
YUI...
IT'S NOT GOING TO END HERE.
PANT

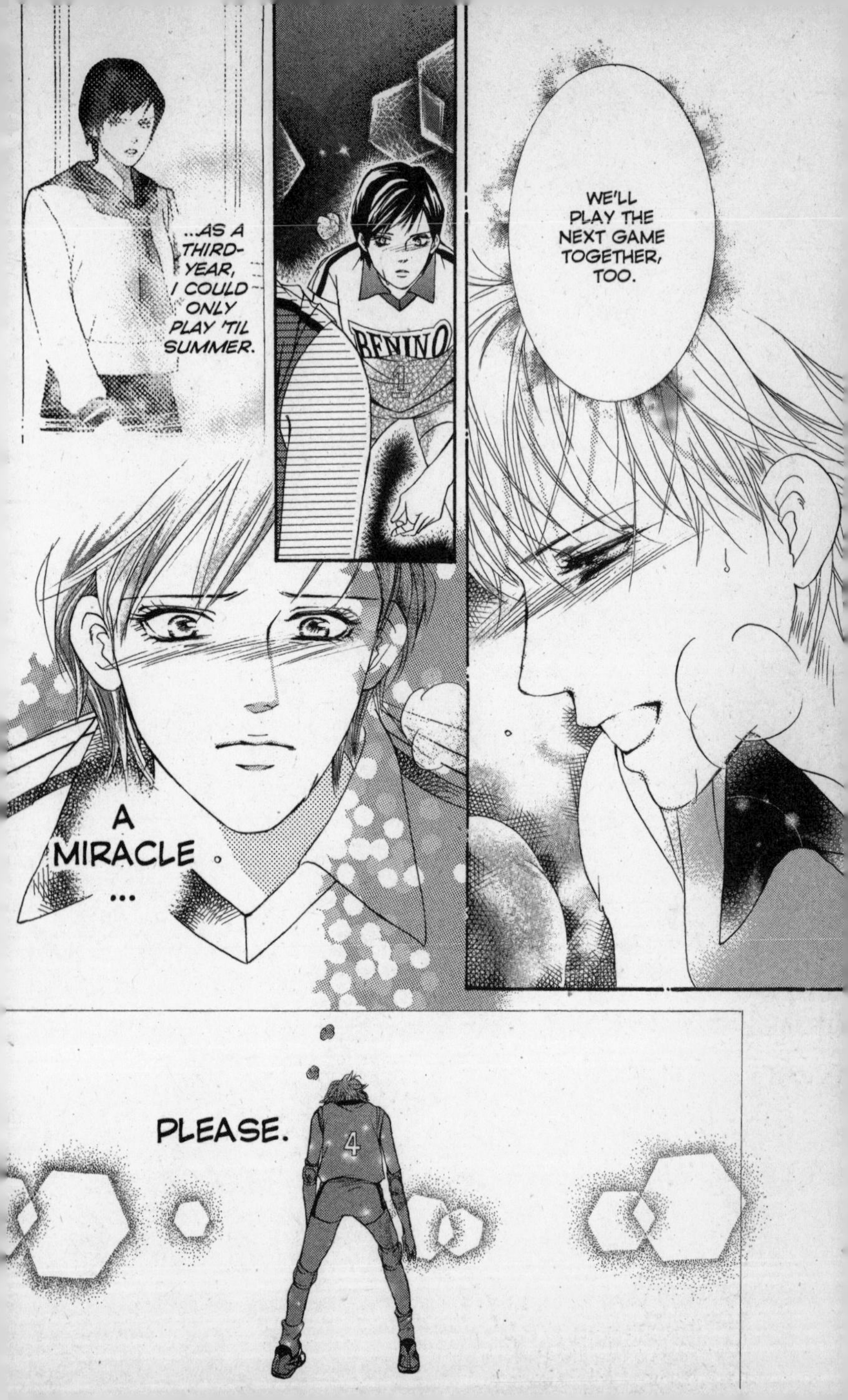
WE'LL PLAY THE NEXT GAME TOGETHER, TOO.
BENINO
...AS A THIRD-YEAR, I COULD ONLY PLAY 'TIL SUMMER.
A MIRACLE ...
PLEASE.

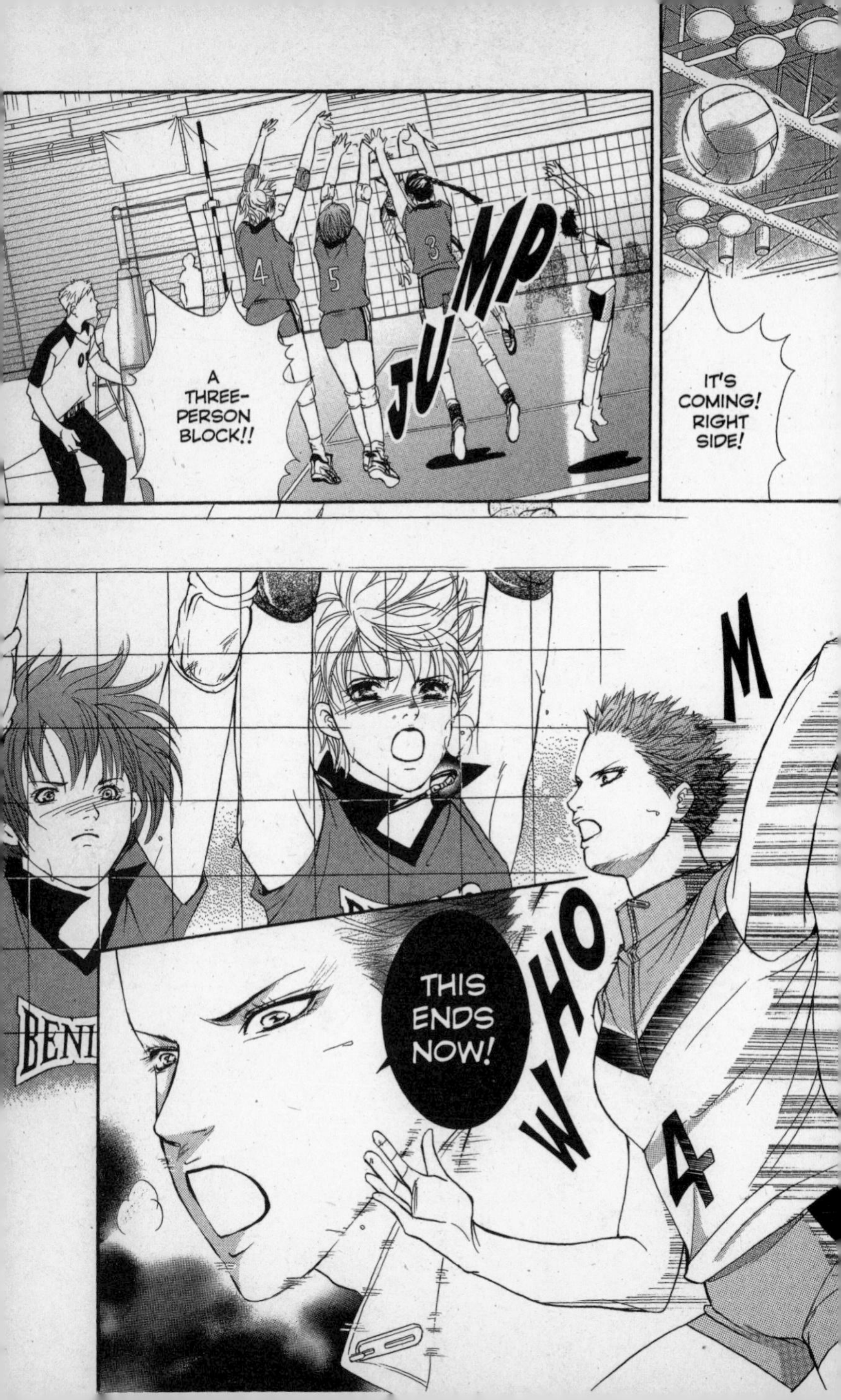
IT'S COMING! RIGHT SIDE!
A THREE-PERSON BLOCK!!
JUMP
THIS ENDS NOW!
WHOM

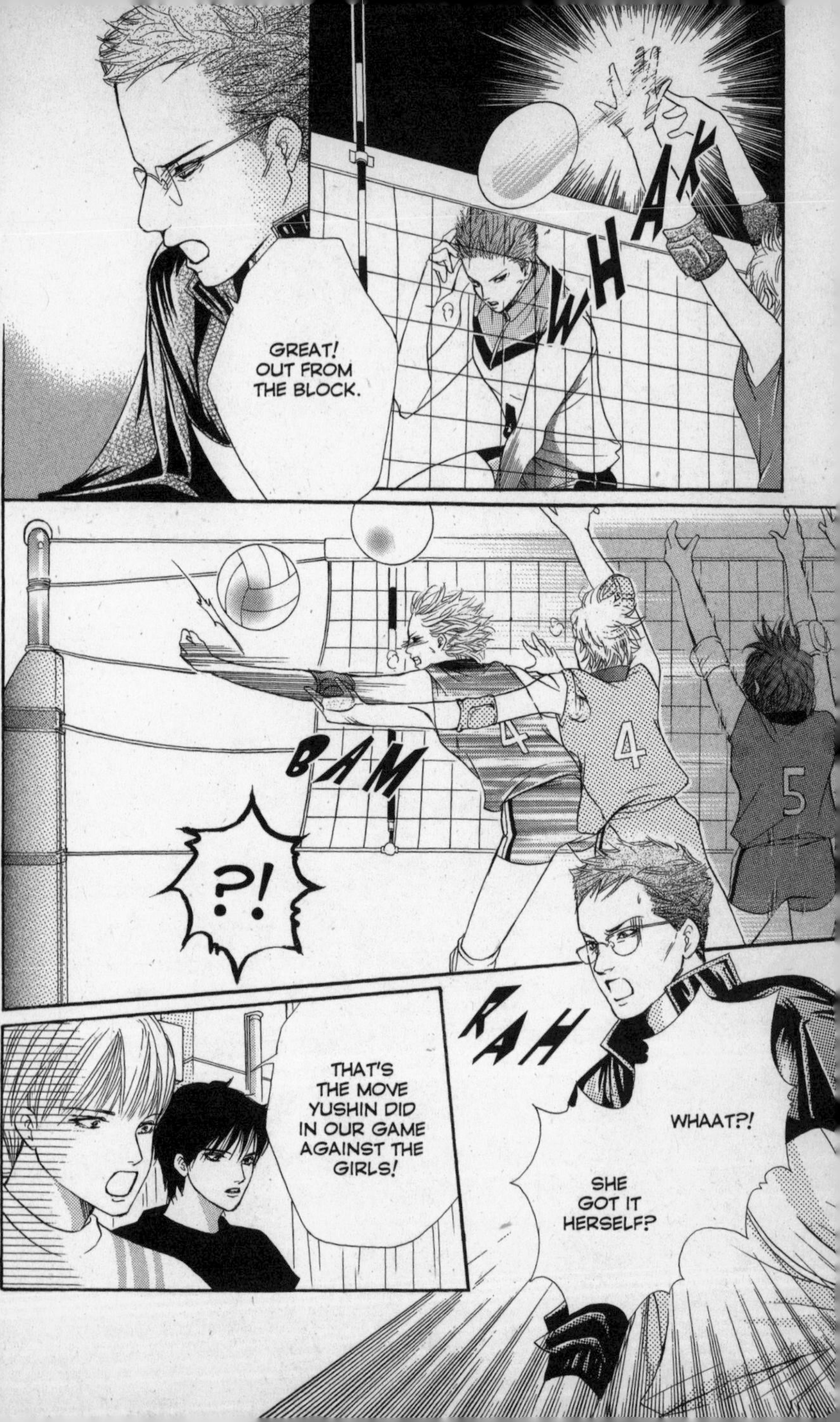
WHAK
GREAT! OUT FROM THE BLOCK.
BAM
?!
RAH
WHAAT?!
SHE GOT IT HERSELF?
THAT'S THE MOVE YUSHIN DID IN OUR GAME AGAINST THE GIRLS!

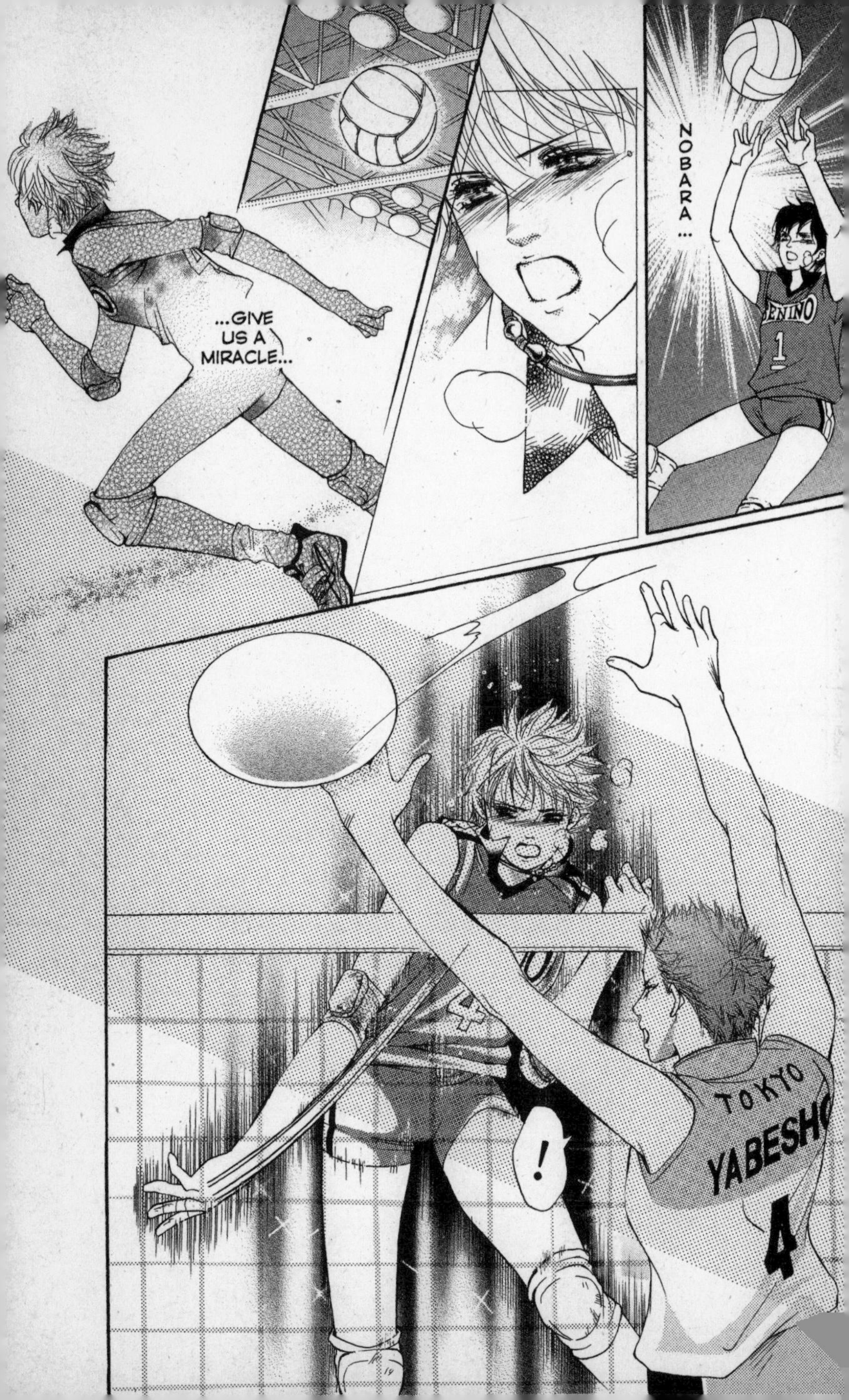
NOBARA...
1
...GIVE US A MIRACLE...
TOKYO YABESHO 4
!

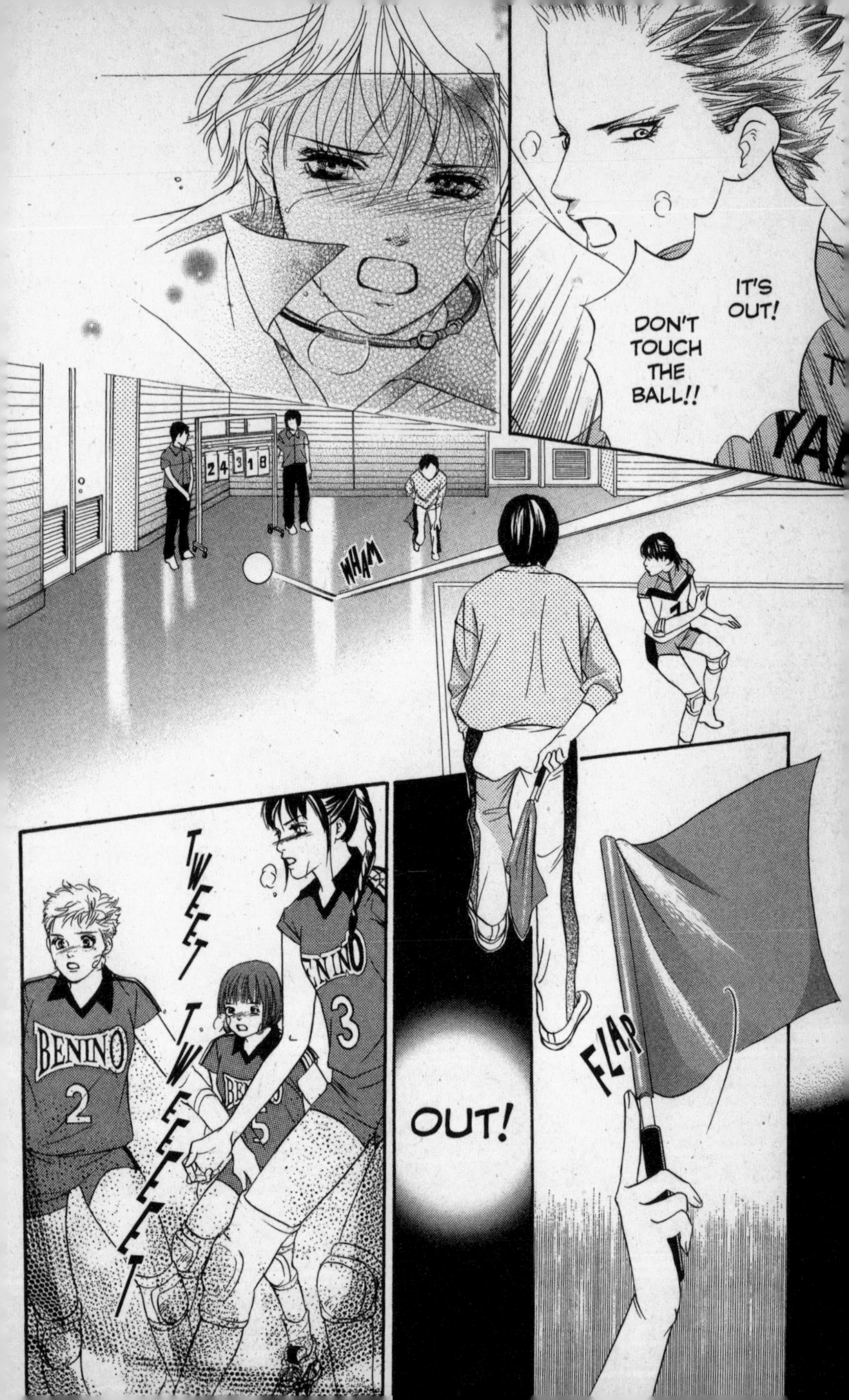
IT'S OUT!
DON'T TOUCH THE BALL!!
WHAM
FLAP
OUT!
TWEET TWEEEEEEET

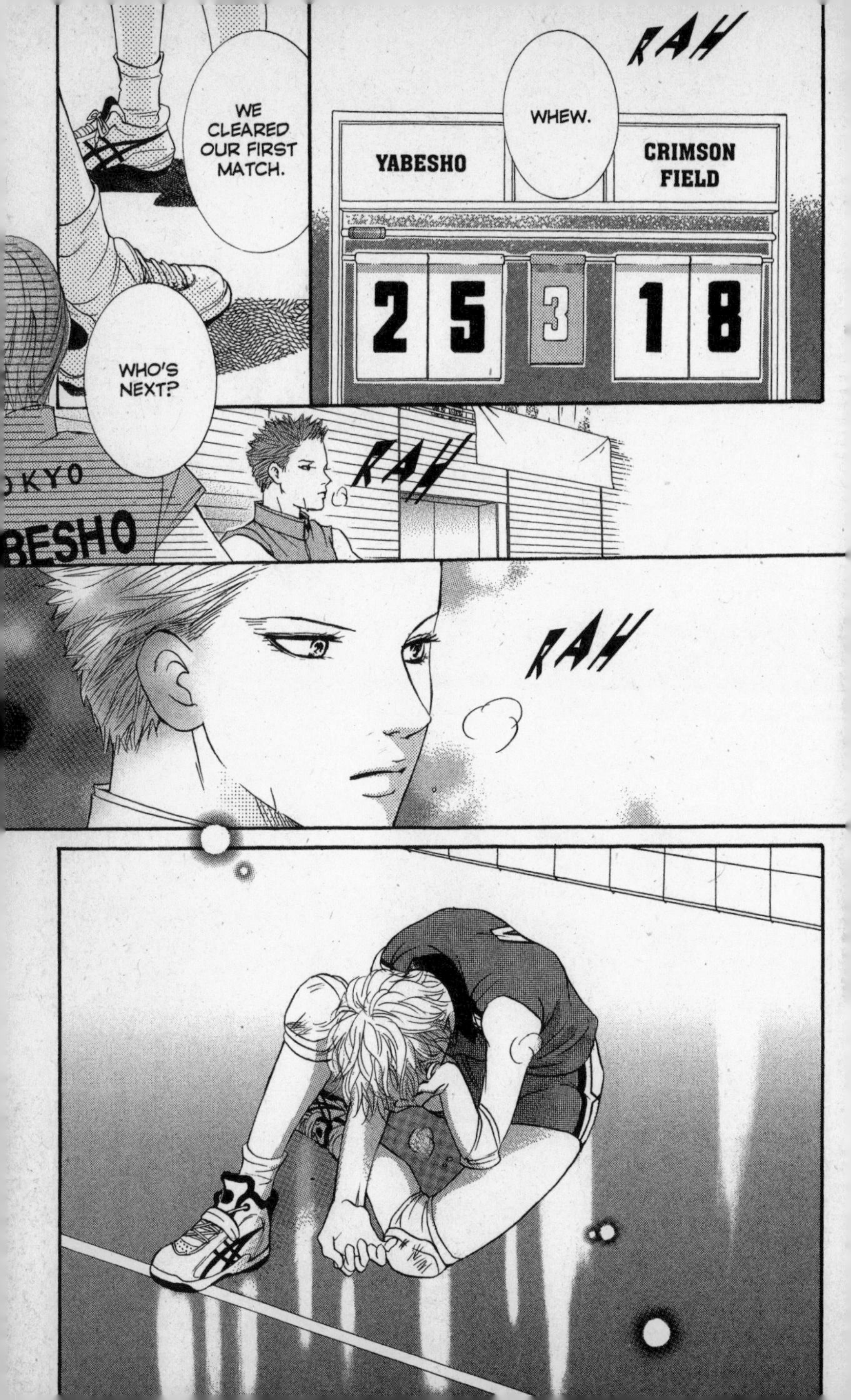
RAH
WHEW.
YABESHO
CRIMSON FIELD
25 3 18
WE CLEARED OUR FIRST MATCH.
WHO'S NEXT?
RAH
OKYO
BESHO
RAH

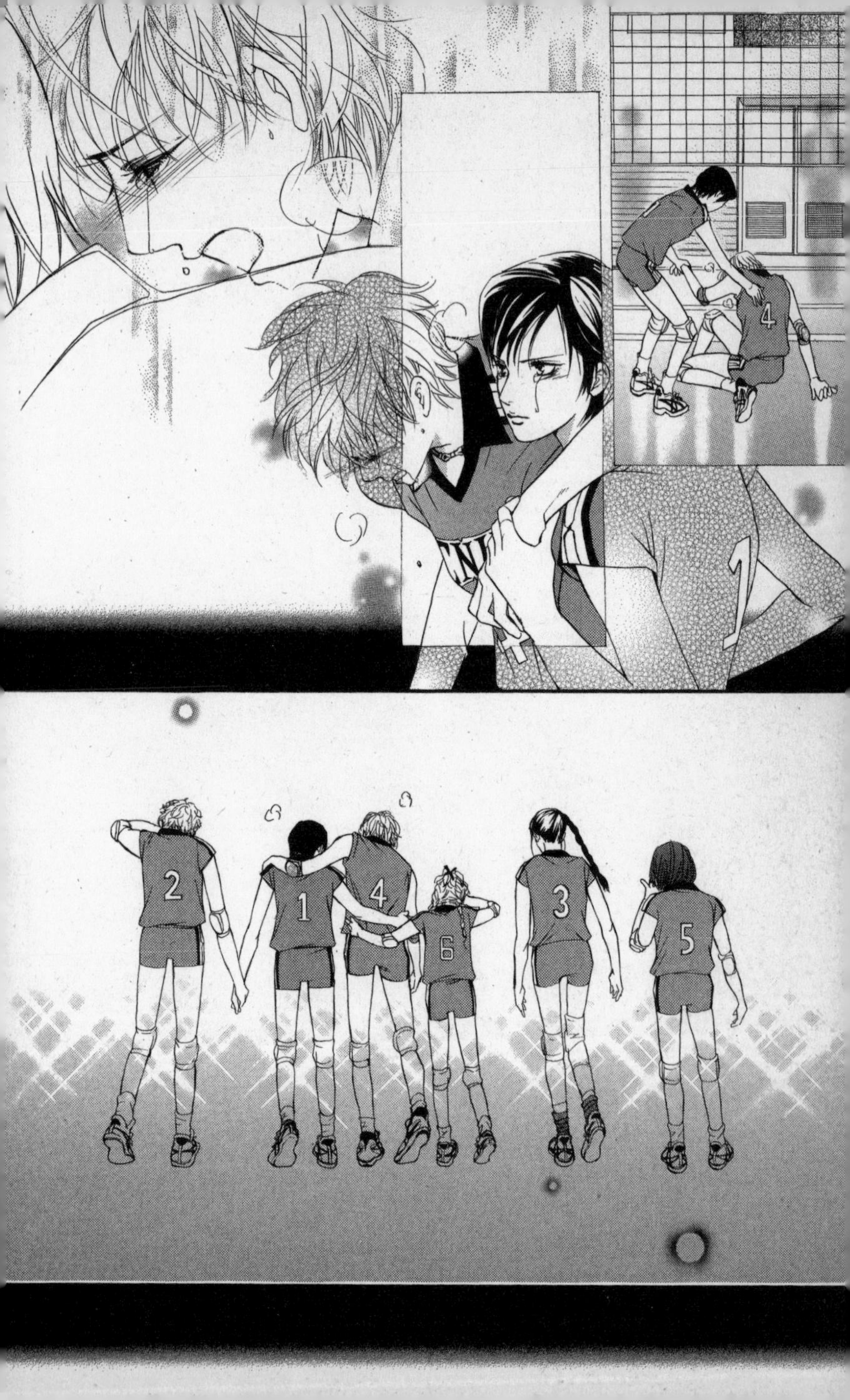

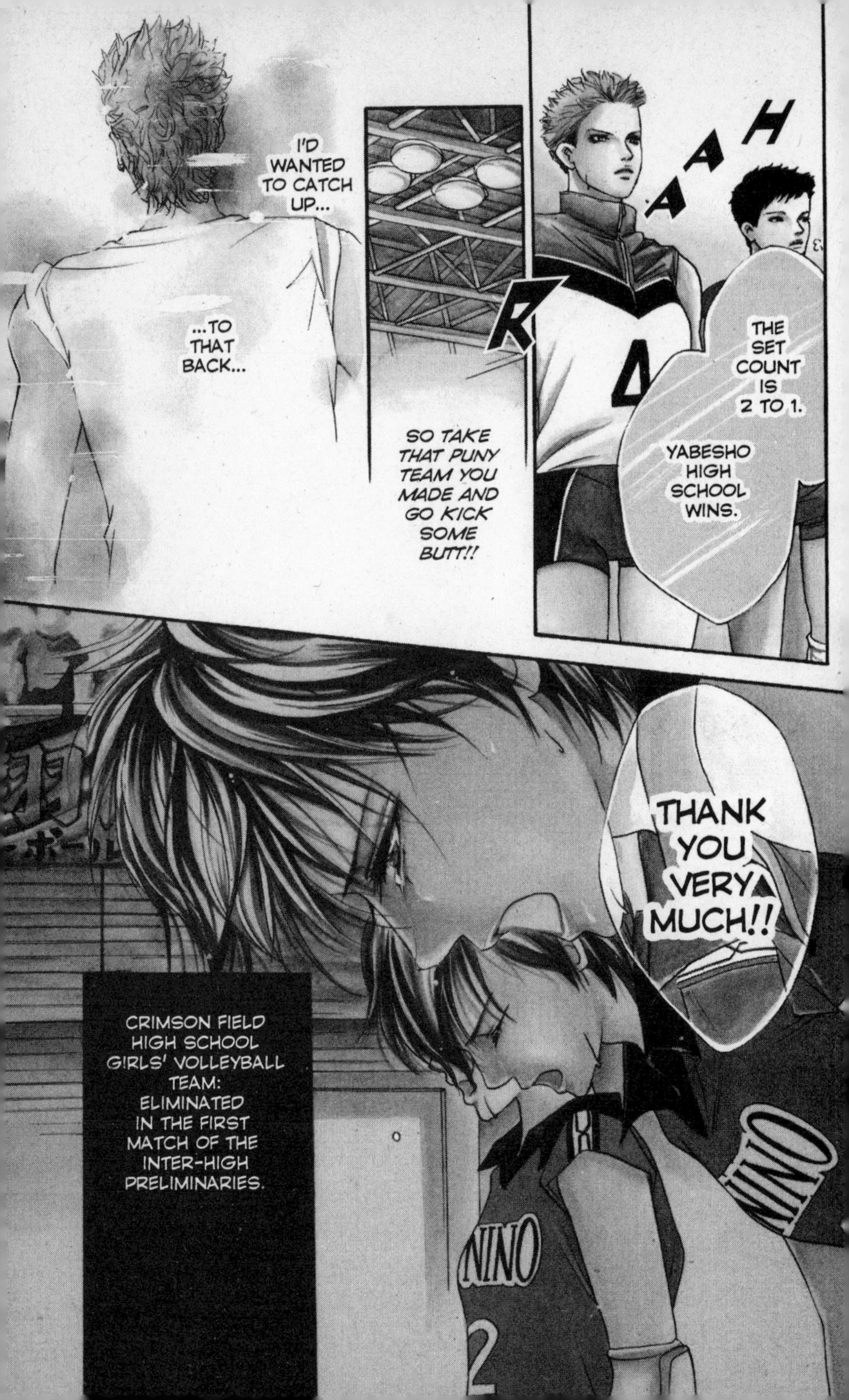
RAAAH
THE SET COUNT IS 2 TO 1.
YABESHO HIGH SCHOOL WINS.
I'D WANTED TO CATCH UP...
...TO THAT BACK...
SO TAKE THAT PUNY TEAM YOU MADE AND GO KICK SOME BUTT!!
THANK YOU VERY MUCH!!
CRIMSON FIELD HIGH SCHOOL GIRLS' VOLLEYBALL TEAM: ELIMINATED IN THE FIRST MATCH OF THE INTER-HIGH PRELIMINARIES.

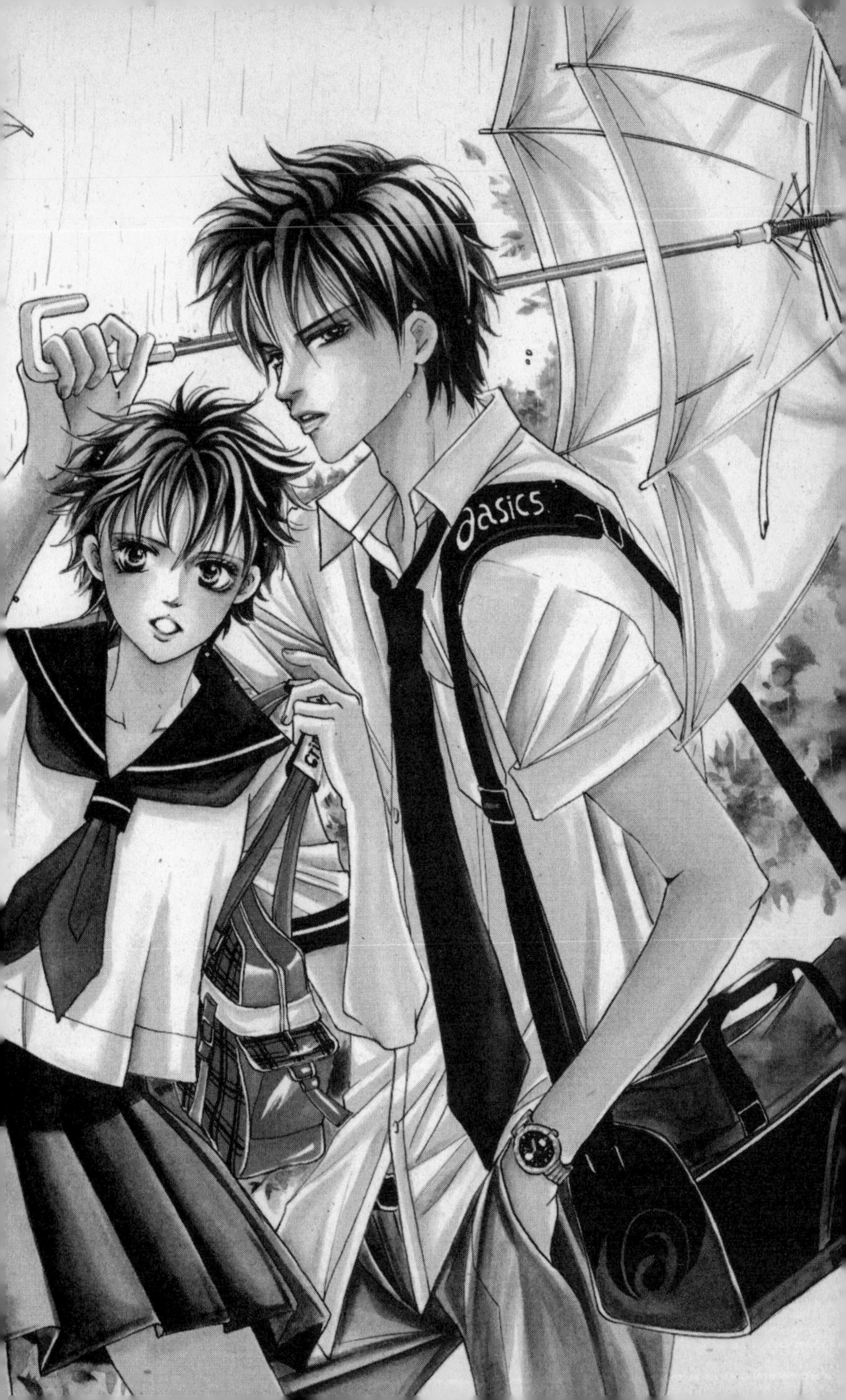
asics

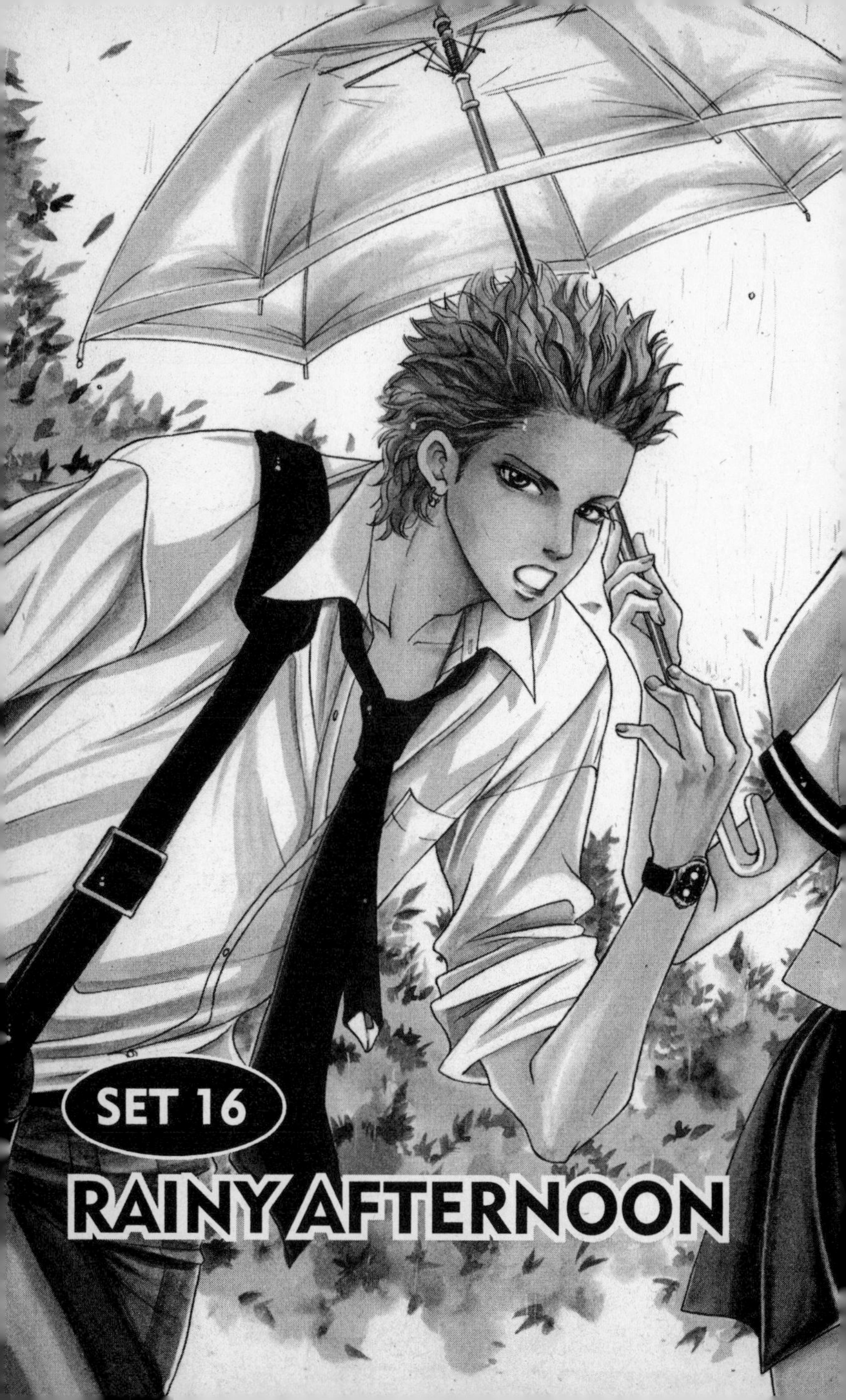
SET 16
RAINY AFTERNOON

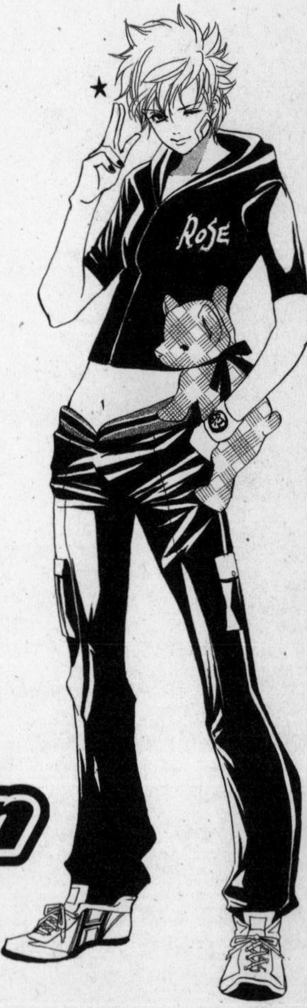
ROSE

Crimson Hero

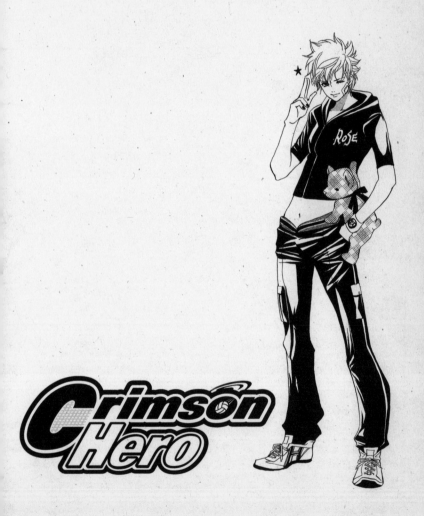

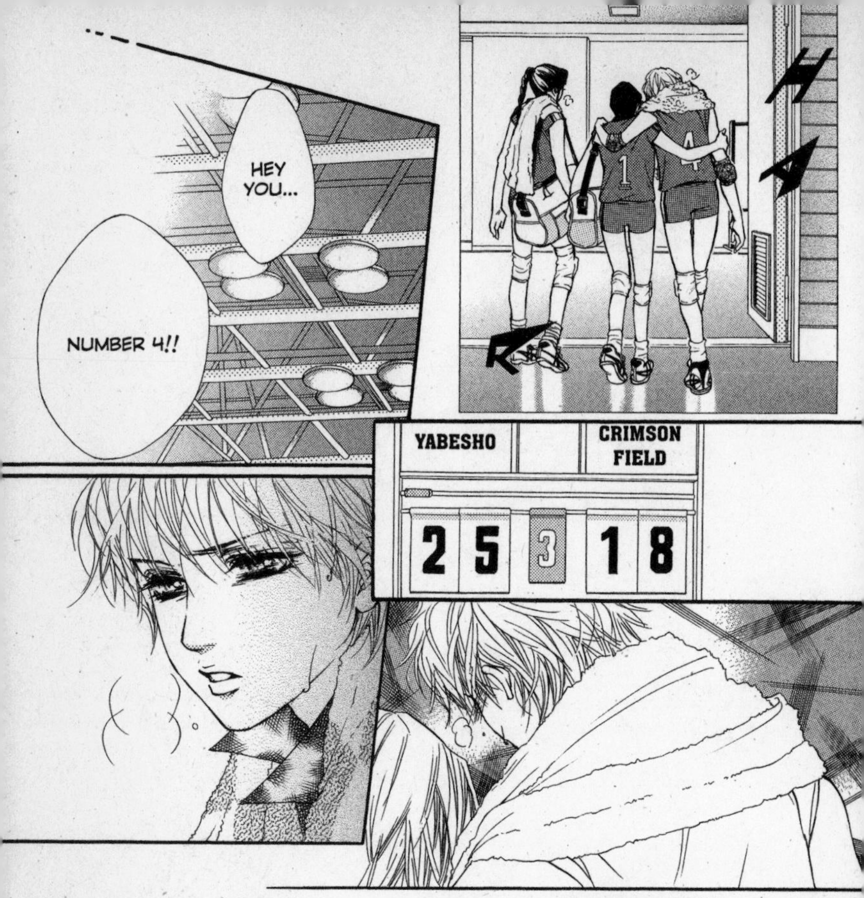
HA
HEY YOU...
NUMBER 4!!
YABESHO
CRIMSON FIELD
25
3
18

THE MAKING OF CRIMSON HERO

Vol.3

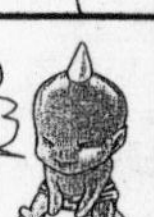

DORM RESIDENTS, PART 2:
IS THAT SO? THE PRETTY TYPE?

KEISUKE HAIBUKI

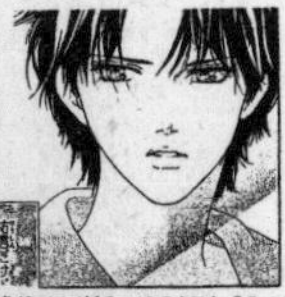

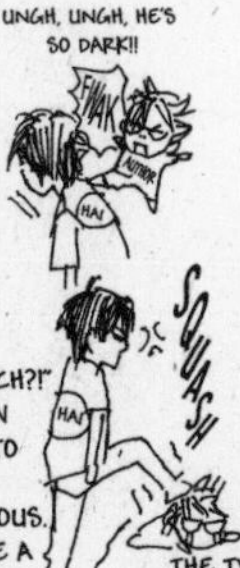
UNGH, UNGH, HE'S SO DARK!!
HAI
AUTHOR
SQUASH

"YOU LIKE NOBARA SO MUCH?!" IS WHAT I THINK AS I DRAW HIM. HIS PERSONALITY IS TO KEEP THINGS BOTTLED INSIDE, WHICH IS DANGEROUS. IT'D BE FUN IF I COULD BE A LITTLE BIT MORE INSPIRED AS I DRAW HIM.

THERE ARE QUITE A LOT OF HAIBUKI FANS. BUT I THINK IF YOU REALLY DATED HIM, IT'D BE QUITE A PAIN. OH, BUT RIGHT. THIS IS MANGA, SO IT'S OKAY. I HOPE HE CAN BE HAPPY SOMEDAY... ANYWAY, HE'S THE TYPE OF GUY THAT'S NOT GOOD AT FOLLOWING THE CROWD.

TOMONORI ICHIBA

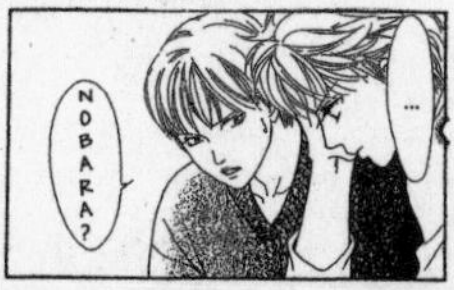
...
NOBARA?

ACTUALLY, HE'S QUITE THE PRETTY TYPE, TOO. I DON'T HAVE MANY OPPORTUNITIES TO DRAW CLOSE-UPS OF HIM. HE WENT TO THE SAME JUNIOR HIGH AS HAIBUKI. HE'S A CUTE GUY-THE TYPE THAT GETS ALONG WITH PRETTY MUCH EVERYONE. AND HE'S A FEMINIST, THOUGH HE OVERREACTS TO THINGS. HE'S GIRLISH, AND I LIKE HIM.

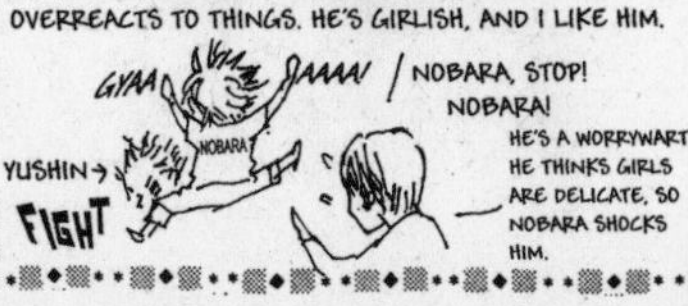
GYAA
AAAA!
NOBARA, STOP! NOBARA!
NOBARA
YUSHIN
FIGHT
HE'S A WORRYWART. HE THINKS GIRLS ARE DELICATE, SO NOBARA SHOCKS HIM.

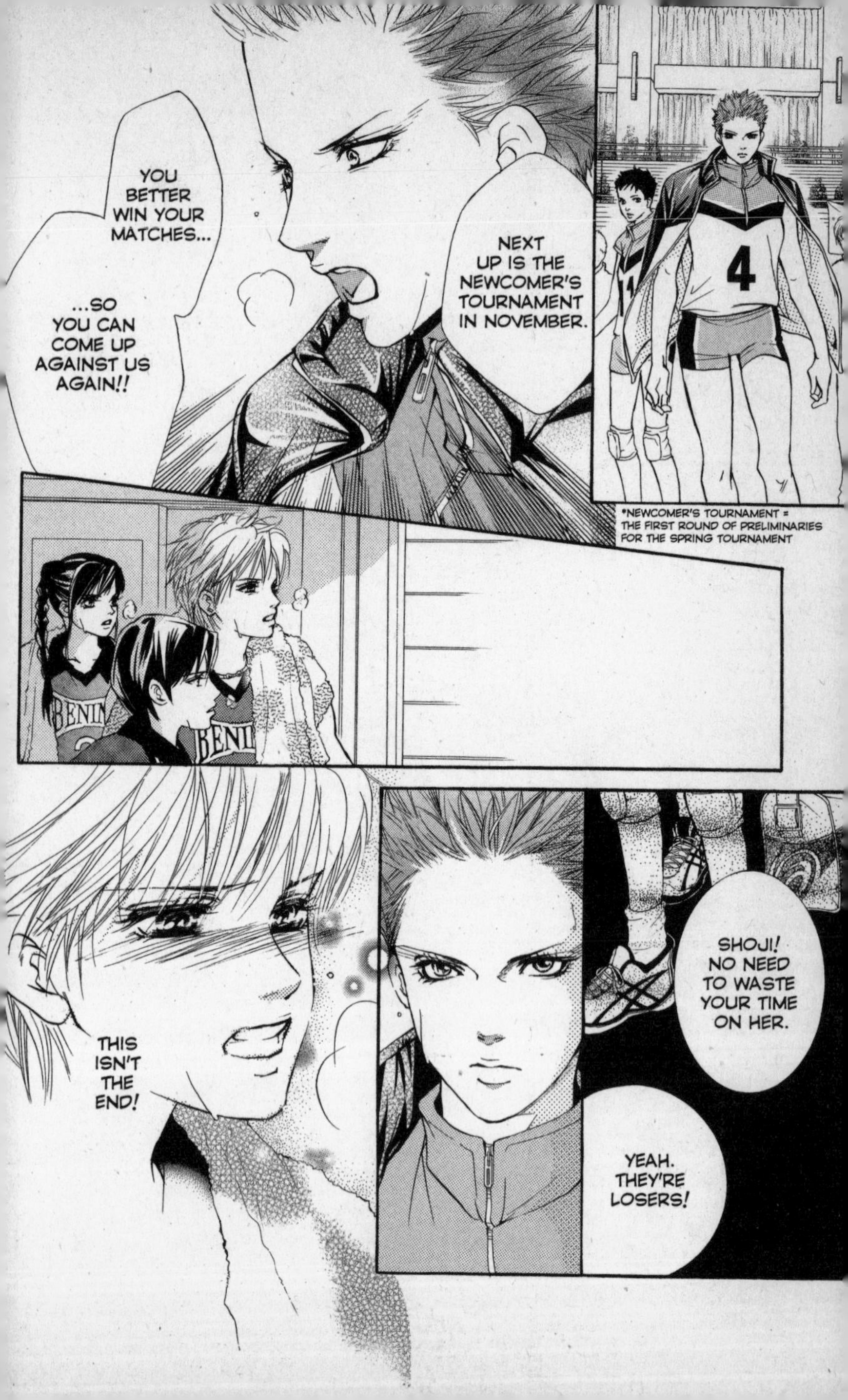
NEXT UP IS THE NEWCOMER'S TOURNAMENT IN NOVEMBER.
YOU BETTER WIN YOUR MATCHES...
...SO YOU CAN COME UP AGAINST US AGAIN!!
*NEWCOMER'S TOURNAMENT = THE FIRST ROUND OF PRELIMINARIES FOR THE SPRING TOURNAMENT
SHOJI! NO NEED TO WASTE YOUR TIME ON HER.
YEAH. THEY'RE LOSERS!
THIS ISN'T THE END!

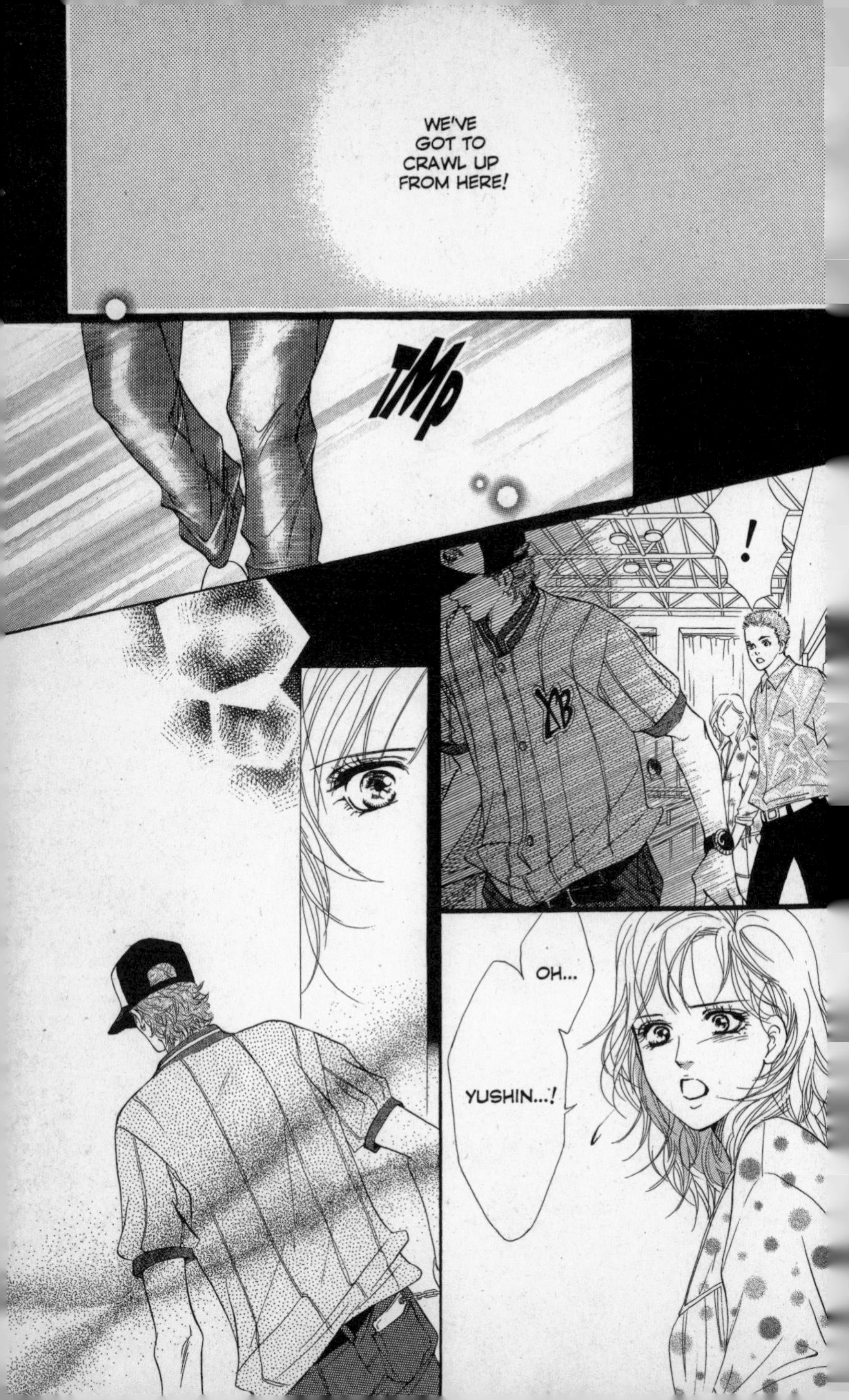
WE'VE GOT TO CRAWL UP FROM HERE!
TMP
!
OH...
YUSHIN...!

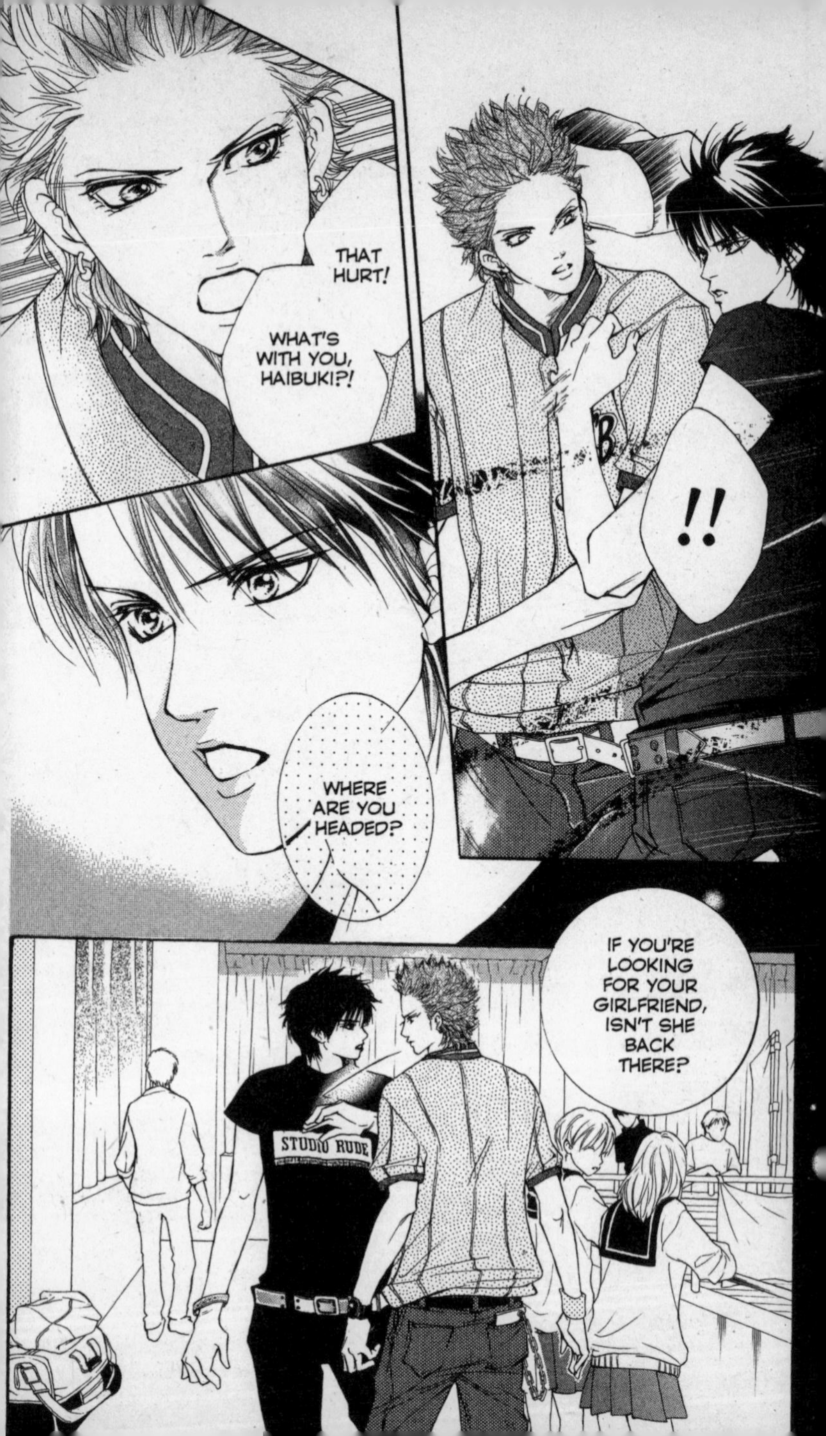
!!
THAT HURT!
WHAT'S WITH YOU, HAIBUKI?!
WHERE ARE YOU HEADED?
IF YOU'RE LOOKING FOR YOUR GIRLFRIEND, ISN'T SHE BACK THERE?
STUDIO RUDE

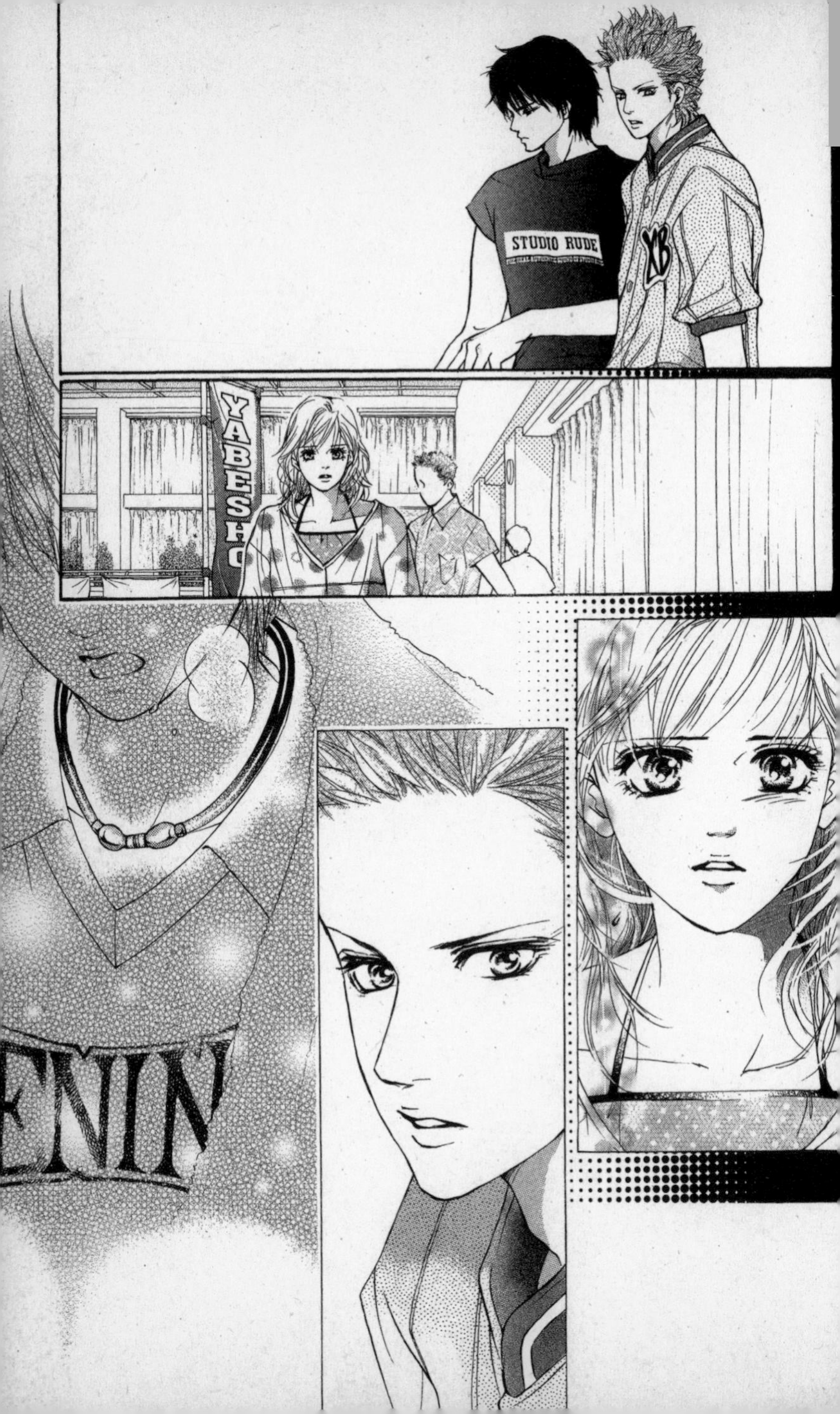
STUDIO RUDE
YABESHO

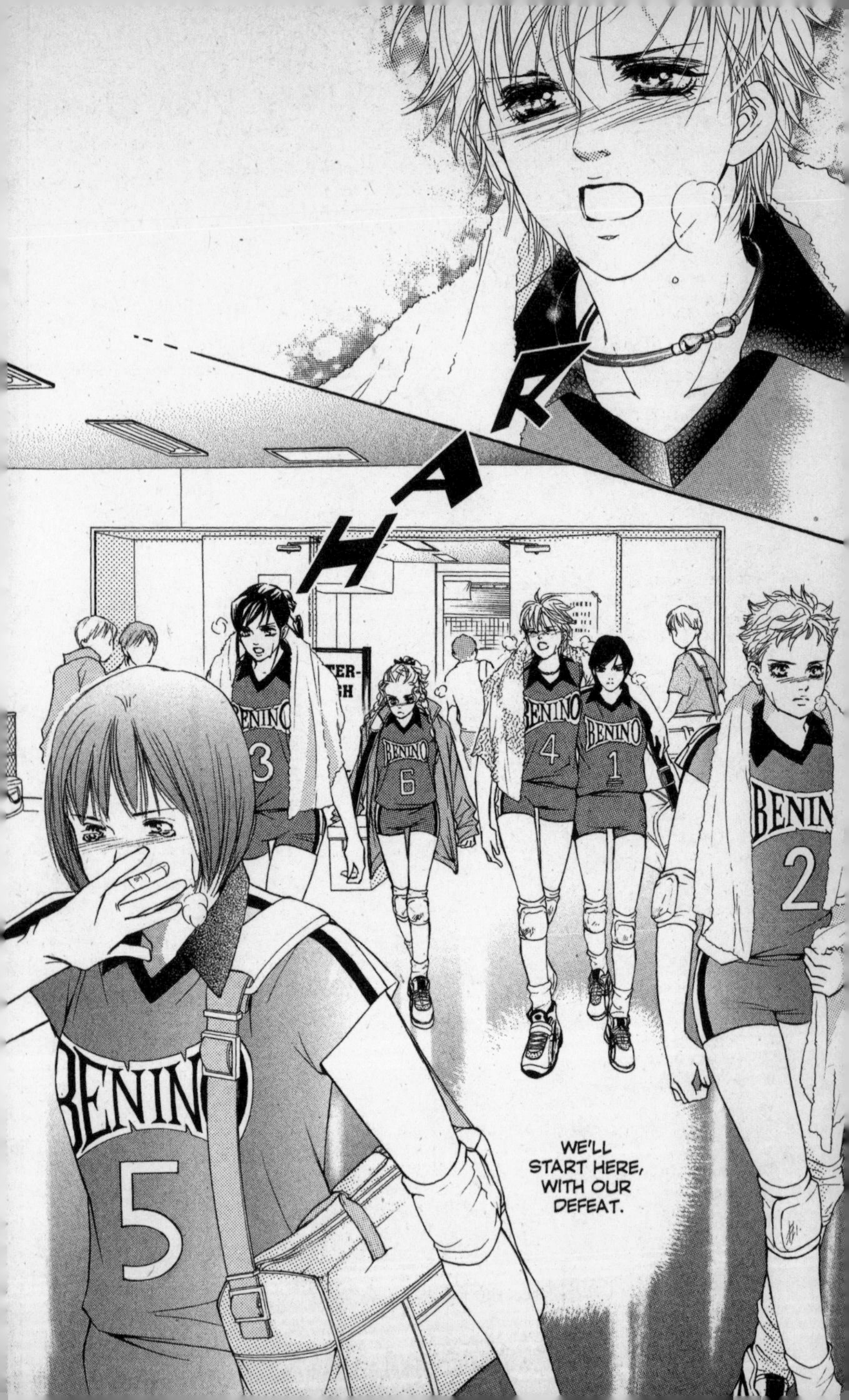
HAR
WE'LL START HERE, WITH OUR DEFEAT.

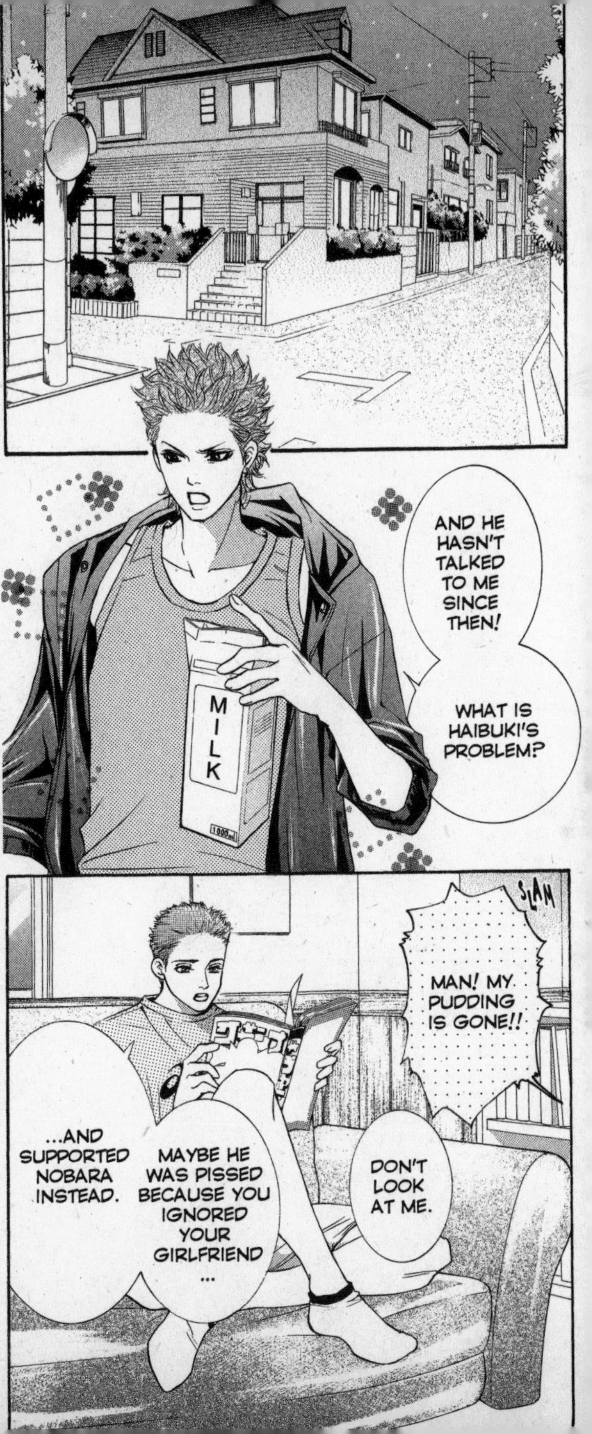
AND HE HASN'T TALKED TO ME SINCE THEN!
WHAT IS HAIBUKI'S PROBLEM?
SLAM
MAN! MY PUDDING IS GONE!!
DON'T LOOK AT ME.
MAYBE HE WAS PISSED BECAUSE YOU IGNORED YOUR GIRLFRIEND ...
...AND SUPPORTED NOBARA INSTEAD.

MITSUBA CLUB

Vol. 4

SO, HOW DID YOU LIKE VOLUME 4? DRAWING ABOUT VOLLEYBALL IS REALLY HARD AND NO MATTER HOW MUCH I RESEARCH OR READ BOOKS, I DON'T KNOW WHAT I DON'T KNOW. SO I'VE DECIDED TO TAKE THE ATTITUDE THAT I'LL ONLY WRITE ABOUT THE THINGS I'VE FELT! I'VE ALWAYS HAD THE BAD HABIT OF WORRYING TOO MUCH, SO I'VE JUST NOW DECIDED TO MAKE THIS MANGA FUN AND CHEERFUL!! (WHERE?!) BASICALLY, NO MATTER WHAT I DO OR WORRY ABOUT, IN THE END I DO THIS BECAUSE I ENJOY IT. IT'D BE GREAT IF THIS WORK BECOMES SOMETHING YOU LOVE AS ONE OF YOUR AMUSEMENTS.

— Special Thanks —

Nina.
Chie. Abe
Ayako. Shitou
Kanon. Ozawa
Sayuri. Kawasugi
+
Aiji Yamakawa
Noriko. Ohtani
Mimi. Tamura
Naomi. Minamoto
Chiharu. Kumagai
+
S. Imai
+
Ryo

--SEND LETTERS TO--

MITSUBA TAKANASHI
EDITORIAL DEPARTMENT
SHUEISHA "BESSATSU MARGARET"
2-5-10 HITOTSUBASHI
CHIYODA-KU, TOKYO
101-8050
JAPAN

WELL THEN, EVERYONE, SEE YOU IN VOLUME 5. MAYBE NOBARA'S LOVE LIFE WILL DEVELOP A LITTLE MORE!!!!

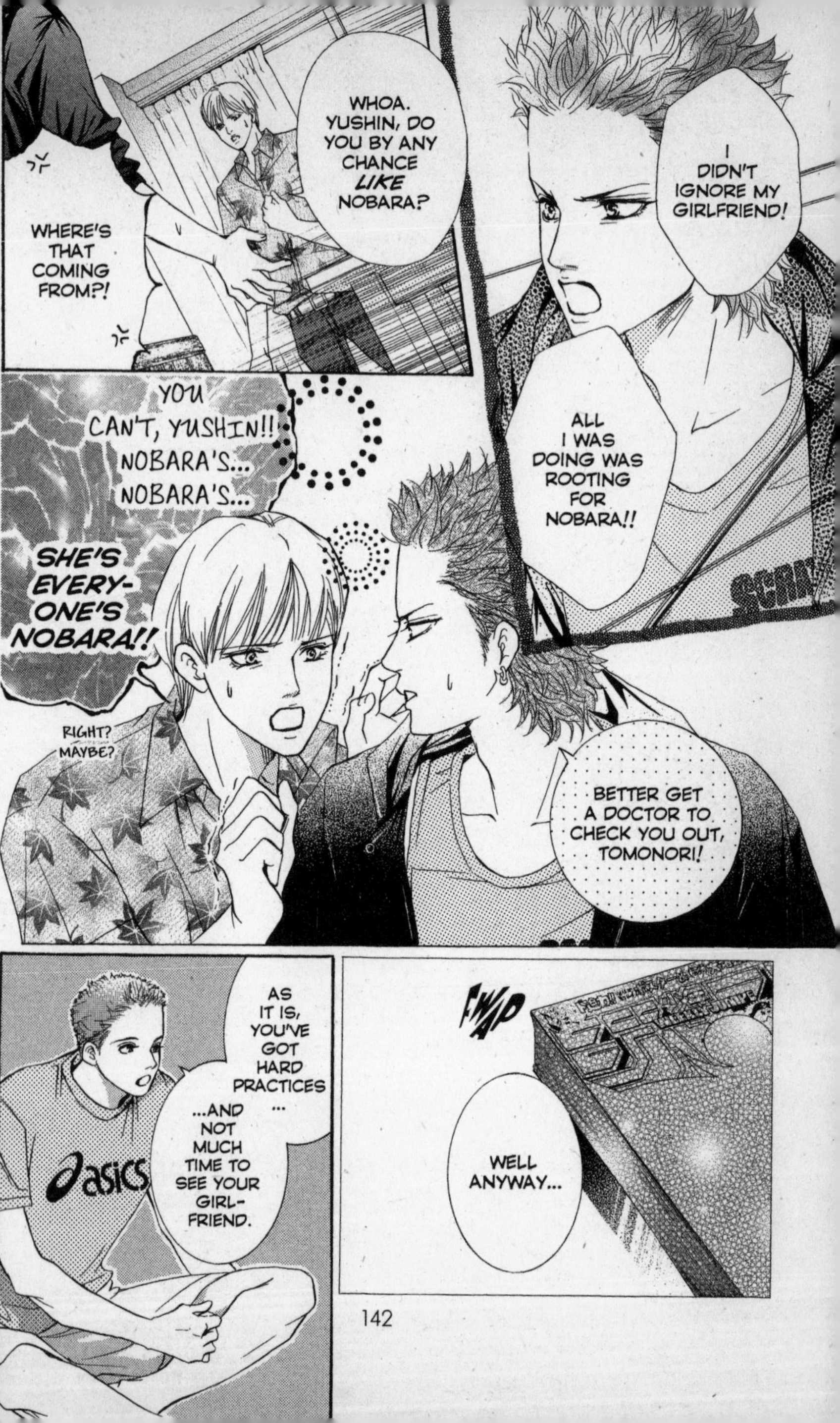

I DIDN'T IGNORE MY GIRLFRIEND!
ALL I WAS DOING WAS ROOTING FOR NOBARA!!
WHOA. YUSHIN, DO YOU BY ANY CHANCE *LIKE* NOBARA?
WHERE'S THAT COMING FROM?!
YOU CAN'T, YUSHIN!! NOBARA'S... NOBARA'S...
SHE'S EVERYONE'S NOBARA!!
RIGHT? MAYBE?
BETTER GET A DOCTOR TO CHECK YOU OUT, TOMONORI!
FWAP
WELL ANYWAY...
AS IT IS, YOU'VE GOT HARD PRACTICES...
...AND NOT MUCH TIME TO SEE YOUR GIRLFRIEND.

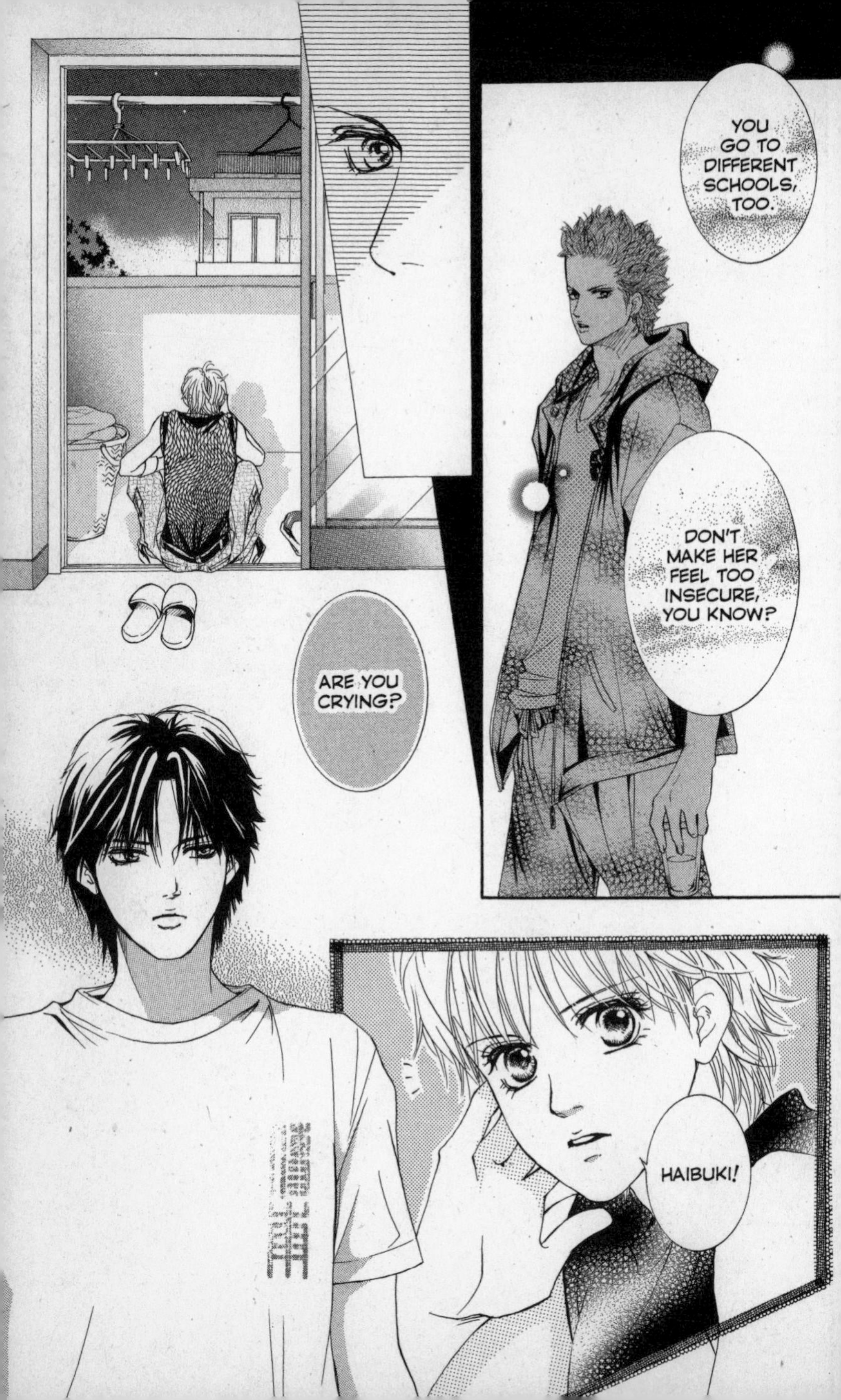
YOU GO TO DIFFERENT SCHOOLS, TOO.
DON'T MAKE HER FEEL TOO INSECURE, YOU KNOW?
ARE YOU CRYING?
HAIBUKI!

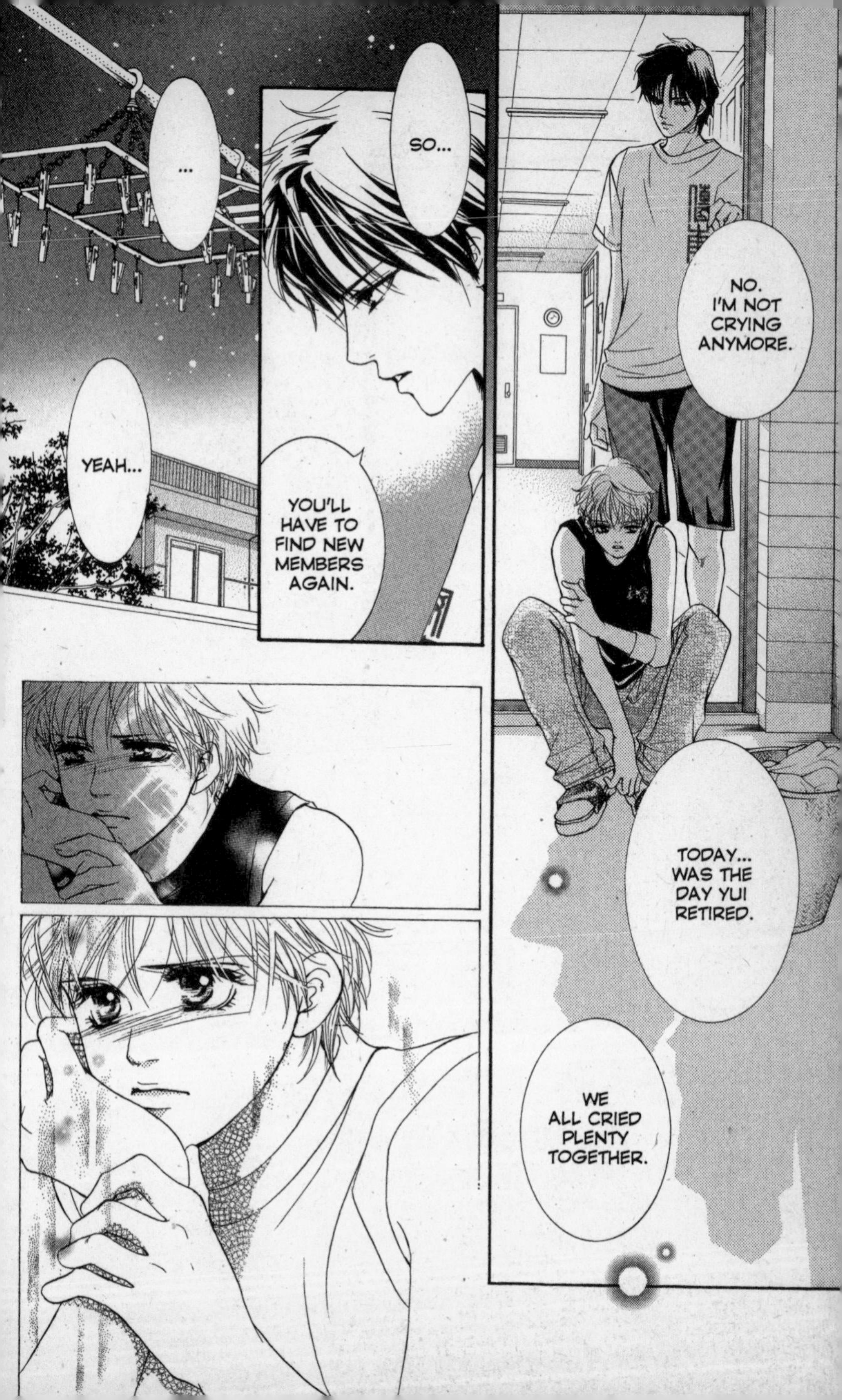
NO. I'M NOT CRYING ANYMORE.
TODAY... WAS THE DAY YUI RETIRED.
WE ALL CRIED PLENTY TOGETHER.
SO...
YOU'LL HAVE TO FIND NEW MEMBERS AGAIN.
...
YEAH...

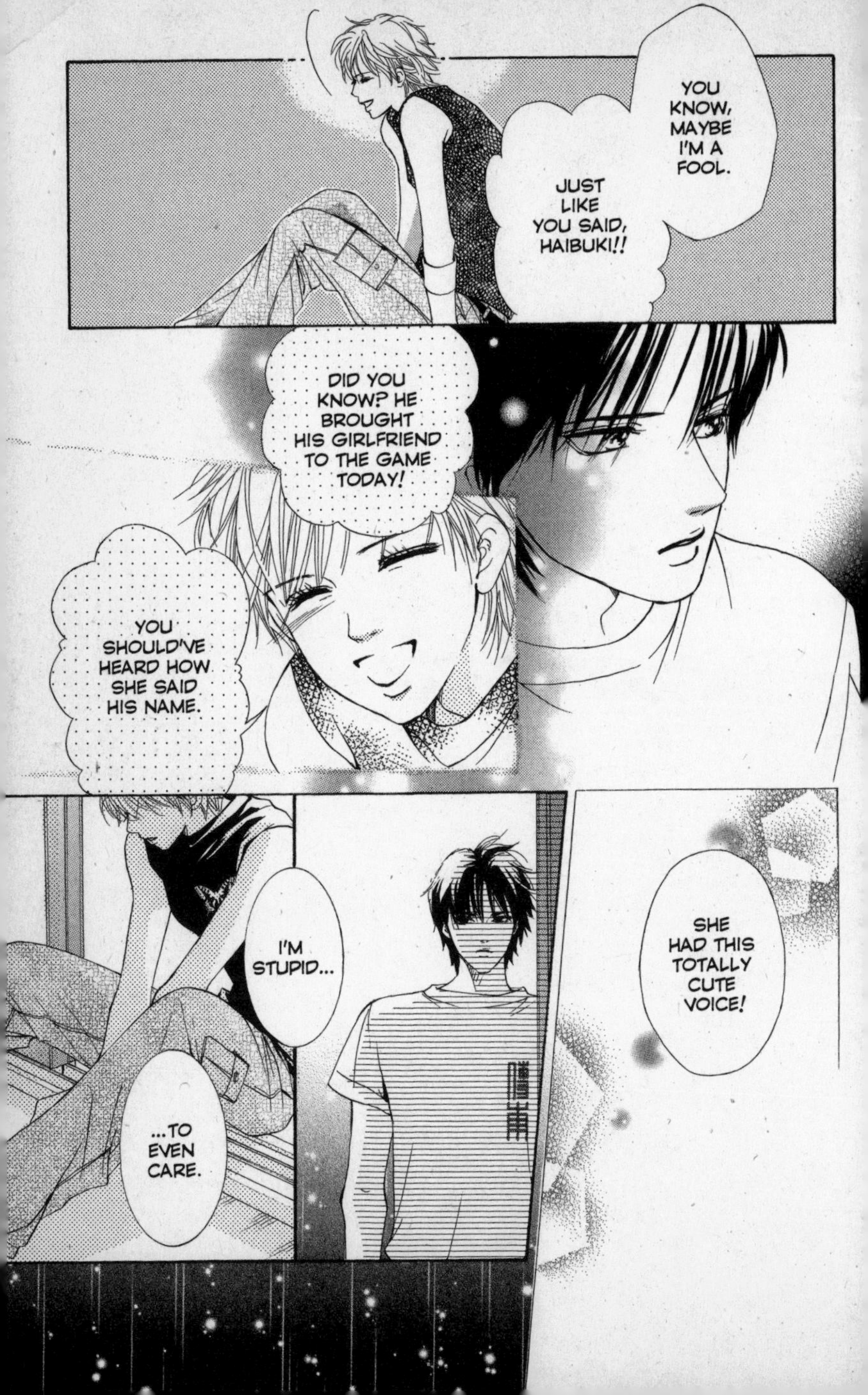
YOU KNOW, MAYBE I'M A FOOL.
JUST LIKE YOU SAID, HAIBUKI!!
DID YOU KNOW? HE BROUGHT HIS GIRLFRIEND TO THE GAME TODAY!
YOU SHOULD'VE HEARD HOW SHE SAID HIS NAME.
SHE HAD THIS TOTALLY CUTE VOICE!
I'M STUPID...
...TO EVEN CARE.

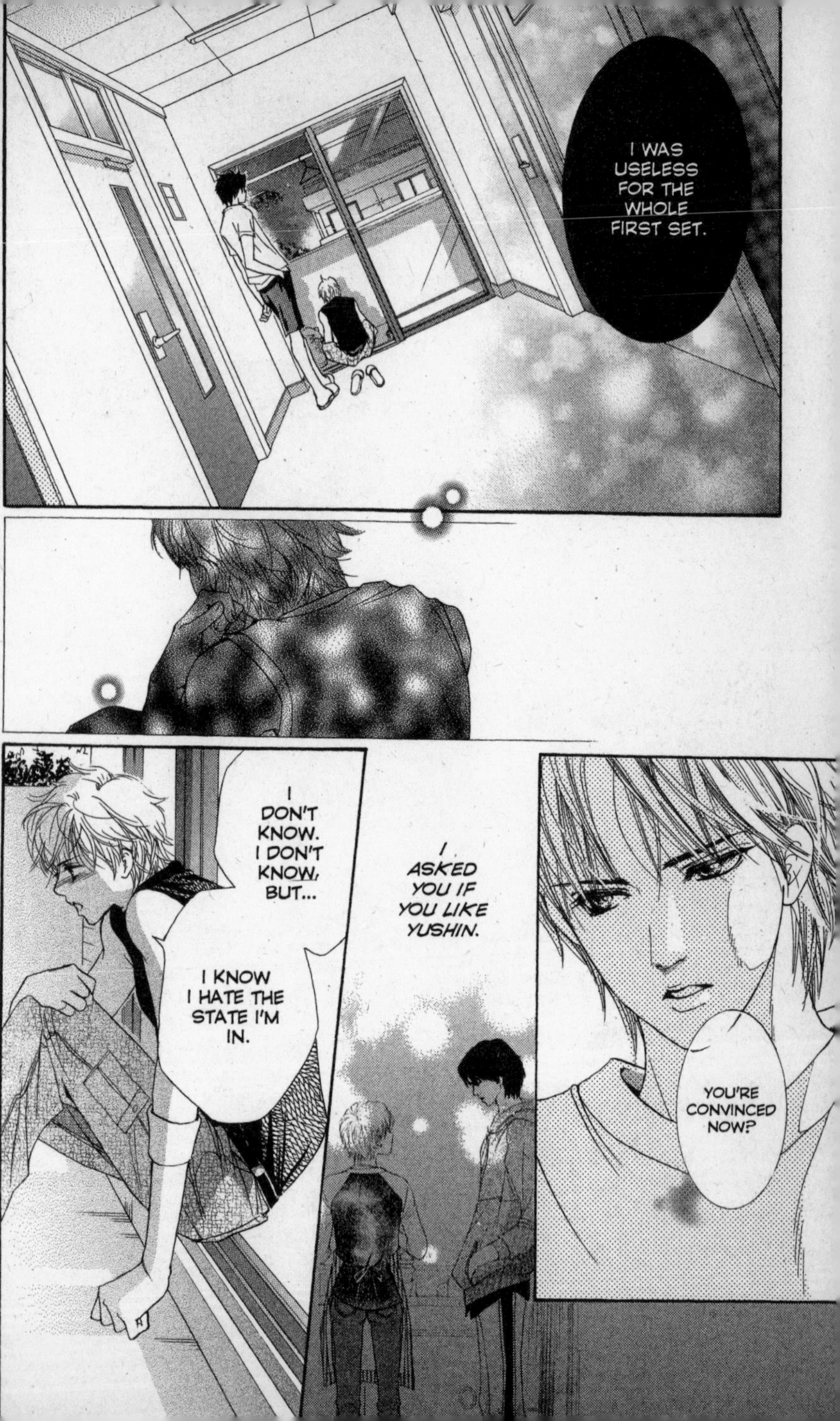
I WAS USELESS FOR THE WHOLE FIRST SET.
YOU'RE CONVINCED NOW?
I ASKED YOU IF YOU LIKE YUSHIN.
I DON'T KNOW. I DON'T KNOW, BUT...
I KNOW I HATE THE STATE I'M IN.

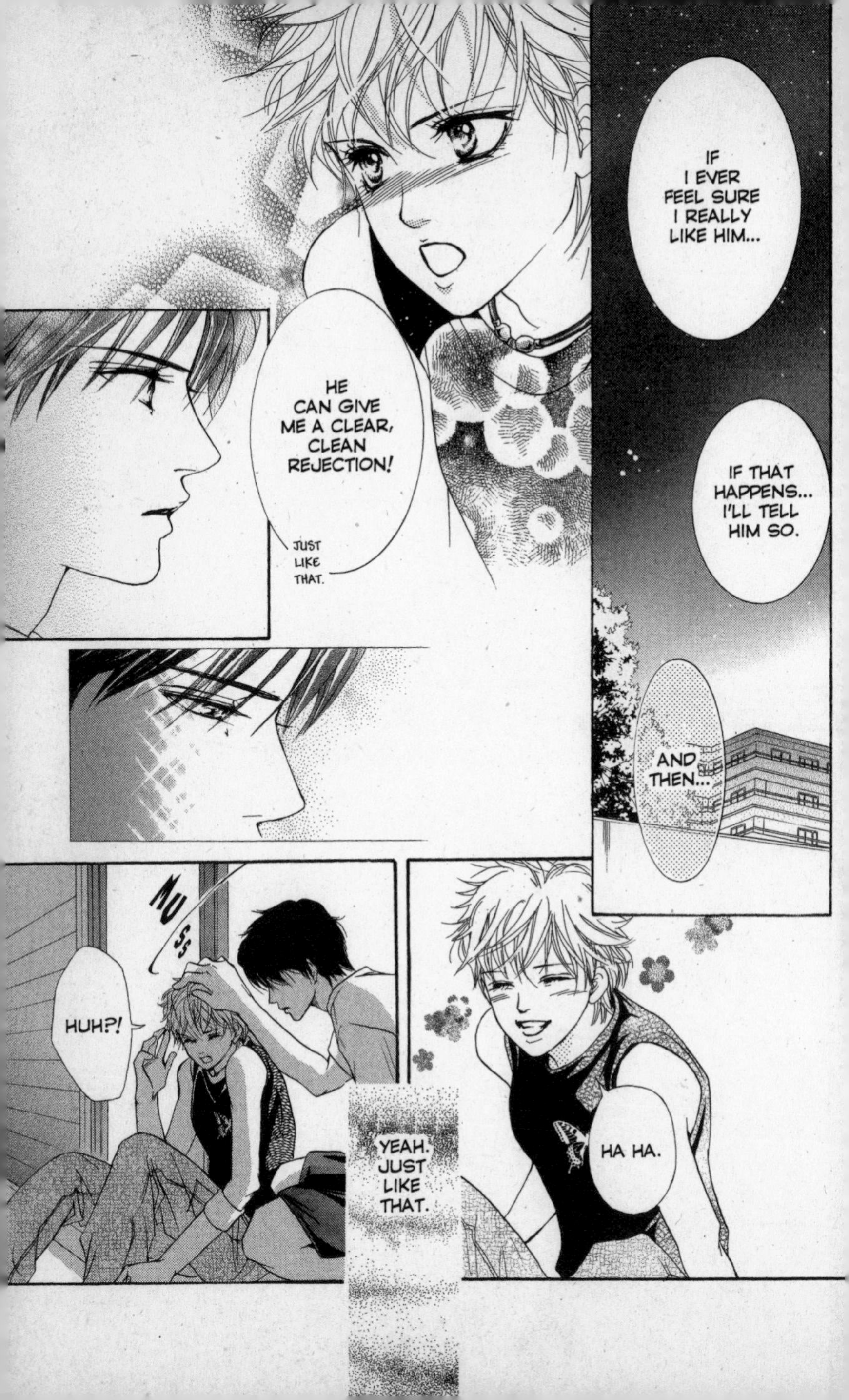
IF I EVER FEEL SURE I REALLY LIKE HIM...
IF THAT HAPPENS... I'LL TELL HIM SO.
AND THEN...
HE CAN GIVE ME A CLEAR, CLEAN REJECTION!
JUST LIKE THAT.
HA HA.
YEAH. JUST LIKE THAT.
MUSS
HUH?!

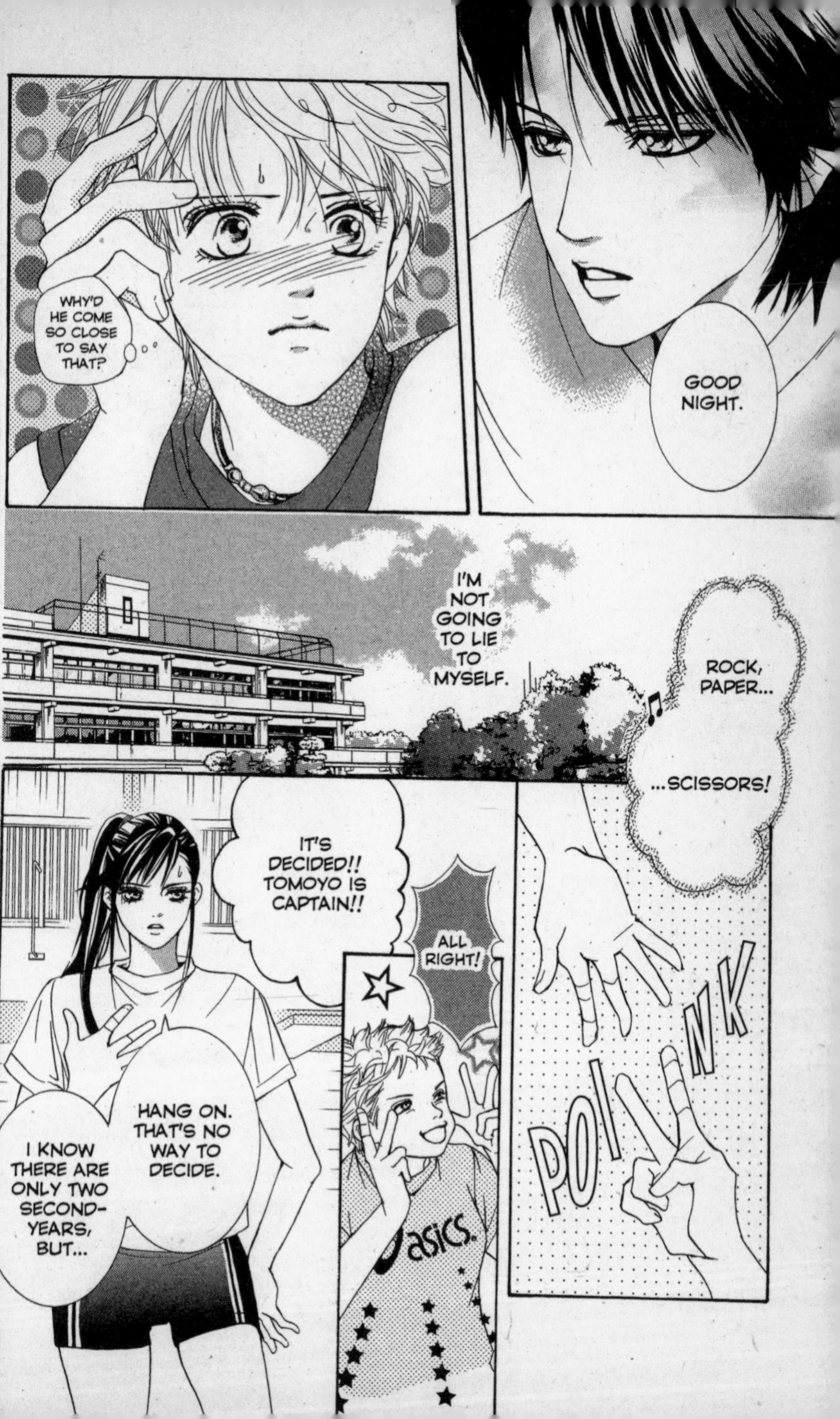
GOOD NIGHT.
WHY'D HE COME SO CLOSE TO SAY THAT?
I'M NOT GOING TO LIE TO MYSELF.
ROCK, PAPER...
...SCISSORS!
POINK
IT'S DECIDED!! TOMOYO IS CAPTAIN!!
ALL RIGHT!
HANG ON. THAT'S NO WAY TO DECIDE.
I KNOW THERE ARE ONLY TWO SECOND-YEARS, BUT...

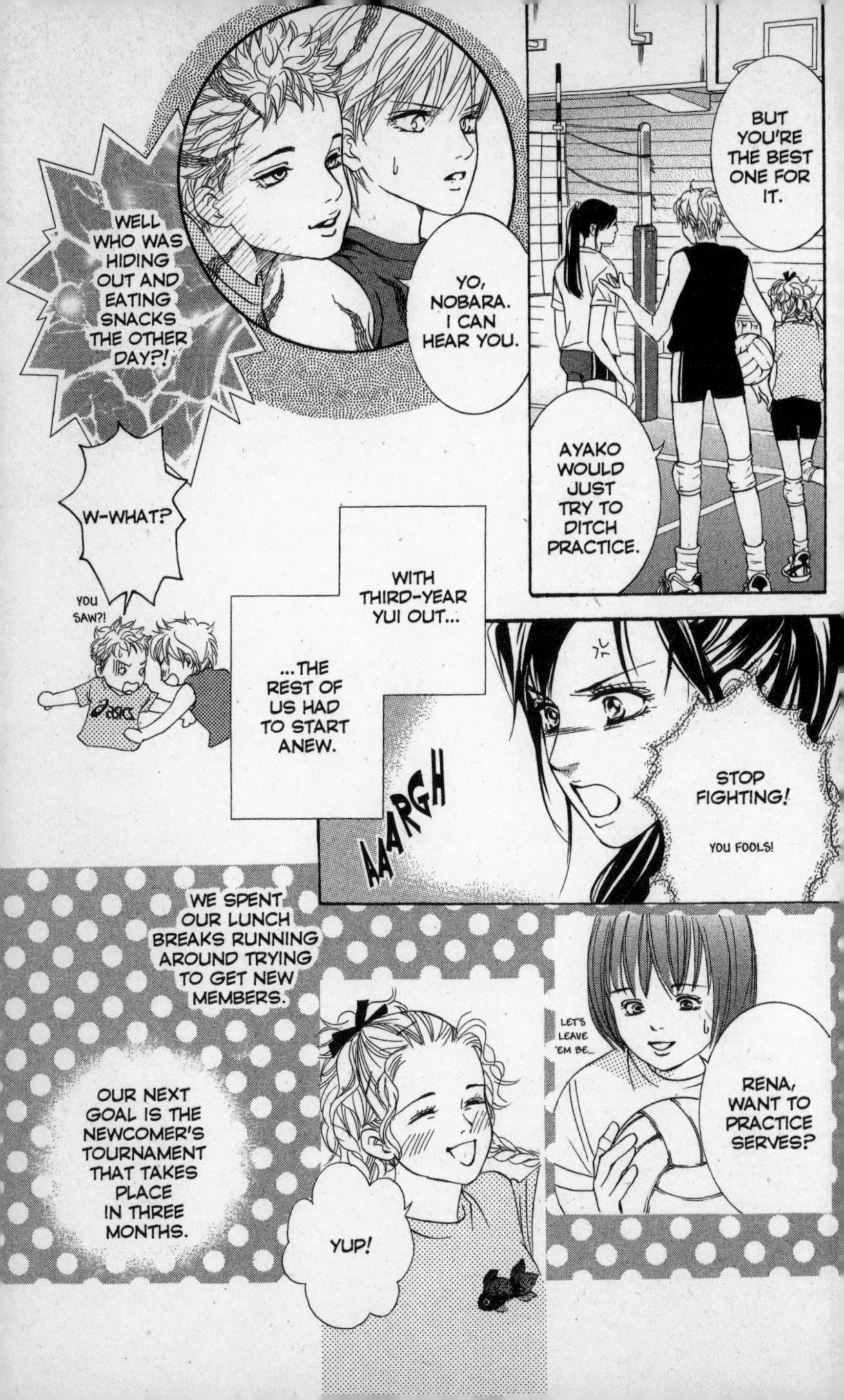
BUT YOU'RE THE BEST ONE FOR IT.
AYAKO WOULD JUST TRY TO DITCH PRACTICE.
YO, NOBARA. I CAN HEAR YOU.
WELL WHO WAS HIDING OUT AND EATING SNACKS THE OTHER DAY?!
W-WHAT?
YOU SAW?!
STOP FIGHTING!
YOU FOOLS!
AARGH
WITH THIRD-YEAR YUI OUT...
...THE REST OF US HAD TO START ANEW.
LET'S LEAVE 'EM BE...
RENA, WANT TO PRACTICE SERVES?
YUP!
WE SPENT OUR LUNCH BREAKS RUNNING AROUND TRYING TO GET NEW MEMBERS.
OUR NEXT GOAL IS THE NEWCOMER'S TOURNAMENT THAT TAKES PLACE IN THREE MONTHS.

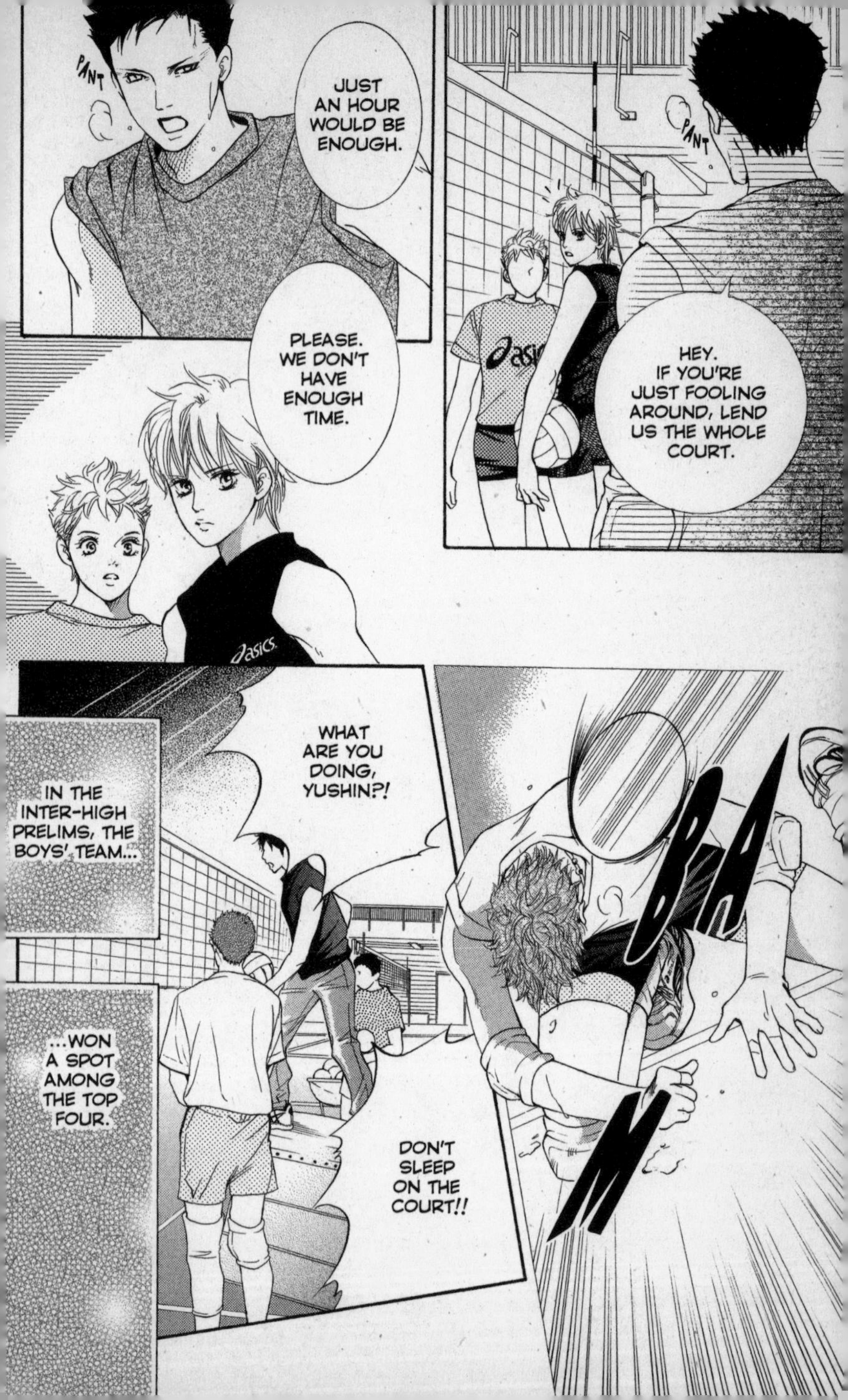
PANT
HEY. IF YOU'RE JUST FOOLING AROUND, LEND US THE WHOLE COURT.
PANT
JUST AN HOUR WOULD BE ENOUGH.
PLEASE. WE DON'T HAVE ENOUGH TIME.
BAM
WHAT ARE YOU DOING, YUSHIN?!
IN THE INTER-HIGH PRELIMS, THE BOYS' TEAM...
...WON A SPOT AMONG THE TOP FOUR.
DON'T SLEEP ON THE COURT!!

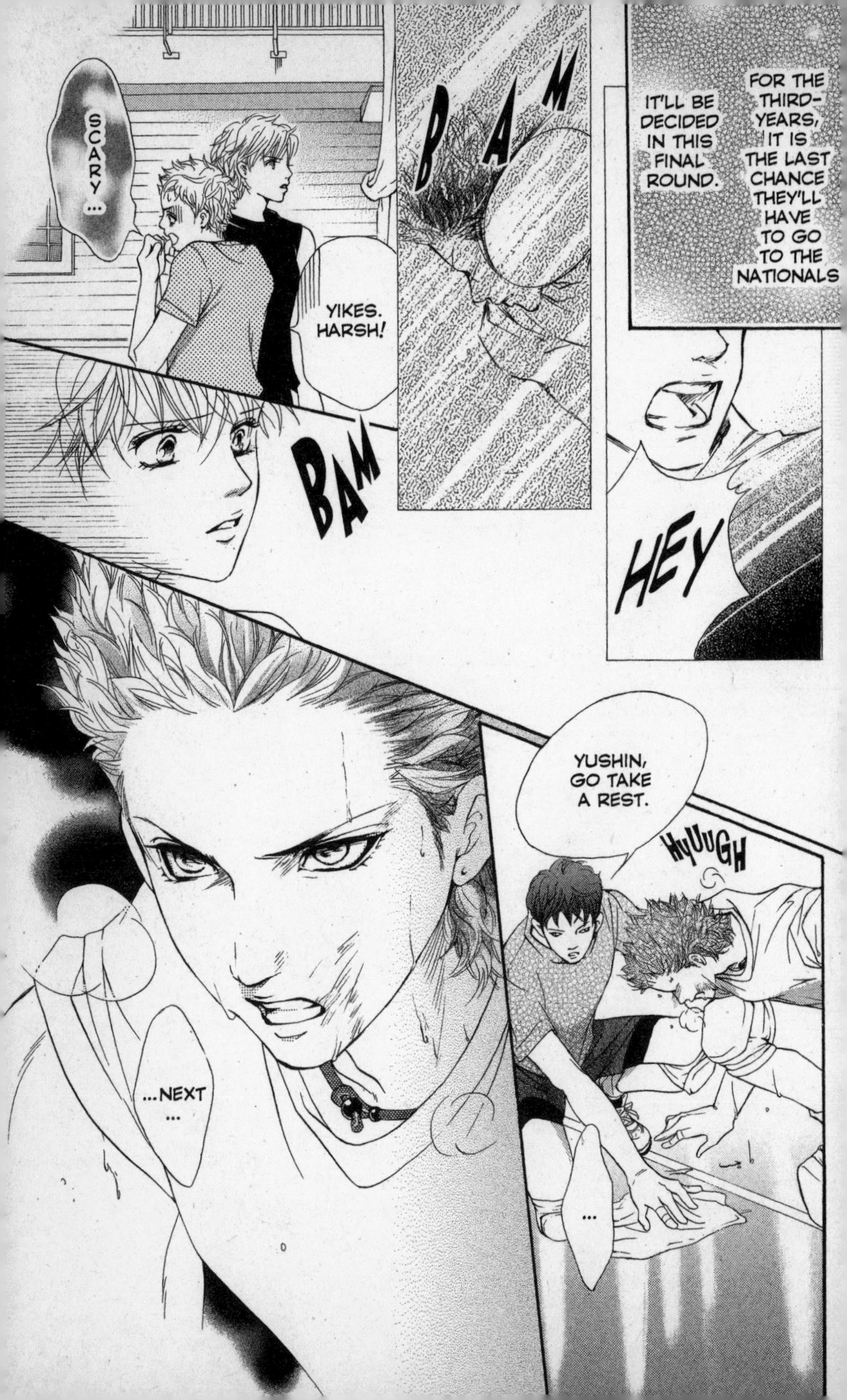
FOR THE THIRD-YEARS, IT IS THE LAST CHANCE THEY'LL HAVE TO GO TO THE NATIONALS
IT'LL BE DECIDED IN THIS FINAL ROUND.
HEY
BAM
YIKES. HARSH!
SCARY...
BAM
YUSHIN, GO TAKE A REST.
HYUUGH
...
...NEXT...

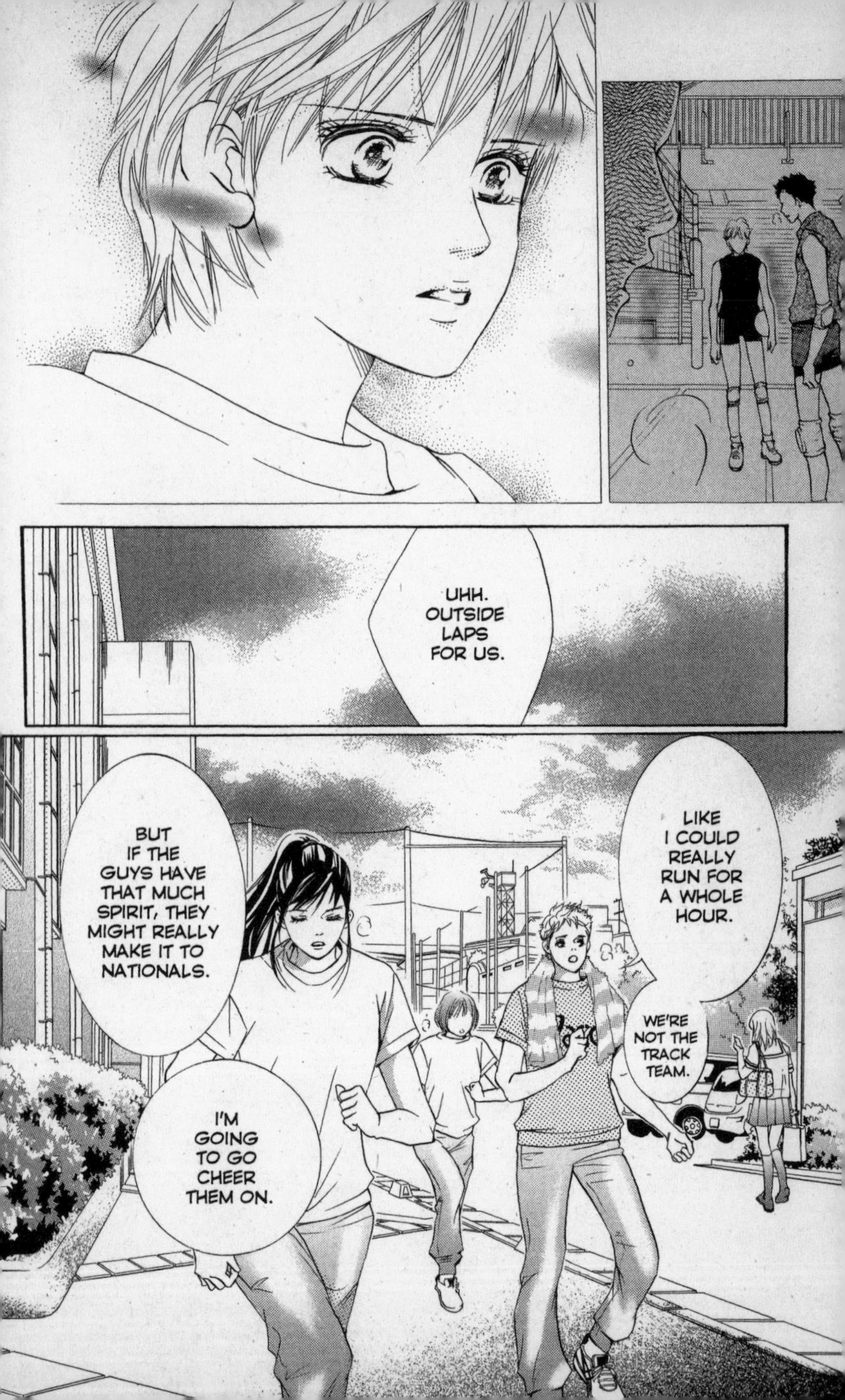
UHH. OUTSIDE LAPS FOR US.
LIKE I COULD REALLY RUN FOR A WHOLE HOUR.
WE'RE NOT THE TRACK TEAM.
BUT IF THE GUYS HAVE THAT MUCH SPIRIT, THEY MIGHT REALLY MAKE IT TO NATIONALS.
I'M GOING TO GO CHEER THEM ON.

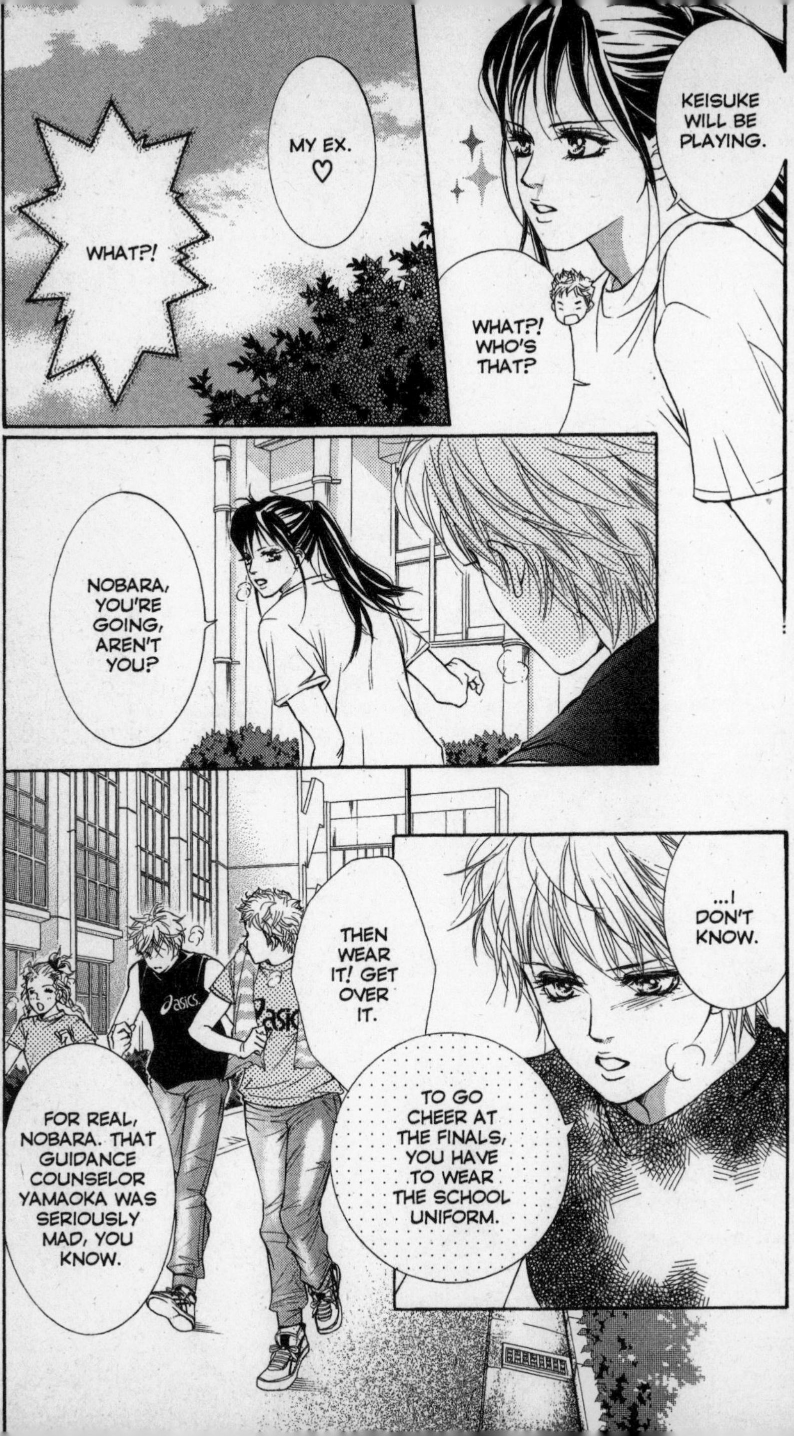
KEISUKE WILL BE PLAYING.
WHAT?! WHO'S THAT?
MY EX. ♡
WHAT?!
NOBARA, YOU'RE GOING, AREN'T YOU?
...I DON'T KNOW.
THEN WEAR IT! GET OVER IT.
TO GO CHEER AT THE FINALS, YOU HAVE TO WEAR THE SCHOOL UNIFORM.
FOR REAL, NOBARA. THAT GUIDANCE COUNSELOR YAMAOKA WAS SERIOUSLY MAD, YOU KNOW.

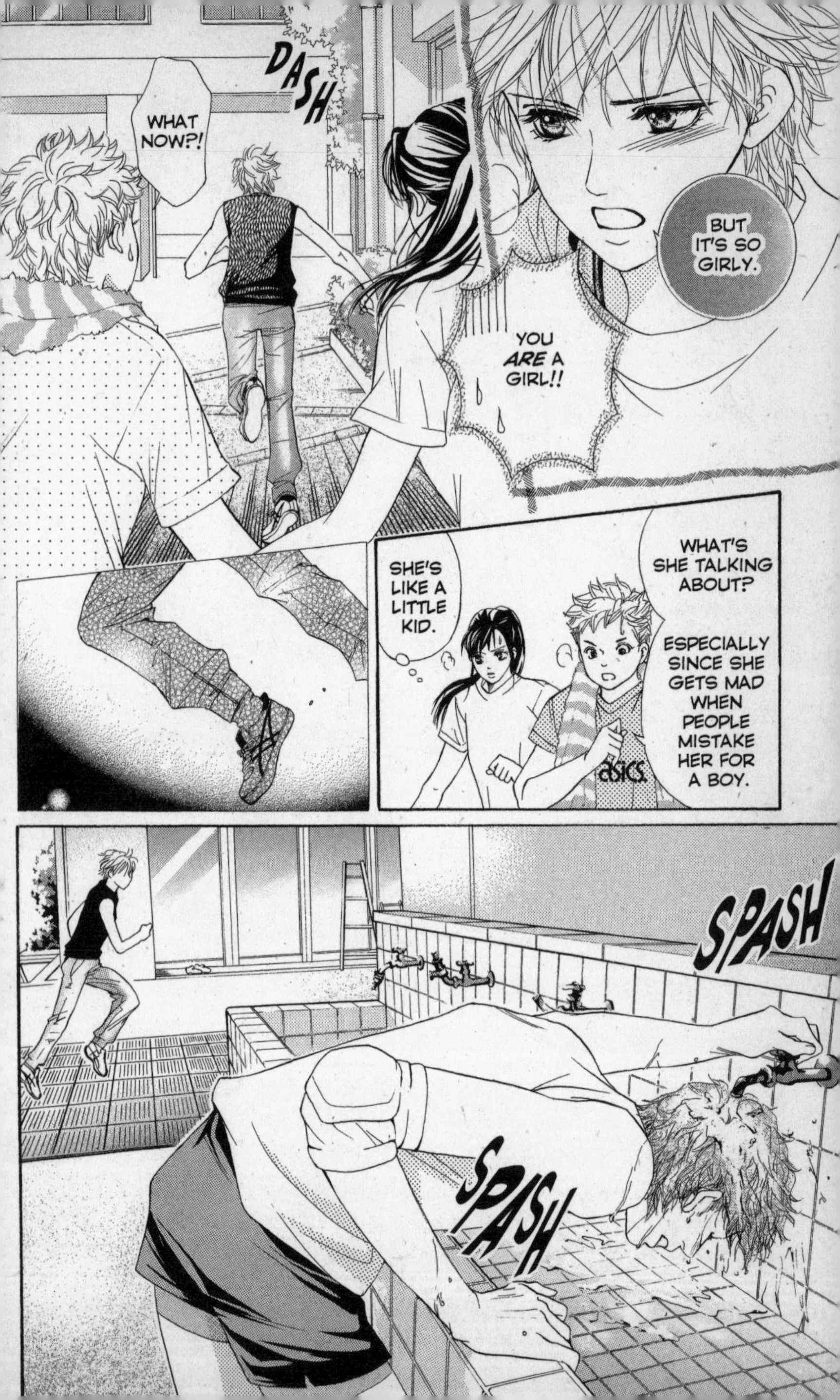
BUT IT'S SO GIRLY.
YOU *ARE* A GIRL!!
DASH
WHAT NOW?!
WHAT'S SHE TALKING ABOUT?
ESPECIALLY SINCE SHE GETS MAD WHEN PEOPLE MISTAKE HER FOR A BOY.
SHE'S LIKE A LITTLE KID.
SPASH
SPASH

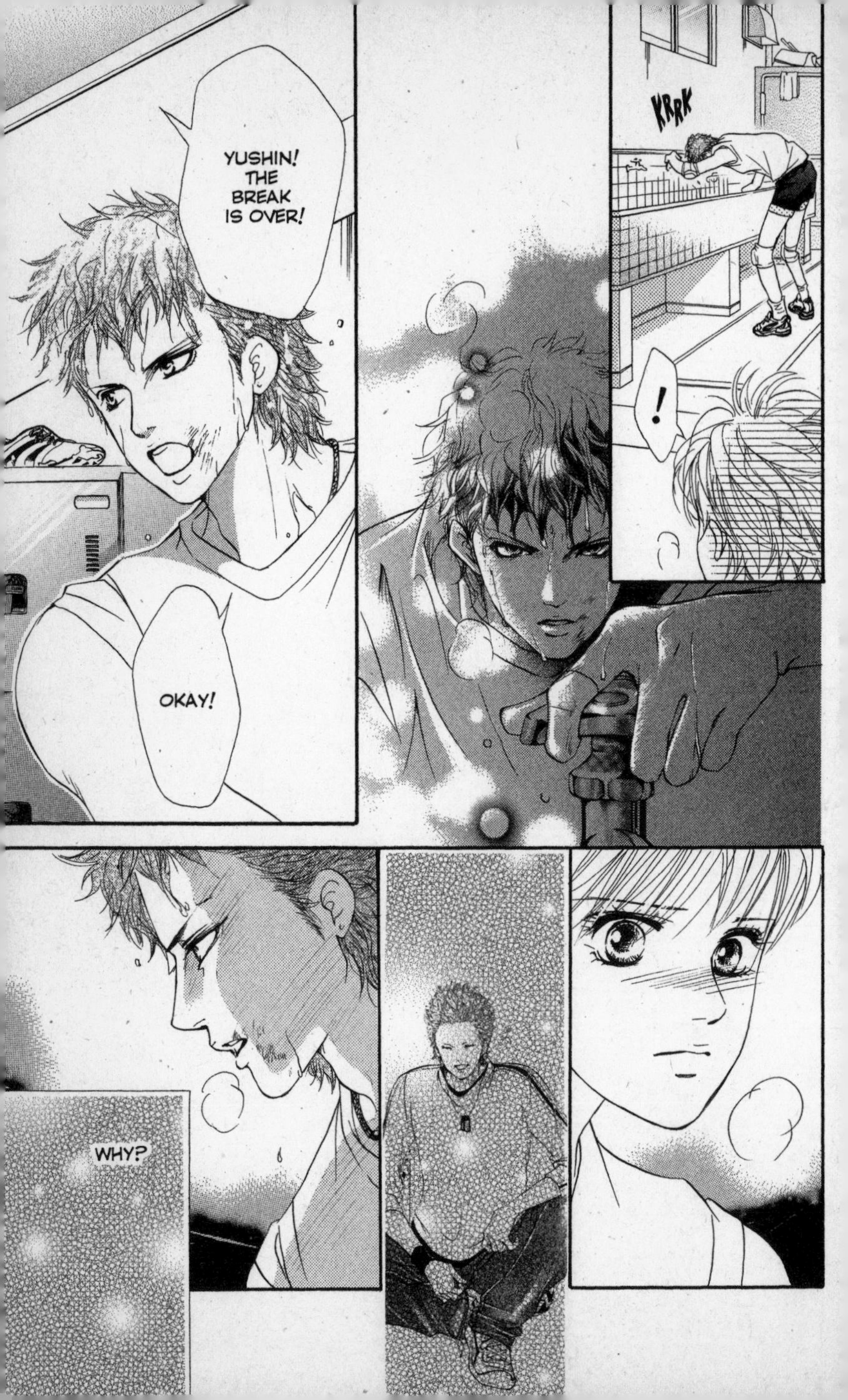
KRRK
!
YUSHIN! THE BREAK IS OVER!
OKAY!
WHY?

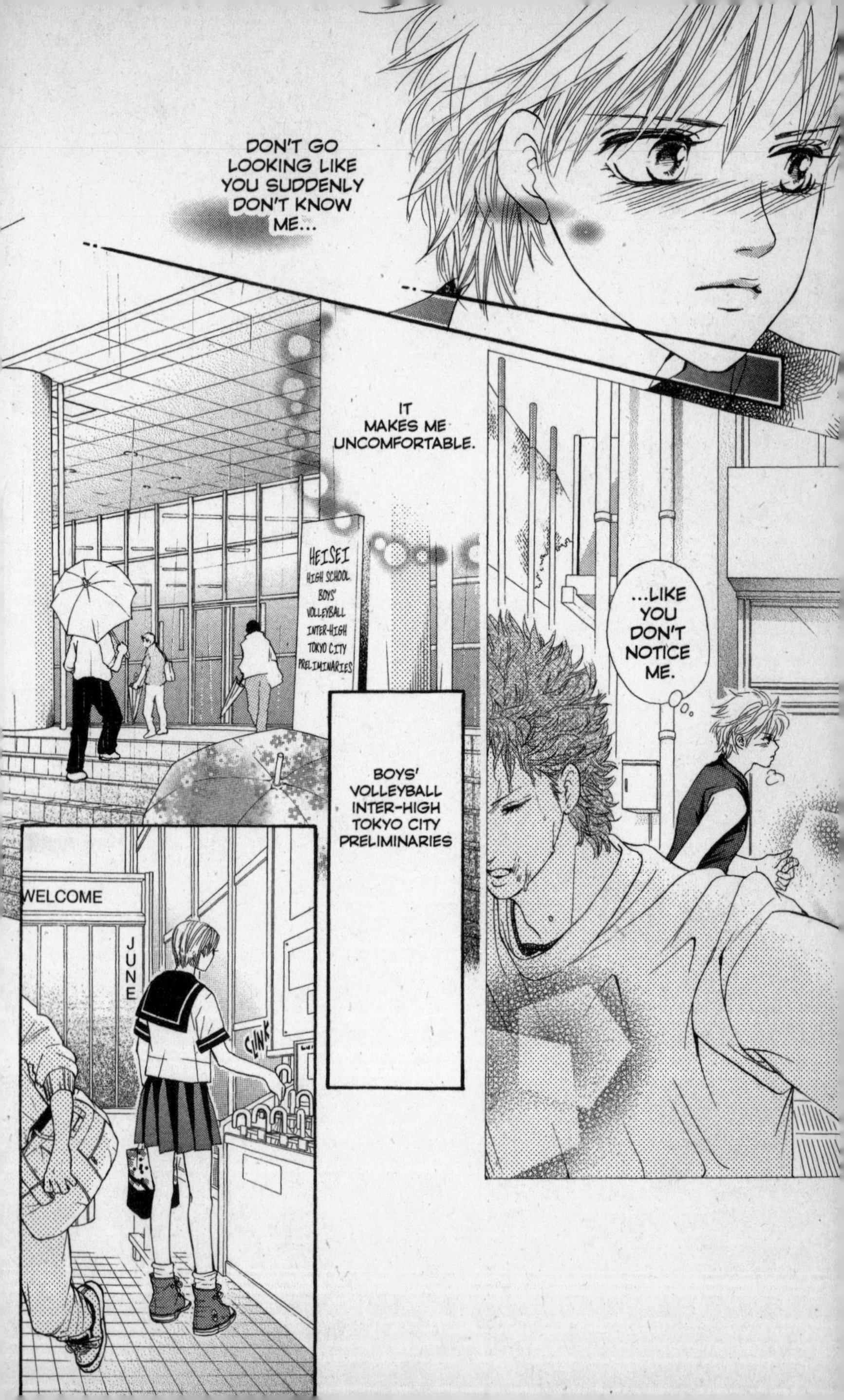
DON'T GO LOOKING LIKE YOU SUDDENLY DON'T KNOW ME...
IT MAKES ME UNCOMFORTABLE.
...LIKE YOU DON'T NOTICE ME.
HEISEI HIGH SCHOOL BOYS' VOLLEYBALL INTER-HIGH TOKYO CITY PRELIMINARIES
BOYS' VOLLEYBALL INTER-HIGH TOKYO CITY PRELIMINARIES
WELCOME
JUNE
CLINK

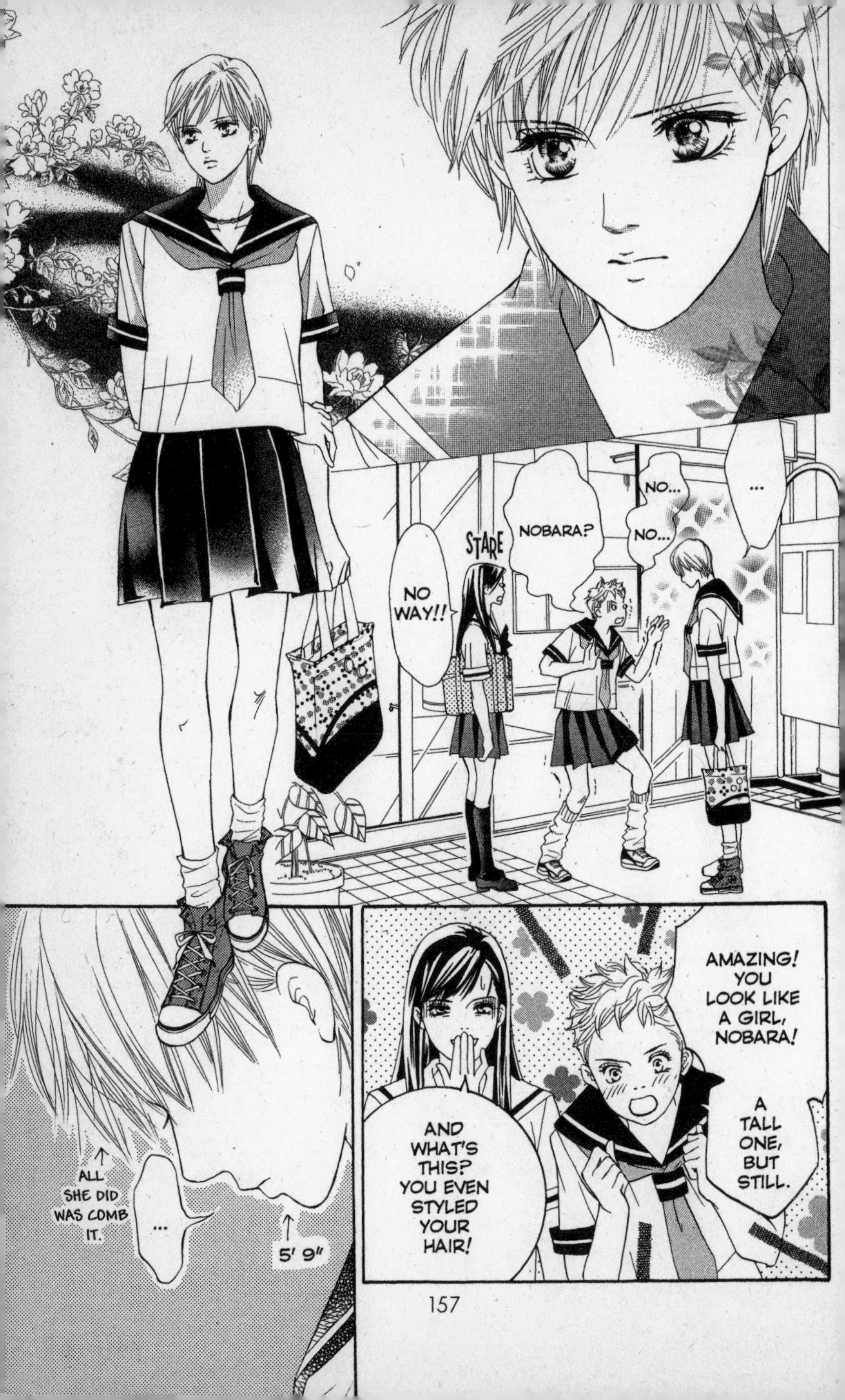
...
NO... NO...
NOBARA?
STARE
NO WAY!!
AMAZING! YOU LOOK LIKE A GIRL, NOBARA!
A TALL ONE, BUT STILL.
AND WHAT'S THIS? YOU EVEN STYLED YOUR HAIR!
5' 9"
...
ALL SHE DID WAS COMB IT.

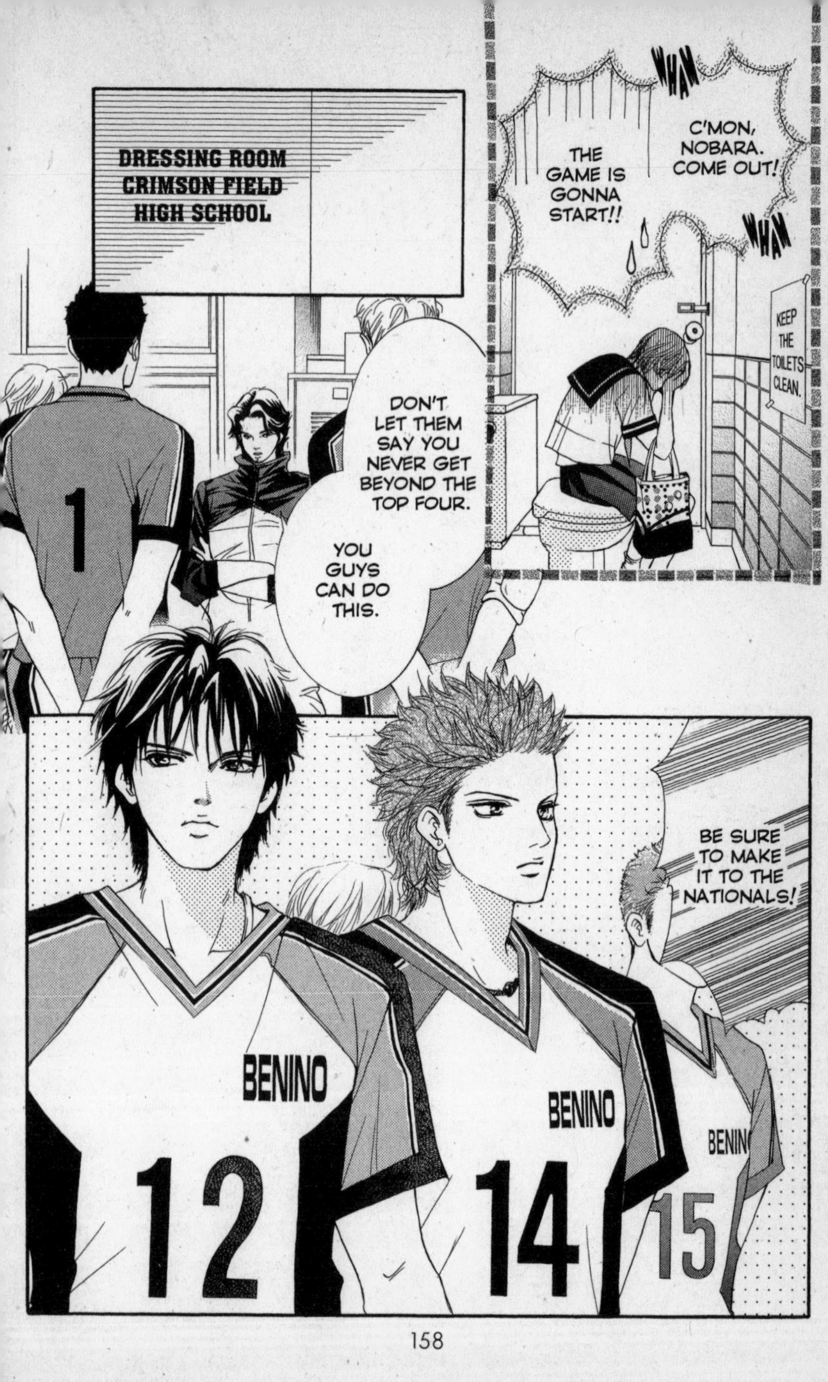
WHAM
C'MON, NOBARA. COME OUT!
THE GAME IS GONNA START!!
WHAM
KEEP THE TOILETS CLEAN.
DRESSING ROOM CRIMSON FIELD HIGH SCHOOL
DON'T LET THEM SAY YOU NEVER GET BEYOND THE TOP FOUR.
YOU GUYS CAN DO THIS.
BE SURE TO MAKE IT TO THE NATIONALS!
BENINO 12
BENINO 14
15

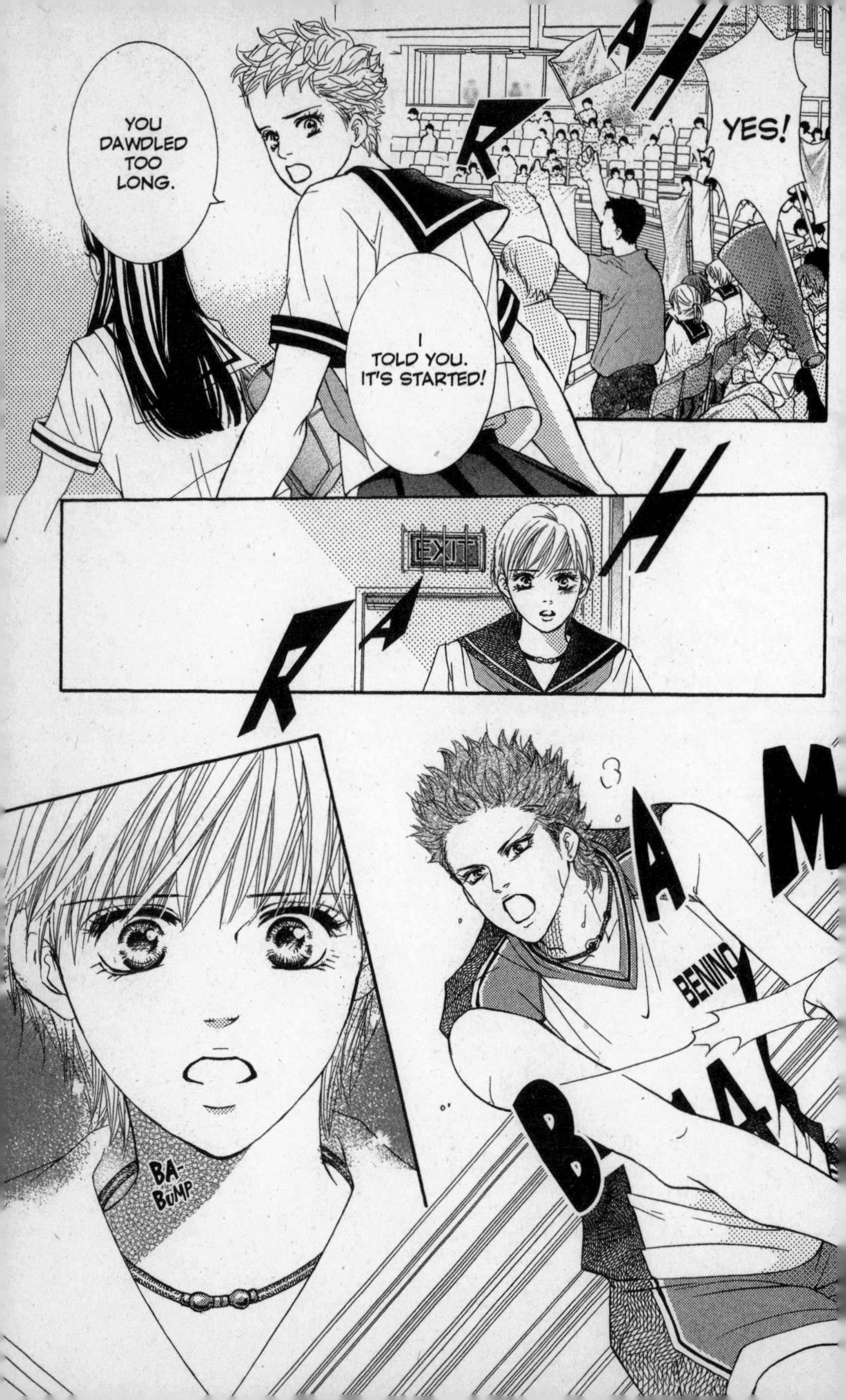
YES!
RAH
I TOLD YOU. IT'S STARTED!
YOU DAWDLED TOO LONG.
RAH
BAM
BENINO
BA-BUMP

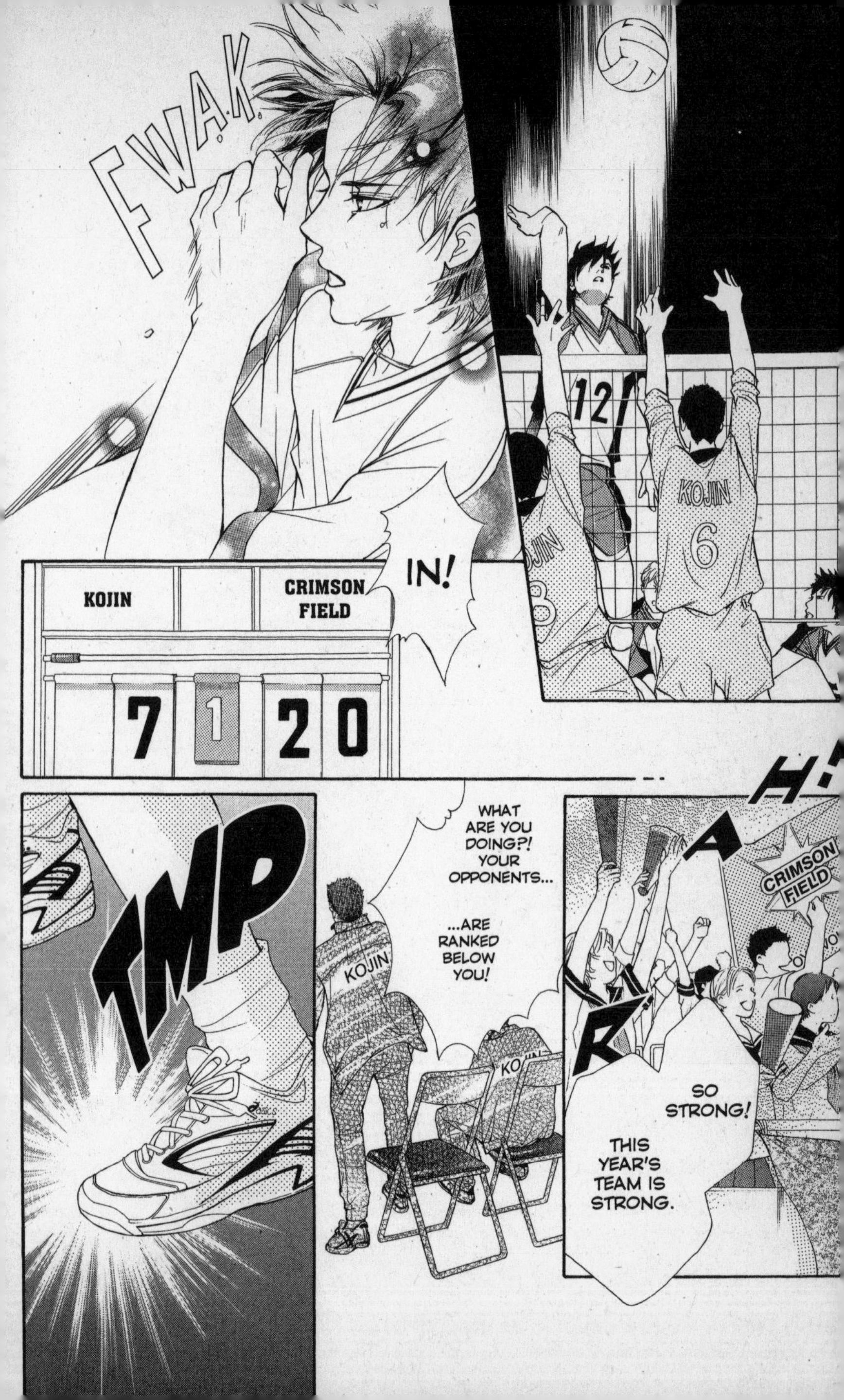

FWAK
KOJIN
12
KOJIN
6
IN!
KOJIN
CRIMSON FIELD
7 1 20
AH!
CRIMSON FIELD
SO STRONG!
THIS YEAR'S TEAM IS STRONG.
WHAT ARE YOU DOING?! YOUR OPPONENTS...
...ARE RANKED BELOW YOU!
KOJIN
TMP

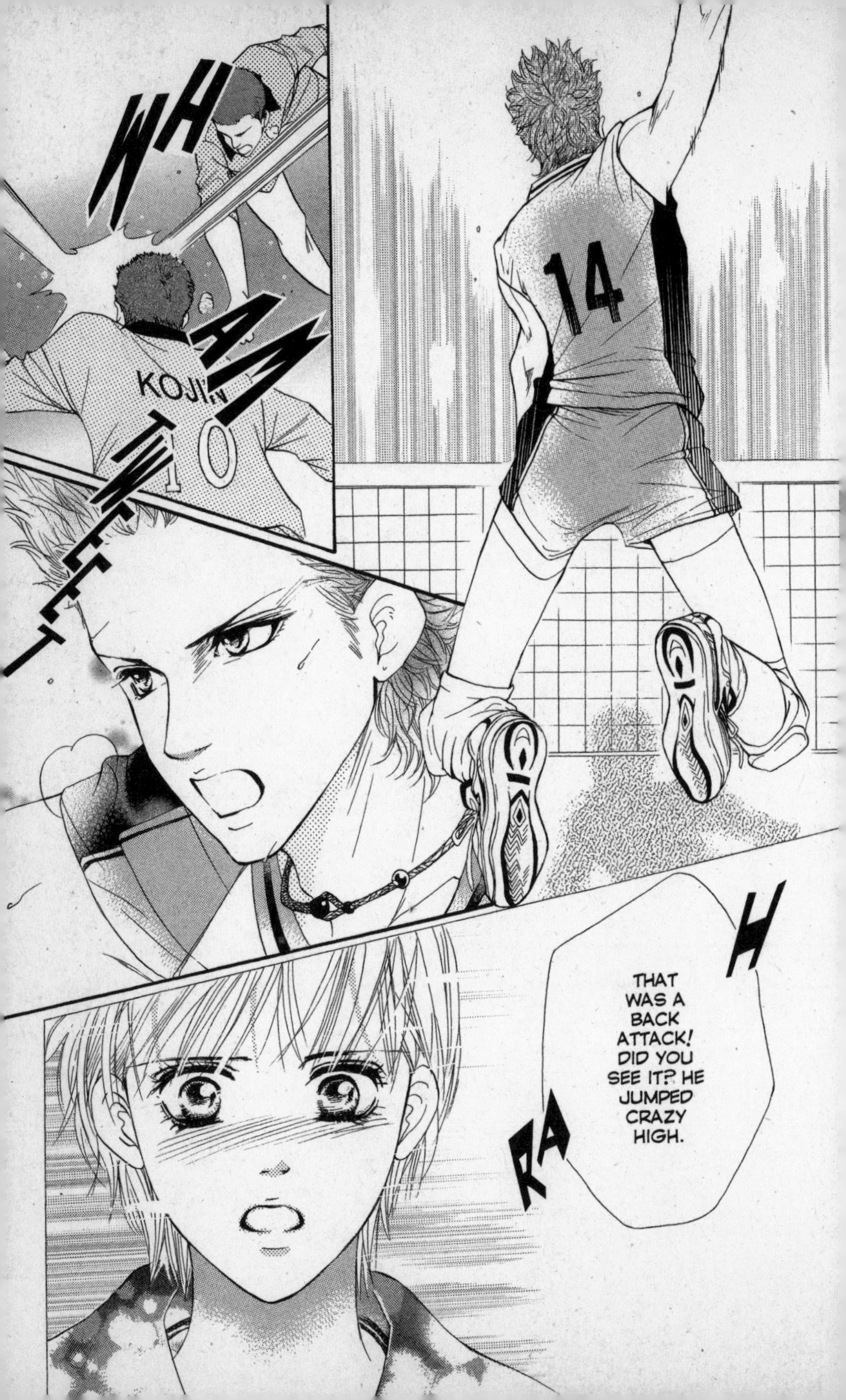
14
WHAM
KOJI
10
TWEEEET
THAT WAS A BACK ATTACK! DID YOU SEE IT?! HE JUMPED CRAZY HIGH.
RAH

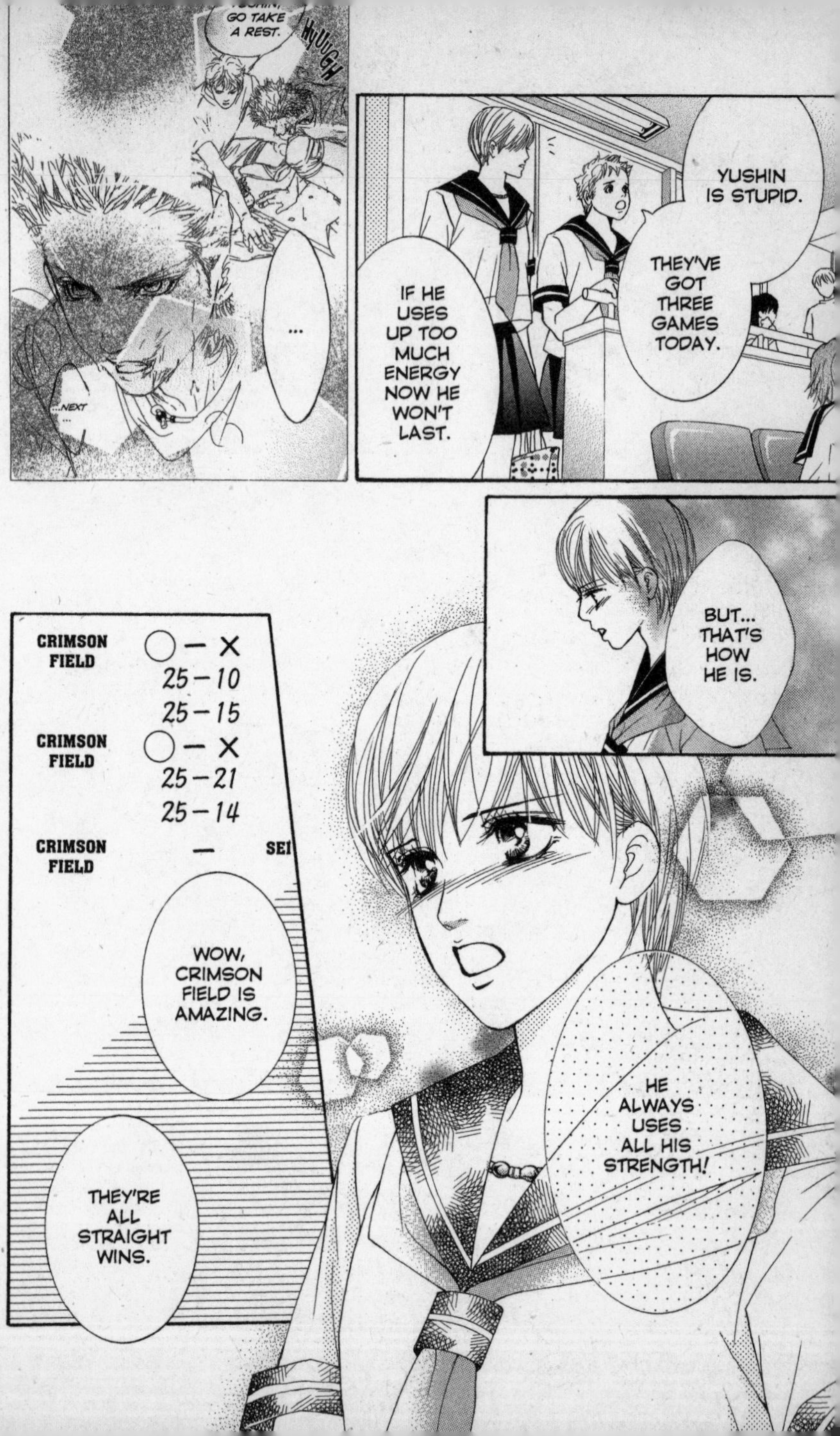

YUSHIN IS STUPID.
THEY'VE GOT THREE GAMES TODAY.
IF HE USES UP TOO MUCH ENERGY NOW HE WON'T LAST.
GO TAKE A REST.
HYUUGH
...
...NEXT ...
BUT... THAT'S HOW HE IS.
HE ALWAYS USES ALL HIS STRENGTH!
CRIMSON FIELD ○ – X
25 – 10
25 – 15
CRIMSON FIELD ○ – X
25 – 21
25 – 14
CRIMSON FIELD – SEI
WOW, CRIMSON FIELD IS AMAZING.
THEY'RE ALL STRAIGHT WINS.

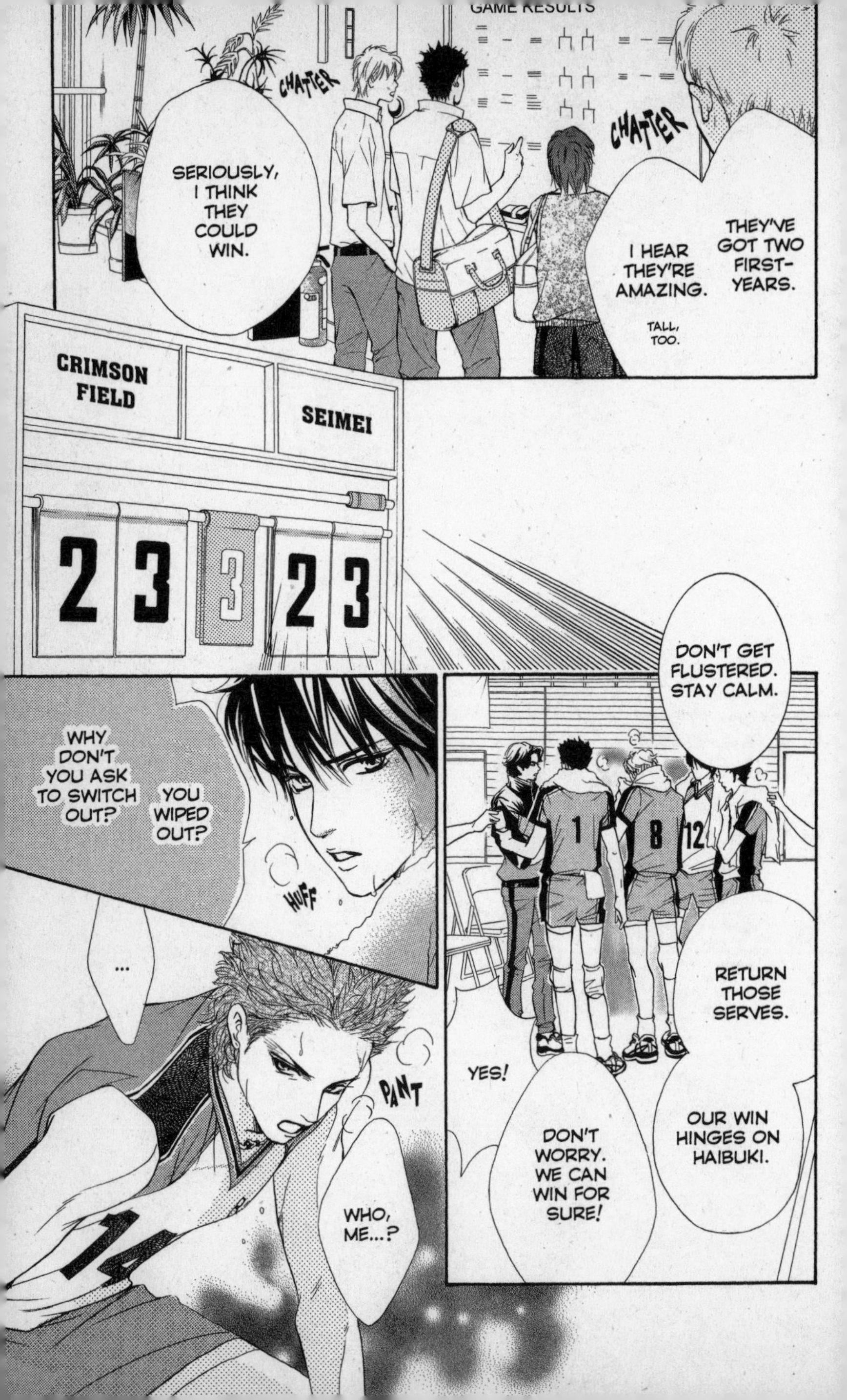
GAME RESULTS
CHATTER
THEY'VE GOT TWO FIRST-YEARS.
I HEAR THEY'RE AMAZING.
TALL, TOO.
CHATTER
SERIOUSLY, I THINK THEY COULD WIN.
CRIMSON FIELD
SEIMEI
23 3 23
DON'T GET FLUSTERED. STAY CALM.
RETURN THOSE SERVES.
OUR WIN HINGES ON HAIBUKI.
DON'T WORRY. WE CAN WIN FOR SURE!
YES!
YOU WIPED OUT?
WHY DON'T YOU ASK TO SWITCH OUT?
HUFF
...
PANT
WHO, ME...?

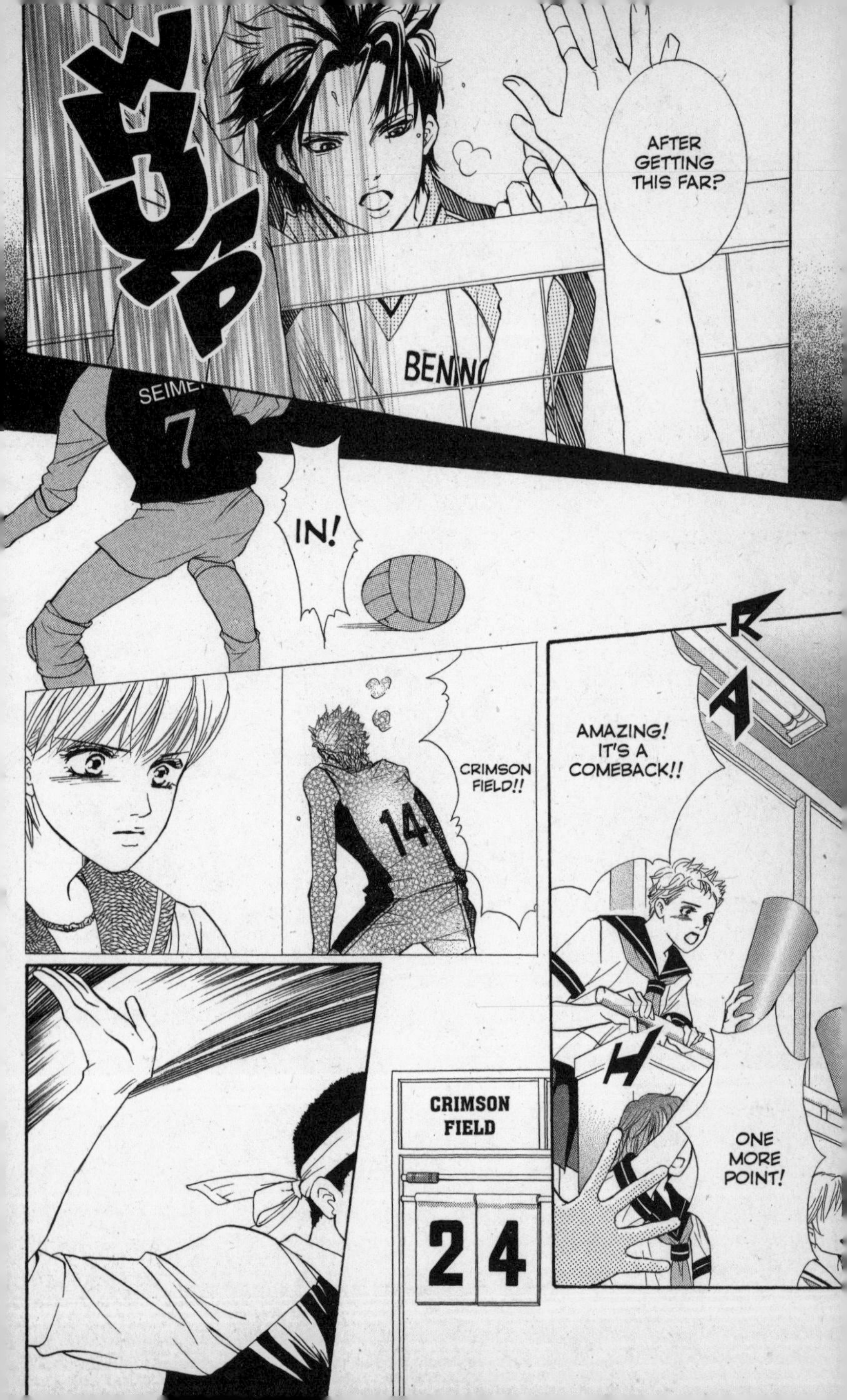
AFTER GETTING THIS FAR?
JUMP
7
IN!
RAH
AMAZING! IT'S A COMEBACK!!
ONE MORE POINT!
CRIMSON FIELD!!
14
CRIMSON FIELD
24

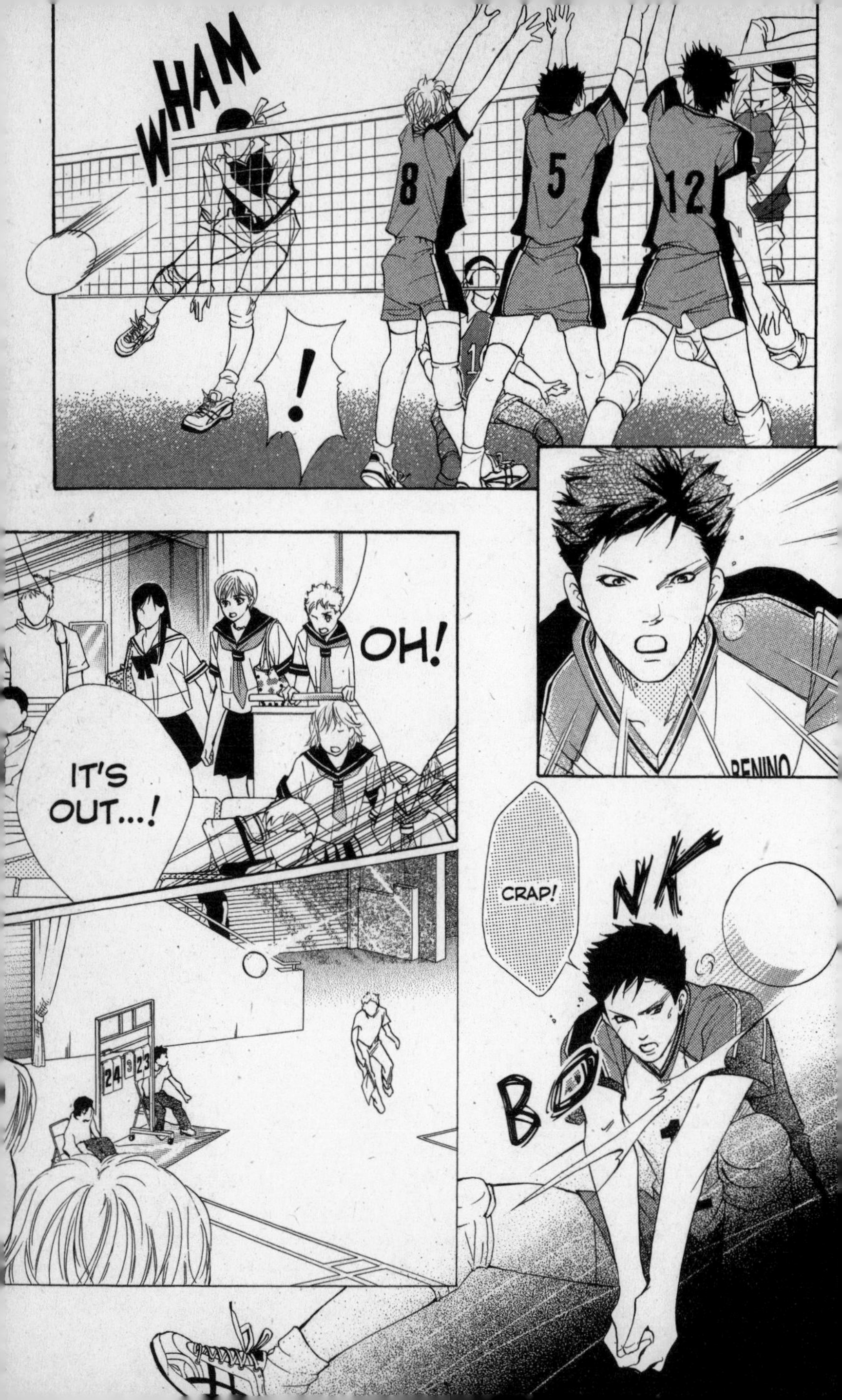
WHAM
!
CRAP!
NK
B
OH!
IT'S OUT...!

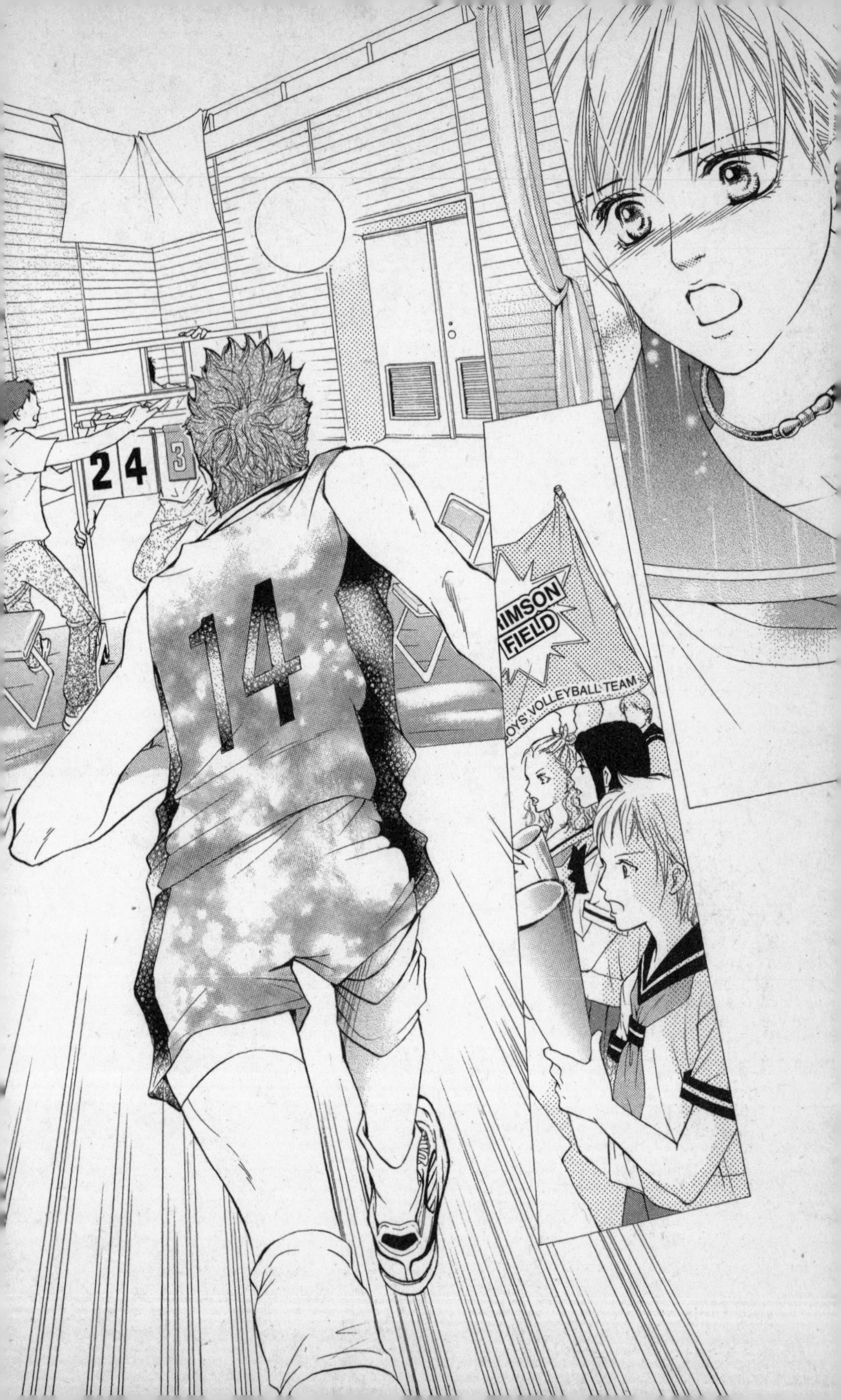
24
3
14
RIMSON
FIELD
OYS' VOLLEYBALL TEAM

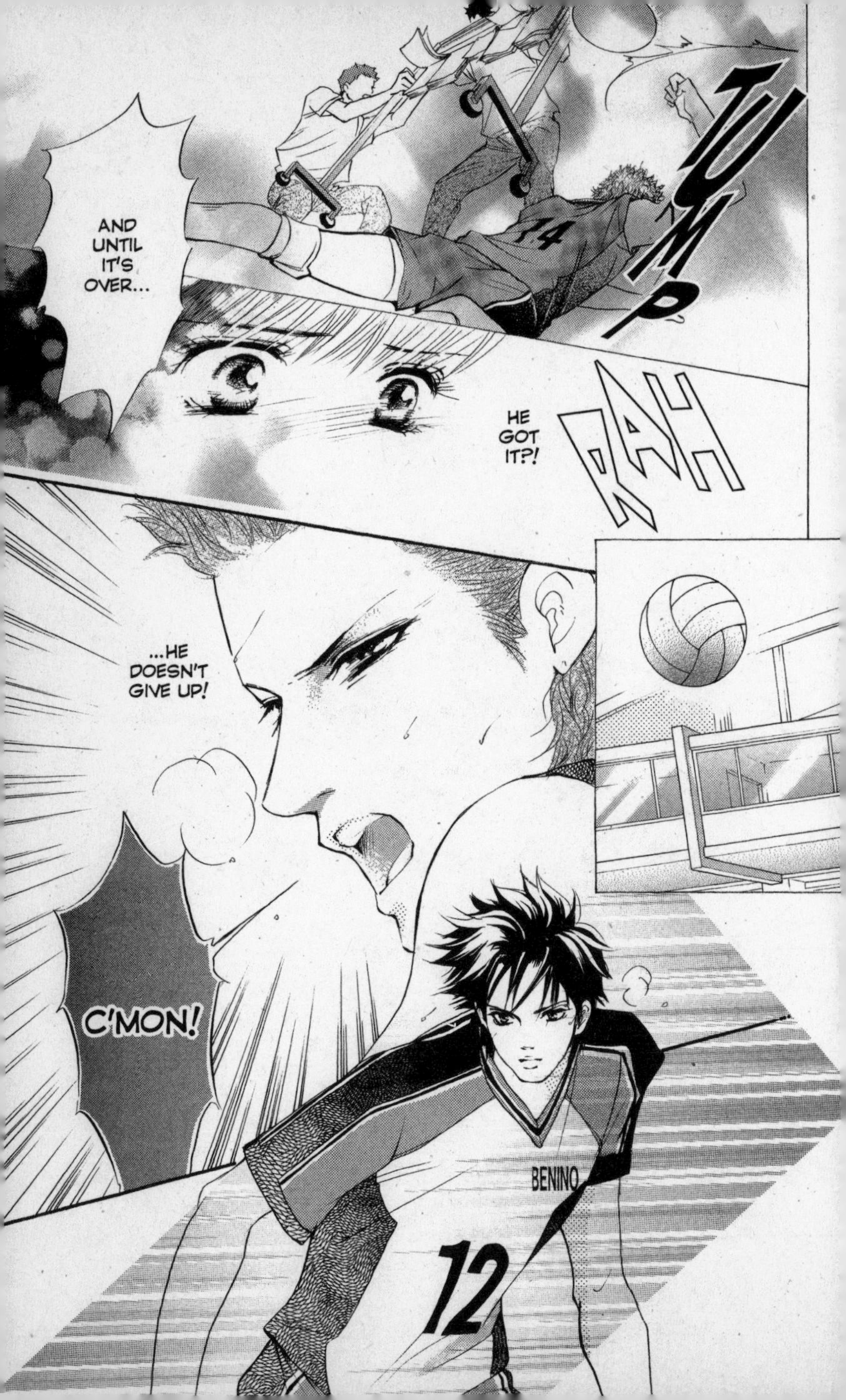
THUMP
AND UNTIL IT'S OVER...
RAH
HE GOT IT?!
...HE DOESN'T GIVE UP!
C'MON!
BENINO

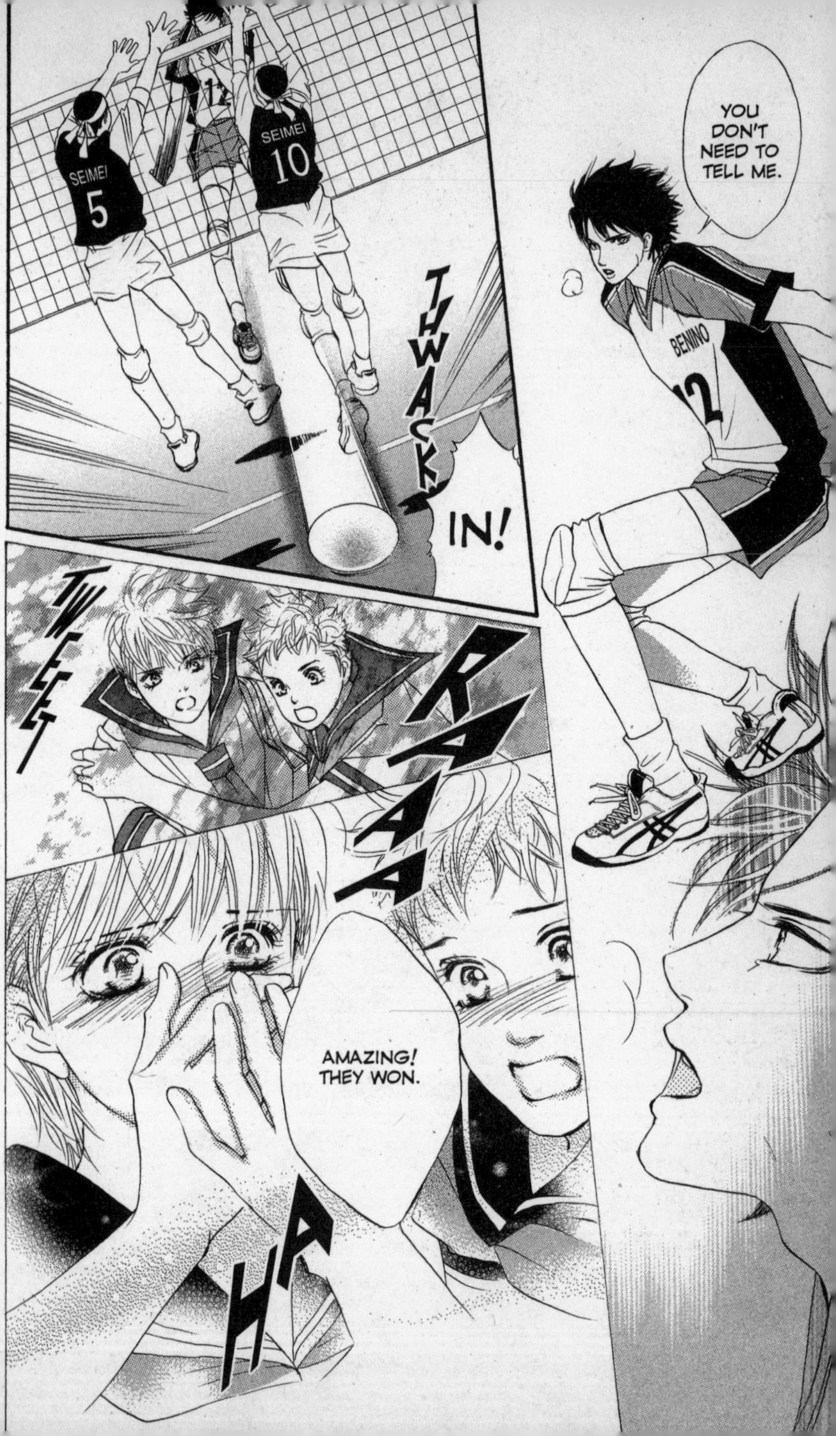
YOU DON'T NEED TO TELL ME.
THWACK
IN!
TWEEET
RAAAA
AMAZING! THEY WON.
HA

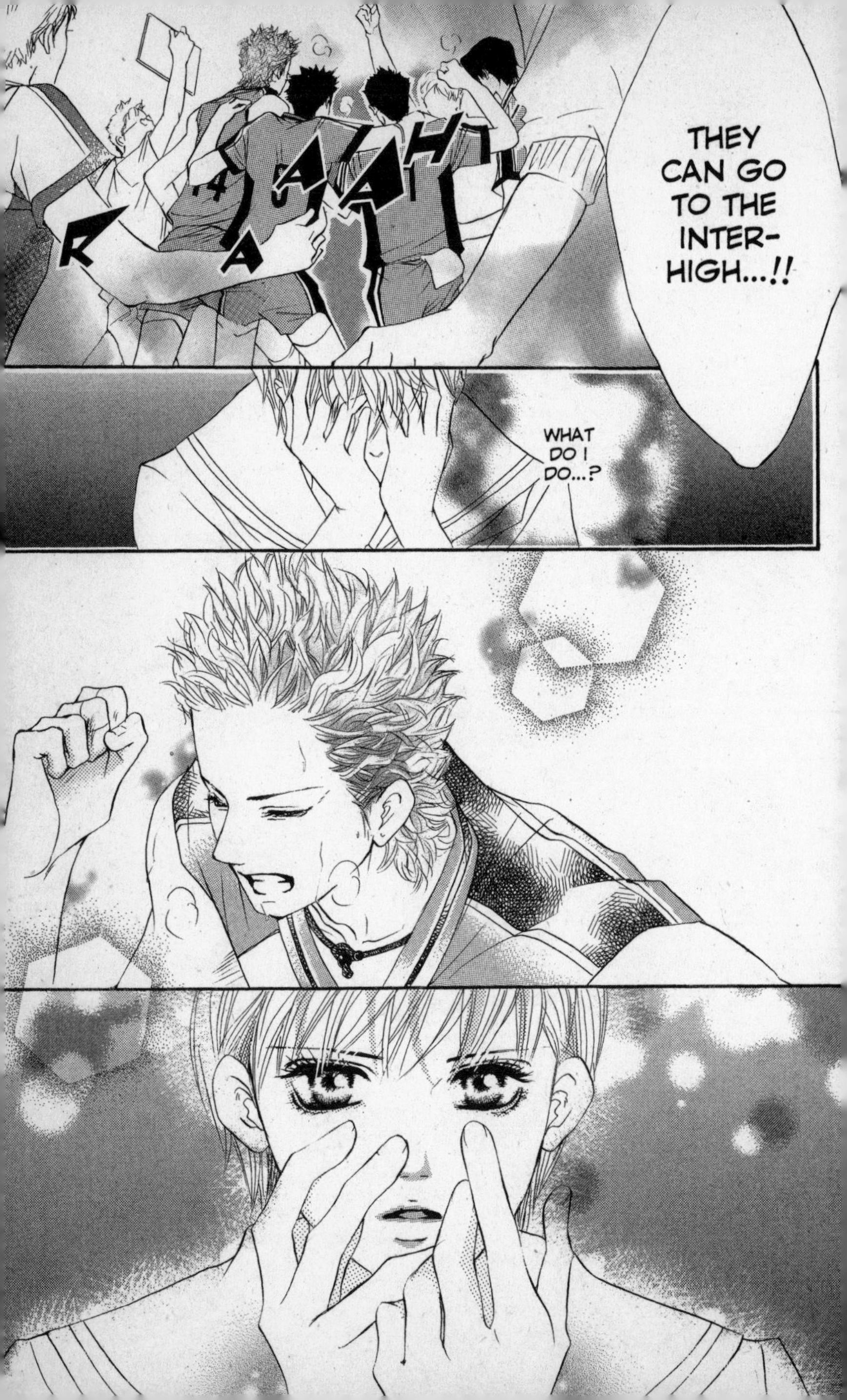
THEY CAN GO TO THE INTER-HIGH...!!
RAAAAH!
WHAT DO I DO...?

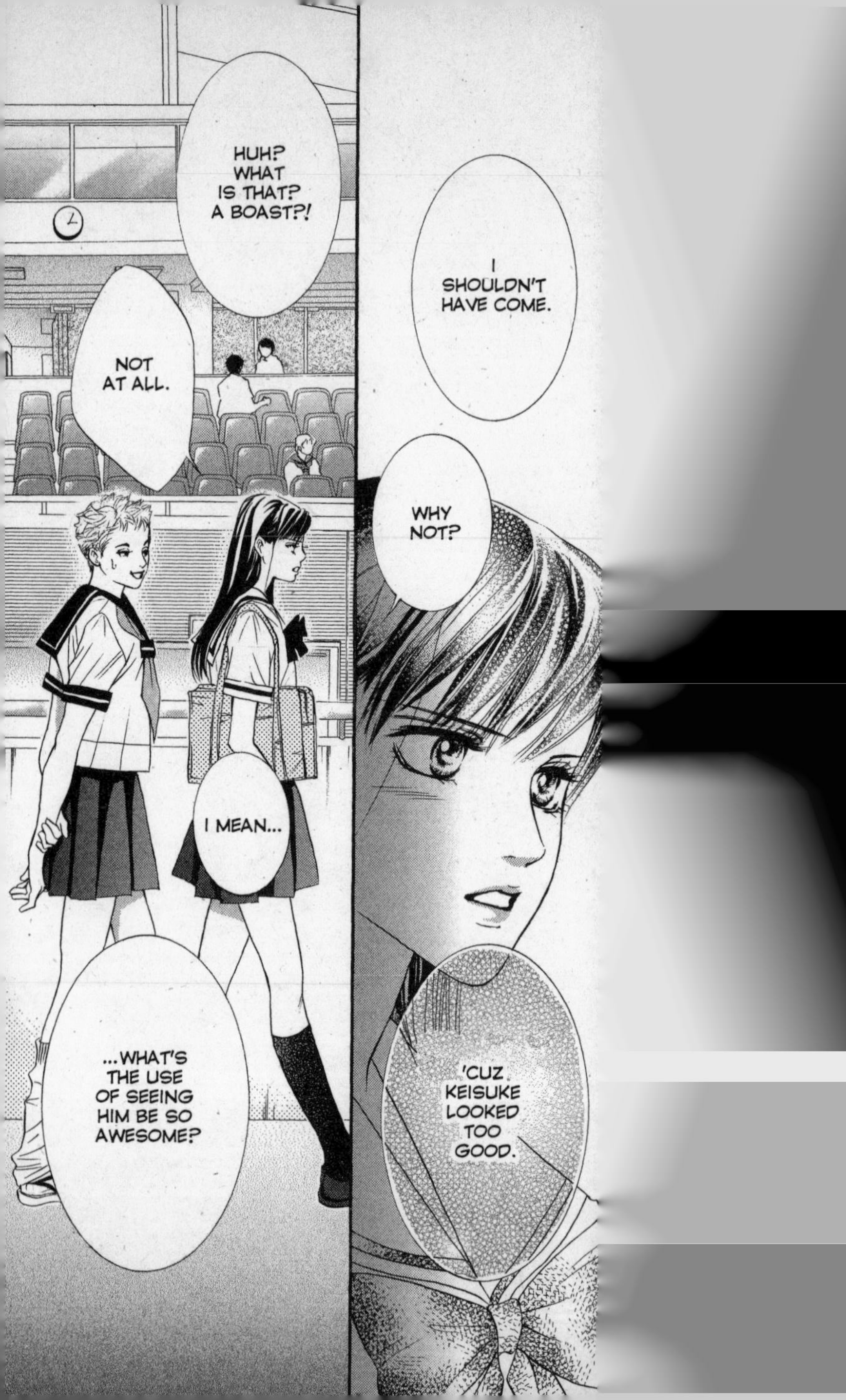
I SHOULDN'T HAVE COME.
WHY NOT?
'CUZ KEISUKE LOOKED TOO GOOD.
HUH? WHAT IS THAT? A BOAST?!
NOT AT ALL.
I MEAN...
...WHAT'S THE USE OF SEEING HIM BE SO AWESOME?

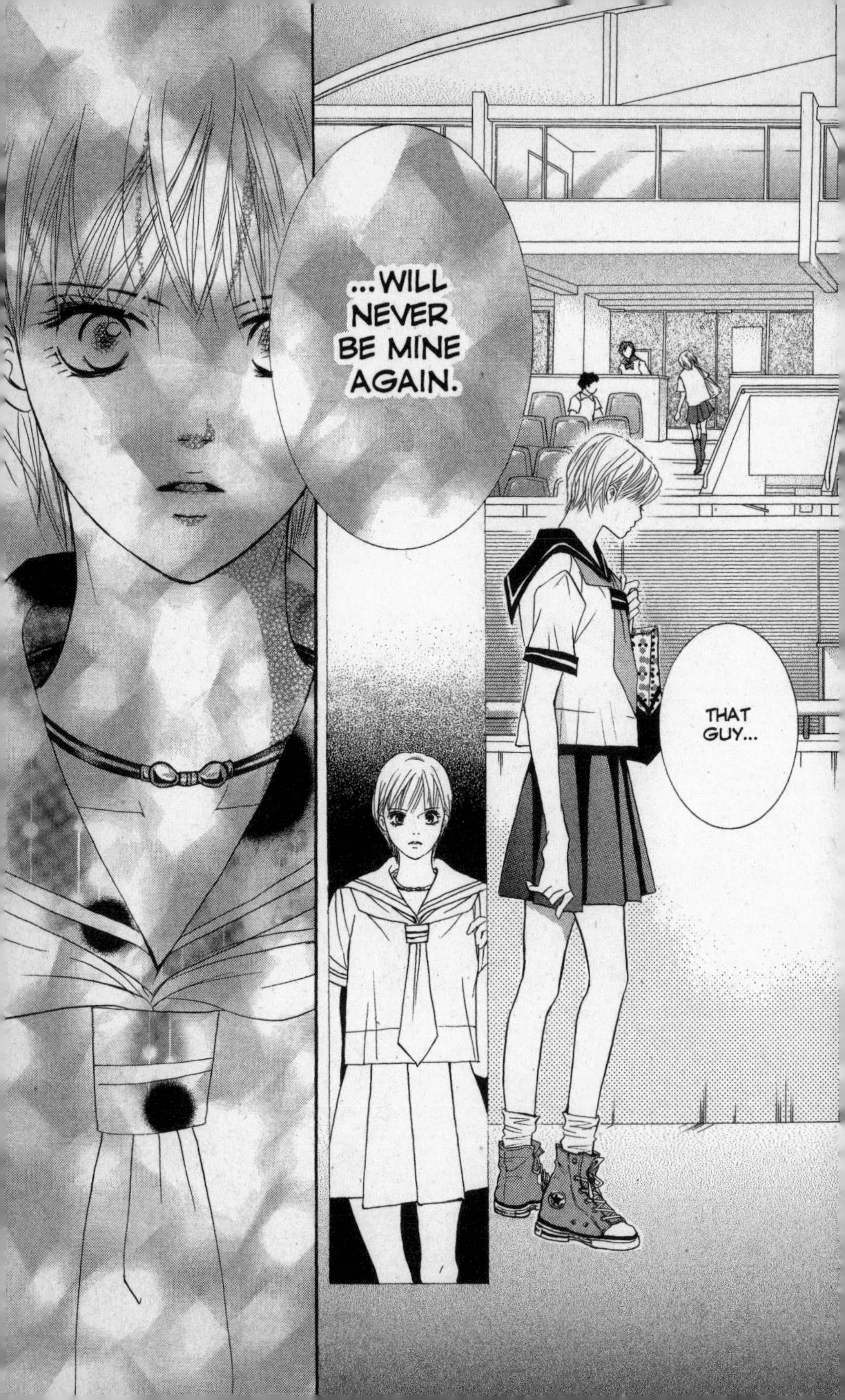
THAT GUY...
...WILL NEVER BE MINE AGAIN.

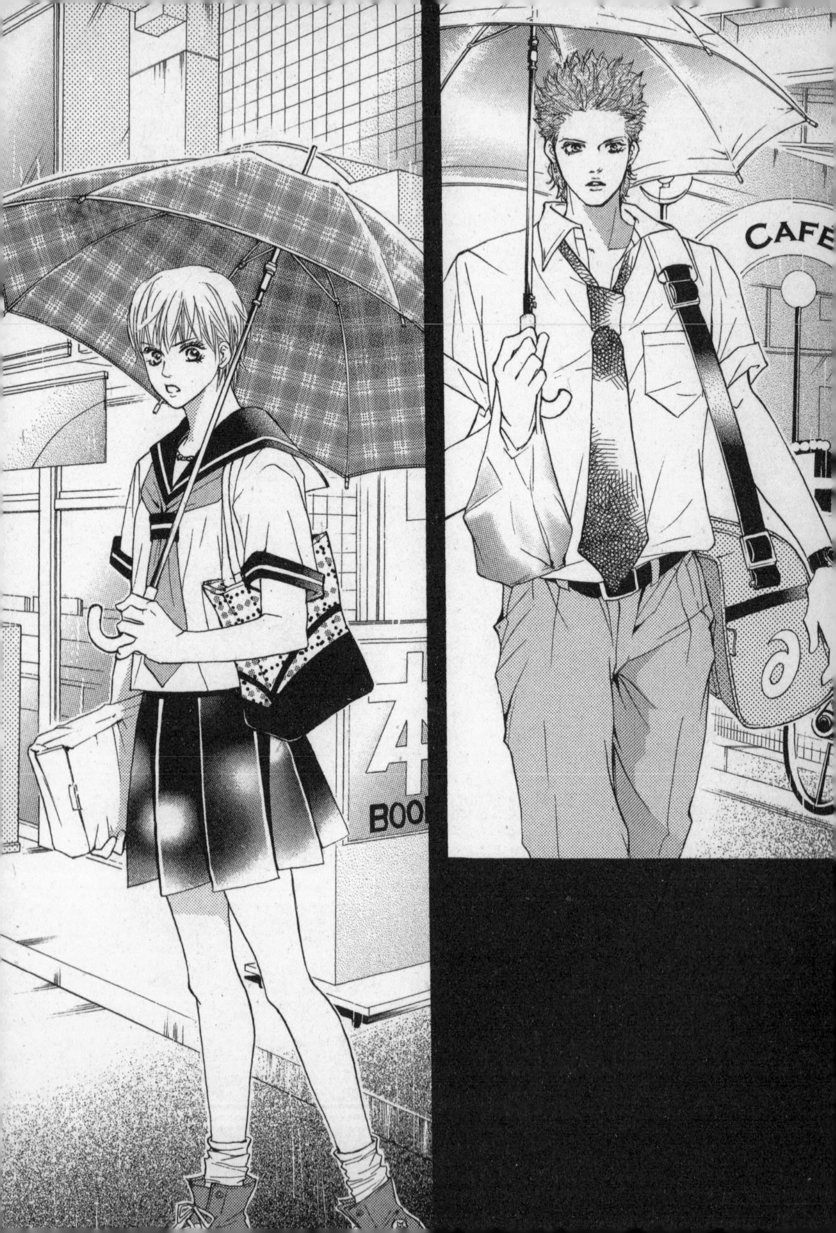
CAFE
本

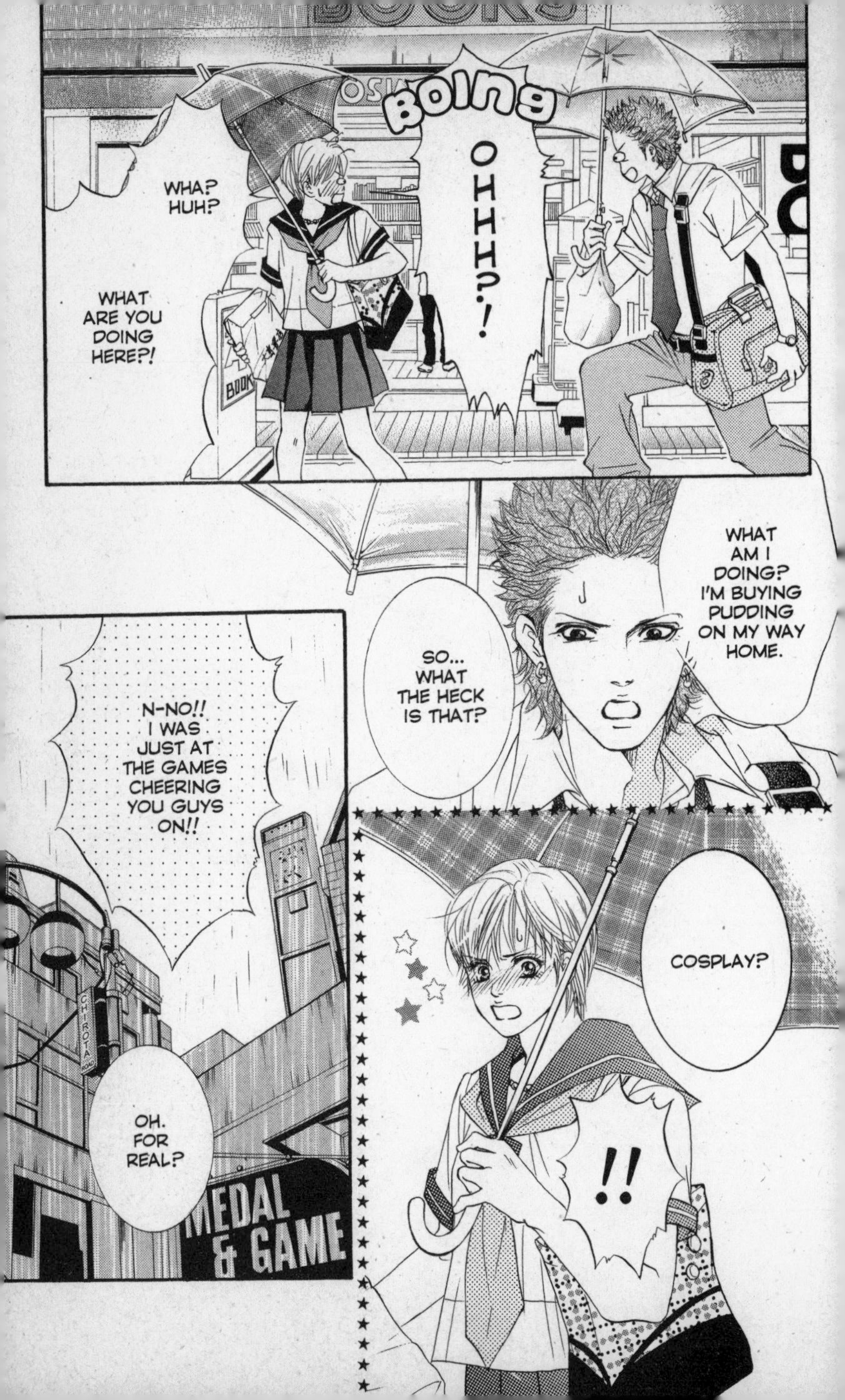
BOING
OHHHH?!
WHA? HUH?
WHAT ARE YOU DOING HERE?!
WHAT AM I DOING? I'M BUYING PUDDING ON MY WAY HOME.
SO... WHAT THE HECK IS THAT?
COSPLAY?
!!
N-NO!! I WAS JUST AT THE GAMES CHEERING YOU GUYS ON!!
OH. FOR REAL?
MEDAL & GAME

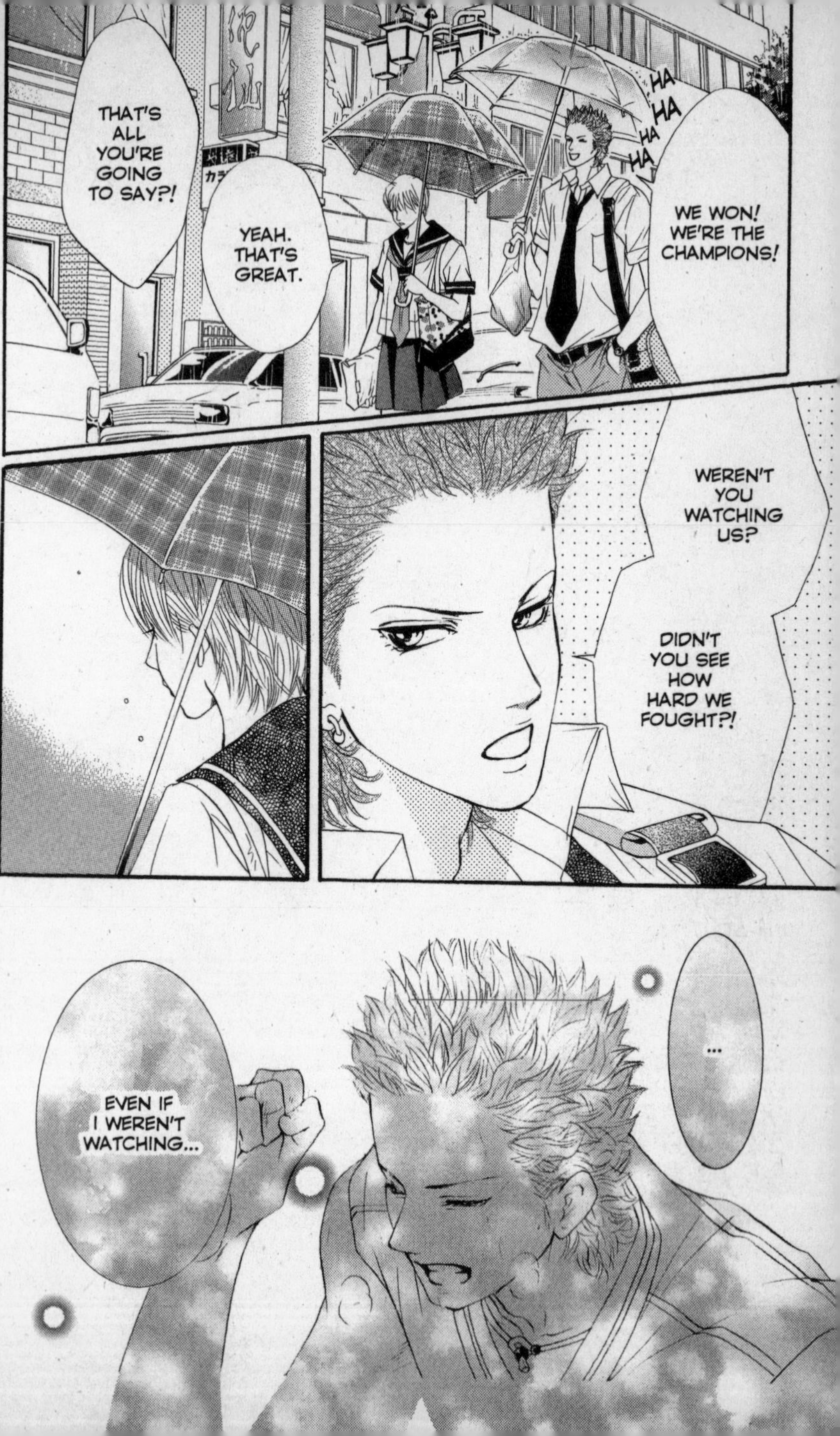
HA HA HA HA
WE WON! WE'RE THE CHAMPIONS!
YEAH. THAT'S GREAT.
THAT'S ALL YOU'RE GOING TO SAY?!
WEREN'T YOU WATCHING US?
DIDN'T YOU SEE HOW HARD WE FOUGHT?!
...
EVEN IF I WEREN'T WATCHING...

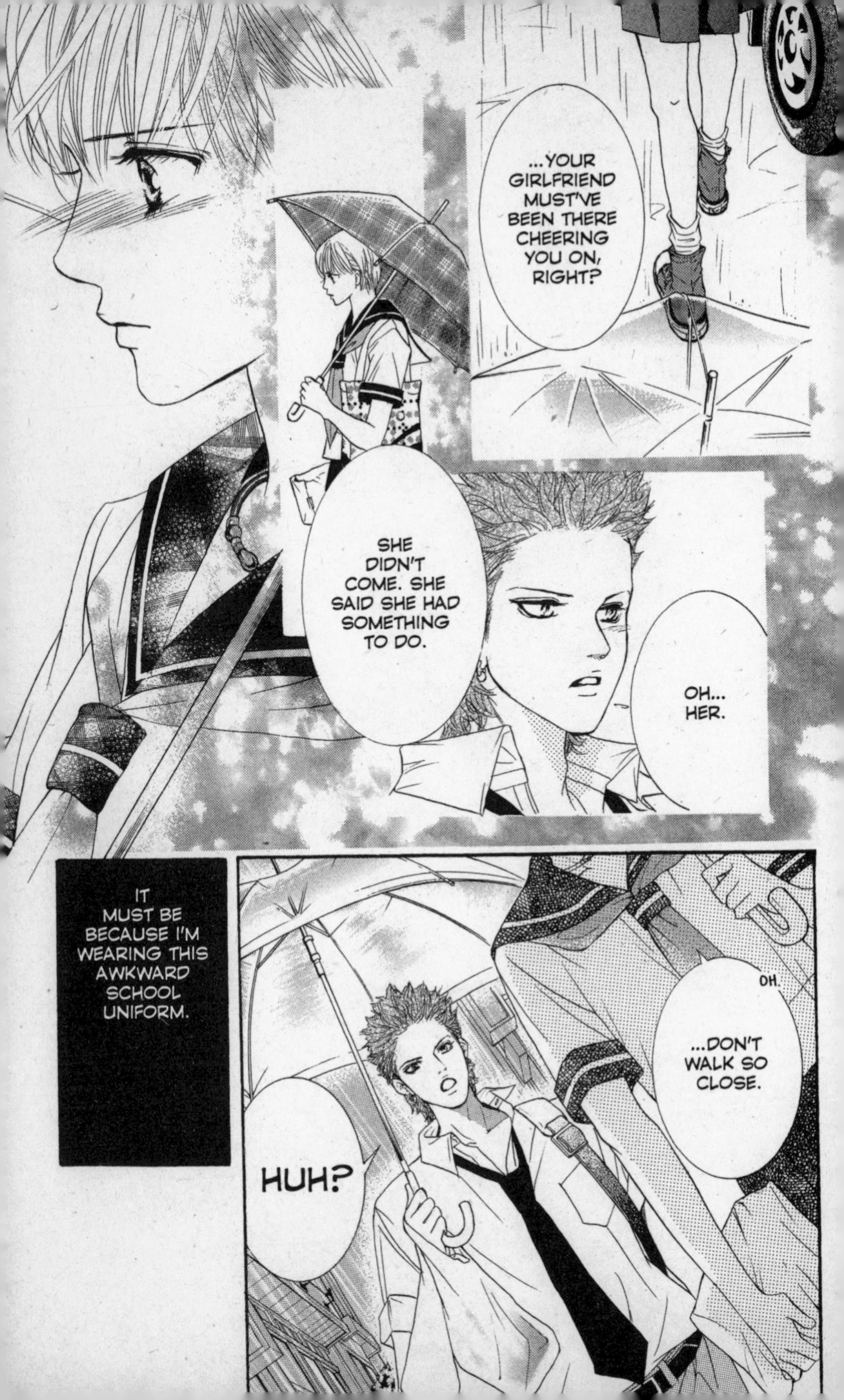
...YOUR GIRLFRIEND MUST'VE BEEN THERE CHEERING YOU ON, RIGHT?
SHE DIDN'T COME. SHE SAID SHE HAD SOMETHING TO DO.
OH... HER.
OH.
...DON'T WALK SO CLOSE.
HUH?
IT MUST BE BECAUSE I'M WEARING THIS AWKWARD SCHOOL UNIFORM.

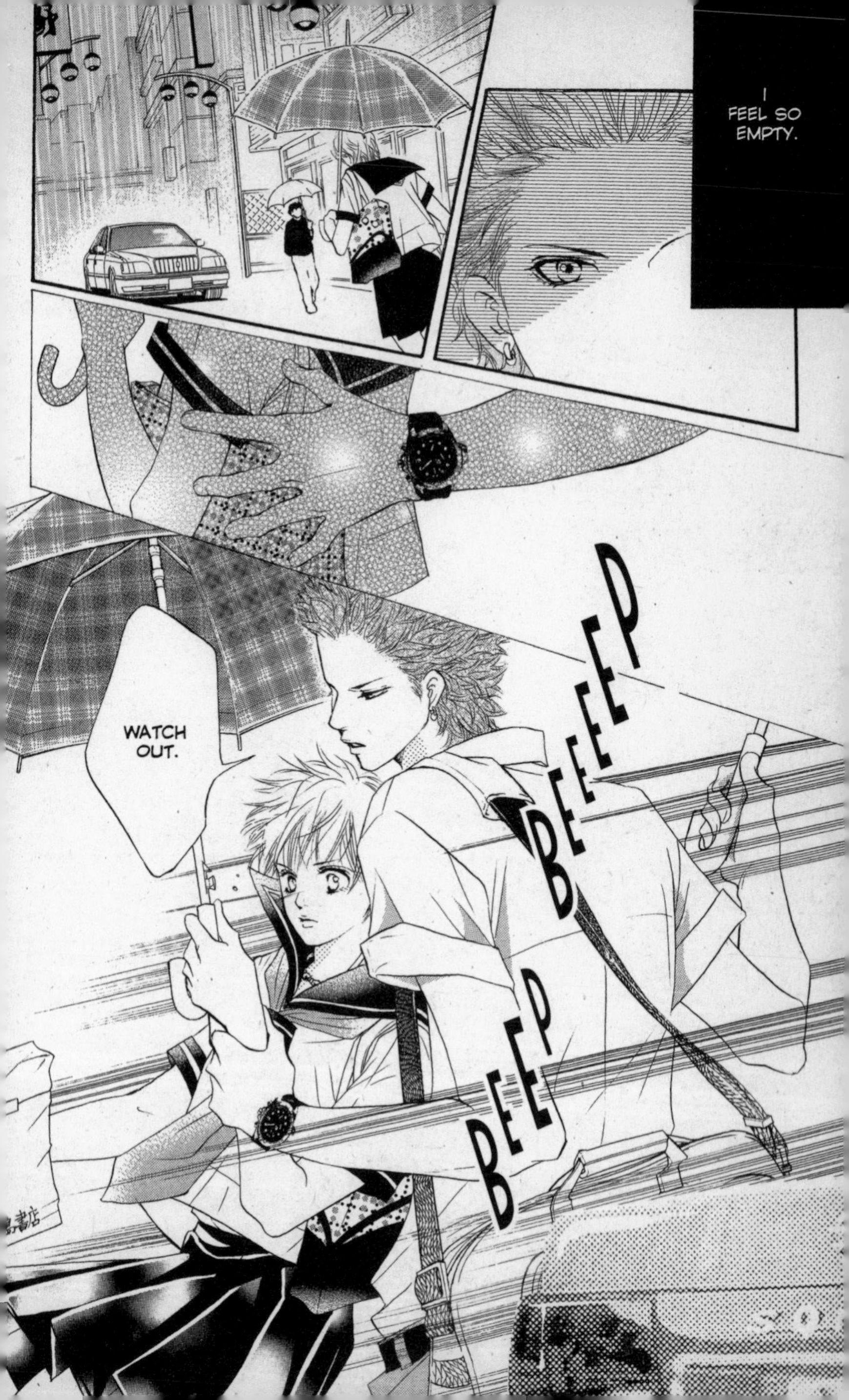
I FEEL SO EMPTY.
WATCH OUT.
BEEEEP
BEEEP

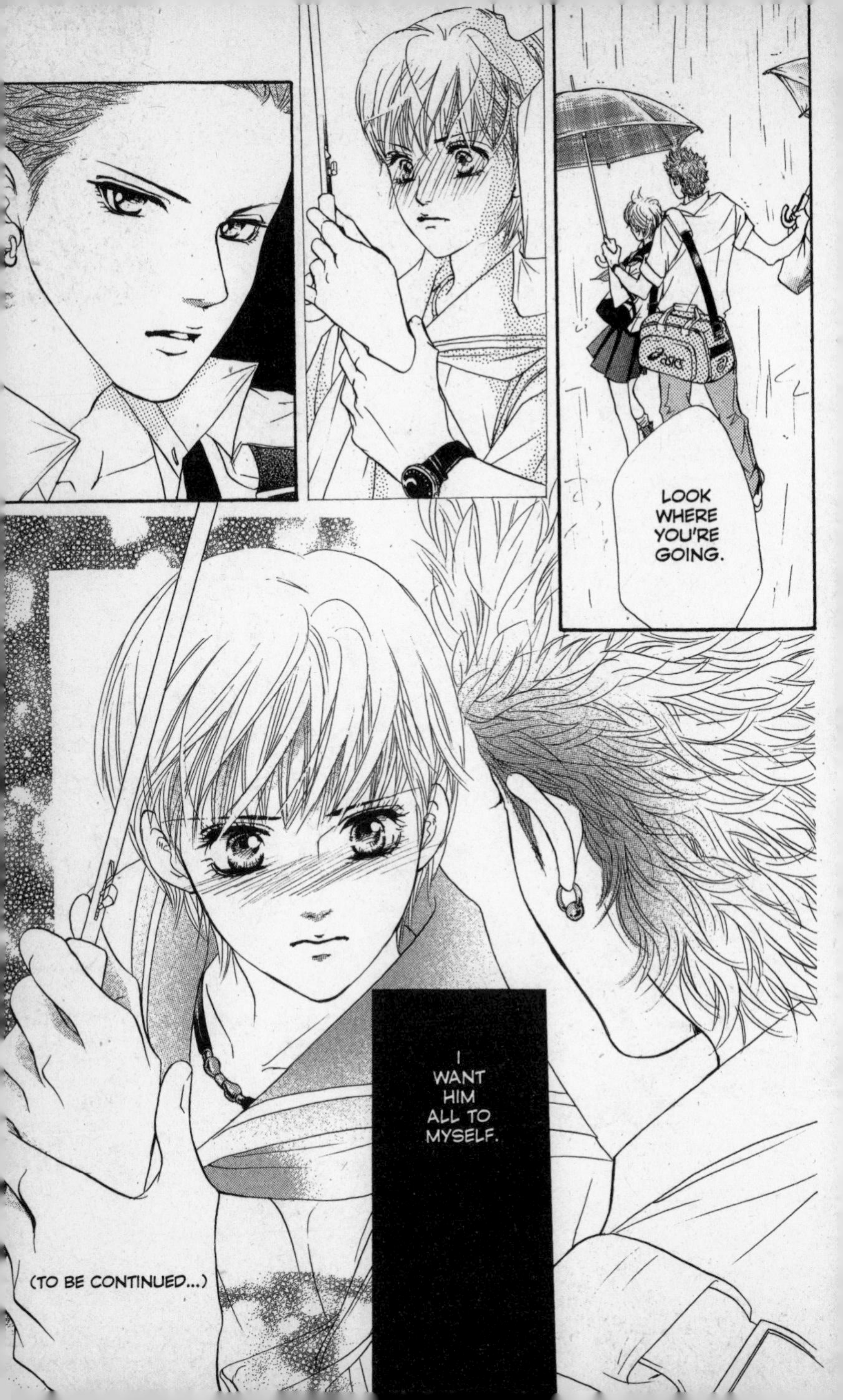
LOOK WHERE YOU'RE GOING.
I WANT HIM ALL TO MYSELF.
(TO BE CONTINUED...)

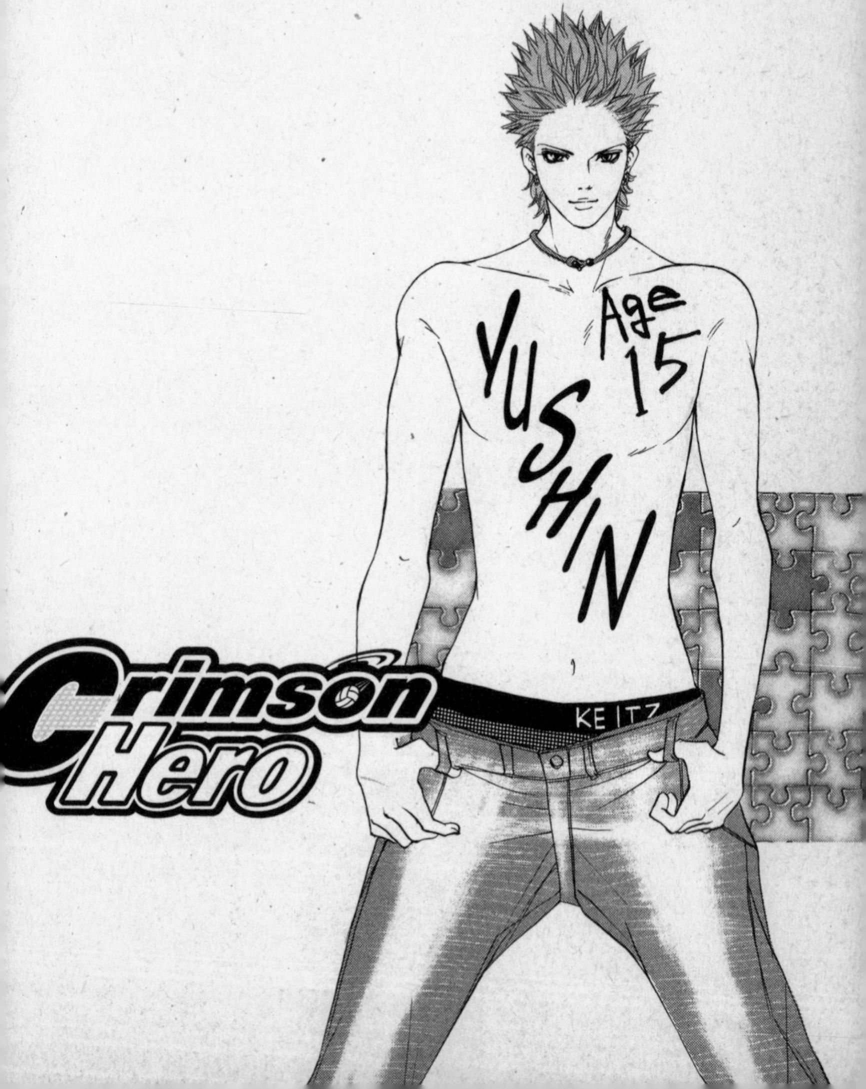
YUSHIN
Age 15
KE ITZ
Crimson Hero

♥When I'm caught up on my manga deadlines (which is rare), I like working marathons and jumping rope into my schedule. But since my body is as out of shape as it could possibly be, I run out of breath after just a few minutes. But I like that moment when I can feel the sweat pouring out. And at those times, even after I've finished my manga pages, my feet feel lighter. At the train station I'll skip the escalator and go up the stairs.

—Mitsuba Takanashi, 2004

At age 17, Mitsuba Takanashi debuted her first short story, *Mou Koi Nante Shinai* (Never Fall in Love Again), in 1992 in *Bessatsu Margaret* magazine and now has several major titles under her belt.

Born in the Shimane Prefecture of Japan, Takanashi now lives in Tokyo, where she enjoys taking walks, watching videos, shopping, and going to the hair salon. Takanashi has a soft spot for the Japanese pop acts Yellow Monkey and Hide, and is good at playing ping-pong.